COMBATING
TERRORISM

COMBATING TERRORISM

Strategies of Ten Countries

Edited by **Yonah Alexander**

with a Foreword by
R. James Woolsey

Ann Arbor UNIVERSITY OF MICHIGAN PRESS

Published in India by

Manas Publications
New Delhi-110002 (India)

MANAS PUBLICATIONS
(Publishers, Library Suppliers, Importers & Exporters)
4402/5-A, Ansari Road
(Opp. HDFC Bank)
Darya Ganj, New Delhi-110 002 (INDIA)
Off. © 23260783, 23265523, Res. © 23842660
Fax: 011-23272766
E-mail: manaspublications@vsnl.com
manaspublications@gmail.com
www.manaspublications.in

2nd Impression 2011 (FP - 2003)

ISBN 81-7049-150-9

₹ 895

Typeset at
Manas Publications

Printed in India at
RK Print Services, Delhi
and published by Mrs Suman Lata for
Manas Publications, 4402/5-A, Ansari Road
(Opp. HDFC Bank),
Darya Ganj, New Delhi-110 002 (INDIA)

Foreword

R. James Woolsey

IF THE WORLD DID not change on September 11, 2001, at least most people's perception of it did. Yonah Alexander has assembled a fascinating collection of pre- and post-9/11 perceptions of terrorism and how it has been dealt with in a number of nations.

This book's insights are derived from professional assessments of what has gone right and what has gone wrong in the struggles of the United States, Argentina, Colombia, Peru, Spain, Britain, Israel, Turkey, India, and Japan with a wide range of terrorist movements in recent years. The nation that has gone through the sharpest transition has been the United States, with its quick movement from a pre-9/11 response heavily rooted in law enforcement and focused on prosecuting individual terrorists to its post-9/11 approach of, essentially, a worldwide war: indeed, designating the Cold War as World War III, Eliot Cohen and Norman Podhoretz have now termed the current struggle against terrorism World War IV.

What works and what doesn't? The jury will be out for some time, and the verdict will not be a simple one. There are, however, some characteristics that successful antiterrorist campaigns have in common: good intelligence; being candid with one's own people; dealing with root causes where practical (as the Spanish have limited the effectiveness of ETA by granting many of the wishes of the Basques regarding language use, schools, etc.); and firm resolve, even ruthlessness, where it can be focused on the terrorists themselves. On the other side, failing counterterrorist programs exhibit brutality toward civilian populations, insensitivity to the need for reforms, rigid and inflexible tactics, intragovernmental rivalries and confusion, and wishful thinking.

Terrorism is developing into the great plague of our post–Cold War age—especially where there is any chance that terrorists may get their hands on weapons of mass destruction—and its multitudinous causes are well chronicled here. Its impact—through both the deadliness of its tools and the vulnerability of its targets—is vastly enhanced by many of the characteristics of modern society.

The modern world is a society of networks of all kinds—the Internet, food production and delivery, oil and gas pipelines, and so on—virtually none of which has been put together with a single thought having been given to the dangers of terrorism. We have now seen two of those networks—civil air transport and mail delivery—turned into mechanisms for killing Americans on and after 9/11. Other networks await such exploitation in this nation and in others.

In any war against terror—in addition to taking the fight to the enemy—it will be vital for government and industry to work together to fix major vulnerabilities in networks and to restructure their incentives so that our societies and economies evolve in more decentralized, distributed, resilient directions. Further, policies that promote efficiency in the absence of terrorism, such as just-in-time delivery of manufacturing components and maintaining hospitals at very high occupancy rates, look very different if, due to terrorism, aircraft do not routinely arrive on time or large numbers of people, stricken by bioterrorism, find hospitals already full.

Another major area requiring a fresh look is the tie between terrorists and states that support them but do so covertly and indirectly. We may well need to move in the future against states for which there is no smoking gun regarding their support of any particular terrorist act but who, nonetheless, must be thwarted. It is wise to remember in such cases that absence of evidence of a given state's specific ties to a particular terrorist act is not evidence of the absence of other types of support. We will have hard decisions to make if we are to drain the swamps from which terrorists come and where they find sustenance and support rather than merely swatting individual terrorist mosquitoes.

Yonah Alexander and his colleagues have assembled an extremely useful collection of the dos and don'ts of fighting terrorism. There is no better way to tell if a perception about terrorism is sound or if a counterterrorist strategy or tactic is likely to be successful than to examine with care the various responses that have been made by serious people. All the rest is hunches and arm waving.

Take a look, with Yonah and his colleagues, at what has worked and what has not in the real world. This is the only way any of us can begin to make sense of the extremely difficult task that will constitute the great struggle of our era.

Contents

Acknowledgments

NUMEROUS ACADEMIC INSTITUTIONS AND individuals throughout the world provided the intellectual framework for developing this comparative study of the counterterrorism strategies of different countries targeted by domestic and international terrorists. I wish to acknowledge the support of several universities and think tanks that have afforded me the opportunity to conduct relevant research since the late 1960s in this important area of public concern: the Institute for Studies in International Terrorism, State University of New York; the Graduate School of Journalism, Columbia University; the Center for Strategic and International Studies, Georgetown University; the Institute of Social and Behavioral Pathology, University of Chicago; and the Terrorism Studies Program, George Washington University.

Special thanks are due to three institutions for assisting me in directing the interdisciplinary research project Counter Terrorism Strategies in the Twenty-first Century: National, Regional, and Global Agenda, which resulted in the publication of this volume: the International Center for Terrorism Studies at the Potomac Institute for Policy Studies; the Inter-university Center for Terrorism Studies; and the Inter-university Center for Legal Studies at the International Law Institute. The support of Michael S. Swetnam, Chief Executive Officer and Chairman, Potomac Institute for Policy Studies, is particularly acknowledged. The encouragement and guidance of Edgar

H. Brenner, Codirector, Inter-university Center for Legal Studies, is appreciated.

The publication of this book could not have been realized had it not been for the extraordinary professional editorial contribution of Herbert M. Levine, Adviser to the Inter-university Center for Terrorism Studies.

In developing the methodology and conducting the research for the study during the past three years, I was ably assisted by two dozen project advisers and a team of interns in the United States and abroad. Generous grants from several foundations also supported the work.

Finally, this book is dedicated to those killed or wounded on September 11, 2001, as well as the victims of terrorism in all societies. It is hoped that our academic work will contribute modestly to national and international efforts in the war against terrorism.

Introduction

Yonah Alexander

AS WE HAVE ENTERED the twenty-first century, terrorism remains a vital threat to national and global security interests. Thus, scores of countries have experienced sporadic and relentless subnational and government-sponsored terrorism. Epitomizing the state of anarchy in contemporary life and increasingly becoming a universal nightmare, terrorism includes kidnapping of businesspeople, assassination of political leaders, bombing of embassies, and hijacking of aircraft. In contrast to its older features, modern terrorism has introduced a new breed of warfare in terms of technology, victimization, threats, and responses.

The most devastating terrorist carnage ever recorded occurred on September 11, 2001. Nineteen terrorists hijacked four U.S. airliners, which they crashed into the Twin Towers of the World Trade Center in New York; the Pentagon in Arlington, Virginia; and a third location, not the intended target, a field in Shanksville, Pennsylvania. The cost in terms of human lives, including the passengers and crew on the planes as well as the persons murdered in New York and the Pentagon, is about three thousand dead and thousands injured.

At 8:45 A.M., American Airlines Flight 11, en route from Boston to Los Angeles with eighty-one passengers and eleven crew members, crashed into the North Tower of the World Trade Center. United Airlines Flight 175, also headed from Boston to Los Angeles and carrying fifty-six passengers and nine crew members, slammed into the

South Tower at 9:03 A.M. At 9:43 A.M., American Airlines Flight 77, scheduled to fly from Washington Dulles International Airport to Los Angeles with fifty-eight passengers and six crew members, crashed into the northwest side of the Pentagon. At 10:10 A.M., United Airlines Flight 93, headed from Newark to San Francisco and carrying thirty-eight passengers and seven crew members, crashed in Pennsylvania during a struggle between the hijackers and passengers.

This unprecedented attack and its grave implications raise a new set of security concerns affecting all civilized nations. Indeed, the coming years will undoubtedly see not only spectacular events such as those of September 11 but also various perpetrators (e.g., nations, organizations, and individuals) with the intent and capability to resort to "superterrorism"—biological, chemical, and nuclear. Exploiting new technologies, terrorists may also attempt cyberattacks against the critical infrastructure systems and economic bases.

These conventional and unconventional challenges to the world's stability require effective national, regional, and global efforts to counter all forms of terrorism. It is not surprising, therefore, that the last four decades have seen a vast amount of literature from governmental, intergovernmental, and nongovernmental perspectives on strategies for responding to terrorism. These conflicting publications and reports, whether official or scholarly, have resulted in confusion and chaos for students, the public, and policymakers, in particular.

The purpose of this policy-relevant research study is to examine the responses of ten selected nations that have encountered terrorist threats, to determine what worked and what did not, and to offer a comprehensive "best practices" counterterrorism strategy agenda for the twenty-first century.

The introduction consists of two sections: first, an overview of the terrorism challenges, focusing on the definitional issue, modus operandi, and future prospects; and, second, a discussion of the rationale as well as the content of the volume. A summary of the experiences of the ten countries' case studies is detailed in the concluding chapter. It should be noted that the ten country-specific chapters were completed before the September 11 attacks. The contributors, however, have added commentaries in the form of "postscripts" based on the impact of these attacks.

Many governments have failed to appreciate the extent and implications of the terrorist threat to modern societies. As a result, a large number of countries, including Western democracies, have not developed strong commitments to deal effectively with the challenge. A major reason for this failure is the definitional and moral confusion over what constitutes terrorism. Every sovereign state reserves to itself the political and legal authority to define terrorism in the context of domestic and foreign affairs.

For example, in November 2001, Syria and the United States disagreed on the status of the Lebanese "guerrilla group" Hizbullah, with Syria arguing that it should not qualify as a terrorist organization. Thus, various countries have developed their own legal definitions of what constitutes terrorism. Canada's description is based on its Security Offenses Act (1984) and its Security Intelligence Service Act (1984). These laws do not explicitly define *terrorism* but apply to "threats to the security of Canada." Such threats include "activities within or relating to Canada directed toward, or in support of, the threat or use of acts of serious violence against persons or property for the purpose of achieving a political objective within Canada or a foreign state."

In its Penal Code (chapters I and II of Title II), France, as another example, ties *terrorist-related act,* defined as "an act by an individual or group that uses intimidation or terror to disrupt public order," to the code's general criminal offenses. Although this definition does not mention political motivation, an act would not be labeled an act of terrorism unless it was linked to some political motive or cause.

In short, an analysis of various governmental as well as academic views on the subject indicates that there is no consensus of what terrorism is. Nevertheless, there seems to be an agreement related to several components, such as the nature of the act (e.g., unlawful), perpetrators (e.g., individuals, groups, or states), objectives (e.g., political), intended outcomes and motivations (e.g., fear and frustration), targets (e.g., victims), and methods (e.g., hostage taking).

On the basis of these elements, the following working definition was suggested to the contributors of this volume: *terrorism* is defined as the calculated employment or the threat of violence by individuals, subnational groups, and state actors to attain political, social, and economic objectives in the violation of law. These acts are intended to create an overwhelming fear in a target area larger than the victims attacked or threatened.

HISTORICAL ORIGINS AND CONTEMPORARY TERRORISM: AN OVERVIEW

Terrorism, as a cost-effective tool of low-intensity conflict that projects psychological intimidation and physical force in violation of law, has ancient roots. Examples are the attacks mounted by the Jewish religious extremists known as the Zealot Sicarii against the Romans in occupied Judea as well as the martyrdom missions of the Hashashin (assassins) targeting the Crusaders in the Middle East. The former were active for seventy years in the first century, and the latter lasted some two hundred years—from the eleventh to the thirteenth centuries. Their experience has proven that terrorism can be attractive, effective, and durable, even if the tools are rather primitive.

In subsequent periods, several European maritime states between the sixteenth and late eighteenth centuries employed pirates, or privateers, to terrorize the seas for the purpose of advancing foreign policy objectives. By the time of the Reign of Terror (1793–94) during the French Revolution, terrorism from "above" and "below" was commonplace. A variety of European groups, nourished by extremist political theories (e.g., left- and right-wing ideologies) and militant nationalism, have attained some tactical successes. Resorting to regicide and other terrorist activities, such as bombing, terrorists assassinated a considerable number of European rulers and officials, including Tsar Alexander II in 1881. Although not intended by the perpetrator, the murder of the Austrian archduke in Sarajevo drew the powers into World War I. The period between the two world wars also witnessed waves of attacks in such regions of the world as Asia and the Middle East, where nationalist groups fought for liberation from colonial rule.

It was not until the late 1960s that terrorism became a constant fixture of international life. Rapid developments in modern technology, improvements in communications facilities, and inexpensive and rapid travel contributed to the proliferation of indigenous international terrorist groups and to the intensification of ideological and political violence (e.g., the rise of Palestinian terrorism following the Arab defeat in the Six Day War of 1967).

More specifically, present-day terrorists have introduced into contemporary life a new scale of violence, in terms of both threats and responses, that makes it clear that we have entered an "Age of Terrorism" with serious implications for national, regional, and global security. Perhaps the most significant dangers that result from modern-day terrorism are those relating to the safety, welfare, and rights of ordinary people; the stability of the state system; the health of economic development; the expansion of democracy; and possibly the survival of civilization itself.

Thus, despite the end of the Cold War and the evolving New World Order, terrorism remains as threatening as ever. Undoubtedly, conflicts emerging from ideological, religious, and national animosities will continue to make terrorism a global problem well into the twenty-first century. The vulnerability of modern society and its infrastructure, coupled with the opportunities for the utilization of sophisticated high-leverage conventional and unconventional weaponry, requires states, both unilaterally and in concert, to develop credible responses and capabilities in order to minimize future threats. Ensuring the safety and interests of its citizens at home and abroad will, therefore, continue to be every government's paramount responsibility in the coming months and years. Understanding the methods of operation employed by terrorists, identifying the threats and specific targets both present and future, and knowing the damage and consequences that may result from acts of terror violence will assist governments in responding to the reality of terrorism.

TERRORISTS' MODUS OPERANDI

Contemporary terrorist groups have utilized a wide range of tactics in order to achieve their political, social, or economic objectives. These methods of operation have included arson, bombings, kidnappings, hijackings, facility attacks, destruction of property, the slaughter of innocent people, and assassinations. The terrorist arsenal comprises not only explosives and arms, such as guns, but includes more sophisticated weapons, such as antitank rockets and ground-to-air missiles.

While a general pattern of criminal behavior may be attributed to all terrorists, the modus operandi of terrorist groups will vary considerably depending on each group's motivation and capabilities. Groups that are small and unsophisticated can be expected to rely mostly on bombings. Those with state support and whose members possess great skills will probably attempt to carry out more complex operations such as kidnappings, assassinations, facility attacks, and hijacking.

What is of particular concern is the fact that "superweapons" are slowly emerging upon the terrorist scene. That is, as technological developments offer new capabilities for terrorist groups, their modus operandi may change. According to various intelligence reports, at least a dozen terrorist groups have shown an interest in acquiring biological, chemical, or nuclear weapons. When the Japanese Aum Shinrikyo terrorist doomsday cult mounted the sarin gas attack on a Tokyo subway in 1995, which killed twelve people and injured more than five thousand, it was seeking more lethal weapons than sarin when its leaders were arrested.

And yet, having attained considerable tactical success during the past four decades, terrorists sometimes find it politically expedient to restrain the level of political violence. It is important to understand that these self-imposed restraints will not persist indefinitely and that future incidents may continue to be costly in terms of human lives and property. Certain conditions, such as religious extremism or perceptions that their "cause" is lost, could provide terrorists with an incentive to escalate their attacks dramatically.

Indeed, future terrorist incidents could be much more costly in terms of human lives and property than in the past. The use of weapons of mass destruction (biological, chemical, or nuclear) as instruments of terrorism could inflict large-scale damage on persons and property. For instance, while the probability of nuclear terrorism remains low in comparison with biological and chemical terrorism, the consequences for mass destruction could be enormous. Thus, if a bomb is stolen (or built by a terrorist group with reasonable resources and talent), an explosion in a major city one kiloton in magnitude (one-twentieth the power of the Hiroshima attack) would cause more than one hundred thousand fatalities and damage totaling billions of dollars. The human, physical, and psychological consequences of such an incident would be far more catastrophic than those of the Three Mile Island or Chernobyl accidents caused by operators who innocently overrode key safety systems of nuclear reactors.

FUTURE PROSPECTS: TWENTY-FIRST-CENTURY TRENDS

The bloody record of terror violence underscores, once again, the fact that terrorism is a permanent fixture of international life, epitomizing the state of anarchy in modern societies that is becoming a universal nightmare. It is safe to assume, therefore, that terrorism will continue into the twenty-first century. This prognosis is born from the reality that many of the causes that motivate terrorists, such as ideological, political, and national animosities, will remain unresolved, thereby encouraging terrorists to instigate violence to achieve political, economic, and social change.

There are several specific reasons why terrorism will grow in the future. First, it has proved to be very successful in attracting publicity, disrupting the activities of governments and businesses, and causing significant amounts of death and destruction. Second, arms, explosives, supplies, financing, and secret communications are readily available. Third, an international support network of groups and states exist that greatly facilitates the undertaking of terrorist activities.

Advances in science and technology are slowly turning all of modern society into a potential victim of terrorism. As such, there is no immunity for the noncombatant segment or nations with any direct connection to political violence motivated by particular conflicts. Superterrorism, then, is likely to have an unprecedented and serious impact on the future quality of life and on orderly, civilized existence.

More specifically, it is conceivable that a highly motivated and desperate terrorist group with technological and financial assets will attempt to improve its bargaining leverage by resorting to mass destructive violence. Such a determined group would be willing to take numerous risks in acquiring and using such weapons.

Because the confrontation is seen by many groups as an "all or nothing" struggle, in case of failure the terrorists are prepared to bring the government to submission, to actually use these weapons and in the process to bring devastation and destruction to many lives, including their own. For these terrorists, the fear of deterrence or retaliation does not exist as it does in the case of states.

It is obvious that the prospects of success for such a group would be enhanced if it had previously demonstrated high technological capabilities and a strong willingness to incur the high risks involved in similar ventures. Even if there were some skepticism about the credibility of the threat, no rational government would lightly risk an unconventional incident. The danger here is that if one subnational body succeeds in achieving its goals then the temptation for other terrorist groups to use, or threaten to use, similar weapons may become irresistible.

In view of these considerations, the arsenal of tomorrow's terrorist might include biological, chemical, and nuclear instruments of massive potential. These weapons are capable of producing from several thousand to several million casualties in a single incident and of causing governmental disruption of major proportions and widespread public panic.

Notwithstanding the assumption that in the short term future biological and chemical terrorism is feasible technologically, the specter of nuclear terrorism, such as the explosion of a nuclear bomb, the use of fissionable material as a radioactive poison, and the seizure and sabotage of nuclear facilities, is seen by many experts as plausible and by others as inevitable. At this time, however, a credible threat or hoax involving a nuclear device, holding for political or economic ransom a reactor or other nuclear facility or shipment of reactor fuel or waste, or the truck bombing of a reactor may be the most likely forms of nuclear terrorism.

Moreover, the evolving threat of cyberterrorism should also be considered. It is the prevailing assessment of intelligence agencies, strategic thinkers, and scientists that not only "hackers" and "crackers" (criminal hackers) but also terrorists (individuals, groups, or state sponsors) are likely to intensify the exploitation of the new "equalizer" weapon as a form of electronic warfare. It is estimated, for instance, that hostile low-risk perpetrators launching a well-coordinated attack with about thirty computer experts strategically placed around the globe and a budget of approximately ten million dollars could bring even the United States, the only superpower, to its knees.

There are numerous other devastating scenarios, including altering formulas for medications at pharmaceutical plants, "crashing" telephone systems, misrouting passenger trains, changing the pressure in gas pipelines to cause valve failure, disrupting the operations of air traffic control, triggering oil refinery explosions and fires, scrambling the software used by emergency services, "turning off" power grids, and simultaneously detonating hundreds of computerized bombs around the world.

In sum, this new medium of communication, and command and control, supplemented by unlimited paralyzing and destructive keyboard attacks on civilian and military critical infrastructure nerve centers, forces us to think about the "unthinkable" with great concern.

When suicidal terrorists hijacked four regularly scheduled passenger aircraft in flight and succeeded in crashing them into the World Trade Center in Manhattan and the Pentagon in Arlington, Virginia, on September 11, 2001, Americans were stunned to learn that terrorists had struck such a devastating blow at symbols of the nation's commercial and military power. Although one of the hijacked aircraft crashed in an open field in Pennsylvania, missing its unknown intended target, the terrorists still succeeded in killing everyone aboard the four aircraft, including themselves.

With the crashes, the toll on lives in buildings and on the ground was horrific. In all, about three thousand people were killed and thousands of others were injured. The twin buildings of the World Trade Center were destroyed, and neighboring property was subjected to much damage as well.

The world in general and Americans in particular asked many questions, not least of which were:

Who was responsible for such an atrocity?

What did the people who committed these deeds expect to accomplish?

How did the terrorists succeed in taking control of the aircraft despite airport security procedures?

Why did the intelligence and law enforcement authorities, particularly the Central Intelligence Agency (CIA) and the Federal Bureau of Investigation (FBI), fail to learn of the operation in advance and prevent it from happening?

Some answers to these questions have been offered. Investigation has revealed that nineteen men participated in the four hijackings and that many supporters—numbering perhaps one hundred or more—helped with the preparations. Almost immediately, the September 11 hijackings were linked to Osama bin Laden's Al Qaeda (the Base organization). This global network, also known as the International Islamic Front for Jihad against Jews and Crusaders as well as the Islamic Army for the Liberation of the Holy Shrines, opposes all nations and institutions that are not governed in a manner consistent with its extremist interpretation of Islam. Since the United States supports some of these "corrupt" governments, such as Saudi Arabia and Egypt, bin Laden has declared war on America as early as the attacks perpetrated against U.S. troops in Somalia and the bombing of the World Trade Center in New York in 1993.

Since these operations, Al Qaeda has been blamed for other operations directed against the United States, including the 1995 car bombing of the American-operated Saudi National Guard Training Center in Riyadh, Saudi Arabia; the 1996 attack at Khobar Towers, a U.S. Air Force housing complex in Dhahran, Saudi Arabia; the 1998 truck bombings outside the U.S. embassies in Nairobi, Kenya, and Dar es Salaam, Tanzania; and the suicide bombings of the USS *Cole* in Aden, Yemen, in 2000. These attacks resulted in the deaths of thousands, including many Americans.

It is against this background that President George W. Bush, speaking before Congress on September 20, 2001, declared a global war against Al Qaeda and terrorism in general. Subsequently, the United States and its international coalition went to war against bin Laden's bases in Afghanistan and against the Taliban regime.

While this military battle has been won, many other issues remain concerning the most devastating terrorist attack in world history. Although they were by no means definitive, government officials and terrorism specialists offered answers to the various questions about the September 11 attack. The terrorists may have believed that they would go to Heaven because they had acted in support of Islam against the American enemy. The terrorists used knives as weapons to take over the aircraft. Finally, intelligence and law enforcement officials had learned that some of the individuals later named as directly responsible for hijacking the aircraft were in the United States. But these officials had no prior knowledge that such a murderous act was planned. Only after the event did investigators put some pieces of the puzzle together and learn that the terrorists had planned and trained for this event for perhaps two years. Some analysts pointed out that it is extremely difficult to penetrate Middle Eastern terrorist groups, just as it is to penetrate Mafia organizations, because of strong personal, family, and traditional ties in the region.

Although time was needed to gather the necessary information about responsibility for the disaster, the nation began to focus its attention on counterterrorism in order to prevent terrorist incidents from occurring in the future or, if they did, to minimize the damage.

The notion that an act of military terrorism could occur was not new to the United States. Indeed, the largest act of domestic terrorism in American history was the bomb blast on April 19, 1995, that destroyed the nine-story Alfred P. Murrah Federal Building in Oklahoma City. This devastating attack perpetrated by two American terrorists claimed 168 lives, including those of 19 children, and wounded 674 people. The explosion, which resulted from the detonation of a 4,800 pound ammonium nitrate fuel oil bomb carried in a truck, not only destroyed the federal building but severely damaged or destroyed twenty-five other structures. In addition, another three hundred buildings were damaged and window glass shattered in a ten-block radius.

Aside from such indigenous domestic terrorist activity, the reality of international Islamic groups operating in the United States in the last decade has become evident. Seeking to achieve common political, social, or economic objectives that transcend national differences, these terrorists, operating under the banner of radical Islam, struck at the United States massively on February 26, 1993. A devastating car bomb explosion occurred in the parking garage at the World Trade Center in New York City, killing 6 people and injuring 1,042 others. The bomb, consisting of approximately twelve hundred pounds of explosives, resulted in a crater of 150 feet in diameter and five stories high. The attack caused considerable damage to the garage, hundreds of vehicles were demolished, and the Vista Hotel, located directly above the detonation site, was badly damaged.

The perpetrators of this attack, considered at that time to have been the single largest international terrorist incident that had ever occurred in the United States, were arrested, convicted, and are currently serving their sentences. They include people from Egypt, Iraq, Jordan, Palestinian Authority areas, and the United States.

Following the World Trade Center attack, members of the international radical Islamic network once again posed a significant threat to American security interests. In June 1993, a group of terrorists consisting of Egyptians, Sudanese, a Jordanian, and a Puerto Rican were apprehended by the FBI in an aborted plot directed at a number of New York City landmarks and various political figures. The terrorists had targeted the United Nations, a New York federal building, the Lincoln and Holland Tunnels, Egyptian president Hosni Mubarak during his 1993 visit to New York, and at least two U.S. political figures. The conspirators were subsequently convicted and sentenced for their criminal activities.

This plot and the 1993 attack on the World Trade Center, as well as numerous attacks abroad, underscored most dramatically the vulnerability of the United States to threats originating from both domestic and international terrorism, with resulting dire human, political, economic, and strategic consequences.

In light of this reality, it is not surprising, therefore, that the United States has adopted an elaborate counterterrorism strategy. The record indicates that while thousands of terrorist incidents were recorded in the past four decades a number of international plots were aborted due to effective intelligence and law enforcement efforts. One of the best-known aborted operations was the plan of groups affiliated with Al Qaeda to destroy a dozen U.S. jumbo jets flying Asia-Pacific routes in 1995. The three terrorists involved in the plot were arrested overseas, brought to the United States, and convicted in federal court.

This successful example is, however, an exception to the victimization of the United States both at home and abroad. As always, new terrorist acts occurred and the nation hoped that it had the personnel and weapons needed to deal successfully with the problem.

It took many measures, such as increasing security in government buildings and at airports, enacting antiterrorism laws, expanding antiterrorism law enforcement authority and operations, promoting antiterrorism treaties, and even taking military action against a state sponsor of terrorism, to prevent attacks on U.S. interests.

In both the executive and legislative branches of the federal government and in state and local governments as well, it was generally believed that acts of terrorism in one form or another would be a continuing threat. And so it was generally agreed that both the American government and the American people ought to be prepared.

In experiencing problems of terrorism, the United States, of course, was not alone. Every country on our planet has a terrorism problem, although some are more serious than others. Names of the organizations remind us of the global reach of terrorism. The Red Brigades in Italy, the Irish Republican Army in Northern Ireland, the Baader-Meinhof gang in West Germany, Hamas in the Middle East, the Kurdistan Workers' Party in Turkey, and the Shining Path in Peru are but a few of the terrorist groups that engaged in violent acts, some of which were so extensive that they threatened governmental authority and in doing so caused governments to appear powerless.

Governments so challenged responded to acts of terrorism in different ways. Politically, one response was to seek political means of conciliation to resolve underlying issues in an effort to undermine popular support for terrorist acts. Another response was the widespread repression not only of terrorists but of innocent civilians as well. Other responses included military attacks and police raids on supposed terrorist sites, freezing the financial assets of individuals believed to be connected to the terrorists, arranging for training in counterterrorism practices, and rallying international support, to name but a few.

In responding to the terrorist challenge, the enemies of terrorism would be helped if they had an understanding of the experiences of many countries. What worked successfully in one country could possibly work in another. To be sure, nations differ in their problems, leadership, resources, and popular support so that a policy that worked in one country might not be successful applied to another. Nevertheless, lessons learned in counterterrorism policies and practices in different countries can offer valuable insights to those officials responsible for setting policy. It is this principle that sparked the interest of the contributors to this volume.

This book presents analyses of counterterrorism policies in ten countries in different areas of the world, including North and South America, Europe, the Middle East, and Asia. Specifically, the countries examined are the United States, Argentina, Peru, Colombia, Spain, the United Kingdom, Israel, Turkey, India, and Japan. The authors include former government officials as well as journalists, academics, and terrorism experts from these countries.

In undertaking this project, guidelines were established. It was recognized, however, that it would be impossible to impose strict rules. In this regard, the participants understood at the outset that they might not even agree on the meaning of certain terms. After all, the term *terrorism* has hundreds of definitions. Even the agencies of the U.S. government do not agree among themselves on the definition of the term. Some observers say, perhaps cynically, "One man's terrorist is another man's freedom fighter." Moreover, the expertise of the authors varies. Still, we thought that we would make a contribution to the study of terrorism by focusing on what does and does not work in counterterrorism. The effort was seen not as a definitive study but as a survey that would be of value to anyone interested in understanding counterterrorism options.

The contributors were asked to consider a number of factors that have an influence on the success of counterterrorism: the political environment, terrorist threats and counterterrorism policies, the legal environment, the public affairs environment, the counterterrorism organizational structure, intelligence, law enforcement, diplomatic methods, economic measures, and military responses.

In addition, the contributors were asked to focus on four questions. First, in a particular country what is the governmental and public perception of the terrorist threat on the conventional and unconventional levels? Second, how successful were the government's policies and actions in combating both domestic and international terrorism? Success was to be evaluated in terms of the following criteria.

Reduction in the number of terrorist incidents

Reduction in the number of casualties in terrorist incidents

Reduction in the monetary cost inflicted by terrorist incidents

Reduction in the size of terrorist groups operating in a country

Number of terrorists killed, captured, and/or convicted

Protection of national infrastructures (e.g., transportation, communications, economic and political institutions, and security installations and units)

Preservation of basic national structures and policies (e.g., the rule of law, democracy, and civil rights and liberties)

Third, what factors influence the government's willingness and ability to cooperate with other nations in combating terrorism? And, fourth, what does the counterterrorism balance sheet of the specific country look like?

In the ten countries under examination, the numbers of terrorist organizations are many and their tactics vary. A brief and select description of some of these organizations and the tactics they have used sets the stage for understanding the problems that government agencies entrusted with counterterrorism responsibilities have to face.

Since the essays in this volume were written, in 1999–2001, terrorist activities in the different countries have continued and at times even escalated. Several updated examples will suffice to illustrate the kind of such attacks in November and December 2001:

Peru: Shining Path terrorists bombed an electric tower near Lima.

Colombia: Members of the AUC murdered fifteen bus passengers.

Spain: An ETA gunman shot and killed two regional Basque police officers.

Israel: A Hamas suicide bomber attacked a civilian bus in Haifa, killing sixteen people and injuring sixty others.

More extensive, updated versions of the essays are provided by the contributors as postscripts to their country chapters.

For its part, the United States has been a frequent target of terrorism both at home and abroad. While the most damaging operation occurred on September 11, 2001, with the hijacking and crashes of four aircraft, there have been many other international attacks. Among the attacks on the United States were the following: the 1979 takeover of the U.S. embassy in Teheran, during which American diplomats were held hostage for 444 days; the bombing of the U.S. embassy and the Marine headquarters in Beirut in 1983; the 17 day hijacking of Trans-World Airlines (TWA) Flight 847 in 1985; and the 1988 destruction of Pan Am Flight 103 over Scotland. The United States has also had to deal with domestic terrorists, including leftist and rightist groups with ideological and political agendas that reject U.S. policy on both the domestic and foreign fronts. Retired ambassador Philip C. Wilcox Jr., who has served as U.S. ambassador at large and coordinator for counterterrorism, considers the U.S. government's role in handling such matters.

Argentina has a tradition of alternating military juntas and democratic governments, a situation that has set the stage for significant state- and nonstate-initiated acts of terrorism. During the peak of the right-wing juntas in the 1960s and 1970s, thousands of civilians disappeared while others were arrested or tortured. This infliction of state violence against certain segments of the populace led to strong reactions among revolutionary factions. During the 1970s, the Montoneros, a left-wing, Peronist, urban guerrilla group, conducted kidnappings of prominent Argentine and foreign businessmen as well as attacks against armed forces' equipment and personnel. Another active left-wing group, which attacked similar targets, was the People's Revolutionary Army (ERP). The key right-wing organization was the Argentine Anti-communist Alliance.

International terrorism struck Jewish and Israeli targets in Argentina during the 1990s. In 1992, the Israeli embassy in Buenos Aires was bombed, killing twenty-nine people. The Islamic Jihad, an arm of the Iran-backed Hizbullah, claimed responsibility. More devastating was the 1994 attack staged by a suicide bomber who detonated a vehicle loaded with explosives in front of Argentina's main Jewish center, resulting in the deaths of eighty-six people and the wounding of more than three thousand. The Followers of God, a previously unknown Middle Eastern group, claimed responsibility for the attack. Dr. Roger W. Fontaine, a journalist for *Tiempos del Mundos* in Washington, D.C., analyzes the Argentine counterterrorism experience.

In the case of Peru, two principal insurgency groups, Sendero Luminoso (Shining Path) and Tupac Amaru Revolutionary Movement (MRTA), inflicted bombings, kidnappings, murder, and mayhem on domestic and foreign civilians and military and political targets. Shining Path, formed in the late 1960s by Abimael Guzmán, sought to destroy existing Peruvian institutions and replace them with a revolutionary peasant regime. Guzmán and other leaders, who were captured in the early 1990s, staged such dramatic terrorist attacks as bombing a location near the Congress building in Lima in 1987, which left forty dead; assassinating provincial mayors in 1986; blowing up electrical towers; and bombing the U.S. embassy in Lima in 1983.

The Marxist MRTA, established in 1984, received support from Nicaragua and Cuba. It carried out various attacks against Peruvian, U.S., and other foreign targets. For instance, it bombed two U.S. Information Service Centers in Lima in 1988 and the Bolivian embassy in 1987. It also attacked the Lima offices of the Texaco Corporation in 1985. It was responsible for the takeover of the Japanese ambassador's residence in Lima in 1996, which involved the capture of hundreds of hostages. In 1997, Peruvian antiterrorist and military forces liberated the remaining hostages and killed the MRTA members. Prof. Alberto Bolivar of the Peruvian Institute for Geopolitical and Strategic Studies in Lima, Peru, reviews counterterrorism strategies in Lima.

Terrorist organizations in Colombia historically consisted of Marxist-inspired insurgent groups such as the Revolutionary Armed Forces of Colombia (FARC), the National Liberation Army (ELN), and several others that over the years were formed and defeated or negotiated settlements with the government. The activities of FARC include bombings, murder, kidnapping, extortion, and hijacking as well as guerrilla and conventional military action against Colombian political, military, and economic targets. Foreign citizens are often kidnapped and held for ransom, which is used to fund these activities. Entities with assets more than a million dollars are "taxed" by FARC. It has well-documented ties to narcotics traffickers, principally through the provision of armed protection. In March 1999, FARC executed three U.S. Indian rights activists on Venezuelan territory after it kidnapped them in Colombia.

The ELN annually conducts hundreds of kidnappings for ransom, often targeting foreign employees of large corporations, especially in the petroleum industry. It also frequently assaults energy infrastructure and has inflicted major damage on pipelines and the electric distribution network.

In recent years, several non-Marxist terrorist groups have

emerged in Colombia. Right-wing self-defense forces such as the United Self-Defense Forces of Colombia (AUC) use terrorist tactics to fight the FARC and ELN. The AUC has been accused of numerous acts of terrorism, including the massacre of hundreds of civilians, the forced displacement of entire villages, and the kidnapping of political figures to force recognition of group demands. In 2000, it committed at least seventy-five massacres, resulting in the deaths of hundreds of civilians, which were designed to terrorize and intimidate local populations into accepting AUC control. It has also committed hundreds of kidnappings, including the abduction of seven Colombian members of Congress in November 2000. Criminal groups like the drug cartels are also known to use terrorist techniques in Colombia. James Zackrison of Oxford University examines Colombia's counterterrorism efforts.

Terrorism has plagued Spain since the late 1950s with the formation of the Basque Fatherland and Liberty (ETA), which aims to create an independent state in the Basque country. This group has been responsible for numerous bombings, assassinations of government officials, and campaigns of terror directed against tourist sites. In all, ETA has killed more than eight hundred people during its existence. Professors Antonio Remiro Brotóns and Carlos Espósito of the Universidad Autonoma de Madrid evaluate Spain's counterterrorism campaign and its successes and failures.

For the United Kingdom, the major terrorism challenge has been the activities of the Irish Republican Army (IRA), also known as the Provisional Irish Republican Army. The IRA was formed in Ulster, Northern Ireland, for the purpose of unifying Ireland. Its activities included bombings, assassinations, kidnappings, extortion, and robberies. Before the 1994 cease-fire, the IRA attacked British targets and Northern Ireland loyalists. Despite the ongoing peace process, Catholic splinter groups as well as Protestant opponents to a political solution continue their violent activities.

The British experience with terrorism is not only related to the Irish problem but is connected to the activities of a variety of foreign nationals, such as Middle Eastern operatives, active in the United Kingdom. For instance, one Palestinian terrorist group attempted to assassinate Israel's ambassador to the United Kingdom and tried to attack an Israeli aircraft. Great Britain has been the target of many acts of terrorism abroad, and tourists traveling outside the country have been victims. Col. Terence Taylor, retired, assistant director of the International Institute for Strategic Studies in London, assesses the British counterterrorism experience.

Israel has been the target of terrorism initiated by various extremist Palestinian, Arab, and Islamic groups at home and abroad. Even after the signing of the Oslo Peace Accord with the Palestine Liberation Organization (PLO) in 1993, the Jewish state continues to be plagued by terrorism.

Hamas pursues the goal of establishing an Islamic Palestinian state in place of Israel. Its military arm, 'Izz al-Din al-Kassam, has conducted many attacks against civilian and military targets. Israeli facilities and citizens have been targets of many attacks outside of Israel, such as the bombing of the Israeli embassy in Buenos Aires in 1992, which was perpetrated by Iranian agents. Other state sponsors of terrorism, including Libya, Iraq, and Syria, have also targeted Israel.

Israel has also faced Jewish terrorism. In 1994, for example, an Israeli religious extremist massacred forty-three Muslims at a historic Hebron mosque. During the following year, a Jewish terrorist and opponent of the peace process assassinated Israeli prime minister Yitzhak Rabin. Gen. Shlomo Gazit, retired, senior fellow at the Jaffee Center for Strategic Studies at Tel Aviv University, analyzes the Israeli counterintelligence effort.

Turkey has experienced terrorism from ideological, religious, and ethnic sources. The Kurds, Marxists, and Islamic fundamentalists have posed the main threats. The Armenian Secret Army for the Liberation of Armenia (ASALA), which is dedicated to an independent Armenian state within a portion of present-day Turkey, has murdered officials, and bombed Turkish targets in Europe and the United States.

The greatest threat posed by terrorists in Turkey, however, is from the Kurdistan Workers' Party (PKK), a Marxist-Leninist insurgent movement seeking to establish an independent Kurdish state in southeastern Turkey. The PKK has conducted a terrorist campaign not only in Turkey but throughout Europe. Its operatives have received financial and training support from Syria, Iraq, and Iran. Turkish ambassador Gunduz S. Aktan, retired, and investigative journalist Ali M. Koknar analyze the Turkish counterterrorism effort.

Three kinds of terrorism in India are analyzed: (1) cross-border terrorism in Jammu and Kashmir; (2) terrorism with internal roots, but supported by external forces, in the northeastern states and Punjab; and (3) domestic terrorism with no external links in Bihar and Andhra Pradesh.

Numerous Sikh terrorist organizations advocating a separate Sikh state of Khalistan have engaged in various violent activities in India and elsewhere. In 1984, Sikh terrorists assassinated Indian prime minister Indira Gandhi. Kashmir is the site of the most intense terrorist activities. The Harakat ul-Ansar organization seeks Kashmir's accession to Pakistan. More specifically, the group is dedicated to continuing an armed struggle against "nonbelievers" and anti-Islamic forces. Although the group has mounted operations against Indian security forces and civilian targets in Kashmir, its members have also participated in attacks in Burma, Tajikistan, and Bosnia. Ved Marwah, research professor at the Centre for Policy Research in New Delhi, describes India's counterterrorism efforts.

The best-known incident of terrorism in Japan was the attack by Aum Shinrikyo, a religious cult, in the Tokyo subway in which terrorists used poisonous sarin gas to kill twelve people and injure five thousand. Before Aum Shinrikyo, Japan's major threat came from the leftist Japanese Red Army (JRA). A Marxist-Leninist group formed in 1971, JRA conducted many activities, including the 1972 Lod Airport attack in Israel in which twenty-six people were killed; the 1975 seizure of the U.S. embassy in Kuala Lumpur, Malaysia; the 1987 rocket attack against the British embassy in Rome; the 1988 rocket attack against the U.S. embassy in Spain; and cooperation with Hizbullah in Lebanon in 1977. Isao Itabashi and Masamichi Ogawara of the Council for Public Policy in Tokyo, and David Leheny, a political scientist at the University of Wisconsin, Madison, analyze Japanese counterterrorism strategies.

It is hoped that this scholarly effort will stimulate further study and research, with a view to devise "best practices" responses to the global scourge of terrorism.

Part I

North and South America

UNITED STATES

Philip C. Wilcox Jr.

TERRORISM HAS PREOCCUPIED ALL U.S. administrations since the 1970s, when international terrorists began major assaults on American interests. These attacks were directed mostly by Arab groups opposed to American policy toward the Arab-Israeli conflict or were carried out by various radical, Marxist, and revolutionary groups that were challenging American influence and power. Before then, terrorism was not viewed as a significant threat, and occasional terrorist acts against Americans were dealt with on an ad hoc basis. In the 1970s, terrorists began a wave of assassinations, hostage taking, aircraft hijackings, and bombings directed against U.S. interests. Washington began to view international terrorism as a national security problem that required a more forceful, effective response. Today, as the threats of nuclear and major conventional war have waned, there is an even sharper focus on terrorism. U.S. policymakers and the public rank international terrorism high among global threats to the United States. Domestic terrorism has also become a major concern since the bombing of the Alfred P. Murrah Federal Building in Oklahoma City in 1995.

The Rise and Decline of International Terrorism

The American response to terrorism in the 1970s and 1980s was varied, as administrations changed, new policies were tried, and terrorist tactics evolved. There was much debate and turmoil over what to do. Policies were sometimes ad hoc and inconsistent, and international terrorist attacks against American and allied interests continued to increase. Between 1968 and 1986, the number of international terrorist attacks worldwide—that is, those involving the citizens or territory of one or more countries—rose from 140 to 666.[1] During the same period, anti-American attacks increased from 54 to 139.[2] After 1987, anti-American and international terrorist attacks worldwide began to decline. In 1998, there were 247 international terrorist attacks overall and 111 attacks against American targets.[3]

Deaths caused by international terrorism are another means of gauging the threat. These numbers have fluctuated widely, from 668 in 1979 to 221 in 1997, but the trend has been downward. There is also a declining trend in the number of Americans killed by international terrorism. Between 1990 and 1999, an average of 9 Americans a year were killed in acts of international terrorism, a relatively small number compared to those killed in other crimes of violence.[4]

There are two geopolitical reasons for this decline in international and anti-American terrorism since 1990. When the Soviet Union collapsed, radical states and revolutionary movements that practiced terrorism lost a major ally. When the Palestine Liberation Organization (PLO) condemned terrorism and joined the Middle East peace process in 1993, the Arab and Islamic states joined in this condemnation, giving increased momentum to a growing international consensus condemning terrorism irrespective of political motives. Another reason for the general decline in anti-American terrorism has been more effective U.S. counterterrorism policies, including greater emphasis on criminal law and law enforcement, a more unified interagency approach to counterterrorism, and more resources than were available earlier.

Defining Terrorism

For many years, ideological and political divisions hobbled international cooperation in the fight against terrorism. The Cold War and the Arab-Israeli conflict, especially, prevented agreement on the definition of *terrorism*. Today there is less concern about a precise definition, and most states now consider politically motivated violence against noncombatants to be terrorism and treat such acts as crimes.

The laws and international treaties of the United States do not attempt to define terrorism precisely but instead focus on the particular act. For policy purposes, the U.S. State Department defines *terrorism* as "premeditated, politically motivated violence perpetrated against noncombatant targets by subnational groups or clandestine agents, usually intended to influence an audience."[5] Under this definition, noncombatants include U.S. military personnel who at the time of the incident are not armed or not on duty. The United States does not define war crimes or actions by states that violate human rights as acts of terrorism and treats these under separate bodies of law.

The Seven Pillars of U.S. Counterterrorism Policy

Today, there are seven basic pillars of U.S. counterterrorism policy and practice.

1. Terrorism is a crime that should be prosecuted, whatever its motivation, and the rule of law should be strengthened as a principal weapon against it. Accordingly, the United States has strengthened its domestic antiterrorism laws and supports international treaties and conventions that address terrorism in its many forms.
2. The United States does not make concessions to terrorists or strike deals.
3. Detection, deterrence, and prevention of terrorism and apprehension of terrorists require intensive and focused collection and analysis of intelligence and cooperation among intelligence and law enforcement agencies worldwide.
4. Diplomacy is essential to encourage international cooperation against terrorism in the form of common policies, training for countries that require assistance, and practical cooperation in apprehending and bringing to justice terrorist suspects and denying safe haven to them.
5. In order to penalize and isolate states and groups that sponsor terrorism, the United States identifies and condemns them and applies economic sanctions and other prohibitions, including criminalization of terrorist fund-raising.

6. Providing physical and technical security measures to protect buildings, aircraft, and other vulnerable installations is essential to discouraging and preventing terrorist attacks.
7. Close coordination and effective teamwork among the U.S. agencies, civilian and military, that share responsibility for counterterrorism are critical to deterring terrorism and responding effectively to terrorist attacks.

Concern about the Future

Although international terrorism and anti-American attacks declined in the 1990s, U.S. officials believe that the terrorist threat today is no less dangerous than in the past, and may indeed be growing, for several reasons. There is an apparent trend toward more lethal and massive terrorist attacks. Modern terrorists are increasingly motivated by hatred, revenge, and religious and cult fanaticism. They are less constrained by the rational political calculus that has influenced most terrorists in the past and that limited mass killing. Above all, U.S. officials fear that terrorists with these inclinations, both domestic and international, may acquire and use increasingly available materials of mass destruction—biological, chemical, and radiological—to carry out unprecedented mass-casualty terrorism.

This threat is sometimes exaggerated and sensationalized, but it cannot be minimized. Some analysts also point out that, although international terrorism has declined, domestic terrorism and political violence in places like Algeria, Pakistan, Russia, the Caucasus, and other areas of conflict may be rising, with potential spillover effects against Americans and U.S. interests.

Terrorism and Public Affairs Policy

The United States warns the public about hazards of terrorism abroad through travel advisories and applies a "no double standard" policy that obliges authorities to publicize, in sanitized form, threat information obtained from intelligence sources when the threat cannot be defended against with confidence. In discussing terrorism and issuing warnings, officials must be careful to avoid creating unnecessary anxiety and disruption by exaggerating the threat, since this enhances the influence of terrorists and the fear

they seek to create. Officials must also be sensitive to the reality that the media often exaggerate and sensationalize terrorism by giving it greater coverage than other forms of violence and mayhem that may represent a greater danger to public safety. Also, care is needed in discussing terrorism carried out by groups claiming to act for religious motives, for example, the current phenomenon of terrorism by extremist Islamic elements, to avoid implying any intrinsic association between religion and terrorism.

U.S. GOVERNMENT PERCEPTIONS OF THE TERRORIST THREAT

The Costs of Terrorism

The U.S. government views terrorism not only as a direct threat to American officials, private citizens, military forces, businesspeople, and property but also as a danger to international peace and stability and American foreign policy interests. For decades, terrorism has caused great damage, for example, in deepening the Arab-Israeli and Northern Ireland confrontations and delaying accommodation. It has exacerbated and prolonged conflicts in Kashmir, Sri Lanka, Colombia, and Algeria. It has alienated the United States from states that have sponsored terrorism such as Iran and Libya. And it has sometimes provoked serious military conflict, for example, the civil war between Russia and Chechen militants.

The United States is also concerned about the economic burden of terrorism abroad and at home. Terrorism has periodically disrupted the economies of friendly states like Egypt and discouraged investment and economic development in Colombia, Sri Lanka, and Pakistan. For the United States, the costs of providing physical security against terrorist attacks on government and military installations and personnel and civil aviation, as well as security protection for the private sector, have been enormous.

The Many Faces of Terrorism

It is difficult to measure the threat of terrorism precisely because it is so varied and fluid. Terrorism has traditionally been the weapon of weak individuals, groups, and pariah states that lack the conventional political or military means to challenge their adversaries. Lone individuals, political opposition groups, and advocates of diverse causes have used terrorism to oppose repressive regimes and attract attention to their agendas. For example, terrorism has been used by ethnic and revolutionary insurgents and fanatical religious groups and cults to promote their causes.

Threat Assessment and Warning

Within the U.S. government, the director of central intelligence and the agencies that report to him are responsible for assessing the threat of international terrorism. The Federal Bureau of Investigation (FBI) is in charge of assessing the domestic threat. During the 1990s, the United States has devoted large and growing resources to the collection and analysis of intelligence on terrorist threats, both international and domestic.

Because terrorists operate secretly, there is a particular need for clandestine intelligence in order to discover, penetrate, and disrupt terrorist groups and operations. The United States has relied heavily on intelligence for both tactical and strategic warnings of terrorist attacks, and some potential attacks have been detected and disrupted. Also, intelligence gathered abroad is often a necessary supplement to information that the FBI collects for the indictment and prosecution of international terrorists.

Threat assessments, however, should not rely entirely on intelligence for warnings. This lesson was underscored by the bombings of the American embassies in Kenya and Tanzania in August 1998. American officials had previously and mistakenly designated these embassies as "low-threat" posts, since there had been no specific intelligence warning of terrorist threats.[6] Since then, Washington has revived its threat assessment system to take greater account of the mobility of today's transnational terrorists, of their practice of seeking out vulnerable targets in areas where they have not previously attacked, and of various environmental factors.[7]

Today analysts focus on various categories of terrorists who have attacked U.S. interests in the past or may do so in the future. These include state sponsors of terrorism; established terrorist organizations; loose networks of transnational terrorists, some of whom are motivated by religious fanaticism; a wide variety of domestic elements that support or threaten terrorist violence; and so-called cyberterrorists, who may attack the U.S. digital infrastructure for terrorist purposes. These categories are discussed in the following pages.

State Sponsors of Terrorism

Beginning in the 1970s various states, usually weak nations in the developing world, began to carry out or sponsor terrorist acts against the United States or other nations. Radical anti-Western ideology or hostility to the United States and Israel usually motivated them. State-sponsored terrorism spread, and in 1979 Congress passed an amendment to the Export Administration Act calling on the secretary of state to annually designate states that consistently support terrorism.[8] This law and others impose economic and military trade sanctions against such states.[9] The State Department has designated Libya, Iraq, Iran, Syria, North Korea, and Cuba as "state sponsors of terrorism," and Sudan was added to the list in 1995. Iraq was removed from the list temporarily in the late 1980s but was redesignated when it resumed terrorist activities.

In recent years, state-sponsored terrorism declined due to the fall of the Soviet Union, which had provided political backing for some of these states, the beginning of the Israeli-Palestinian peace process in the early 1990s, and growing international rejection of terrorism. The U.S. law is flexible enough to allow policymakers some discretion in designating state sponsors of terrorism. It also permits designated states to redeem themselves. But all seven countries remain on the list, although their continuing support for terrorism varies from significant to negligible. Cuba, for example, remains on the list, although it is no longer an active state sponsor of terrorism. Some U.S. analysts believe that because of the growing asymmetry of power between the United States and small, hostile states, such adversaries may turn to terrorism again to redress this imbalance.

Terrorist Organizations

The Department of State also keeps and annually reviews a list of nonstate foreign terrorist organizations designated by the secretary of state, as required by the Anti-terrorism and Effective Death Penalty Act of 1996.[10] Under this law, members of and activists in these organizations are denied entry into the United States and are subject to deportation if they are found there. The law also enables the Treasury Department to seize the funds of these organizations in the United States. To date, few funds have been seized, but the law has apparently deterred terrorist fund-raising in the United States. As of the end of 1999, there were fifty-five organizations on this list.[11]

Terrorism by many of the organizations active in the 1970s and 1980s has declined or ceased. For example, the radical secular Palestinian groups associated with the PLO are now more or less inactive, since the PLO's leader Yasser Arafat has committed the Palestinians to make peace with Israel. The Irish Republican Army (IRA) has accepted the peace process in Northern Ireland. And many, though not all, of the Latin American and European radical leftist groups are now extinct or moribund. Some ethnic insurgent organizations, like the Tamil Tigers in Sri Lanka and, to a declining extent, the Basque Fatherland and Liberty Party (ETA) in Spain, still practice terrorism. The Revolutionary Armed Forces of Colombia (FARC) and the National Liberation Army (ELN) of Colombia are still deeply involved in terrorism.

Radical Islamic Terrorists: Osama bin Laden

As of the year 2000, U.S. analysts viewed terrorist groups—either organized or loosely linked—that claim to act on behalf of Islam as the most dynamic threat in international terrorism. These elements include such established groups as the Gamaat Islamiyya in Egypt; the Harakat ul-Mujahideen in Kashmir, Afghanistan, and Pakistan; and Hamas and the Palestinian Islamic Jihad in the West Bank and Gaza. Even more active among radical Islamic terrorists are militants linked to the Saudi dissident Osama bin Laden. Some of these fought with the Mujahideen guerrillas during the Afghan war against the Soviet Union in the 1980s or have received terrorist training in Afghanistan. Bin Laden is in direct control of several hundred terrorists in Afghanistan and influences and finances a network of militants known as Al Qaeda that extends to many countries. The U.S. Department of Justice has indicted bin Laden and some members of

his Al Qaeda group for the bombings of the U.S. embassies in Nairobi and Dar es Salaam in 1998.

The United States regards bin Laden and his allies as the most pervasive and dangerous of the radical Islamic terrorists. There is some debate about whether bin Laden's leadership in terrorism outside Afghanistan is primarily operational or whether his main role is financial and inspirational. He has issued a *fatwa* (religious-based order) calling for the deaths of American officials and civilians. Some private analysts think that U.S. officials may be exaggerating his operational role in radical Islamic terrorism, which in the past has been inchoate and widely dispersed.[12] Bin Laden is a dangerous terrorist leader, but the phenomenon of extremist Islamic terrorism is a much larger problem, which cannot be attributed to bin Laden alone. He is also a sophisticated publicist and self-promoter who thrives on the aura of fear and power that surrounds him. Excessive and sometimes lurid publicity by the media and the tendency of some officials to encourage this by speculating that he is associated with virtually every terrorist act have tended, inadvertently, to increase his stature and influence in radical Islamic circles.

American officials believe that terrorism by radical Islamists and other religious fanatics is especially dangerous because of their tendency to carry out attacks that inflict very many casualties using massive explosive charges.[13] They cite, for example, the bombing of the World Trade Center in New York City in 1993, the bombings of U.S. embassies in East Africa in 1998, and the bombing of U.S. Air Force personnel at the Al Khobar barracks in Saudi Arabia in 1995. Unlike traditional, secular terrorists, fanatical religious terrorists lack a rational political calculus for their acts.[14] They preach hatred and dehumanize their victims and are thus inclined to kill more people. In contrast, traditional, secular terrorists have more calculated political agendas. They are usually more interested in attracting attention to their causes than in killing for motives of hatred, revenge, or some messianic religious purpose.

American officials are aware that throughout history fringe groups from many religious faiths have claimed divine sanctions for violent acts. They have sought to make clear that there is no link between terrorism and Islam or any other religion and that those who justify violence on religious grounds are betraying their faith. Nevertheless, the attention given to radical Islamic terrorism has caused unease in the Islamic world and the Arab-American and Islamic-American communities.[15]

Domestic Terrorism: Christian Extremists

Americans tended to associate terrorism with foreign countries until the bombing of the Murrah federal office building in Oklahoma City by a right-wing extremist American in 1995. In fact, politically motivated violence has been a problem in the United States for generations. Although such violence has not often been described as such, domestic terrorism has included violence against racial or religious groups and revolutionary and anarchist bombings and assassinations. Today, antiabortion killings and attacks by radical environmental groups also qualify as terrorist acts.

Law enforcement officials are most concerned today about antigovernment terrorism by right-wing hate groups and some associated Christian fringe elements, who preach racism, antisemitism, and hatred of the United Nations (UN) and government, especially the federal government. Many of these elements are armed, and Internet chat groups have strengthened their cohesion. Federal guidelines for law enforcement officers protect such groups from surveillance if they have not committed illegal acts and there is no evidence indicating that they are preparing to do so.[16] In addition, the law allows them to own firearms. Nevertheless, within carefully defined limits the FBI and local authorities are now devoting greater resources to monitoring potential domestic terrorists.

Terrorism and Weapons of Mass Destruction

By 1998, the threat of terrorist acts using chemical; biological; and, to a lesser extent, nuclear or radiological weapons of mass destruction (WMD) had become a major concern to the U.S. counterterrorism community. Concern has grown because of the increased availability of technologies for making such weapons, for example, through the Internet. The precedent set by the Japanese Aum Shinrikyo cult in 1995 when it staged a sarin gas attack in a Tokyo subway is another cause of concern. Analysts believe that the new breed of terrorists, including religious fanatics and hate groups, is no longer constrained, as traditional terrorists were, and seek mass

casualties as an end in itself. There is also concern that radical states like Iraq, whose commitment to its biological and chemical warfare programs is tenacious, notwithstanding UN sanctions, may attack the United States or American forces abroad using materials of mass destruction delivered by clandestine terrorists under the direction of a radical state or perhaps via long-range missiles.[17]

The perception of a new WMD terrorist threat has been given weight by studies and expert commissions calling this the Achilles' heel of America's defense strategy. The Clinton administration launched various programs for deterring or mitigating the effects of such a devastating attack. Officials acknowledge that the probability of such an attack is low, but they believe it is growing and that the potential consequences are so devastating that more preparation is needed.

The WMD terrorism threat is an especially difficult issue for policymakers because of the virtual impossibility of preparing in a comprehensive way for the huge variety of potential attacks and the many toxic and chemical substances that might be used. Massive resources would be needed for such preparation. And there are inherent difficulties in creating a coordinated program given the U.S. federal system and the thousands of government entities and jurisdictions that would be involved. For this reason, a more selective, "risk management" approach in which limited resources are invested where the risk appears to be greatest is probably needed. There is also a need for more restraint in official commentary about the WMD terrorist threat to avoid creating needless anxiety and provoking costly hoaxes.

Cyberterrorism

In recent years, the U.S. government has become increasingly concerned that terrorists might use computers to attack the digital infrastructure of the federal government, state and local authorities, the armed forces, public utilities, and other facilities using critical digital networks, including those in the private business and financial sectors. This potential threat, dubbed "cyberterrorism," has been widely publicized in the press. President Clinton appointed a Commission on the Protection of Vital Infrastructure to study the vulnerability of infrastructure in general and make recommendations.

There is little history of efforts by terrorists, international or domestic, to penetrate or disrupt sensitive cybernetworks for political purposes, although some terrorists doubtless possess the knowledge needed to do this. On the other hand, there have been hundreds of attacks on cybernetworks by mischievous hackers and criminals. Thus, the current problem in cyberspace appears to be crime rather than terrorism. It is conceivable that in the future such attacks will be made for political reasons and thus will qualify as terrorist violence. Some imaginative analysts and fiction writers have described scenarios in which cyberattacks cause airplanes to crash, dams to burst, and bridges to open, causing many deaths. There is no evidence to date that terrorists are contemplating such complex crimes, but cyberterrorist attacks are a serious potential threat.

COUNTERTERRORISM LAWS AND LAW ENFORCEMENT

Domestic Law

In searching for the best way to combat terrorism, the United States has relied increasingly on law and law enforcement. The basic principle of American policy today is that no political cause or grievance, even one with some legitimacy, can justify the killing of innocent civilians and that any such act must be considered a crime. Traditionally, most acts of violence committed by terrorists in the United States were subject to prosecution under conventional criminal laws against murder, assault, arson, and kidnapping. But prior to the last twenty years the United States had few legal tools for the investigation and prosecution of terrorist crimes against Americans abroad.

In the absence of such "extraterritorial" jurisdiction, the United States was forced to rely on foreign governments to deal with such acts at a time when terrorism against Americans overseas was growing. Often even friendly governments, because of their sympathy for the terrorists' political agendas (e.g., the Palestinian cause) or out of fear of reprisals, failed to prosecute terrorists aggressively. Nor could they arrest the terrorists and hand them over to the United States since at that time extraterritorial terrorist acts were not crimes under U.S. law. A case in point was the murder of Leon Klinghoffer, an American, in 1985 aboard the Italian cruise ship

Achille Lauro by a Palestinian radical group led by Abu Abbas. When the *Achille Lauro* docked in Alexandria, Egyptian authorities were unwilling to arrest Abbas. Nor could they hand him over to the United States, which had no jurisdiction in the case. When Egypt allowed him to escape on a commercial flight, U.S. military aircraft in a desperate maneuver forced the plane to land in Italy, hoping that the Italians would arrest him. Like the Egyptians, they chose not to do so, and Abbas was allowed to escape.

The lesson of this episode and other terrorist acts against Americans was that new laws were needed to authorize prosecution in the United States of terrorists acting against Americans abroad when the United States could gain custody of the suspect. As a result, the Congress passed many new statutes and today the United States has a wide variety of antiterrorism laws that confer extraterritorial jurisdiction. In many cases these laws impose tougher penalties for such crimes than for similar acts committed without terrorist motives in the United States.[18]

International Law

While domestic American antiterrorism law has expanded, the United States and its allies have also enlarged the reach of international law against terrorism in a growing series of treaties and conventions, a list of which follows. These treaties, now numbering eleven, address specific terrorist acts. They oblige signatories to pass domestic laws criminalizing the terrorist act defined in the treaty and to either prosecute or extradite the suspect to the country of the victim.

- 1963 Tokyo Convention on Offenses and Certain Other Acts Committed on Board Aircraft
- 1970 Hague Convention for the Unlawful Seizure of Aircraft
- 1971 Montreal Convention for the Suppression of Unlawful Acts against the Safety of Civil Aviation
- 1973 Convention on the Prevention and Punishment of Crimes against Internationally Protected Persons
- 1979 Convention on the Physical Protection of Nuclear Materials
- 1979 Convention against the Taking of Hostages

1988 Protocol for the Suppression of Unlawful Acts against the Safety of Fixed Platforms Located on the Continental Shelf

1988 Convention for the Suppression of Unlawful Acts against the Safety of Maritime Navigation

1991 Convention for the Marking of Plastic Explosives for the Purposes of Detection

1998 Convention for the Suppression of Terrorist Bombings

1999 Convention for the Suppression of Financing of Terrorism

The United States has greatly expanded its bilateral extradition treaties with other nations in order to strengthen further antiterrorism cooperation through international law. It has also upgraded old treaties, for example, by eliminating the "political exception" clause found in many old extradition treaties that had enabled terrorists to escape extradition by claiming that their crimes were political. Mutual legal assistance treaties (MLATs) are another device providing for mutual cooperation in the investigation and prosecution of crimes, and the United States has signed many of these in recent years.

Increasing reliance on the rule of law and criminalization of terrorism has greatly strengthened Washington's ability to investigate and prosecute terrorist crimes against Americans abroad. In recent years, U.S. authorities, with the help of foreign governments and treaty partners, have arrested many terrorist suspects abroad and brought them to the United States for trial and conviction.

By adopting law enforcement and criminalization as the central elements in its counterterrorism policy, the United States has had less reason to resort to unilateral or covert operations that are dangerous or controversial in order to apprehend terrorists abroad. It has seldom acted unilaterally, although some believe that it should do so regularly.

There is a dilemma in the criminalization and law enforcement approach to counterterrorism that Washington has not yet, but may someday, encounter. Terrorist organizations occasionally reform themselves and make peace with their adversaries. The IRA and the PLO are cases in point. If the senior political leaders of the PLO and the IRA had been indicted for the terrorist crimes of their subordinates, it would have been difficult for the United States and Israel, in the case of Yasser Arafat and the PLO, and the United

Kingdom in the case of the IRA leadership, to accept their former adversaries as peace partners. This problem is unlikely to arise in cases in which the political cause or grievance that motivates terrorism has no merit, and there is no reason to expect that it might be addressed in the future through a political or negotiating process.

Counterterrorism Sanctions

Laws and executive orders impose a wide variety of sanctions against states that the United States designates as sponsors of terrorism. These sanctions prohibit trade, military sales, and other economic transactions, and they vary among countries. Some laws contain waiver and licensing provisions for special cases. Most require the United States to oppose loans by international financial institutions to state sponsors.[19]

The impact of these sanctions has been mixed. Although they deprive state sponsors of valuable economic ties with the United States, Washington has been unable to persuade its European and Japanese allies to join in sanctions and companies in those countries have profited accordingly. This weakness has sharply reduced the impact of sanctions and harmed U.S. business interests.

In 1996, Congress passed the Iran-Libya Sanctions Act and the Helms-Burton Act concerning Cuba, which require the United States to sanction foreign companies that engage in certain economic relations with these states.[20] These laws are counterproductive. Their full implementation would seriously inflame the relations of the United States with its friends without significantly curtailing support for terrorism in the targeted states. Fortunately, the laws contain waiver provisions, which the president has exercised for broader reasons of foreign policy. The policy of widespread unilateral sanctions needs a reappraisal, and the State Department has undertaken this effort. The value of sanctions should be measured by whether they work and impose costs on other interests of the United States that outweigh the benefits for counterterrorism, not the short-term political satisfaction they may bring.

Unilateral U.S. sanctions as a counterterrorism tool have had little international support. In contrast, multilateral UN Security Council sanctions have been quite successful, as shown by the sanctions against Libya. When all nations join in sanctions, they provide powerful leverage. Libya, which was subject to heavy sanctions for the bombing of Pan Am Flight 103 in Scotland in 1988, finally yielded to these sanctions in 1999 by handing over the two Libyan suspects to prosecutors for trial in a Scottish court sitting in the Netherlands.

Debate over the Assassination of Terrorists

During the administration of President Ronald Reagan, following reports that the Central Intelligence Agency (CIA) had attempted to assassinate Cuban leader Fidel Castro in the 1960s, the president signed an executive order forbidding the use of assassination as a weapon of U.S. foreign policy or counterterrorism. Since then, some critics who advocate tougher counterterrorism measures have urged the repeal of this order, arguing that killing foreign terrorists or officials who are responsible for terrorist acts against American interests is justified for reasons of self-defense and deterrence. These critics have focused on such leaders as Saddam Hussein, Mu'ammar Qadhafi, Slobodan Milosovic, and Osama bin Laden as especially loathsome and dangerous figures whose elimination, it is argued, would bring about a safer and more stable world. Assassination, they claim, is a simpler and more certain counterterrorism weapon than the costly and uncertain processes of diplomacy, law enforcement, and sanctions.

Opponents of assassination argue that it is contrary to the rule of law, which is now at the center of U.S. counterterrorism policy, and would undermine the edifice of domestic and international criminal law that the United States has worked to promote throughout the world. They point out that assassination cannot substitute for criminal prosecution based on legal evidence, that it is very difficult and dangerous, that it risks collateral casualties or even killing of the wrong person, and that it can provoke retaliatory assassinations or terrorist acts directed against innocent Americans. Assassination practiced by a few states has indeed led to bloody reprisals. Opponents argue, above all, that the United States should not sink to the level of terrorists and engage in murder, however heinous the enemy. The latter arguments are compelling, and there is little chance that the United States will change its anti-assassination policy.

COUNTERTERRORISM DIPLOMACY AND INTERNATIONAL COOPERATION

Growing World Consensus against Terrorism

The globalization of terrorism in the last generation and a growing consensus that it should be criminalized have led to increased international cooperation, especially in the last decade. This international cooperation has required intensive diplomacy, multilateral and bilateral, and close and coordinated relationships among foreign ministries and intelligence and law enforcement agencies.

Before the last decade, U.S. efforts to create a common, international approach to terrorism were crippled by two major geopolitical divides, the Cold War and the Arab-Israeli conflict. Efforts to win support for condemnation of terrorist acts committed on behalf of Marxist or anticolonial revolution or the Palestinian struggle against Israel often foundered over these ideological and political fault lines.

Many governments, especially in the developing world, were unwilling to condemn revolutionary or anticolonial terrorism because of sympathy for the political agendas of the terrorists or fear of breaching their commitment to nonalignment. When terrorism issues were raised in multilateral bodies or bilateral discussions by the United States, these governments often excused terrorist acts on the grounds that these were the desperate efforts of oppressed "freedom fighters" whose circumstances had forced them to resort to terrorism. For example, states sympathetic to the Palestinian cause argued that its militants should be viewed as freedom fighters, not terrorists.

As a result of this political and ideological gap, other governments often declined to cooperate with the United States by arresting and prosecuting terrorists. Washington was also unable to persuade the UN General Assembly and other multilateral groups to condemn terrorists because of the perception that "one man's terrorist is another man's freedom fighter."

The fall of the Soviet Union and the renewal of the Arab-Israeli peace process changed this attitude. The end of revolutionary Marxism as a popular cause and the PLO's stand against terrorism and for peace with Israel enabled governments to deal with terrorism more objectively. A consensus that terrorism is a crime that cannot be justified under any circumstances began to grow. Arab and Islamic governments, some of which were under attack from local terrorists who sought to overthrow or destabilize them, also began to view terrorism as a threat to their internal stability and to condemn it forthrightly.

Multilateral Action

There were many signs of this new international consensus. In recent years, after failing for decades to condemn terrorism, the UN General Assembly passed and annually reiterated a strong resolution condemning terrorism and calling on nations to cooperate in opposition to it. In 1995, the Organization of the Islamic Conference did likewise. Other multilateral groups joined this trend, and there were counterterrorism conferences sponsored by the Philippines, Japan, Argentina, and Peru. In 1996, after a series of bus bombings in Israel threatened to abort peace talks between Israel and the Palestinians, American, European, Israeli, Arab, and Palestinian counterterrorism and law enforcement officials met as a working group in Washington, as a sequel to the Sharm-el-Sheikh Summit, to discuss cooperation in the struggle against all forms of terrorism.

The United States and the Group of Seven (G-7), whose terrorism subgroup had met annually before G-7 summits to consider new forms of counterterrorism cooperation, also intensified consultations. Russia was invited to join the group, which now became the Group of Eight (G-8), and Canada and France both sponsored special G-8 conferences on terrorism. The G-8 also continued to take the lead in proposing new international conventions on terrorism, for example, the Convention on Terrorist Bombing, which was approved by the UN General Assembly in 1997, and a draft convention on terrorist fund-raising, which the General Assembly completed in 1999.

Bilateral Cooperation

The United States has also intensified a series of periodic bilateral consultations with European Union states, Japan, Turkey, and Israel and new consultations in the Middle East, South Asia, East Asia, and Latin America. New bilateral counterterrorism ties were also cre-

ated with Muslim and Arab states, the Palestinians, and Russia. These consultations are led by the Department of State's coordinator for counterterrorism and are joined by experts from the intelligence, defense, and law enforcement communities. The FBI and U.S. intelligence agencies also carry out more informal and specialized consultations with counterpart agencies abroad.

Overseas Investigations, Extradition, and Rendition of Suspects

For the United States, application of its broad extraterritorial jurisdiction to investigate and prosecute terrorism against Americans abroad depends on close cooperation with foreign governments. In some cases, the state where the terrorist act occurred may choose to prosecute the crime under its own laws. But in other cases states have been willing to extradite suspects to the United States, pursuant to multilateral or bilateral treaties. In recent years, as a result of close counterterrorism ties forged with foreign governments, thirteen terrorist suspects have been extradited, or in some cases "rendered" (an informal handover of suspects to a foreign government) for prosecution in the United States. These extraditions have included terrorists responsible for the World Trade Center bombing, a conspiracy to blow up American passenger aircraft over the Pacific, attacks on American embassies in Asia and Africa, and various other attacks on U.S. interests.[21]

THE NO CONCESSIONS POLICY

Rationale and Application

The basic goal of U.S. counterterrorism policy is to punish all terrorist acts directed against American interests, thereby deterring further acts and reducing the level of terrorism. A fundamental tenet of this policy is that the United States will not yield to terrorists' threats or attempts to intimidate or extort concessions. The purpose of the "no concessions" policy is to put all potential attackers on notice that using terrorism to extract concessions or ransom is futile, thereby discouraging similar acts in the future.

This policy has been brought to bear in incidents of aircraft hijacking, bomb threats, the seizure of embassies, and the holding of Americans hostage for ransom or to extract concessions. This policy does not mean that the United States refuses to "negotiate" with terrorists. Indeed, U.S. officials seek to establish a dialogue with terrorists in threat situations in order to gain the release of hostages, to dissuade the terrorists from acting, or to buy time. If U.S. officials are unable to communicate with terrorists in such situations abroad, they encourage foreign governments to establish a dialogue.

The United States violated the no concessions policy in 1985 when it sold arms to Iran in the expectation that Iran would instruct its protégé, the Hizbullah in Lebanon, to release Americans whom it was holding hostage. The result was a fiasco. Not only did Iran not help to obtain release of the hostages, but the Hizbullah took more hostages, almost certainly under the direction of the Iranians, who were emboldened to raise the ante after seeing that the United States was willing to bargain. There have been other cases in which the United States came close to making concessions in terrorist crises, but for the most part the no concessions policy has been maintained. The policy may have been a factor behind the virtual abandonment by terrorists of the practice of seizing U.S. officials for ransom or political concessions since the early 1980s. In contrast, terrorists have continued to abduct private American citizens, knowing that their families and companies are often willing to pay a ransom.

Tension between Humanitarian Need and Denying Terrorist Gains

The no concessions policy is difficult to apply and is controversial in practice, especially when the lives of hostages are at stake. There is usually a conflict between the humanitarian urge to rescue the victims and the need to avoid encouraging further terrorist acts by making concessions or paying a ransom. The United States encourages all Americans to support this policy, but it is binding only on U.S. government officials in dealing with terrorists. Often when private citizens are taken hostage abroad their employers or families, who are not responsible for public policy, establish contact with terrorists and negotiate ransom settlements. There is no U.S. law forbidding such acts. In countries like Colombia, where

ransom payments are common, kidnapping is frequent and in many cases should be defined as common crime or extortion rather than politically motivated terrorism.

Dealing with the tension between the no concessions policy and immediate humanitarian needs is all the more difficult when terrorists demand concessions by the U.S. government and the family of the potential victim urges the government to bow to the terrorists' demands. As the United States learned during the hostage crises in Iran and Lebanon, reconciling the need for compassion with the need to protect other public interests and adhere to principle is not easy. Some governments, including several that otherwise pursue tough counterterrorism policies, make concessions in order to save lives and thus expose themselves to further acts of terrorism.

THE MILITARY'S ROLE IN COUNTERTERRORISM

Public Support

Military force has always been an element in the U.S. arsenal of counterterrorism tools, together with law enforcement, sanctions, and diplomacy, and the United States maintains highly trained, specialized forces for use in a variety of terrorism crises. But in practice force has seldom been used because of the difficulties and drawbacks in applying it effectively.

On the few occasions when the United States has used force to punish or preempt terrorism, the public response has been very positive. A swift, strong, military reaction has an immense cathartic effect in satisfying the anger and outrage Americans feel about terrorist killings of innocent citizens. Force is regarded as an effective message that the United States will not be intimidated by terrorism and a warning to others that such attacks will be avenged. Compared to the tedious and uncertain alternative of using criminal law in response to terrorist crimes, the military option offers the appearance of swift justice.

Cases in Which the United States Has Used Force

In recent decades, major military force has been used against terrorism only a few times. In 1981, an effort to rescue Americans held hostage in the U.S. embassy in Teheran with helicopter-borne troops ended in disaster when everything went wrong and a helicopter and troop transport aircraft collided after landing in the Iranian desert.[22] This abortive mission revealed the need for better intraservice coordination and training. It led to the creation of the U.S. Special Operations Command, which is responsible today for the military's counterterrorism role and many other difficult, specialized missions.

Following the release of the American hostages in Iran in 1982, President Reagan announced that thereafter the United States would impose "swift and effective retribution" against terrorists. As terrorist attacks multiplied and public concern mounted, National Security Directive 138 was adopted, announcing the policy of using force against terrorists and moving from "defense to offense." Secretary of State George Shultz warned terrorists that they would pay a price for further attacks on the United States and that America was prepared to take "preventive or preemptive actions" against terrorists. In 1986, Washington exercised this new approach after intelligence clearly established that Libyan agents had bombed the La Belle Discotheque in Berlin, killing an American soldier and wounding 220 others. The U.S. Air Force bombed military facilities and other sites in Tripoli, including a dwelling of President Mu'ammar Qadhafi in Tripoli.

In 1985, the United States used force after the killing of Leon Klinghoffer on the cruise ship *Achille Lauro.* When Egypt allowed the killers, a radical Palestinian faction leader, Abu Abbas, and his gang, to escape Cairo in an Egyptair passenger aircraft after the *Achille Lauro* landed in Alexandria, U.S. fighter planes intercepted the flight and forced it to land in Italy. Although Italy prosecuted Klinghoffer's killer, it chose not to prosecute Abu Abbas and allowed him to leave the country. In 1991, after coalition forces reversed Iraq's invasion of Kuwait, a car bomb, believed to have been planted by Iraqi intelligence officials, was placed at a point on the motorcade route of visiting president George Bush. It was discovered before it detonated, and the United States responded with cruise missile attacks on Iraqi security installations in Baghdad.

The United States also responded with force in August 1998 after terrorist suicide bombers, believed to have been guided by Osama bin Laden, destroyed the American embassies in Nairobi and Dar es

Salaam. The United States responded with simultaneous cruise missile attacks against terrorist training camps associated with bin Laden in Afghanistan and the Al Shifa pharmaceutical plant in Khartoum, Sudan, which Washington believed contained a chemical weapons facility connected to bin Laden.

Disadvantages of Military Force

The infrequent use of American military force in combating terrorism reflects various practical problems inherent in using force effectively. Contrary to popular belief, it is difficult and dangerous, and often impossible, to send U.S. ground forces against terrorists in sovereign states where terrorists have been given or have established a safe haven. Nor is it usually possible for aircraft to accurately target and attack terrorists on the ground. Training camps and other terrorist "infrastructure," such as Osama bin Laden's camps in Afghanistan, are usually makeshift, rudimentary operations in rural areas that are easily moved and replaced.

When a state employs its agents or contractors to attack American targets, as Libya and Iraq have done, and the purpose of a military response is to deter and punish the guilty government, targeting is less of a problem than it would be against groups that lack state sponsorship, since military or other sites associated with terrorism are usually available. The U.S. cruise missile attack against Iraq in 1991, launched in response to the plot to assassinate President Bush, apparently accomplished this purpose, judging from the lack of subsequent Iraqi terrorism directed against U.S. targets. However, the U.S. bombing of Libya in 1986 failed to deter Libyan-sponsored terrorism. Indeed, the bombing of Pan Am Flight 103 in December 1988 by terrorists whom the United States and the United Kingdom have identified as Libyan intelligence agents was probably carried out in retaliation against the U.S. raid on Tripoli, which killed several dozen civilians.

The risk of unintended civilian casualties when using military force against state sponsors of terrorism or nonstate terrorists is often high. This factor and the chance that such attacks may provoke further terrorism against American civilian targets, as was apparently the case with the bombing of Flight 103, are major drawbacks to the military option.

Another drawback of the use of force against terrorists is finding a persuasive legal justification. This problem has been cited by European allies of the United States and other critics who claim that unilateral military action is incompatible with the growing trend, which the United States itself has championed, of dealing with terrorism through the rule of law, especially when the target is not a state. A military response to an act of terrorism sponsored by a state can be justified as self-defense. The legal issue becomes more acute when military action is taken against nonstate targets in sovereign foreign countries without the consent of the host government.

When considering the use of force against terrorists—both state and nonstate actors—governments must anticipate that other governments and critics may expect strong evidence of guilt, of the kind that would withstand scrutiny in a court of law, as justification. For retaliatory action, this explanation can present problems since such evidence is often derived from sensitive intelligence sources and methods. For example, the inability of the Clinton administration to present convincing proof that the Al Shifa pharmaceutical plant was linked to Osama bin Laden and was really a disguised chemical weapons plant exposed the U.S. government to the embarrassing criticism that the attack was neither a legal nor a proper response to the terrorist bombings in East Africa.

The United States was able to present a plausible legal case that it was essential to attack the terrorist training camps in Afghanistan. Washington argued that intelligence showed that terrorists associated with Osama bin Laden and these camps were preparing to strike other U.S. targets in the period following the bombings of the U.S. embassies in Nairobi and Dar es Salaam, and that the Taliban government in Afghanistan had refused to close these camps or expel bin Laden. The United States claimed it had therefore acted legally in self-defense, and few faulted this rationale.

A Necessary Option

Fighting terrorism at this stage in history cannot yet be confined entirely to diplomacy and law enforcement. Given the existence of states that operate outside the norms of international law and that tolerate or support terrorism, the United States needs to keep open the option of using military force, albeit on rare occasions. The fact that the United States has highly trained military assets that at times have been used can serve as a strong deterrent to potential terrorists. In late 1995, terrorists seized the Japanese ambassador's residence in Lima, Peru, and took hostage dozens of foreign diplomats, including seven Americans. The Americans were released within a few days, many weeks before Peruvian Special Forces rescued the others. At the time, a rumor was circulating in Lima that American Delta Force commandos had arrived in town and were preparing to storm the residence. The rumor was false, but it is possible that the terrorists released the Americans because they feared a U.S. attack.

Highly trained U.S. special forces are capable of carrying out many other complex missions that may or may not be associated with terrorist emergencies. They have provided critical support over the years, for example, in emergency evacuation and rescue situations in which official and civilian Americans were in danger. Military assets have also been an integral part of delicate operations involving the apprehension of terrorist suspects abroad by foreign governments in cooperation with the American government and the extradition (or informal "rendition") of the suspects to the United States. In many such cases, U.S. military aircraft are used. The Department of Defense also provides expert training to special forces of other nations in order to improve their ability to deal with terrorism and other complex emergencies and to collaborate, if need be, with U.S. forces.

COUNTERTERRORISM ORGANIZATION AND COORDINATION

The Need for Teamwork

Over the years, the United States has developed, through trial and error, a process of coordinating the assets of many different government agencies to combat terrorism. Prior to the 1990s, disagreements within the government sometimes hobbled counterterrorism efforts and led to confusion about U.S. policy abroad. The system was badly shaken during the Reagan administration when staff members of the National Security Council took secret and unilateral action in terrorism matters without informing other agencies, including the Departments of State and Defense. The most dramatic example was the secret deal that provided weapons to Iran in exchange for the release of hostages in Lebanon held by the Hizbullah and the use of funds from these transactions to support the anticommunist "Contra" militia in Nicaragua. The Iran-Contra scandal involved violations of both U.S. law and counterterrorism policy and led to a congressional investigation and the conviction of various U.S. officials.

The lesson learned from this debacle was that dealing effectively with terrorism requires close teamwork among the many agencies whose skills must be integrated in a collective process. There were occasional proposals for the creation of a counterterrorism "czar" in the White House to centralize all counterterrorism policies and operations. But, because the roles of many agencies are required and all agencies have their own personnel and budgets, a highly centralized process seemed neither practical nor desirable. Instead, a process of coordination evolved among cabinet agencies and the White House.

The potential always exists for friction and bureaucratic competition among agencies involved in combating international terrorism, given the high political concern about this issue in the United States and the sensitive foreign policy issues it presents. This places a premium on high-quality, professional personnel and teamwork. In contrast to the situation in former decades, coordination today is quite effective. The targeting of terrorists and terrorist suspects using the combined resources of diplomacy, intelligence, and law enforcement, often with military support, has made possible many operations in which terrorists have been arrested abroad and brought to the United States for trial and conviction.

U.S. Agencies with Counterterrorism Responsibilities

By means of a presidential directive, the Department of Justice (including the FBI, which is an arm of the department) has been designated the "lead agency" for domestic terrorism, that is, for policy and operations concerning terrorism within the United States, including terrorist acts by foreigners within the United States.

The response to acts of international terrorism directed against U.S. citizens and targets abroad requires more complex organization than does the response to similar acts committed in the United

States, since the resources of many agencies are needed and foreign governments are involved. In this realm, the president has designated the State Department as the lead agency. The Office of the Coordinator for Counterterrorism (S/CT) is in charge of overall coordination of policy and operations for international terrorism. The head of S/CT is a presidential appointee with ambassadorial rank who reports directly to the secretary of state. Frequent consultations by S/CT, which often leads an interagency team, are conducted with foreign governments to enhance international cooperation. The office also represents the United States in various multilateral bodies such as the counterterrorism subgroup of the Group of 8.

Within the State Department, S/CT works closely with the Bureau of Diplomatic Security (DS), which is responsible for the protection of American officials abroad. The DS administers the Anti-Terrorism Assistance Program, which trains foreign security personnel in antiterrorism techniques and has trained more than twenty thousand foreign officials from more than one hundred countries.[23] It also runs the department's Terrorism Rewards Program, which offers payments of up to two million dollars for information leading to the arrest and conviction of terrorists.[24] The Bureau of Consular Affairs assists American citizens abroad and issues warnings concerning terrorism and other hazards to travelers.

The CIA and other elements of the U.S. intelligence community are responsible for collecting and analyzing information about international terrorism. The Counterterrorism Center at the CIA, which reports to the director of central intelligence, combines counterterrorism personnel from various agencies. It works closely with the Department of State and the FBI. Intelligence officers also maintain liaisons and intelligence-sharing relationships with friendly foreign governments that are critical to combating international terrorism.

The Department of Justice and the FBI also take part in Washington's international counterterrorism apparatus. Their role has grown, as the United States has turned increasingly to law enforcement as its principal weapon against terrorism and has enacted new laws that provide "extraterritorial jurisdiction" for investigation and prosecution of terrorist crimes against American interests abroad. The senior Justice Department official in this process is the assistant secretary for terrorism and violent crime, and the FBI's representative is the head of the International Terrorism Directorate.

Legal attachés from the FBI serve under ambassadors at a growing number of American embassies. They provide liaison between the FBI in Washington and its foreign law enforcement counterparts. They also work with host government officials to investigate terrorist and other crimes perpetrated against Americans over which the United States has extraterritorial jurisdiction.

The Department of Defense is also a key player. Counterterrorism policy at Defense is the responsibility of the assistant secretary of defense for special operations and low-intensity conflict (OSD/SOLIC). Operational support is handled by a flag rank officer representing the Joint Chiefs of Staff.

Because U.S. civil aviation has been targeted by terrorists, the Federal Aviation Administration (FAA) has been charged with responsibility for aviation security. Together with its parent, the Department of Transportation, it is an important part of the counterterrorism community.

The Department of Energy, which has sophisticated technical resources for dealing with nuclear terrorism, participates in this process. The Department of Treasury and its affiliate, the U.S. Customs Service, also play various roles in counterterrorism law enforcement, for example, administering and enforcing economic and financial sanctions and providing security at ports of entry.

Under the Clinton administration, the National Security Council assumed a larger role in counterterrorism than most previous administrations through the Office of the National Security Advisor for Global Affairs. This official chairs the Counterterrorism Security Group (CSG), which meets frequently to deal with major counterterrorism policy and operational issues. The chairman of the CSG was designated by the president as national coordinator for security, infrastructure protection, and counterterrorism to coordinate, among other things, policy and planning dealing with potential domestic terrorist attacks using materials of mass destruction.

Research and Development of Counterterrorism Technologies

The United States also has an active and increasingly well-funded program for research and development of counterterrorism technologies under the direction of the Technical Support Working

Group (TSWG). This interagency group is chaired by a staff member of the State Department's Office of the Coordinator for Counterterrorism and is staffed and financed largely by the Department of Defense. It has developed dozens of technologies for enhancing counterterrorism communications, surveillance, detection of explosives and weapons, defensive measures, building security, and the identification of chemical, biological, and radiological substances. It also maintains joint research and development programs with several friendly foreign governments.

SECURITY AGAINST TERRORISM

Protection of U.S. Embassies and Diplomats

Security against terrorist attacks has been an important element of U.S. counterterrorism policy, and during the last thirty years government and the private sector have spent billions of dollars on security measures. Nevertheless, investment in secure U.S. embassies abroad has fallen short of the need because of budget constraints and perceived higher priorities.

In the fifteen years that followed World War II, when terrorist attacks against American officials abroad were rare, Washington began a massive program of building new embassies to show its commitments to the world and demonstrate the best in modern American architecture. Many of these buildings were monuments to style, but they were vulnerable to attack. By the late 1960s, terrorists and protestors were targeting U.S. embassies as symbols of American power and prestige, especially in Latin America, Europe, and Vietnam. The Department of State began to realize that it could no longer maintain adequate security without some compromises in the image of openness and accessibility that Americans wished to project in the design and location of their embassies.[25]

In the 1970s, terrorists struck American embassies and diplomats with growing frequency—in Khartoum in 1973, Athens in 1974, Kuala Lumpur in 1975, Beirut in 1976, and Tehran in 1979. As it became clear that the United States could no longer depend on host governments for protection, the State Department increasingly fortified embassies with retrofitted walls, concrete perimeter ballards, sentry posts, surveillance cameras, vehicle barriers, and other protective devices. Searches of vehicles and personnel were increased and mirrors, security lights, and warning and communications devices were installed. Many embassies began to hire and train local guard forces to supplement their American security officers and Marine security detachments, and all embassies were instructed to prepare emergency response and evacuation plans.

But the stark dimensions of the terrorist threat did not become clear until a series of suicide truck bombings in 1983 destroyed the U.S. Marine barracks in Beirut and later the American embassy there, killing hundreds of Americans. As a result, an Advisory Panel on Overseas Security, chaired by retired admiral Bobby Inman, recommended a massive increase in funds for building safer embassies and establishing tough new security standards.[26]

For a few years, Congress responded with increased funds. But as the Cold War ended and terrorism seemed to abate, memories faded about vulnerability to truck bomb attacks. Congress, preoccupied with budget cutting and domestic concerns, progressively slashed the Department of State's budget for security and embassy construction as part of deep cuts in the foreign affairs budget.

In 1996, a devastating truck bomb killed nineteen U.S. Air Force personnel and wounded more than five hundred others at the Al Khobar barracks in Dhahran, Saudi Arabia, a reminder of U.S. vulnerability. Yet there was no restoration of funding or renewed momentum for the Department of State's security and embassy-building programs. Although Washington should not have been surprised, it was shocked when radical Islamic terrorists associated with the Saudi dissident terrorist Osama bin Laden used suicide truck bombers to destroy the U.S. embassies in Nairobi and Dar es Salaam on August 7, 1998, killing 220 people, and wounding more than 5,000.

The lesson of these bombings was that high standards of physical security are necessary for all U.S. embassies, even in areas like Africa, where such attacks were previously unknown. Today's terrorists are more mobile than in the past and seek out vulnerable targets for surprise attacks worldwide.[27]

Some have proposed that because of its vulnerability and the expense of building safe embassies the United States should reduce its profile abroad and conduct more diplomacy from Washington. Such a retreat would be a major victory for terrorists. The United States is

quite capable of paying for adequate protection for its officials, and an active overseas presence provides essential "eyes and ears" and the influence needed to protect America's many interests abroad.

After the embassy bombings in East Africa, accountability review boards chaired by retired admiral William Crowe recommended major increases in funding for diplomatic security and safe embassy buildings.[28] Although some new funds were appropriated, the Clinton administration, under pressure from Congress to reduce nonmilitary spending, did not request sufficient funds to meet this need.

Terrorist attacks on American embassies and diplomats are attacks on the United States. The cost of such attacks should be measured not just in lives and property damage but in lost prestige for the United States and victories for terrorists. The failure of successive U.S. administrations and congresses to provide adequate funds for safe embassies is a shortcoming in U.S. counterterrorism policy that needs to be remedied.

Protection of U.S. Military Forces

The Department of Defense gave the highest priority to protecting American armed forces abroad following the Al Khobar barracks attack in 1996, and a similar, less costly attack in 1995 on a U.S. military office in Riyadh. The Pentagon is investing heavily in physical defense, antiterrorist technologies, and training for the rank and file, preaching the message: "Security is everyone's business." This investment has been quite effective.

Civil Aviation Security

Because of the wave of terrorist hijackings and other attacks on U.S. civil aviation, beginning in the late 1970s the FAA instituted sweeping security requirements for American airlines and airports. These include, for example, scanners to detect weapons and explosives in luggage and stringent controls on access to some airport areas. The FAA tightened aviation security after the bombing of Pan Am Flight 103 in 1988 by suspected Libyan terrorists, for example, by requiring "baggage matching," which prevents loading luggage unless its owner also boards the aircraft.

Many other nations' airlines have been targeted by terrorists, and as a result there has been extraordinary international cooperation. The center of this process is the International Civil Aviation Organization (ICAO) in Montreal, a UN body, which formulates worldwide standards. Airlines in countries that do not abide by ICAO standards, or by those of the FAA, which are sometimes stricter than ICAO's, are not permitted to land in the United States. And foreign airports that are not certified by the FAA cannot be used by U.S. airlines. As a result of tougher aviation security measures, terrorist attacks against aviation targets declined sharply in the 1990s.

Security for the Private Sector

Terrorism also poses a major challenge to American businesses and other private organizations that operate abroad. Indeed, attacks against U.S. businesses overseas now exceed attacks on official targets. In response to this threat, a large security consulting industry has emerged in the United States, and American companies spend billions for security at home and abroad. Although terrorism has discouraged trade and investment in some countries, American business has coped well and is more active abroad today than ever before.

The State Department has created an effective mechanism for consultation and information sharing with the business community called the Overseas Security Advisory Council (OSAC). Through the Internet and an electronic bulletin board, information on terrorist threats and defensive measures are shared.[29]

TERRORISM, THE PUBLIC, AND THE MEDIA

The Need for a Balanced Declaratory Policy

All U.S. administrations have shown strong concern about terrorism because of the threat it poses and because it evokes such strong public concerns and emotions. Political leaders understand, quite rightly, that failure to do so would bring charges of weakness and indifference from the press and political adversaries. Since the end of the Cold War, the speeches and statements of American officials on the subject of national security have given an even higher profile to international terrorism as one of the major "global threats" facing the United States. A tough, resolute policy toward

terrorists that emphasizes a high level of vigilance is therefore an important part of the U.S. public affairs posture.

There is some danger that with their comments on the threat of terrorism and the issuance of warnings political leaders and officials may inadvertently increase public anxiety to levels that exceed the reality of the threat. By exaggerating the threat of terrorism in order to demonstrate the resolve to combat it and show sympathy for its victims, officials can increase the level of fear and disruption, thus giving terrorists an unearned psychological victory.

Media Sensationalism

Public officials must also carefully anticipate the way the media will treat official comments and public warnings. Terrorism is among the most compelling human interest stories, and the media give it very full (and sometimes exaggerated and hyperbolic) coverage. Even officials' modest comments or warnings are sometimes inflated by the media, thus creating an unintended level of fear that may not be warranted by the underlying danger.

Travel Advisories

The Bureau of Consular Affairs of the Department of State issues periodic travel advisories warning citizens of particular or general threats that have come to the attention of U.S. authorities.[30] The FAA also issues warnings to air travelers. In both cases, warnings are published only in cases in which the United States believes that threatened attacks cannot be prevented with assurance.

In recent years, travel advisories have been issued with increasing frequency. After the bombing of Flight 103 in 1986, the Department of State was criticized for not making public in advance confidential intelligence that indicated there might be an attack on U.S. civil aviation. The result was the "no double standard policy," which requires the release of sanitized versions of threat intelligence when assured countermeasures are not feasible. In fact, no precise intelligence foreshadowed the Flight 103 bombing, and U.S. officials were among the victims.

As in other public statements about the threat of terrorism, a fine line must be drawn in deciding whether to issue travel advisories in order to avoid unnecessary fear and disruption. Terrorists realize that they can frighten thousands or millions of people simply by issuing threats. Indeed, the U.S. intelligence community receives hundreds of threats annually that turn out to be false. This fact places a difficult burden on analysts, who must separate the credible threats from hoaxes perpetrated by malicious pranksters and the false threats of genuine adversaries. Travel advisories also must be precise enough (with respect to the time and location of threats) to offer helpful guidance. Threats that are too general cause anxiety without providing any practical guidance and can cause unnecessary disruption, offense to foreign governments, and economic loss.

Discussing WMD Terrorism

Terrorism that uses materials of mass destruction—nuclear, chemical, and biological—is frequently mentioned by U.S. officials as a looming threat to national security. In addressing the practical and declaratory aspects of this threat, officials must measure the potentially drastic consequences of such attacks against the low probability, based on historical experience, that they will occur. Officials must also be aware of the special concern that the specter of such attacks arouses in the public mind and temper public comments accordingly without neglecting or minimizing the problem.

War against Terrorism?

Officials often declare that the United States is "waging war against terrorism." While the war metaphor expresses the determination to defeat terrorism, it suggests that all of it will ultimately be defeated, which is unlikely. A more serious problem is that war rhetoric is seen by terrorists and their supporters as giving them the status and prestige they seek as warriors against a powerful, hated adversary. Terrorists are not warriors. They are criminals.

POSTSCRIPT

THE CATASTROPHIC TERRORIST ATTACKS against the United States on September 11, 2001, confirmed the worst fears of American analysts that the twenty-first century would bring a new epoch of mass-casualty terrorism. These suicide attacks were carried out by radical Islamic terrorists associated with the Al Qaeda international terrorism network led by Osama bin Laden. The terrorists flew commercial airliners into the World Trade Center and the Pentagon, killing approximately three thousand people and inflicting incalculable economic damage. These attacks, unprecedented in the history of terrorism, demonstrated that fanatic, ideologically driven, transnational terrorists have the discipline, organization, and technical skills needed to inflict immense damage on the United States on a scale that experts had not anticipated. September 11 revealed that, notwithstanding major U.S. counterterrorism efforts in recent years, America is more vulnerable to terrorist attacks than anyone had realized. Other terrorist attacks in the United States in the fall of 2001, which involved lethal anthrax spores enclosed in letters sent through the public mails, revealed another serious vulnerability.

In response to the September 11 attacks, President George W. Bush declared that the United States is at war with global terrorists and that this will be the highest priority of U.S. foreign policy until victory is won. Recognizing the need for strong international support, the United States forged an international coalition against terrorism and expanded intelligence and law enforcement cooperation abroad. On the basis of compelling information that the Osama bin Laden group was responsible for September 11, the United States launched military attacks against the militant Islamist Taliban regime in Afghanistan, which had given refuge to bin Laden and his senior Al Qaeda henchmen. The United States took other initiatives to strengthen its counterterrorism capabilities at home and abroad. Some of these depart from past counterterrorism policies and practices. Others reinforce traditional approaches.

It is too early to identify with any certainty the failures of U.S. policy that contributed to the September 11 debacle, but some preliminary conclusions can be drawn. First, aviation security practices, although they had been upgraded in recent years, were inadequate. Analysts knew that Islamic extremists had established a record of suicidal and mass-casualty attacks. However, because aerial hijacking had sharply declined and there had been no previous use of passenger aircraft as suicide bombs, such attacks were not included in threat scenarios. New airport measures for screening passengers and baggage and onboard security practices have since been adopted. If rigorously implemented, these steps should prevent further mass-casualty attacks of the September 11 variety.

The September 11 attacks also revealed the weakness of American border and visa controls and demonstrated that intelligence sharing among the FBI and other U.S. authorities must be improved, notwithstanding efforts in recent years to correct these problems.

Many commentators claimed that September 11 was the result of a serious failure of American intelligence agencies to anticipate threats and provide warnings. Surely, more can be done to improve intelligence collection and analysis, and the Bush administration is taking steps to meet this need. But it is not realistic to expect that U.S. intelligence can become omniscient about the plans of foreign terrorist groups. These are the most difficult targets to penetrate. One obvious problem that needs attention is inadequate foreign language expertise among the employees of U.S. agencies.

The September 11 and anthrax by mail incidents proved that the United States needs better coordination among agencies to help prevent terrorist attacks and deal with their consequences. The president has appointed a coordinator for homeland security to coordinate the counterterrorism functions of a multiplicity of federal, state, and local agencies and jurisdictions. This is a formidable task. The anthrax attacks proved that improved systems of diagnosis and emergency treatment and medication are needed as well as means for dealing with mass biological attacks. To date, most U.S. experts have assigned a low probability to such attacks, but the apparent ability of terrorists to obtain minute particles of "aerosol" anthrax has increased concerns about this danger.

In the area of law and law enforcement, the Bush administration requested and received legislative authority for various new counterterrorism tools. It also issued a strengthened executive order for monitoring and blocking terrorists' financial assets, although past experience suggests that such measures cannot stop their financing altogether. Other, more controversial initiatives include mass questioning of Muslim and Arab Americans; prolonged, secret detention of aliens; the right to monitor communications between lawyers and terrorist suspect clients; and the creation of military tribunals for trying foreign terrorists in place of the civilian trials that the United States has used in the past. The Bush administration, in response to critics who claim that some of the new measures are unnecessary and harmful, believes that such measures are appropriate, given the severity of the terrorist threat. As of the end of 2001, this debate was continuing.

It is not clear yet how the proposed military tribunals will be used. Some friendly foreign governments have announced that they will not extradite terrorist suspects to the United States for trial in military tribunals. This could create an obstacle to U.S. counterterrorism efforts in the future, assuming the United States will continue to rely heavily on prosecution of foreign anti-U.S. terrorists apprehended abroad with help from foreign governments. In any case, the United States has decided to try the first foreign suspect in connection with the September 11 attacks, who was arrested and indicted in the United States, in a civilian court.

The main new emphasis in American counterterrorism policy after September 11 has been a declared preference for greater use of military force to preempt, punish, track down, or apprehend terrorists. President Bush has announced that hereafter the United States will regard any state that harbors terrorists "of global reach" as supporters of terrorism, and other officials have warned that such states might be subject to U.S. military action. Some commentators have suggested that military force, which enjoys strong public support, should become the new paradigm of U.S. counterterrorism policy.

The use of U.S. air and ground forces in Afghanistan to defeat the Taliban regime and help Afghan forces pursue Osama bin Laden has, as of this writing, been quite effective, although bin Laden is still considered at large. But the circumstances are unusual. Afghanistan is a broken state, and the Taliban regime was widely hated. American forces have had Afghan military allies on the ground, and neighboring Pakistan and Uzbekistan have given vital support. There has also been broad international sympathy and support for, as well as participation in, the American military effort.

In the future, there may be similar situations in which terrorists take refuge in foreign countries whose governments decline to hand them over to the United States or where the United States identifies potential terrorist threats. However, in most of these cases it will be more difficult for the United States to use force to apprehend or preempt terrorists against the will of the host government because of sovereignty concerns, tactical and logistical problems, problems of legal justification, and lack of regional and international support. It is likely, therefore, that in the future the United States will continue to rely on diplomacy and cooperation among intelligence and law enforcement officials to obtain custody of foreign terrorist suspects and bring them to justice in the United States. The United States will nevertheless maintain effective military counterterrorism assets for overt or covert use when and where the gravity of the crime and the need for self-defense are clear, military action is feasible, and other options are not available. The very presence of this capability can also serve as a deterrent to terrorism.

The September 11 attacks proved again that, in addition to destroying lives and property, terrorism inflicts enormous psychic damage. American officials, for the most part, have acted wisely in rallying public morale. Some officials could be faulted, however, for a series of public warnings of further terrorist attacks, without specifying the time, the place, or how citizens might protect themselves. Such warnings are of dubious value and contribute unnecessarily to fear and economic loss. It should be emphasized, notwithstanding the enormity of the September 11 attacks, that the probability of becoming a victim of terrorism is still quite low.

There is also a danger that official promises to achieve "victory in the war against terrorism" will create exaggerated expectations of total victory. While it is important to mobilize and sustain strong support for more effective counterterrorism efforts, especially against catastrophic attacks like those of September 11, the recurrence of conflict throughout history suggests that even such heightened efforts are unlikely to stop all terrorism, especially against an open society like ours.

Finally, as the U.S. government broadens and strengthens its policies aimed specifically at preventing terrorism and apprehending terrorists, a comprehensive American counterterrorism strategy should include efforts to address and ameliorate the root causes of terrorism.

At the beginning of the twenty-first century, the most prominent terrorist threat comes from within the Muslim states of the Middle East and South Asia where political and economic development lags far behind that of the developed world. Political alienation in autocratic states, poverty, poor education, and unemployment breed humiliation, hatred, and despair. These conditions create fertile ground for political violence and terrorism. Grievances in troubled societies are exploited by demagogues and religious charlatans like Osama bin Laden and are frequently directed against the United States and the West. The long-festering Israeli-Palestinian conflict is another source of Arab and Muslim anger against the United States and discourages closer counterterrorism cooperation from governments in that region.

It is not yet clear whether the Bush administration will decide, as some are recommending, to create and provide adequate resources for a second track in its counterterrorism policy intended to address the root causes of terrorism through more expansive foreign policies. Such a strategy would use diplomacy, more vigorous intervention in incipient conflicts, economic development assistance, and other tools to help ease the sources of strife. These efforts should aim to affect conditions that generate political violence and terrorism, not just in the Arab and Muslim worlds but in troubled areas elsewhere. A redefinition of American national security that deals with conditions that breed terrorism, in addition to more effective traditional counterterrorism efforts, is necessary if we are to develop a comprehensive strategy to fight terrorism and reduce the risk of more tragedies like that of September 11.

ARGENTINA

Roger W. Fontaine

THE TERM *PYRRHIC VICTORY* readily comes to mind in describing Argentina's decade-long war with multiple organizations that sowed terror and reaped counterterror, all of which continues to haunt the country's politics. Like the ancient king of Epirus, the Argentine authorities of the time may have wiped out the terrorist groups with near finality, but they did so at an exorbitant cost for which the Argentine nation is still paying.[1] To be explicit, the governments of Argentina defeated, indeed eliminated, the terrorist threat but at such a price in lives and legality that democratically elected regimes will still be plagued by the past, leaving, among other things, Argentina's ability to combat similar or related threats now and in the future a very open question.[2]

How could the Argentines get it so wrong? To be sure, combating a determined terrorist force is never easy or free of mistakes. Innocent lives will be lost or damaged no matter how the war is conducted. In Argentina's case, however, this commonsense assessment cannot be plausibly argued. Why the security forces got it wrong, meanwhile, may be a simple question for which there is no equally simple answer. But searching for that answer in a cool and dispassionate manner may tell us much about how to meet a terrorist threat efficiently and humanely anywhere in the world, far more so, in fact, than any "successful" counterterrorism campaign could ever do.

In saying all that, the following will serve in no way as an apologia for the violent left-wing groups that sought a new Argentina, aping the revolutionary movements and governments that proliferated in the 1960s and 1970s. Much of the literature on Argentina's so-called *guerra sucia* criticizes governmental authorities, the military and police in particular, and conveniently minimizes or ignores altogether the atrocities of the Left. That said, however, minimizing the responsibility of the security forces simply plays into the agenda of those who have no interest in fostering a genuine respect for human rights—especially (and being the most basic), government resting on the consent of the governed.[3]

In any just and settled judgment on those years, that one-sided approach cannot be left unchallenged. It should be remembered that the war of the Argentine armed groups that sought the overthrow of authority—whether elected civilian or military—was conducted without a shred of legality or concern for human rights. The war they waged was neither a good nor just one. It was a war in which the leadership, at least, fled the country when threatened, ordering their followers to commit suicide rather than risk capture and interrogation.

A question remains, however. How could a war against terrorism that had the overwhelming support of the Argentine people, at least in the beginning, prove to be the worst managed in the hemisphere? To begin answering this question requires a clear understanding of the war's background, which runs deep into Argentine society.

BACKGROUND TO TERRORISM

Argentina's inability to combat terrorism effectively is in part a result of the fact that Argentina remained, ironically, largely untouched by guerrilla violence during the 1960s and 1970s. At the time, this situation was not thought to be remarkable. After all, Argentina did not resemble the smaller and poorer nations of the hemisphere in Central America and the Caribbean or the northern tier of South American states, Colombia and Venezuela, much less the impoverished Andean nations, Peru and Bolivia.

Argentina, it was said, was too middle class, too urban, too developed economically and socially, too European (and, dare we say, too white) to be seriously threatened by rural-based *guerrilleros* (guerrillas) following a strategy of war involving small mobile groups of insurgents, despite the existence of one of that strategy's crown princes, Ernesto Che Guevara, himself an Argentine, albeit a peripatetic one. A brief and disastrous attempt at rural insurgency based in Argentina's far north in 1963 only seemed to confirm the conventional wisdom. To Guevara, the key to South America was Bolivia, not Argentina, which led him, on his rendezvous with destiny, to that Andean nation in 1967.[4]

To the extent that the hemispheric guerrilla convulsions in the Americas were voluntarist in nature rather than the result of social forces and conditions—which for the most part they were—suggests would-be revolutionaries felt the same way about their opportunities and where they could best expend their scarce resources. That place, in effect, was not Argentina, which they believed was simply not poor or brown enough for another one of Guevara's celebrated "two or three Vietnams." Argentina, in fact, would have to wait for the second wave of revolutionary upheaval before it found itself in an internal war for which it was not prepared. Even then, in the so-called era of the urban guerrilla (which remained largely terrorist in tactics), Argentina lagged behind its immediate neighbors—Brazil, Uruguay, and, after the fall of Salvador Allende in September 1973, Chile as well. In all three, furthermore, the terrorist threat was both less and more ephemeral in nature and consequently did much less damage to each society, then and now. Finally, although the South American dirty wars are usually lumped together—those of Brazil, Chile, Uruguay, and of course Argentina—it is the last country that was scarred most deeply by an internal war fought over a decade.

Uruguay could have provided an especially apt warning for the Argentines, who prefer peaceful over violent change. Uruguay, too, shared Argentina's Europeaness, not to mention its middle class mores. If anything, Uruguay had less of a gap between rich and poor than Argentina, and, moreover, it boasted a democratic tradition that Argentina could hardly emulate. Uruguayans, then and now, point out with satisfaction their country's steadfast support of the democratic allies of World Wars I and II, in contrast to Argentina's spotty neutrality in both conflicts. Yet Uruguay would be afflicted with the violence-prone leftist Tupamaros, who attacked a government and society that, although middle class to the core, had long fallen into economic stagnation thanks in large part to the costs of a welfare state that its largely agro-livestock economy could no longer afford.[5]

Although in many ways Argentina's terrorist groups, the Montoneros especially, resembled the Tupamaros in background and motivation, not to mention tactics and strategy, they preceded them by half a decade. Many members and most of the leadership were middle class and university trained, with no particular outlet for their political ambitions or careers despite extra years of higher education. The system also produced a large number of university dropouts who could only acquire menial positions in the service sector (mostly in banking), which only added to the discontent. In Ernst Halperin's acute judgment: "It is understandable that such an experience and such prospects may cause them to regard a total, revolutionary change of the social order as the only solution."[6]

Revolutionary change, the Tupamaros thought, would come through action in the cities (in Uruguay's case, one city, the capital, Montevideo) rather than the countryside, which had been the graveyard for many a *guerrillero* in the 1960s, including Che Guevara, who died in Bolivia in October 1967. After all, the Tupamaros reasoned, the instruments of state power (the army and the police especially) were located primarily in urban not rural areas. Attacks on police and soldiers were therefore conducted there. To finance the revolution, for awhile the Tupamaros successfully resorted to kidnappings and bank robberies, which they conducted on a grand scale—their first appearance on the national stage was a raid on the casinos of the resort town of Punta del Este. In so doing, the Tupamaros could strike out at what they considered to be imperialism, which included the kidnapping of British ambassador Geoffrey Jackson (later Sir Geoffrey), who lived to tell his story and U.S. Agency for International Development worker Daniel Mitrione, who did not.[7]

Nearly all that applies to Uruguay's Tupamaros, who reached the peak of their popularity in 1970, could also be ascribed to Argentina's insurgents. The primary difference between the two is that the Tupamaros were a single (and single-minded) organization while Argentina could boast a number of terrorist groups. They came from a variety of ideological backgrounds—including left-wing Peronism and Trotskyism—always with a touch of Cuban-inspired *fidelismo,* the early *fidelismo,* it might be added, the kind found, for example, in Castro's *Second Declaration of Havana,* a rousing call to arms against U.S. imperialism in the 1960s. They all—whether Montonero (Peronist) or ERP (Trotskyite)—shared the Tupamaro penchant for direct, armed action with activities financed by kidnappings of the wealthy (foreign as well as Argentine) and the robbing of banks as well as murder and general mayhem, including an ERP raid on Argentina's Atucha nuclear power plant in 1973. Indeed, kidnappings became nearly an art form with the ERP, which pulled them off regularly (178 in 1973 alone). Significantly, while the ransom demands escalated—the top figure being $60 million for three Bunge and Born executives—most were paid and none of the kidnappings was ever solved by the police.[8]

Nor was all this violence nihilistic in nature. The better organized, more coherent ERP (in contrast to the Montoneros) had a relatively clear notion of where they were going in this prolonged war against the Argentine state. The ERP leaders believed in combining legal and illegal activities aimed at persuading a majority of Argentines that regime change could only take place through a revolution, not by means of "meaningless" elections. Moreover, they also believed that a victory in Argentina was only possible in the context of a continent-wide struggle that would distract and overwhelm even the resources of the United States—a theme made familiar by Che Guevara.[9]

Most of these ideas, including the virtues of urban over rural guerrilla warfare, were taken from the work of Abraham Guillén, a Spanish civil war veteran who wrote extensively on Latin America in the 1950s and 1960s.[10] Guillén was an ideological eclectic arguing that a revolutionary vanguard could and should consist of various movements and not be confined to one sectarian group. The struggle, too, should be throughout Latin America in order to counter what he called "the Pentagon strategy" of picking off revolutionary movements one by one. Guillén's focus on a united front strategy was nothing new, but it did reject the unqualified leadership of any party, that is, one of the Soviet-oriented communist parties that could be found in every Latin American country and whose leaders had a penchant for asserting their status as primus inter pares. Above all, even though the leadership and cadres ought to be socialist in doctrine, socialism itself should be downplayed until victory is achieved. In any case, the main thrust of the revolutionary movement must be in urban areas, where a rapidly growing percentage of the region's population was to be found. The focus on the city followed, of course, the failure of rural-based revolutions in Latin America after the single success in Cuba (the Sandinista victory in Nicaragua would occur more than a decade after Guillén's major writings).[11]

Although critics of the Argentine repression of terrorism like to focus on the year in which the military took command once more (in March 1976), Argentine terrorist groups had been at work in the early 1970s during three different military regimes. When Juan Perón returned from political exile and resumed his presidency in September 1973, ERP continued its operations, although the Peronist Montoneros declared a cease-fire until Perón's death and the assumption of power by the country's vice president and his widow, Maria Estela Isabel Martínez de Perón. Indeed, one of the central objectives of the terrorist groups, including the Montoneros, was to escalate the violence during the Isabel years precisely to force the military into retaking power through the *golpe*, the classic coup d'état, which they hoped would prove unpopular as well as providing a huge boost in support for them from what they patronizingly referred to as "the masses." These groups succeeded in doing this. But (as is often the case when getting what one wishes for) ultimately, the new military government lasted long enough, now that the Peronist option had seemingly vanished with the general's death, to crush the rebels once and for all. But at what price?

PROLEGOMENON TO ARGENTINA'S LONG, DIRTY WAR AGAINST TERRORISM

The repression did not begin or end with the ascension to power of Gen. Jorge Videla in 1976, nor did the mayhem. By the first quarter of 1976, Argentines had already been subjected to five years of bombings, assassinations, and kidnappings of police and military officers, judges, trade union leaders, and businessmen as well as to extortion, robberies, and incessant propaganda as to why the violence would eventually make them happier at a time when they were also subjected to falling standards of living and inept government, both civilian and military. They had also begun to lose all hope after the less than inspired return to rule of Juan Perón (after a nearly twenty year absence) and eighteen months of disastrous governance by his wife, Isabel, a former nightclub dancer.

Confronted with this onslaught, which many analysts at the time, both in Argentina and abroad, believed would lead to a civil war of catastrophic proportions, the various governments—military, then civilian, and then military again—waged a counterterrorist war of increasing ferocity. Perón himself made clear to the Montoneros that it was time for them to retire from direct action or face the consequences. They refused. With Perón's passing in July 1974, the war against terrorism escalated under Señora Perón, whose advisers, the sinister José López Rega in particular, remained largely in charge. López Rega was, among other things, Isabel Perón's personal astrologer.

Indeed, under the second Perón government, a textbook example of how not to conduct antiterrorist operations was introduced in the form of the Alianza Anticommunista Argentina (AAA), better known as the Triple A. To its few defenders, the AAA was presented as a kind of vigilante organization dedicated to killing communists and other insurgents who seemed beyond the law and the police. In fact, they were the police, or, more precisely, they were recruited, armed, and abetted, not to mention instructed, by the federal police and then López Rega—a dark and mysterious man whose death date to this day remains uncertain. Nevertheless, López Rega, as minister of social welfare (and himself a former police corporal), ran the AAA out of his own office.

As a set of vigilantes operating outside any semblance of the law, the Triple A more than lived up to its sinister reputation. Its agents, out of uniform, carried out their "duties" at night, moving in unmarked, made in Argentina Ford Falcons, sans license plates, and detaining and usually murdering their "suspects" with no regard to legal procedures. It should come as no surprise that the history of the AAA has never been written owing to the utter lack of documentation. If any exists, it would probably reveal that the AAA seldom if ever liquidated any real terrorists. At most, it may have struck at suspected supporters and sympathizers of the armed Left, but the entirely innocent were also involved. How many and what the percentages were will probably never be known. But experience with undisciplined and undeterred operators with a license to kill from the nation's highest authorities invariably reveals a pattern of gross misconduct, as that power is often used to settle private grudges under the cloak of counterterrorism. And finally it should be noted that no member of the Triple A was ever arrested, as the Argentine government turned a blind eye to its activities.[12]

The Triple A would eventually vanish, along with its chief patron, López Rega, after the fall of the second Perón administration, although the date of its demise and his whereabouts after a brief stint as Argentina's ambassador to Spain were never (and are still not) clear, typifying the shadowy character of this peculiar war in all its unsavory aspects. But the Triple A, for all its counterproductive efforts in fighting terrorism, was only a part of the picture—and as time went on a relatively small one at that.[13]

HOW NOT TO WAGE WAR AGAINST TERRORISM: PART ONE

For the second half of the 1970s, the military, principally the army, held direct power in Argentina. In fact, it did so until it was displaced by democratic elections in 1983 brought about by Argentina's defeat in the 1982 Falklands War against Great Britain and its redoubtable prime minister, Margaret Thatcher.[14]

It is now conveniently almost forgotten how welcome the military takeover in March 1976 was to most Argentines at the time. General Perón had been dead for nearly two years, and the ship of state seemed rudderless under the inept command of his chosen successor, the widow Perón. Not only was Argentina subjected to the incessant and unstoppable attacks from multifarious armed groups, but the economy, once the pride of Latin America, was rapidly disappearing into a vortex of galloping inflation and agro-industrial decline. In her last and most turbulent year in office—March 1975 to March 1976 prices, for example, shot up at the then unheard of rate of 738 percent and exploded to nearly a 1,000 percent per annum increase two months later.[15]

It is little wonder that most Argentines felt relief after the bloodless coup that ended the brief rule of the erratic Señora Perón and her adviser López Rega or that Argentina's best-known writer, Jorge Luis Borges, would pronounce: "Now we are governed by gentlemen," an assessment a large majority no doubt shared at the time.[16] Alas, good government was not to be.

What, then, explains the ineptitude and the counterproductive use of raw state power to suppress the terrorist threat that so affected the 1970s in Argentina and left that nation years later divided and embittered over who and what were responsible for it all? The answer, or more precisely the answers, to that question form the balance of this essay.

The most fundamental reason why Argentina's experience with counterterrorism was less than satisfactory was its lack of preparation by the security forces and an inability to learn from past mistakes. Argentina's first serious brush with revolutionary terrorism came more than a decade after Fidel Castro's seizure of power in Cuba. The Argentines, who at all times are and were preoccupied with events at home, paid little attention to what was occurring throughout much of the hemisphere, where guerrilla-led insurgencies were expected to take place in "tropical" countries but not in modern societies like that of European Argentina.

How badly prepared Argentina was to fight terrorism is clearly seen in the nature of its security forces. The police, both federal and provincial, were poorly educated and trained and badly equipped and led, with resulting low morale. All of this combined with minimum wages and low public opinion and respect to make the police forces in Argentina and elsewhere in the region both corrupt and incompetent. In many cases, these forces were and remain commanded by former military officers with no experience in legitimate police work. The police forces were (and still are) largely incapable of dealing with criminals and were always seen—as elsewhere in Latin America—as a first line of defense against civil disorder. In Argentina, that meant preventing the country's labor unions from getting out of control during their frequent strikes and *manifestaciones,* that is, noisy protest demonstrations.[17]

But if the nation's police lacked the ability to collect and analyze intelligence and crime scene evidence, Argentina's armed forces—army, navy, and air force—were no less well prepared for the onslaught of organized terrorism. Even as a conventional fighting force, the Argentine military lacked any semblance of competence in the twentieth century. For one thing, by 1970 it had not fought a war in a hundred years—other than seasonal expeditions aimed at the nation's troublesome frontier Indians—despite chronic border disputes with its two most powerful neighbors, Brazil and Chile.[18]

To be sure, the Argentine armed forces—the army in particular—had no lack of theories about their role in society, a role that grew steadily in size until the Falklands disaster. Juan Perón as a relatively young officer, for example, wrote extensively on Argentina's need for a well-trained force if it were to survive in the jungle of world politics. But that meant more than guns, tanks, and planes. Perón and his adherents argued that Argentina must transform itself from a nation with an agro-pastoral, export-minded economy into a highly industrialized country that could be nearly self-sufficient, especially in wartime. These ideas did not remain on the pages of military journals but in fact were transformed into policy in the 1940s and 1950s at heavy cost to Argentina's economic health—a bill that Buenos Aires is still paying.

Exactly how unprepared the armed forces were can be judged from Argentina's defeat in the Falklands War. On almost every level, that failure was manifest. In fact, the one major achievement of the Argentine military was obtaining the advantage of surprise. Neither the United States nor the United Kingdom appreciated what would happen in the South Atlantic until the eve of the invasion, and then, owing to distance, there was little London or Washington could do to prevent it other than deliver a last-minute warning from President Ronald Reagan to Gen. Leopoldo Galtieri, the then junta chief, that the occupation of the islands by force would not be recognized by the United States or accepted by the British government without a fight and an all-out effort on the part of London to recover them.

President Reagan's observations proved prescient—far more so than the Argentine high command's ability to decipher British intentions and capabilities. First, the Argentines underestimated the enemy—a fatal mistake for anyone employing military force against an adversary. Second, once the islands were occupied, they had little ability to collect intelligence on the approaching forces. Third, although Argentine Air Force pilots conducted operations with almost reckless courage, the bulk of the armed forces—mostly poorly motivated interior army conscripts—lacked the will to fight once the Royal Navy landed highly trained, thoroughly professional commandos and marines. Fourth, the armed forces had a difficult time properly coordinating the Falklands operation even from the beginning. After the sinking of the Argentine cruiser *Belgrano,* the navy, from the beginning the most belligerent of the services in the fight for the Falklands, withdrew from the fray, hoping to preserve its remaining capital of ships far from the scene of action.[19]

Finally, if the Argentine armed forces could not wage a conventional war on their own ground properly, they could not wage a highly advantageous peace settlement either. In fact, before British forces arrived at and on the islands, Washington, working through President Belaúnde Terry of Peru, crafted a negotiated solution to the problem that Prime Minister Thatcher had accepted after much doubt and foot dragging. With U.S. Secretary of State Alexander Haig serving as a tireless interlocutor, the arrangement would have provided a gradual transfer of the Falklands to Argentina under the auspices of the United Nations. In fifteen years, the islands would have become the Malvinas in fact, and by now the Falklands would have become a distant memory.

It was not to happen. Why? Because the Argentine junta was fearful of taking yes for an answer. The junta members were intimidated because at the time they were afraid of their own troop commanders, who would accept nothing less than an immediate transfer of the islands and also held veto power over every decision of their nominal superiors. This perverse chain of command fully reveals the extent to which the Argentine military was an institution riven by faction and a lack of basic discipline. It would be no different in the security forces' war against terrorism.[20]

As for the Falklands campaign, that defeat, completed in mid-June 1982 when the Union Jack was once again hoisted over Port Stanley, was the beginning of the end of the military junta and marked the return to elected civilian rule under the Radical Party politician Raúl Alfonsín at the end of the following year. More important, defeat revealed the deeply flawed capabilities of the Argentine armed forces—considered at one time to have been the most professional in Latin America. But the loss to a determined

Margaret Thatcher (with considerable assistance from the United States) reveals only some of the Argentine inability to put together an effective security force aimed at either a conventional or unconventional armed foe, the latter bent on revolution, largely through indiscriminate terrorism.

HOW NOT TO WAGE WAR AGAINST TERRORISM: PART TWO

Although none of Argentina's various insurgent groups ever came close to achieving victory or even one of its lesser goals—persuading a majority of Argentines, for example, that they were engaged in a legitimate attempt to seize power—the terrorists gained one important advantage. They succeeded in depriving the authorities of any moral advantage due to the government's response to terrorism in kind until the moment sometime in 1979 when they were no longer capable of armed action. That failure on the part of Buenos Aires was multifaceted. But all these various failures resulted in Argentina conducting the kind of counterterrorism that helped buoy the terrorists for so long and for so dark a purpose.

What were these failures and how did they contribute to the discrediting of Argentina's counterterrorist war? First, there was a failure of leadership. Second, there was a failure in intelligence, *the* most effective weapon against terrorism. Third, there was a failure in tactics and strategy. Finally, there was a failure to rely on legal procedures and humane methods in dealing with the illegal and manifestly inhumane.

The leadership failure, too, appeared in many ways. First, and foremost, Argentina's political leadership in those years—from 1970 to 1983—was unstable and often short-lived, to say the least, and at best shakily legitimate. This was not a war to preserve constitutional democracy; it was only a war against terrorism. Compounding that problem, Argentina in less than fifteen years had no less than ten changes in heads of government, none of which were ever quite normal, constitutionally speaking. No less than seven military regimes sandwiched three civilian ones. Even the civilian governments were somewhat questionable in terms of legitimacy besides being outright failures at everything else. For example,

Héctor Cámpora, who was elected president in 1973 after seven years of military rule, was seen by everyone as a mere stand-in for Juan Perón, who remained in exile in Madrid during the election. But with Cámpora's victory in March 1973 came the understanding that the loyal Peronist would resign and Perón himself would return to assume the presidential sash after a constitutionally dubious special election. Nevertheless, an increasingly desperate electorate welcomed the opportunity of having him back, given that Perón had won more than 60 percent of the vote in the September 1973 balloting. It was only a majority of Argentines who hoped the old leader would put things right; even the general's ardent military critics believed that he alone could command the respect and provide the political cover necessary for its "to the death" struggle against terrorism.

To the satisfaction of the counterterrorists in the military and police, Perón initially proved to be a godsend. In one of his first acts in office, the new president outlawed the ERP and virtually declared war on the Montoneros. But Perón, then a man in his late seventies and in failing health when he returned from Spain for good, was well past his prime. His increasingly poor political judgment was most revealingly demonstrated by his insistence that his wife, Isabel, become Argentina's vice president, a post she was manifestly unprepared for, as her twenty-one-month, disaster-prone presidency would prove after the death of her husband in July 1974. Isabel, in brief, was not his first wife, Evita, who had once hungered for the vice presidency but had been denied it by Argentina's generals. Isabel's emotional and physical collapse in office mirrored the crisis-wracked state of Argentina, and by nearly universal consent the military moved once more into direct control of the nation's affairs, a control they would retain for another seven years.[21]

Latin American militaries have a reputation, at times well earned for all their faults, for at least imposing stability on often unstable societies. Imposing law and order—or at least order—suggests that military governments themselves are strong in contrast to weak and wavering, not to mention ephemeral, civilian rule. After all, what else can soldiers with weapons be? It is simply in their nature. The Argentine experience in the 1970s, however, suggests something else. Neither Gen. Juan Carlos Onganía nor any of his immediate successors, generals Roberto Levingston or Alejandro Lanusse, was able fully to impose his authority as Gen. Augusto Pinochet did in Chile after September 1973. Indeed, a student-led revolt in the provincial capital of Córdoba in 1969 was enough for Onganía to be deposed by his fellow military officers. In fact, all military presidents also served at the pleasure of the senior commanders, from Onganía to Gen. Leopoldo Galtieri. Their removal from office could be precipitated by single events—the Córdobazo in 1969 or the failure in the Falklands in 1982—or a general sense among the *oficiales* that the current officer-president had lost their confidence or in some cases the nation's. In any case, leadership did not flow from the top down but rather the reverse. But that in effect meant no real leadership at all since the power wielders—troop commanders, in effect—were often divided themselves and often held their official positions for only brief periods of time before retirement or promotion.[22]

Revolving door presidencies—military or civilian—with only two (Cámpora's and then Perón's) supported by the ballot box (the latter for another dozen years), suggest several related flaws that account for, in large part, Argentina's inability to wage a just war against terrorism. First, weak and ephemeral leadership at the top meant that little could be expected in the way of a rational chain of command or accountability. Although nine Argentine military chiefs, including Jorge Videla, Roberto Viola, and Emilio Massera, were later tried and jailed during the Alfonsín administration for their part in waging the *guerra sucia,* to this day there is no certain knowledge of what they knew, what they ordered, or what was done in their names. In addition, it is not clear how much they chose not to know, thus skirting responsibility and accountability.[23]

What is clear enough, however, is how fractured the security forces were as each arm of it—federal and provincial police, army, navy, and air force—carried out its own war, often a personal vendetta against those whom officers thought were killing brother officers and often enough members of their families. Whether any of this was coordinated is doubtful given the factional nature of these services and the secrecy with which they carried out their often sives against terrorists, real and imagined. Some services engaged in counterterrorism, of course, became better known—or more notorious—than others, although for years their existence was officially denied. The Argentine Navy and its New Mechanics School, ESMA, were among the most infamous, and suspects tortured and murdered at the school were for the most part never identified. By some accounts, some five thousand individuals met that grisly end. The New Mechanics School and the navy were then under the command of Adm. Emilio Massera, who had long cultivated an image of political moderation, which fit well with the Argentine naval tradition of being pro-democracy—in contrast to the army, which had in the 1930s and 1940s flirted with fascism.[24]

Little by little the facts—but only some of them—have emerged. We have stories of those who were picked up—*arrested* implies some kind of legal process when often there was none—and disappeared forever. We have stories of victims flown to sea and dropped in the River Plate or the Atlantic Ocean by Argentine Navy personnel. We have accounts of men and women placed in prison without charge, left to languish, and then released with no explanation.[25]

What we have, in short, is almost everything but a coherent account of how to fight the evil of terrorism without engaging in the same practices. The inability to concentrate on the real criminals is another aspect of the terrible price exacted by the authorities. Thus, not only was the official response to terrorism fractured and uncoordinated, curbed by no sense of proper legal procedure, but it was pursued in a random, hit and miss way, suggesting that the security service had only a rough idea of what they were fighting.

This suggests that these services lacked the most basic tool of those asked to fight terrorism: intelligence, in every sense of the word. Again there is no proper documentation—itself a significant indicator of the problem. But the problem is apparent even to the less-experienced observer. The Argentine military and police over nearly twenty years never acquired the ability to collect, analyze, collate, and act upon accurate intelligence regarding the strengths and vulnerabilities of the groups they fought. They had a rough idea regarding the identity of the leaders but not the members. They could not distinguish—or didn't care to—between the fighting cadre (which always proves to be a constantly changing group) and supporters and sympathizers. Indeed, the authorities seemed to be unable to distinguish between the supporters and sympathizers and the wholly innocent, prominent and obscure alike.

The lack of intelligence is evident on another aspect of fighting terrorism. The Argentine authorities, in fact, greatly exaggerated the fighting strength of their enemy. To be sure, bean counts, when it comes to irregular warfare, are often off the mark—as the United States discovered in Central America, particularly in the early 1980s—but in the Argentine case the numbers were apparently wildly wrong. Instead of five hundred or so armed terrorists, Buenos Aires thought (or claimed) that it was battling twenty-five thousand. Of course, the terrorist groups themselves share part of the blame, as they exaggerated their numbers, but propaganda aside it is clear that the authorities had little idea as to how many they were actually battling in this *guerra prolongada.*[26]

The lack of intelligence (without which no antiterrorist program can succeed) was only one part of a broader failure of strategy and tactics. At its broadest level, the Argentine government and its various military governments from 1976 to 1983 talked incessantly about defending Western values, including democracy, but did little to exemplify those values themselves. At their most obvious, the various juntas never made a serious effort to restore civilian government through an election until the Falklands defeat deprived the military of its last shred of legitimacy. Instead, the armed forces (the army in particular) were determined to solve Argentina's many problems with a hard hand and the firm smack of authority under their so-called National Reorganization Program. That they lacked an economic or political game plan was apparently beside the point. They severely undercut the legitimacy of their war by pursuing antidemocratic forces using antidemocratic means.[27]

If strategy failed, however, so did the government's tactics. One glaring example will suffice. Along with intelligence, the most effective weapon against terrorists is the ability to infiltrate the various groups. That takes patience and skill, not to mention strong nerves mixed with a bit of luck. In the long battle against the Montoneros and the ERP, there is no evidence that either the police or the armed forces were able to do that, leaving them with the indiscriminate approach of sweeping up anybody and everybody who could possibly be a terrorist or terrorist supporter, with the judgment often left to the manifestly incompetent. On that point, the breakdown of the chain of command from top to bottom left armed men in (and out of) uniform ready and able to settle their own private scores under the guise of antiterrorism. After all, with no accountability and legal curbs, why not?

In Argentina, this was not just a theoretical possibility.

What would today's Argentina look like if it had escaped the ravages of terrorism or at least the excesses of counterterrorism that occurred throughout the 1970s? The short answer is very different, indeed. Positing an alternate history of the Argentine Republic is nothing new. Domingo Cavallo, former foreign minister and then economics minister in the Menem government, and two of his colleagues, Roberto Domenech and Yair Mundlak, wrote an influential work in 1989—the year of Argentina's economic collapse—a book entitled *The Argentina That Could Have Been* (La Argentina que pudo ser). In it, the authors describe in detail an Argentina that, had it followed sensible economic policies, would rank among the wealthiest of countries in per capita terms.

Cavallo and his collaborators first document the familiar belief that at the turn of the century Argentina, with its abundant natural resources and Europeanized population, was one of the planet's most advanced countries, equaling Australia, Canada, and the United States, nations with similar expansive territories and growing populations. Its growth was not simply due to these factors, however, Cavallo and his coauthors argue. Rather it was because of Buenos Aires' classically liberal economic policies put into practice in the mid–nineteenth century and followed scrupulously in the first part of the twentieth.[28]

Argentina's economic decline began in 1930 when its governments, *both* military and civilian, replaced its export-oriented, low-tax, minimum-interventionist model with its opposite. They replaced wealth creation with a national security state in which the economy was directed to support the armed forces, just as it was in prewar Japan, Germany, and Italy (and the Soviet Union) instead of the other way around. Military defeat in World War II freed the Axis powers from this model, but Argentina until 1990—the same year in which communism fell—continued to impose capital controls, discourage foreign investment, punish agriculture with export taxes, force import substitution by protecting inefficient industries (often state-controlled), and impose high marginal tax rates to finance a federal budget that was out of control, say Cavallo, Domenech, and Mundlak.[29]

Only in the last decade has Argentina, under presidents Carlos

Saul Menem (a Peronist) and Fernando de la Rua (a Radical), changed course and allowed the country to recover (albeit slowly) from the ravages of *dirigisme.* The cost has been high, and much remains to be done—government budgets at the federal and provincial levels are not yet under complete control and tax policies prescribed by the International Monetary Fund remain, as they have always been, antigrowth—but Argentina in a decade or so could still join the family of mature economies provided that there are no major reversals in policy. So Cavallo and company showed in their work.

Economic well-being is important, but wealth creation and distribution is not enough. Argentine governments for eight decades presided over a once-rich economy and ran it into the ground. For nearly two decades, it fought the terrorist fire with counterterrorist fire and largely destroyed the already fragile fabric of Argentine society along with the terrorists, factors that economists like Cavallo rarely consider. This has meant that Argentina remains a polarized society with the question of the "disappeared" still on the agenda. It is almost certain that the bulk of those responsible will never be brought to trial or before a South African–style truth commission. Nor is it clear that they could be—such is the nature of a secret war. This means that Argentina's political wounds can never heal as long as any part of the population has a living memory of these events. That, too, only reinforces cynicism about politics, politicians, and the nature of legal justice. It also gives a weapon to what remains of the Argentine Left—albeit a nonviolent one that can turn a legitimate issue of responsibility and legal safeguards into a potent weapon against any government that may be following an economically liberal course but cannot or will not meet the demands of the moment.

The Argentina that could have been may not have escaped from all the political problems that the country has encountered but never resolved in this century. But it would have been free of a past that has been poisoned by the *guerra sucia,* not to mention sparing thousands of lives and the hundreds of thousands who were indirectly affected by the atrocities committed on both sides. Argentina, without the terror and counterterror it generated, would have made civilian government more stable and kept the military in the barracks at an earlier date. Perhaps, and even more likely, the

Falklands War would have been avoided as well. The Argentina that might have been can only have been a vast improvement over the Argentina that was and is.

CONCLUSION

Argentina's bitter experience with terrorism and its equally terrible twin, maladroit counterterrorism, should provide a useful warning for Argentines or anyone concerned with the first question of politics: how to ensure order but not at any cost. Terrorism does not simply happen in poor and benighted societies. It can happen anywhere, as Italy, Spain, and Argentina have proved. Although a society may be relatively wealthy and well educated, it only takes a few to cause mayhem. That mayhem is magnified when security officials and their leaders (elected or otherwise) do not have the tools to combat the terrorists surgically rather than taking a "round up the usual suspects" and take no prisoners approach. To be sure, the war eventually can be won, but at what cost? In Argentina, to this very day, the peace has yet to be won.

This raises the troubling question, could it happen again? The likelihood of a Marxist-based insurgency may be dubious, but it is not impossible. Terrorism is and always has been a hydra-headed monster. Its sponsors can come from any part of the ideological spectrum or from any part of the world. The two bombings in recent years aimed at Jewish institutions in Argentina are a reminder of that. Violent crime with terrorist overtones is on the rise in Argentina, and the police seem no more capable of combating it than in the past when terror was overtly political. One reason for this is that the criminals are often part of the state security services. The authorities' inability to find the perpetrators, in short, shows how ill equipped the Argentine state is in combating terrorism. Ironically—or, more precisely, tragically—the inability to come to terms with its past has led to paralysis in fashioning an effective, legally bound, counterterrorist capability. Meanwhile, Argentina's political and legal structures seem no better equipped to withstand an all-out assault of terror and counterterror than they did twenty years ago.

POSTSCRIPT

THE SEPTEMBER 11 TERRORIST disaster has had very little impact on Argentina despite its history of homegrown terrorism. The reasons for this are varied and throw considerable light on Argentina as a nation and a people.

First, Argentina remains, for all its European trappings, an insular society preoccupied with its own concerns. Moreover, it has never been, even in the Menem years or on the whole, particularly close to the United States—and that is an understatement. Argentine leaders since the turn of the twentieth century have seen their country as a rival to the United States, not a partner in any common endeavor. More than a century later, little has changed. According to well-informed observers, little empathy was shown in Argentina for Americans after the September 11 loss of three thousand largely civilian lives. Indeed, within the country's elite, including the military, there was a suggestion that somehow the United States had brought the disaster on itself and the Bush administration would either show little or no resolution in hunting down and destroying the perpetrators or would strike out blindly against the entire Muslim world.

Since the fall of Fernando de la Rua's government and the establishment of Eduardo Duhalde's presidency, that sense of *schadenfreude* and indifference about America's terrorist problem has only increased in the River Plate Republic. Ordinary Argentines, besieged by grinding daily economic uncertainty and sudden impoverishment, have no time for or interest in foreign terrorism. Nor does the new Duhalde government, an untested regime that fairly breathes an old-fashioned Peronist xenophobia.

As Argentina plunges further into economic and political chaos, that operational indifference to September 11 will no doubt remain the case. Moreover, even if the Duhalde government or any of its eventual successors were to do more than extend an obligatory expression of concern about terrorism it would not be supported by many Argentines, who have learned to revile their entire political class, often with good reason.

The roots of Argentina's failure run deep into the country's history and need not detain us for long. Still, the recent shocks of recession and national bankruptcy have proved particularly painful for a nation perpetually at war with itself. Argentines have long been preoccupied with their own internal problems—primarily economic but also political—which in the last year have sparked the worst crisis since mid-1989. At that time, inflation went into overdrive, with prices doubling every month and no end then in sight. Many fear it will happen again—and it could. At the beginning of 2002, Argentines had seen their government collapse with the sudden, unexpected resignation of President De la Rua after food riots had broken out in Argentina's largest cities.

This time, however, De la Rua was not forced out by the military, much less a political cabal, but only because of the pressures of the job, whose responsibilities he so clearly was unable to shoulder. De la Rua, the second failed Radical president in little more than a decade, presided over a two-year presidency that turned difficult but surmountable economic difficulties into a world-class crisis sparking national insolvency, deepening recession, and possible hyperinflation, not to mention panic in the streets.

De la Rua's ruined presidency was succeeded in rapid-fire fashion by several provisional governments headed by political lightweights, one of them a former governor of one of Argentina's lesser provinces who proposed that the solution to the nation's problems lay in yet another currency. He in turn was succeeded by former senator Eduardo Duhalde, whose new administration is supposed to last two years, after which time new elections are to take place. Few analysts believe that will happen given the size and difficulty of Argentina's economic problems. Historically, Argentina's temporary governments of the day have nearly always lacked authority and decisiveness or even a clue as to an effective policy. As a consequence, a more permanent government may be years, certainly months, in the future.

If conditions continue to deteriorate radically—and they probably will—the military, reluctantly but eventually, could be forced to step in, although it is discredited, has a poor record in managing the economy, and would in doing so most likely spark a violent reaction. The high command is well aware of its limitations. During the rioting of last December and January, the military high command made it clear to the civilian authorities that it would not intervene to prevent looting and rioting since it was not equipped to do so short of using lethal force. In this milieu, then, with no end in sight or painless solution available, we must place what the Argentine government has said so far about the events of September 11.

Finally, it would be unfair to suggest that the De la Rua government did not respond at all to the attacks on New York and Washington, D.C. It did. But whether commitments made to combat Islamic fundamentalist terrorism will be sustained by any succeeding Argentine government remains very much to be seen. On the diplomatic grace note level, then, President De la Rua and his government's representatives in the Foreign Ministry and Argentina's missions to the Organization of American States and the United Nations made repeated statements of support for America's stand against terrorism in the wake of the September 11 attacks.

Moreover, that government further pledged its cooperation in pursuing an investigation of alleged Hizbullah activity in the so-called tri-border area that connects Argentina, Brazil, and Paraguay. How much De la Rua's successors will be willing to cooperate on this issue also remains very much to be seen. The Paraguayan border area in particular has long been considered virtually lawless, and many suspect that Lebanese Hizbullah used it as a base for their terror attacks on the Israeli embassy and a Jewish community center in Buenos Aires.

This raises a final ambiguity about the Argentine position on terrorism. The De la Rua government pledged in the spirit of his predecessor, Carlos Saul Menem, to cooperate with the United States and the United Nations in committing a battalion of Argentine peacekeepers to Afghanistan under the command of the British. That surely is an irony in view of the 1982 war over the Falkland/Malvinas Islands. Nevertheless, the De la Rua promise of six hundred men, a pledge that attracted harsh criticism within the Argentine Congress as being unconstitutional when it was first proposed last December, will be difficult to sustain in the present atmosphere of economic uncertainty, tight budgets, and political turmoil. And that is quite aside from the problem of a more nationalistic Duhalde government simply ignoring the pledge of a discredited predecessor.

Thus, the degree, if any, to which an Argentine government can be concerned with international commitments remains highly uncertain. Only time will tell, and in this case it may well be a very long time.

PERU

Alberto Bolivar

THIS DOES NOT PRETEND to be a story of the twenty years of political violence in Peru that left more than thirty thousand dead and $25 billion in damages but is instead a critical analysis of the actors involved in this revolutionary war process and the strategic successes and mistakes that led to the war's conclusion. Primarily, the conflict involved Sendero Luminoso (SL, or Shining Path), the smaller Movimiento Revolucionario Tupac Amaru (MRTA), and the Peruvian state. Both insurgent and state forces made serious and decisive mistakes during the conflict. But in the end the former were defeated because they committed more mistakes than the state forces and also because the latter, almost a decade after the beginning of the armed struggle on May 17, 1980, developed a different and more or less efficient counterinsurgency strategy than they had devised previously.

The strategic defeat of SL and MRTA would not have been possible without the critical participation of the rural civil population, which forged an alliance with the security forces as part of that new approach in the late 1980s. This was, of course, the organization of self-defense committees (or *rondas campesinas*), which in the end broke Sendero's strategic backbone.

In the late 1980s and early 1990s, Peru was on the brink of collapse. The existence of the state, the survival of the nation, and the stability of a region were at stake. A small, ruthless, but organized and dedicated revolutionary organization almost destroyed the country. How did this happen? Why was the response so ineffectual until 1988–89? Carlos Tapia, a Peruvian counterinsurgency expert, says that in only a few instances in Latin American history has there been a case in which frivolity, inaction, or covert conciliation in the face of terrorist subversion took a country to the edge of collapse. Also there have been few cases in which one can find so many mistakes committed by politicians and military leaders who had the responsibility for fighting the subversion and who facilitated its expansion and development over several years.[1]

From the beginning of the insurgency, both the civilian and military leaders failed to understand the real nature of the threat as a revolutionary war machine whose main objectives were political, although the primary symptoms felt were the military actions of the Ejército Guerrillero del Pueblo (EGP, or Popular Guerrilla Army), the armed branch of the SL. Sendero leader Abimael Guzmán structured the SL as an iceberg: the EGP acted on the surface, but the most important action took place under it.[2] The Peruvian security establishment failed to understand that this insurgency was different from the one that took place in 1965, which was easily infiltrated and destroyed. Consequently, it required a new counterinsurgency approach.[3] As this essay will demonstrate, Sendero also managed to wage a very efficient asymmetrical war that provoked and made the state's initial response late, disproportionate, flawed, and counterproductive.

AN ATYPICAL INSURGENCY

Wars, conventional and unconventional, are never fought in the same way. In 1965, Peru suffered an insurgency inspired by the doctrine and strategy of Che Guevara, the Latin American revolutionary. The intention of the insurgents was to mobilize, organize, and lead the peasants to an armed uprising. The problem was that they lacked the organizational structure, ideological coherence, material means, and intelligence concerning the sociopolitical environment to perform that kind of task. As indicated previously, the insurgents were easily infiltrated and were promptly destroyed by the security forces. Che Guevara became a legend but not an example.[4] From the early stage in the organization of the armed party to conduct revolutionary warfare against the Peruvian state and society, Guzmán kept in mind the mistakes committed in 1965. He then set about creating a war machine within the framework of Marxism-Leninism-Maoism. According to the American counterinsurgency specialist William Ratcliff, Shining Path is one of the most unusual guerrilla organizations in Latin American history. Maoist parties have existed in the Western Hemisphere since the early 1960s, but no Maoist guerrilla force has ever caused as much unrest and destruction as this originally provincial group from the Andes.[5]

SL strategy also differed from traditional theoretical and experiential frameworks because the interplay of variables in Peru contradicted the existing scholarly theories of revolution developed during the Cold War. According to some of these theories, political exclusion was a key impetus to revolution. In the case of Peru, however, political exclusion was not a key factor. Rather, between 1980 and 1991, elections in Peru were fair and the electoral process was inclusive. Marxist parties participated in the political process, electoral and otherwise. Whereas the Marxist Frente Farabundo Martí (FMLN) participants in El Salvador frequently cited political exclusion as the main reason for their decision to join the movement, participants in Shining Path did not say that political exclusion caused them to join that organization.[6] It was not pure serendipity but cold reasoning that led Guzmán to choose the proper political and strategic moment for the Inicio de la Lucha Armada (ILA, or Beginning of the Armed Struggle). "Silvia," a Sendero member interviewed by American political scientist Robin Kirk, pointed out that Guzmán's genius resided in his ability to choose the moment for his political project.[7] The declaration of war was issued with the Chuschi attack of May 17, 1980, one day before the elections that were to mark Peru's return to democracy after twelve years of military rule (1968–80). The candidates included the center-leftist Armando Villanueva of the Aprista Party and Fernando Belaúnde Terry, the very person who had been overthrown by the military in

1968. Belaúnde Terry won in a landslide and began the transition to democracy, coming to power on July 28, 1980.

The Sendero leader knew that there was going to be great distrust between the government and the military. This was especially true in the case of Belaúnde Terry, who thought that the intelligence he was receiving about an insurgency was a ruse to allow the military to retain some degree of power. In reality, the military did not pay much attention to what it regarded as a minor insurrection, certainly no worse than the uprising that had occurred in 1965. What the military could not imagine was that Guzmán's plan for the ILA would fully exploit the mistakes in organization, tactics, security, and mobility that were committed by the 1965 insurgents. Sendero insurgency was atypical and could not be found in the classical standards and manuals of counterinsurgency. Silvia was right. The political environment was ideal for Guzmán: the civil and military authorities distrusted each other and lacked exact knowledge of the real nature of the threat. Some of these problems would continue during Alan García's administration (1985–90).[8]

ORGANIZATION OF THE SHINING PATH

Guzmán created a very closed, secretive organization, described by British expert J. Bowyer Bell as one hidden within a *protective ecosystem,* an underground that both protects and punishes.[9] Joining the Shining Path had elements of a rite of initiation into a religious sect or, worse, an armed sect of true believers driven by what Bell calls *the dream.*[10] These elements were not only the source of the energy driving the armed struggle, but they also largely determined the dynamic of that struggle.

Few security or military analysts study or understand the sociological phenomenon of true believers or their dreams. All movements that opt for the armed struggle are shaped and circumscribed in large part by the need to turn a dream into reality. Rebels have great dreams, and Sendero was no exception. Its dream was transcendental and commanding, with promises of salvation and redemption. It offered an end to grievances and a future appropriate to a new reality. Never was the absolute dream impure for the true believer. Others may find flaws outside the organization, but the rebels see none.[11]

But besides the dream Guzmán needed a different kind of revolutionary organization. Peruvian anthropologist Carlos Iván Degregori says that most classic guerrilla groups clearly underestimate the role of bureaucratic organization in the making of their movements and in shaping society in general. Guzmán represented the culmination of a shift from romanticism to calculation. He built an authoritative organization and converted it, by its own definition, into a war machine. He coldly planned for mass death because the triumph of the revolution would cost a million deaths, as he said in a televised appearance days after his capture on September 24, 1992.[12]

Although *revolutionary organization* is seldom defined, for many scholars the term includes the organization's ideology, strategy, structure, and leadership. In one model, American political scientists Raj Desai and Harry Eckstein emphasize the importance of visionary and innovative ideas that are advanced with zeal as well as of a combat party that can make fervor efficient—that is, identify where the party is likely to gain adherents, mobilize and retain members, identify friends and enemies, and plot a plausible path to power.[13] Guzmán's recognition of the need for such an organization was also caused by the fact that terrorist and guerrilla groups have an organizational momentum that works in their favor in the face of government countermeasures. Guerrillas tend to plan well in advance, conduct detailed reconnaissances, and have the forces deployed for operations of prolonged and enhanced activity. Guerrillas are engaged in a war of attrition, and only after time and multiple demonstrations of countermeasures will they give ground.[14] Sir Robert Thompson, one of Britain's main counterinsurgency strategists, says that the individual in a threatened society could have been attracted during the first phase by the original cause—the dream. But in the second phase there will be much less attraction, and the individual will be most influenced by the efficiency of the revolutionary organization and the tensions that revolutionary war creates.[15] The March 2, 1982, Sendero assault on the Huamanga prison—located in Huamanga, the capital city of Ayacucho—freed dozens of imprisoned guerrillas, provided a great attraction, and resulted in many new recruits. With this spectacular military action, SL proved that it was not an "armchair" revolutionary organization but a real and efficient one. From that date, it was seen as com-

pletely different from previous revolutionary organizations and the static rhetoric of the Peruvian Left.

When insurgents can demonstrate relative military and organizational achievements, their chances for gaining support increase, especially if the government is inept, lethargic, and incompetent. This concept, advanced by the U.S. National Defense University's Bard E. O'Neill, may sound trite, but it is a truism that people generally gravitate toward the side perceived to be winning.[16] Unfortunately, the Peruvian state was inept, lethargic, and incompetent.

The Sendero developed a rigorous system of internal discipline that ensured its growing success in the first years of the war. Each new candidate for membership submitted entirely to the party's authority, writing out the fullest possible self-criticism and waiting humbly for the party's judgment of it. Again and again, recalls the journalist John Simpson, "I was to notice a certain look about Shining Path's true believers: a calmness, a total certainty which came from the complete relinquishment of personal ideas, ambitions and feelings, and a wholehearted acceptance of Gonzalo's—Guzmán's nom de guerre—thinking."[17]

There was a dream, there was an organization, and also there was a revolutionary elite. Michael Radu, a scholar at Philadelphia's Foreign Policy Research Institute and one of America's leading counterinsurgency experts, defines *revolutionary elite* as the group of individuals who have political, military, or ideological control over decision making within revolutionary movements. *Revolution* is summarily defined as a political, economic, ideological, and social project, not necessarily fulfilled but at least characterized by one overall goal: the radical restructuring of the entire society, from the distribution of wealth and property to the level of individual mentalities. Revolutionary elites are ideologically aware, decision-making, revolutionary professionals.[18]

Sendero reflected one of the most important features of Maoism: the dependence upon a highly charismatic and unchallenged leader. From the start, Guzmán built up his personality cult. After he went underground, his megalomania and his pro-Maoist and pro-Stalinist ideological bias permitted him to transform his already unchallenged control over Sendero into a godlike, mythical omnipresence.[19] When men with such a makeup are either perceived to have supernatural qualities or manifest impressive speaking skills and a dynamic, forceful personality, they frequently are able to motivate others to join their cause through their example and persuasiveness, as was the case with Guzmán.[20]

One of his maxims was: "strategic centralization, tactical decentralization." No decision was made without his consent at the strategic level. Before his capture, American scholars William and Sandra Hazleton mentioned that analysts agreed that he was the chief architect of a very hierarchical and bureaucratic party that was, at the same time, decentralized to a considerable degree. This meant that long-range strategic planning and major political decisions were made by the national leadership but implementation was generally left in the hands of the regional zone commanders and sector and local cells.[21] In the end, as Boston University's terrorism expert David Scott Palmer says, one of the factors limiting Sendero was its dependence on a single leader. This is one reason why Guzmán's organization began to crumble almost immediately after his capture on September 12, 1992.[22]

The Rand Corporation's Gordon McCormick correctly described the importance of Guzmán as the force behind the scene. In retrospect, it can be said that Guzmán carefully cultivated an image of genius and omnipresence among his followers, who often appeared to be as enamored of the man and his image as of the goals and objectives of the organization. Authority and control within Sendero, in this respect, appeared to hinge on some variant of what has been termed by Ann Ruth Willner as "the charismatic leader-follower relationship." Such a relationship is based on four elements.

The group leader, in this case Guzmán, is believed to possess a unique vision of the future and superhuman qualities.

Group followers unquestionably accept the leader's views, statements, and judgment.

They comply with his orders and directives without question.

They give the leader unqualified devotion.

McCormick continues by saying that, although this relationship can be subject to a breakdown over time, when it is operative it results in a unique bond between the leader of an organization and its rank and file membership. The leader under this condition is much

more than the mere head of the group. For a period of time, at least, he commands absolute authority and is regarded as a historic figure by his followers, who assume the role of disciples. A relationship of this nature will result in close group unity. It will also tend to limit the role of the organization's secondary or midlevel leadership, whose principal role in the eyes of the membership will be to serve as a link between the leader and those who are sent out to do his or her bidding.[23]

That is why when Alberto Fujimori took office as president of Peru in 1990 he decided that the two pillars of his government would be international economic and financial reassertion and a counterinsurgency strategy at every level of government rather than just a focus on military aspects. But his main weapon would be the intelligence that allowed him to target the leaders of Sendero through the combined efforts of the National Directorate against Terrorism (DINCOTE) and the National Intelligence Service (SIN). He knew that the key to the strategic defeat of Sendero was to behead the organization, that is, to capture Guzmán. As mentioned previously, this strategic objective was spectacularly achieved on September 12, 1992; after that, the organization crumpled like a house of cards.

THE GOALS OF SENDERO LUMINOSO

As a political and military organization, SL had from the beginning a single goal: to take over the national government of Peru by applying an adaptation of Mao's strategy to surround the cities from the countryside. Thompson reminds us that in revolutionary war the aim is always political. As Mao stated: "Politics is war without bloodshed: war is politics with bloodshed."[24]

According to Robin Kirk, Guzmán's plans responded to a revolutionary ideal that did not envision a reformed Peru but rather a destroyed Peru, thus extirpating every last vestige of capitalism from Peruvian soil.[25] For Gerónimo Inca, Sendero's first stage (democratic revolution) was to take power through a prolonged or unitary people's war, by which war was conceived as a combined assault. Again, Mao's strategy of dominating the countryside and then encircling the cities was at the heart of Guzmán's plan.[26] This prolonged war had three components: strategic defense, strategic equilibrium, and strategic offensive. The plan was for the military arm, now called the Ejército Popular de Liberación (EPL, or Popular Liberation Army), to establish the República Popular del Perú, or People's Republic of Peru. It is interesting to note that when Sendero began its people's war the objective was to establish a República Popular de Nueva Democracia, or People's Republic of New Democracy.[27] This change, according to Peruvian expert Carlos Tapia, indicates that Sendero's initial philosophy of struggle was poorly conceived and had abstract and ideological political objectives not well understood by the peasant masses.[28] Thus, Guzmán adapted his rhetoric and developed a new plan more acceptable to his target constituency.

STRATEGY OF THE SENDERO LUMINOSO

Sendero's revolutionary warfare was the embodiment of the Maoist definition: a form of warfare that enables a small, ruthless minority to gain control by force over the people of a country and thereby to seize power by violent and unconstitutional means.[29] French military analyst Col. Georges Bonnet has advanced the following equation to explain revolutionary warfare:

$$RW = G + P,$$

where RW stands for revolutionary war, G stands for guerrilla tactics, and P stands for political and psychological activities. Bonnet and other French military analysts concluded that in revolutionary war the military tactics of the guerrilla are secondary to the central strategic objectives of destroying the legitimacy of the target government through the establishment of a counterideology and counterinstitutions. Thus, it was the objectives sought, and the central importance placed on political warfare and psychological operations in achieving them, that differentiated revolutionary war from other forms of irregular combat. Mao Zedong was the first person to systematically apply this formula.[30]

Prior to 1990, Peruvian civilian and military authorities missed the most important point of Guzmán's movement. As a result, they

countered Sendero only in the military aspects of its actions and did not seek to affect what was below the surface of the Peruvian revolutionary reality. Thus, Peruvian government forces militarized what from the start should have been a mainly political approach to containing the insurgents.

Sendero's main strategy was the use of terrorism in the countryside. As British counterinsurgency expert Sir Richard Clutterbuck points out, rural populations are psychologically very vulnerable to terrorism. Ancient China's military thinker Sun-Tzu encapsulated the concept as "kill one, frighten ten thousand." When terrorists prowl through villages at night or jump out of the bushes when people are at work in the fields, the rural population feels very insecure and far more isolated than someone who is enveloped in the bustle of a city or shanty town.[31] American counterterrorism expert Ernst Halperin describes terror against civilians as a necessary and inevitable component of guerrilla warfare. In order to survive, the guerrillas must eliminate popular support for the opposing side in the contested area. Therefore, guerrilla warfare is first and foremost warfare against the civilian supporters of the opposing side. Harassment of enemy forces is only a secondary objective.[32] For Bard E. O'Neill, insurgent terrorism is purposeful rather than mindless violence because terrorists seek to achieve specific short-, mid-, and long-term goals.[33]

According to American counterinsurgency experts Michael Radu and Vladimir Tismaneanu, the guerrillas never lost sight of their ultimate aim, which was not only to replace the existing government but to destroy its base of support and to introduce already defined revolutionary changes to control the populace.[34] Sendero's terrorist actions were directed mainly at civilian authorities outside of the cities, seeking to displace and destroy the state in the hinterland as part of a strategy of creating a political vacuum.[35] A secondary purpose was to obtain popular support by demonstrating the government's weakness.

According to O'Neill, an insurgent's success depends in large part on two factors: the target of terror and the length of the campaigns. However, as Kirk says, prolonging and intensifying terrorism may be counterproductive because it can disrupt traditional lifestyles, as happened with Sendero's first actions against peasant fairs and market participation, which ignored the mercantile and cultural needs of the inhabitants.[36] In O'Neill's opinion, failure to replace terrorism with more effective military operations can create the impression that the insurgents have lost the initiative and their chances of success are remote. Even worse, as terrorism continues there is a danger that it will become indiscriminate, and the insurgents can end up alienating potential domestic and international support.[37]

As general governor of Algeria in 1957, Jacques Soustelle noted: "Terror is a psychological weapon of unbelievable power. Confronting bodies with severed throats and the grimacing, mutilated faces of the victims, all capacity for resistance ceases. Nonetheless, terrorism is not an efficient type of warfare. The revolutionaries cannot gain permanent support of a population by force. Terror may drive people into supporting the administration if the governing authorities can offer them security. Smart terrorists will dispense such violence sparingly to avoid this adverse reaction."[38] Apparently, Guzmán was not one of the smart ones, for his use of terror as a main weapon favored Sendero's expansion only in the midterm. The violence provided the backdrop against which the popular armed organizations (*rondas*) were created in the countryside and cities that would later be the basis for Sendero's strategic defeat. The sixteen massacres of twelve persons or more between December 1987 and February 1992 are evidence that Guzmán did not change his strategic approach to terrorism.[39] In other words, for twelve years Sendero never could make the qualitative leap toward its main objective of taking power but instead relied only on terrorism in and of itself.

One dramatic but illustrative case of Guzmán's strategy is the way SL treated the Asháninka people in the central jungle. It created concentration camps where the natives were forced to work for the party under subhuman conditions and endure privations, including corporal punishment and death for disobedience and flight. The majority of the natives rescued by the Asháninka *rondas* and the armed forces showed symptoms of critical malnourishment.[40] More than two thousand people, including *colonos* (Peruvians who had migrated to rural areas) and Asháninka prisoners, died over the course of Sendero's presence in the Ene River valley. They were either assassinated or died from malnutrition and disease resulting from the inhumane conditions to which they had been subjected. In August 1994, several mass graves were discovered.[41]

STATE VACILLATION, LOST TIME, AND AGGRAVATION OF THE SITUATION

Peruvian counterinsurgency experts Carlos Iván Degregori and Carlos Rivera wrote that in the countryside just before the involvement of the armed forces in the war against Sendero (December 1982) there were signs of discontent between the peasants and the insurgents. In one case, nine journalists in the Quechua community of Uchuraccay were killed in January 1983, according to a commission headed by the writer Mario Vargas Llosa. The reporters were traveling to investigate a villagers' rebellion against Sendero in the neighboring village of Huaychao. Inside the Peruvian armed forces there is now acknowledgment of the grave error represented by the indiscriminate repression that they conducted, as for years it lessened the perception of Sendero's own propensity for violence. Due to this state use of violence, Sendero was viewed as the lesser evil until the second half of the 1980s.[42] The armed forces fell into the trap of repression because of Guzmán's strategy of forcing a repressive state response that would alienate the populace and make it more receptive to his message, says David S. Palmer. This popular reaction should not be interpreted as support for Sendero; it was primarily a reaction against the terrorism of the government.[43]

Related to Sendero's use of terrorism came the discussion in the first years of the war on how to classify and cope with the violent organization. In 1990, Peruvian journalist Santiago Pedraglio argued that it was a grave error to consider SL as a mainly military force. This error, which goes hand in hand with proposals for a military solution, undervalues Sendero's strength because it minimizes its political impact on sectors of the population and reduces the problem to a surgical matter or at best a psychosocial one. For Pedraglio, SL is not only a military organization but one of the most important political parties that has ever existed in the country. This does not contradict the fact that SL is a militarized group prepared for war, but it is primarily a party, an organizational and ideological entity with a project for the country.[44]

ASYMMETRIC WARFARE EFFICIENTLY WAGED AGAINST A SUPPOSEDLY STRONG STATE

In 1980, Peru supposedly was a strong country. The military government that had ruled since 1968 had enlarged the size and scope of the state apparatus. Notwithstanding, Guzmán noted that despite that strength both Peruvian society and the state were disorganized at the time. That is why he always referred to the government as a big elephant that could easily be trapped in the mud. The problem in Peru was the lack of an effective government throughout the country. The military government increased the size of the bureaucracy, but it remained concentrated in the coastal departments, especially in Lima.[45]

Due to the perception of threat and traditional geopolitical preconceptions, the Peruvian armed forces grew to become one of the most powerful military establishments for conventional warfare in Latin America. It was organized, trained, and deployed to fight a potential war against Chile and Ecuador. Billions of dollars were spent purchasing weapons systems in Europe, mainly from the Soviet Union. Peru had the ability to wage a two-front external war, but it had no domestic concerns because the military had taken power and, remembering the traumatic events of 1965 as a product of injustice and poverty, began a political and social revolution that it believed would prevent any future insurgency. The military government was promptly infiltrated by all kinds of leftists. The regime of President Juan Velasco began what he called the Peruvian Revolution, which would improve the country's status in South America and serve as an example of a third option for a noncapitalist and noncommunist government.

The Peruvian Left skillfully infiltrated the state structure, including organizations that Velasco created, such as the National System for Support of Social Mobilization (SINAMOS), a gigantic bureaucratic entity that on paper was to channel the social demands of the population but in fact frustrated such efforts as the land reform of 1969. This was a result of the extreme ideological treatment given to all aspects of Peruvian life. Velasco reinvigorated the Confederación General de Trabajadores del Perú (CGTP, or General Confederation of Peruvian Workers), a labor structure controlled by the pro-Soviet Peruvian Communist Party, to oppose the labor organization

efforts of the rival Aprista Party. He did not realize that he was creating monsters everywhere, which (indirectly) included SL. Guzmán and his followers were camouflaged as another radical group because being progressive was the mood. At one stage, he worked in SINAMOS, which gave him and his cadres the opportunity to know their enemy's organization from within, especially its weakest parts.[46]

The centralized Peruvian state that was attacked in 1980 gave the impression of strength, but in reality it was structurally very weak. American political scientist Philip Mauceri thinks, however, that a centralized state is not synonymous with a powerful state and argues that Sendero's rapid growth in the 1980s and early 1990s was directly related to limits in the state's organizational capacities and influence in society. The SL organization followed the classic Maoist model used by many other groups in Peru, but it was far more successful in taking advantage of the state's weakest points.[47] Paraphrasing American colonel Charles Dunlap Jr., we can say that Sendero may have perceived vulnerable asymmetries in what the Peruvian state viewed as its virtues, that is, a huge bureaucratic apparatus, but one centralized and not identified with the people of he hinterland and powerful armed forces perfectly suited to wage a conventional war.[48] Low-intensity conflict is a more subtle and complex kind of challenge than those to which most governments and armed forces are accustomed, and SL knew this.[49] According to American counterterrorism expert Neil Livingstone, from a military perspective, the chief problem faced by major Western powers in ghting terrorism is that of dealing out small amounts of force. Western arsenals are structured to fight big wars, as was the case in Peru, not counterinsurgency operations. As a consequence, in reent years there has been a tendency to employ these weapons to trike back at terrorists, which can be compared to using a sledgeammer to kill a bothersome fly.[50]

Guerrillas often frustrate regular military forces, as the United tates and the Soviet Union found out in Vietnam and Afghanistan nd Russia is now learning in Chechnya. Heavy firepower and large nit maneuvers are irrelevant, not cost effective, and sometimes ounterproductive.[51] The use of conventional armed forces in counrinsurgency operations almost always leads to huge collateral amage; conventional forces always engage in excesses that harm the civilian population. Peru was no exception. The armed forces forgot Sir Robert Thompson's accurate words: "It's all very well having bombers, masses of helicopters, tremendous firepower, but none of these will eliminate a Communist cell in a high school which is producing fifty recruits a year for the insurgent movement."[52]

Moreover, in 1980 it was hard to believe that a handful of fanatic followers of Mao, armed with (in Guzmán's words) "humble dynamite," would have a chance against the solid, modernized army Velasco had built to fight a conventional war against Chile or Ecuador.[53] In retrospect, the tactical lesson in this case was that the lowest of low-tech weapons used with panache by skilled and disciplined combatants on their home turf can be brutally effective.[54]

Sendero prepared itself to wage asymmetrical warfare, which in Defense Intelligence Agency analyst Paul F. Herman's words is "a set of operational practices aimed at negating advantages and exploiting vulnerabilities rather than engaging in traditional force-on-force engagements. The incentive to engage in asymmetric warfare is usually greatest for the weaker party in defense against a stronger foe. Asymmetric concepts and moves seek to use the physical environment and military capabilities in ways that are atypical and presumably unanticipated by more established militaries, thus catching them off-balance and unprepared."[55]

Shining Path simply did not fit into the classical standards and manuals of counterinsurgency, so it became unconventional and atypical even within the realm of unconventional warfare. The Peruvian armed forces felt frustrated and responded with violent intervention in Ayacucho, which only favored Sendero and prompted its expansion to other departments throughout the country.

A COUNTERPRODUCTIVE AND MISTAKEN STATE RESPONSE

When Sendero's actions began to mount, President Belaunde put the police in charge of the operations in Ayacucho and referred to the insurgents as cattle rustlers and delinquents.[56] Belaunde's approach to insurgency was the same in 1965 and 1980. In 1965, he announced that sensational reports could harm the credit of the country. There were armed groups, but the police could control the situation. There could be no guerrillas where there is a democratic government.[57] It took him fifteen days to order the military to mount operations against the insurgents. Against Sendero, he waited twenty-nine months before calling on the armed forces in December 1982.

It was *too late,* and the reaction would prove to be *too much.* Belaunde's decision to call on the armed forces was motivated by the total defeat of the current police forces (a unified national police was not created until 1988) to which the military overreacted between 1983 and 1984 with a body-counting approach. Apparently the military had no knowledge of the British experience in Malaya, where, faced with an equally powerful Maoist insurgency, the colonial authorities never went so far as to claim enemy casualties based on statistical probabilities, as later became the misleading practice of the U.S. military in Vietnam.[58] The United States' involvement in Vietnam was another experience that the Peruvian military should have studied. By 1983, the toll in Peru was very high, with 1,486 deaths, and it was even higher, with another 2,651 deaths, in 1984.

With assassinations or threats, Sendero managed to eliminate several local mayors, governors, and lieutenant governors in remote rural districts. Although it is true that many small police posts were attacked in those remote places, the great majority of the almost five hundred posts were deactivated as a preventive measure. In this way, the power vacuum that existed at the moment when Sendero was trying to settle down strategically in the rural zones was not the product of victories achieved in military confrontations but rather, as in soccer, the product of default.[59] Thus, the Peruvian state ceded power and further debilitated the traditionally weak positions it had in the hinterland. The British example in Malaya consisted of an opposite policy, one that placed greater emphasis on government: "government," Thompson said, "that not only functioned, but was seen to function, so that the births, marriages and deaths still get registered."[60]

Peruvians forgot that of all the variables that have a bearing on the process and outcome of insurgencies none is more important than government response. O'Neill asserts that governments can control their own destinies, largely because they are normally in an advantageous position during the incipient stages of violence because of their higher degree of political institutionalization and their control of the instruments of coercion by the police and military. Also, O'Neill continues, when a government misunderstands the type of insurgent movement it is facing, it can blind itself to policy options that could end the insurgency at a lower cost.[61]

A key point to be addressed when evaluating a counterinsurgency program is how well the government knows its enemy. As self-evident as this may seem, historical and contemporary data reveal instances in which governments have misdirected policies because they misunderstood or falsely portrayed the goals, techniques, strategies, and accomplishments of their opponents. Whatever the reasons (inflexibility, sloppy thinking, ignorance, biases, bureaucratic imperatives, or a psychological aversion to acknowledging one's own weaknesses), the outcome is flawed, costly, and sometimes fatal. To begin with, it is important to find out whether the authorities have made a conscious effort to identify the type of insurgency with which they are dealing by carefully examining all information at their disposal—statements, publications, and internal documents of the insurgents as well as intelligence from human and electronic sources, if it is available. Failure to do this can lead to false pictures of the adversary. It is a matter of taking into account Clausewitz's advice: "The first, the supreme, the most far-reaching act of judgement that the statesman and commander have to make is to establish the kind of war on which they are embarking, neither mistaking it for nor trying to turn it into something that is alien to its nature. That is the first of all strategic questions and the most comprehensive."[62]

"The governing power," says American counterinsurgency expert John McCuen, "must take a careful estimate of the situation, evolve realistic long-term plans, and commit sufficient resources in time to regain the initiative."[63] Instead of coping with it politically and psychologically, the Peruvian government took a purely militaristic approach to the problem, forgetting that if political and psychological warfare plays an important role in revolutionary insurgency the same can be said for counterinsurgency strategy. The objectives of such a strategy include denying the insurgents access to the population, establishing and maintaining government legitimacy, mobilizing the population, and delegitimizing the insurgents and those governments that support them.[64] In militarizing the war, the Peruvian government went against the logic of this kind of war-

fare. Sir Henry Gurney, the high commissioner in Malaya, decided that on no account must the armed forces have control over the conduct of the war. This, he argued, was a war of political ideologies. He believed that what was needed was armed support for a political war, not political support for an army war.[65]

In Peru, the problem was thought to be purely military. Belaunde and García failed to see it in its real dimension: as a political problem. Paradoxically, as Mauceri says, the increased political role of the armed forces acquired over the coming years resulted more from civilian pressures than the military's appetite for a return to power. At the end of military rule, the Peruvian armed forces were demoralized, divided, and intent on restoring their shattered unity by depoliticizing the institutions. However, civilian officials openly encouraged the military to increase its role in counterinsurgency planning and operations.[66]

These were the same civilian officials who were offended when military and police officers talked about the existence of guerrillas in Peru in late 1980 and early 1981. Law 24150, the Law of the Politico-Military Commands, allowed the armed forces to coordinate the public and private sectors in the zones declared to be in a state of emergency and gave them administrative control over local authorities and rights to propose political measures to the executive branch.[67]

Lacking political objectives and a counterinsurgency strategy, the armed forces occupied Ayacucho as if it were enemy territory. Military leaders did not have in mind that in such cases the objective of the security forces is to regain control of the population and not just to occupy terrain. The purpose of territorial consolidation must be to establish contact with the people, says McCuen, in order to protect them, not to treat them like presumed terrorists and thus alienate their support.[68] Most of the populace consisted of frightened peasants in need of protection. In Clutterbuck's opinion, there is a myth that the winning side always has the support of the people. In practice, 80 percent of the people do not want to get involved with either side for fear of retribution by the other side against themselves or their families. They prefer to see and hear nothing. Usually, 10 percent at most will actively support the guerrillas (although more may be coerced by terror into doing so), and 10 percent at most will actively support the police, army, and local government, often encouraged by incentives and rewards.[69]

In Peru, such incentives and rewards were established as late as mid-1992. In Malaya, big money was the simplest way to tempt informers to talk. The results were immediate. British general Harold Briggs wisely stated that the people matter, they are vital, but you can't expect support from people you can't protect.[70] For him, security was the vital ingredient, for security leads to confidence, confidence leads to better information, better information leads to greater security force success, and greater success leads to more security.[71]

Security must be apparent, effective, and stable so that the people recognize its existence, can depend upon it, and will be confident of the future.[72] So the primary task of the security forces in rural guerrilla conflict is to build up the rural community's confidence in its own security and the inevitable defeat of the guerrillas. With this sense of security, they will cooperate by giving information to the military, thus serving as an intelligence force multiplier.[73]

Again following with the successful Malayan experience, it was a matter in Peru of *winning the hearts and minds of the people.* In most instances, a combination of diplomacy, medical assistance, and acts of kindness is sufficient to win over the people, who probably have little love for the revolutionary intruders anyway. But this cannot be done without giving them a permanent sense of security. In Indochina, during the Red River delta operations, the local people, who had twice seen French occupation, also saw them depart twice and leave the inhabitants at the mercy of the Vietminh. They became hostile to further French clearing operations.[74] In Ayacucho, the troops provided only sporadic protection. Thus, the terrorists returned frequently, inflicting reprisals on the villagers.

The Peruvian security establishment also forgot that since the prime purpose of destabilization is to break the rule of law, the first essential element in countering terrorism is to ensure that soldiers, police, intelligence officers, and others claiming to support the government themselves act within the law.[75] In other words, the insurgent uses police repression as a tool to win popular support by catalyzing the population and intensifying counterterrorist operations, a tactic that further alienates the authorities from the local population. The insurgents try to provoke arbitrary and indiscriminate government reprisals, calculating that this will increase local resentment against the government, which they hope to convert into support for their insurrectionist cause.

The success of such insurgent ploys depends on the nature of the government's response and the social groups involved. Excessive violence by military and police units and government-sponsored vigilantes (death squads) is generally recognized as a factor accounting for increased support for insurgents.[76] When repressive measures are left almost entirely in the hands of military or police forces without adequate civilian control working for an eventual political solution, there will be an excess of force and brutality. In the end, the population may be controlled but it will not be won.[77] Jean Vaujor, director of the Sûreté (the French security service) during the war in Algeria, correctly asserted: "To send tank units, to destroy villages, to bombard certain zones, this is no longer the fine comb; it is using a sledgehammer to kill fleas. And what is much more serious, it is to encourage the young, and sometimes the less young, to join in the maquis (as the French guerrillas were known in World War II)."[78] As will be seen later, it is a matter of not committing regular forces to this kind of war. For Washington's Center for Strategic and International Studies scholar Edward Luttwak, low-intensity conflicts cannot be won solely through the application of mass firepower. They require more subtle tactics and special forms of politico-military expertise: low-intensity-conflict wars are all different (e.g., compare the 1965 Peruvian insurgency to that of 1980), and each requires an ad hoc set of operational procedures. Thus, a key task for forces seeking to suppress terrorists or insurgents is to develop one-place/one-time adaptive doctrines and methods.[79]

The troops that were sent to Ayacucho in late 1982 were not only conventional, but they were not informed of their mission's purpose. What McCuen calls "the counter revolutionary troops and militia" should be carefully indoctrinated so that they will realize that their ultimate objective is not to destroy the revolutionary forces but to mobilize the population in support of the government.[80] If they fail to do this, they will lose just as surely as if they were defeated by the superior mobility and firepower of an opposing army. This indoctrination has to be part of an overall counterinsurgency strategy that did not exist in Peru until 1991–92 as a product of President Alberto Fujimori's determination to defeat the Sendero and the MRTA, which focused on a strategy and plan based on the use of good intelligence. Fighting without good intelligence consists at best of mindless campaigns of destruction conducted in the hope that indiscriminate damage to the opponent's arms and body will affect vital but unknown pressure points.[81] No state can protect the population from guerrilla warfare without good intelligence.[82] But the creation of an intelligence system and building up the flow of information through it are long and arduous processes.[83]

In sum, when massive numbers of troops entered Ayacucho they should have followed a plan. The Briggs Plan in Malaya was no magic wand but a coherent plan with a painstaking eye for detail, hard work, application, and professionalism instead of grand gestures and sweeping strategic maneuvers.[84] Besides, apart from a few legal norms (such as the Peruvian counterterrorist law or the law of the politico-military commands), the security forces lacked a general legal framework in which to confront the insurgents. The dismal situation originated in the reluctance of the legislative branch to enter into a serious discussion about political violence and was compounded by the failure to establish firm bases or integrate political and military strategies.[85] Fujimori would use this issue in April 1992 as one of his reasons for closing the Congress.

A FAILED INSURGENCY

During its first years, Sendero achieved a certain degree of popular support in Ayacucho. In September 1982, some ten thousand people attended the burial of Edith Lagos, the Sendero leader who boldly directed the assault on the Huamanga Prison in March of that year. Because of the nature of Shining Path, many analysts did not like to acknowledge the evidence of popular support for the movement, despite the evidence.[86] But Sendero acted with precision because of the information it received from various segments of the population, what the Vietminh called "the popular antennae." This flow of information resulted from its excellent organization. In describing this phenomenon, Peruvian journalist Gustavo Gorriti wrote in March 1990: "In the history of guerrilla insurrections, there are few, indeed if any, in which the factor of political will, supported by exhaustive planning, has been so preponderant. If this is a war of apparatuses, SL will win because it is more efficient, better organized and has better intelligence."[87]

For O'Neill, there are two types of popular support: passive and active. Passive support comes from individuals who quietly sympathize with the insurgents but are unwilling to provide material assistance. Although at first glance passive supporters may seem inconsequential, at minimum they are not apt to betray or otherwise impede the insurgents. This is important because a key aspect of counterinsurgency strategy for government units combating elusive terrorists and guerrillas is to acquire information from such people. Thus, passive support is a valuable commodity for insurgents. Active support is the most important kind of support the people can render to the insurgents.[88]

The Peruvian state was lucky that most of Sendero's popular support never became active. Why was this? One of the answers is the chronic terrorism inflicted upon the population. The SL allegedly was looking for support, but the reality is deeper. Some analysts saw a certain degree of racism in Abimael Guzmán, such as when he referred to the people in remote jungle villages as *chutos* (*sallqas*, in the Quechua language of the highlands, means "dirty," "savage," or "pagan"). For Guzmán, these people were not equals but masses to be commanded to overflow, flood, and inundate the enemy on demand. They were less a human force than a natural phenomenon to be pooled, directed, and worked once the dam of revolution had been erected.[89] Sendero simply tried to gain support through violent coercion.

Painstaking efforts to acquire support by relying on various combinations of techniques other than coercion can be rapidly undermined by actions that victimize the population. Mao recognized this and clearly articulated it in a code of conduct for dealing with the people. Guzmán deviated from Mao's admonitions, and in the end this kind of conduct backfired against him.[90]

According to American scholar Timothy Lomperis,

> The essential error of SL is that it had picked the wrong Mao for its ideological beacon. Rather than the pragmatic young Mao bent on power from the Yanan caves, Guzmán fixed on the radical old Mao bent by his fanaticism into the self-destructive purge of the Cultural Revolution in the hands of his overzealous confederates, his wife and the Gang of Four radicals. Guzmán's error has been to eschew a united front approach and confine his movement to the radicals of his carefully nurtured cells. This made it difficult for him to broaden the base of his insurgency, and it has left him without allies in the far

more competitive political terrain of the cities. In fact, this urban myopia led to his capture.[91]

In another view, American counterinsurgency expert Thomas Marks notes correctly:

> Reality, especially as concerns Maoist insurgency, lies in the relationship between the mechanisms of grievance-driven recruitment, infrastructure and terror and the manner in which these change over time in their relative importance in the maintenance of the insurgent movement. Maoist insurgency has become increasingly divorced from the masses it purports to serve. Few cases illustrate this as well as does Sendero Luminoso.[92]

Through rural and urban terror, Sendero pushed the government to the brink of collapse. Shortly before Guzmán's capture, journalist John Simpson spoke with a former minister, who impressively said: "In a few months' time this country will have no government. It will have collapsed. And the SL will be the only force capable of governing. It will be like Year Zero in Cambodia."[93] Most government officials and middle-class people were profoundly depressed by the state of the country, and a disturbing number seemed to agree that SL was close to victory.

Only in retrospect did it seem obvious that Sendero had lost the war between 1989 and 1992, despite appearances to the contrary.[94] In those years, the profound alienation of peasants crystallized as organized resistance to Sendero's politics, facilitated by a certain rapprochement between the military and the peasants.

A NEW STRATEGIC APPROACH AND THE DEFEAT OF THE INSURGENTS

Why was SL defeated, despite all its seeming advantages? From the perspective of peasant society, the armed forces followed a positive trajectory: while SL became more distant from peasant society, the military forged closer ties with it. As Sendero grew more external to peasant society, the armed forces became more internal to the population. The armed forces did not seek total control of everyday life. To be sure, the obligatory weekly visits to the peasants' commands, the marches, and the attention paid to the visiting army patrols were inconvenient for the peasants. But the armed forces did not otherwise interfere in the daily life of the population and certainly did not exercise the level of control imposed by Sendero. Sendero, on the other hand, grew more distant from the peasants, causing a change in popular support from pragmatic acceptance to resistant adaptation and finally to overt rebellion.[95]

Paradoxically, the increasing role of the military was favored by the same weakness of the state presence in the hinterland that favored Sendero's expansion. In other words, the military presence became the only real presence of the state in the countryside, although that was not the military's mission. This issue stimulated a discussion about how to cope with the insurgency.[96] In Mauceri's opinion, one of the most important problems the military confronted between 1983 and 1986 was a lack of consensus over the basic approach to counterinsurgency.[97] Within the Peruvian armed forces, this is known as the struggle between the French and British schools of counterinsurgency. The British school focused more on the nonmilitary aspects of counterinsurgency. The French school gave more importance to the military steps needed to defeat an insurgency. In 1984, General Adrián Huamán tried a version of the British approach as commander in chief in Ayacucho, but his efforts clashed with Belaunde's general philosophy of governance. He was promptly replaced and posted to Mexico as military attaché. But by the late 1980s one could say that the British approach was winning. The Peruvian nongovernmental organization Instituto de Defensa Legal said:

> Nevertheless, without basic changes in the political matrix of the countersubversive strategy, in 1989 a search for a more regional counterinsurgency approach emerged to overcome obstacles to achieving support and action from the population. The more relevant examples are those of generals Howard Rodríguez in Ayacucho and Alberto Arciniega in the Huallaga River valley. In both cases, the countersubversive strategy was blended with a political strategy in an attempt to win the support of the civil society through its recognition of the military as a valid representative of the state.[98]

This proved to be a new and innovative approach to combating Sendero.[99]

Informally, midlevel officers began to change their approach toward the population, helping, protecting, and organizing it, creating the *rondas.* In 1976, these self-defense groups were created in Cajamarca and Piura to fight cattle rustlers. But in the late 1980s they were redesigned and armed by the military to fight Sendero. They not only created serious tactical and (in the end) strategic problems for Sendero, but they became a great source of intelligence. Many of these sources were villagers who had escaped Shining Path's control. For example, Friar Mariano Gagnon, a priest who protected the Asháninkas from SL in the Ene River valley, wrote:

> I was awash in a sea of information. Some of the new arrivals had, at great risk, escaped from the terrorists, and as they told their stories, the climate of panic increased. From what I could gather, a large number of native families had been conscripted into terrorist ranks. The community of Camantavesti was completely taken over, as well as other settlements along the Ene and its tributaries. The escapees were a mine of military intelligence, and I somehow had to get their information back to the authorities.[100]

Francisco Reyes, a Peruvian sociologist, says: "The *rondas* have plucked out the 'thousand eyes and ears of Guzmán's men,' and what is more they have infiltrated their enemy's territory with their own eyes and ears. They move like fish in water, because they do not wear uniforms and have learned to move unseen, becoming part of the environment and extending their espionage system."[101] For Tapia, in the confrontations with the *rondas* the EGP columns not only suffered important military setbacks but for the first time confronted armed peasants of their own region. At the same time, a significant number of members of Sendero's and MRTA's local forces realized that their struggle was wrong, and they defected, becoming repentants long before the Repentance Law was passed.[102] This law, similar to the one the British applied in Malaya, allowed thousands of Sendero and MRTA cadres to defect and give all kinds of information to the government about their leaders and organization.

According to Peruvian anthropologist Nelson Manrique, the *rondas* represent a reaction to Sendero's myopic inflexibility and planned use of mass violence. By the beginning of the 1990s, more than thirty-five hundred villages in the departments of Apurímac, Ayacucho, Huancavelica, and Junín had organized *rondas* to fight

Sendero. Despite the assassination of hundreds of members, or *ronderos,* the alliance of the peasants and the military pushed the Maoists almost completely out of such former strongholds.[103]

The Peruvian armed forces' process of change was similar to that of the French in Algeria. There the excesses directed against the population were caused as much by frustration as by the inability to tell friend from foe. The excesses occurred long before adoption of the French strategy of 1956–57. This strategy was developed as an alternative to repressive military and police actions, which obviously were not working. Fundamental to the concept is winning popular support rather than alienating the people.[104] It was a *doctrinal reaction* to the initial flawed approach that materialized on August 9, 1989, when the armed forces adopted a new counterinsurgency manual, which replaced American strategic planning documents.

In Peru, the first example of serious change was probably in Puno, where the army distributed its forces with discretion and caution, without committing the repressive excesses of the Ayacucho campaign and with an astute use of intelligence and civic action.[105] A veteran journalist in Ayacucho discussed this change with Robin Kirk, stating that as a strategy it left much to be desired but at least the soldiers could see the advantages of getting the peasants on their side and had devoted time and energy to the committees (the *rondas*). Sendero's trained soldiers were still out there, but their ability to move and find support in the countryside had eroded dramatically. Among other things, the journalist pointed out that before the exodus tapered off there had been a sense, fragile but persistent, that the worst of the war was in the past.[106]

The achievements of the *ronderos* in establishing a precarious social peace, a winding down of political violence, and a rebirth of civil society created a consciousness that they had won the war despite the inadequacies of the military and the state.[107] Peasants and *comuneros* (people from the villages) were citizen-warriors who had led the nation from the abyss, not hapless victims and marginals rescued by military patrons. Degregori wrote in 1996:

> The peasants are proud of having won the war. They are proud of being better combatants than the military. Proud, but at the same time prudent, claiming for the presence of the state for the

reconstruction of their villages and claiming for the military protection, more like some kind of rear guard, than as an umbrella: a last line of defense.[108]

The strategic defeat of Sendero could have been achieved before 1992 if the Peruvian state had developed a different counterinsurgency strategy during the previous decade. But why did success not come earlier? Probably one good reason is the military leader's lack of knowledge of successful historical counterinsurgency experiences and something as simple and dramatic as the lack of foreign language skills. Many books were published about Malaya, Algeria, Vietnam, and so on, but these were mainly in English. Peruvian military strategists simply could not read them. Thus, their learning process was painful, bloody, and entirely avoidable.

WHAT COULD HAVE BEEN DONE?

During the first stages of Peruvian insurgency, a comprehensive and politically oriented strategy should have been developed, one that included the following seven concepts.

1. *Intelligence.* The immediate centralization and unification of all intelligence efforts, as was done by Fujimori in his first administration (1990–95), was required to win the war.

2. *Laws.* The proper legal framework that could have given the security forces the legal support to break down the insurgents' organization was required to create an environment of law and order to preempt Sendero's reason for existence. Fujimori provided that legal framework after his much-criticized closing of the Congress on April 5, 1992.

3. *Indoctrination of the forces that were being sent to Ayacucho.* Special forces should have been the primary forces deployed. Although they have important applications in both conventional and unconventional wars, special forces operations are the most useful.[109] They can play a selective role in the actions, for which other army units are neither suited nor trained, because sometimes special operations, more than paramilitary ones, can be described as parapolitical.[110] That is why special forces' use of violence is selective.[111] These kinds of forces can achieve success by reducing the

asymmetry between the opposing forces and altering their manner of operation. For example, full security in what had been the U.S. frontier sometimes came at the price of approximating the Indians' own tactics, as army general George Crook did in his war against the Apaches in the 1880s. In the Philippines, U.S. forces were effective, especially with the Moros, because they adapted to the way war was waged by their enemy.[112]

Although small detachments should establish operational bases, they should not be garrisoned in posts but rather should be continuously nomadic, using whirlwind-type tactics. That is, the detachments should keep constantly on the move within their assigned zones—attacking, ambushing, patrolling, searching, establishing an intelligence system, and, perhaps most importantly, contacting and assisting the people. In the words of French general Raoul Salan, "These units create a constantly insecure climate for the adversary."[113] In Algeria, the *commandos noir* of French general Jacques de Bollardiére, lightly equipped semiguerrilla detachments, lived like nomads with the Muslim population. Contrary to the sadly accepted norm in the army, they pledged themselves to regard every Muslim as a friend and not a suspect, except when proved to the contrary. With this policy of never shooting first, they were often involved in situations of high risk as well as being viewed with some suspicion by the conventional authorities. These units ruthlessly hunted down the hunter.[114]

In Malaya, the Special Air Service (SAS) did incredible work, forcing the communists to face another guerrilla army, one that was perfectly willing to confront them on their own terms.[115] On many occasions, the SAS patrols forced the guerrillas to the jungle fringes and into ambushes by the infantry battalions and the police. These strategies made the interior unsafe for the enemy through a long-term presence and the winning over of the aborigines.[116] Only special forces in Ayacucho could have adapted, adjusted, and compromised as needed to cope with the unfamiliar modes of resistance.[117]

4. *Prisoners.* Mao reportedly made the following comment when talking to Ferhat Abbas during the Algerian rebel chief's 1960 visit to China: "Instead of killing them, convert them to your way of thinking."[118] The British in Malaya called them surrendered enemy personnel (SEPs). With their help, it was possible to develop an increasingly detailed picture of the insurgents' order of battle, who

the important leaders were, what their strengths and weaknesses were, which units they commanded, and where they operated.[119] In the words of Thompson, "The main basis of a successful psychological warfare campaign will depend on a clear and precise government surrender policy towards the insurgents. Such policy has three main aims: first, to encourage insurgent surrenders; second, to sow dissention between insurgent rank-and-file and their leaders; and third, to create an image of government both to the insurgents and the population which is both firm and efficient but at the same time just and generous."[120]

That policy was officially nonexistent in Peru until the May 1992 Repentance Law (no. 25499). The only successful infiltration action by the security forces in the first years was that of army captain José Colina, who, disguised as a French leftist (he spoke French), infiltrated Sendero in 1982. Two years later he was killed by an army patrol in Ayacucho after he was captured alive as part of a guerrilla column. He died before gaining the total confidence of Sendero's leadership.[121]

5. *Political warfare.* Peru could have affected Sendero's organization through the use of political warfare. In its purest form, a political party of radical bent like Shining Path is simply a political warfare capability looking for a permanent geographic home. As practitioners of political warfare, its members are themselves most vulnerable when it is conducted against them.[122] Their cadre and support structure are targets for political and psychological operations. Certain areas are especially ripe for exploitation: the ideological and political system of the insurgent organization, the central organizational infrastructure, and the support apparatus. Based on up-to-date intelligence, a variety of operations could be directed against each of these targets, including deception, psychological warfare, and activities meant to influence local or national politics. In each of these activities, it is important to adhere to the most basic principle of strategy, the identification of the appropriate vulnerabilities.[123] Political warfare seeks to demoralize the terrorists and their supporters. It yields more defectors, the flow of information becomes a flood, and the whole movement begins to crumble.[124]

6. *Mobilization.* If the insurgents consider mobilizing the masses as a scientific and fundamental principle of revolutionary

warfare, it follows that for the governing authorities to win they not only must defeat the revolutionaries' attempts to mobilize the people, but they must mobilize the people themselves.[125] In other words, the government seeks to limit the terrorists' efforts more than the activities of the population: to do less than an adversary is to invite failure. The counterrevolutionary strategist should recognize that the decisive element in a revolutionary war is that the great majority of the population is normally neutral and initially uncommitted to either side. Of course, his or her other objective must be to mobilize this majority so that it supports the governing power.

7. *A new kind of state.* One of the reasons for Sendero's growth was the absence of the state in the hinterland, a severe problem that Colombia, for example, is facing now in its war against the guerrillas of the Fuerzas Armadas Revolucionarias de Colombia (FARC) and the Ejército de Liberación Nacional (ELN). The Peruvian security forces could have easily prevented Sendero expansion by merely staying in the area. Peru should have provided a state presence that was motivated, honest, and efficient—one identified with the population it was supposed to serve and protect.

POSTSCRIPT

ANOTHER FACE OF GLOBALIZATION arrived the hard way for Peru and the Latin American countries when New York City and Washington, D.C., were attacked in such a devastating way on September 11: global terror. The realization is that a new kind of war has begun, one in which there are no clear boundaries and open battlefields, one with ruthless and faceless enemies who in the name of lesser gods will use any available means to achieve their ends.

The impact was felt almost instantly after the attacks in the form, among other things, of the contraction of the worldwide tourism market. For Peru, one of the main macroeconomic bases for its 2001–6 development program was supposed to be attracting more foreign tourists.

Also, remembering the 1992 and 1994 attacks in Argentina against Jewish targets, there came the realization that something similar could happen on Peruvian soil: attacks against American,

Israeli, British, or any moderate Arab country's interests but with the casualties being mostly Peruvians, especially if weapons of mass destruction are used.

The potential use of weapons of mass destruction complicates everything for several reasons.

1. Our intelligence communities lack the training, equipment, and language skills required to meet the threat of these extraregional terrorists. Apart from a June 1988 joint Mossad and Peruvian counterterrorist unit—DINCOTE—operation that captured a cell of Abu Nidal terrorists and the late November 2001 capture of a group of alleged Pakistani terrorists in southern Peru, we Peruvians lack experience.
2. The security system in our airports is not technologically advanced, and its personnel are not trained to detect biological or chemical agents. Worse is the condition of both equipment and personnel in the border posts.
3. Our regional armed forces have not developed any biological or chemical weapons. Thus, they lack the equipment and training to cope with such an eventuality. In the summer of 1991, Peru suffered the equivalent of a biological attack: a cholera outbreak. On that occasion, our precarious health system performed heroically and the effects of the outbreak were diminished relatively rapidly. Today, it would be impossible to cope with a massive biological or chemical attack. We would face the 1991 problems in an exponentially increased way.
4. Al Qaeda may try to establish some kind of cooperative link with regional terrorist groups such as the Colombian FARC or the Peruvian Sendero Luminoso. With these groups, Osama bin Laden has something in common: the drug business. Poppy crops, and consequently heroin traffic, are increasing in Peru and Colombia. Basque and Irish terrorists have been captured in Colombia on training missions. Why wouldn't bin Laden try to expand his worldwide terrorist web in this region?

If we Peruvians and Latin Americans agree that twenty-first-century terrorism is decentralized, transnational, and willing to use any means at its disposal anyplace in the world, we have also to realize that it is a global threat that knows no boundaries; therefore, the response also has to be transnational.

To meet the terrorist challenge with success, I propose the following measures.

1. Create subregional centers of intelligence—Southern Cone countries, Andean countries, and Central American and Caribbean countries—choosing central headquarters and allocating specialized personnel from the intelligence services of the respective countries.
2. Increase the bilateral and multilateral exchange of intelligence.
3. Get advisory help in the form of training, language skills, and new intelligence technologies from countries like the United States, Great Britain, and Israel.
4. Reformulate the tasks and structures of the regional intelligence services so that they will be able to collect information on extraregional terrorists and perform joint intelligence operations against an unfamiliar, decentralized, and more technologically advanced foe. For the latter, the advisers of Spain and France would be very important because of the expertise they have in joint operations against the Basque terrorists.
5. Allocate the proper budgetary resources to increase and improve the abilities of health systems to face a biological or chemical crisis.
6. Make concrete the spirit of the September 12, 2001, Lima Declaration, which was formulated during the General Assembly of the Organization of American States, in the form of a regional counterterrorist convention.
7. Reformulate the 1947 Inter-American Treaty of Reciprocal Support to adapt it to current circumstances, which are very different from the conditions of the Cold War that created it.
8. Establish strategic complementary agreements between regional armed forces so that they can increase levels of mutual confidence and intelligence-sharing and share the expertise in asymmetrical situations.

Latin American peoples have to realize that the tragedies of New York City and Washington, D.C., mark the beginning of a new kind of war: a global one against terrorism, one in which anybody can be a victim. On September 11, the victims were innocent citizens living in those cities. Tomorrow the victims could be innocent citizens living in any Latin American city.

COLOMBIA

James Zackrison

COLOMBIA IS KNOWN AS a violent country. Never in its history has it had a lengthy period of peace. One particularly violent period in the twentieth century was given the ultimate name in the terrorism game—La Violencia, "the violence." Conducting a study of terrorism is difficult in a country with such a history and doubly so because Colombian society does not recognize or admit that terrorism exists. Indeed, research for this essay began with an attempt to locate a specialist on terrorism in Colombia, only to find that the academic community in that country denies the existence of such a specialty. The most one could find were specialists known as *violentologos* (violentologists), although even these were careful to specify that they were not specialists on terrorism because Colombia has had so little terrorism in its past. In fact, the current phase of terrorism has claimed more than thirty thousand lives and shows no signs of slowing down. This anecdote is presented as evidence of the difficulty of defining the multifaceted aspect of political violence in Colombia. Merely describing the various types of terrorism and terrorist acts there would take up all the allotted space in this book.

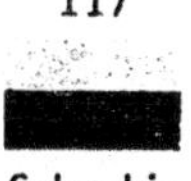

Colombians have developed many methods of coping with high levels of violence, ranging from constantly ducking for cover to leaving the country. This essay attempts to define the various manifestations of terrorism and the counterterrorism strategies of the national government in attempting to carry out its mandate to provide protection and dignity for all of its citizens. It will analyze the best practices evident in Colombia as well as present a discussion of which strategies have not worked.

DEFINITIONS AND LIMITATIONS

The general definition of *terrorism* given as a starting point for this essay is codified in the Geneva Conventions, that is, violence carried out by subnational groups intended to impose fear and through that fear achieve political objectives. The term *terrorism* (or *terrorist act*) indicates a premeditated, politically motivated violence against noncombatant targets by subnational groups, usually intended to influence the targets. The term *terrorist group* means any group (or a subset of a group) that practices terrorism to achieve political goals. The term *noncombatant* includes civilians as well as military, police, or government personnel who are unarmed at the time of the terrorist act. In Colombia, many terrorist acts are part of a larger phenomenon of politically inspired violence, which includes acts of war as well as terrorism. At times, this line between acts of terrorism and acts of war is difficult to distinguish.

VIOLENCE AND TERRORISM IN COLOMBIA

Colombia's violence is deeply ingrained in the history of the country. On July 20, 1810, a representative council was created in Bogotá in an act of repudiation of the authority of the Spanish king in Madrid. Three years later Colombia declared its independence, although it took another six years to achieve. Gran Colombia's first president was Simon Bolivar,[1] who presided over an area that included Venezuela, Ecuador, Panama, and Colombia. His vice president was Francisco de Paula Santander, who founded what later became the Liberal Party. Bolivar himself led the Conservatives.

Colombia's history is one of conflict between these two parties, which includes two major civil conflicts—the War of One Thousand Days (1899–1902) and La Violencia (1948–65)—one said to have resulted in the deaths of more than four hundred thousand Colombians. Nonetheless, there have been only three periods of military government: in 1830 when Ecuador and Venezuela seceded from Gran Colombia, in 1854 during a civil war, and in 1953–57, when an attempt was made to stop La Violencia. Civil government and open elections have been traditional in Colombia despite this history of violence. This development is an odd juxtaposition of violence and democratic practice that often defies common historical patterns.[2]

During La Violencia, the internecine political fighting became violent as the political parties followed the previous pattern of fighting civil wars to establish political supremacy. This time, however, a new element was introduced: Marxist communism as an ideology among some of the Liberal Party groups. When Gen. Rojas Pinillas was given political power as president with the collusion of the main political parties, the communist guerrillas refused amnesty and took to the hills to fight against the entire political system. These guerrilla groups later coalesced into what is now known as the Revolutionary Armed Forces of Colombia, or FARC.

Other armed bands appeared on the scene as well, proclaiming variations on the Marxist communist agenda. The National Liberation Army (ELN) followed the Cuban model of revolution, hoping to attain in Colombia what communist leader Fidel Castro had achieved in Cuba. The M–19, a guerrilla group with no clearly discernible ideology, was founded by middle-class students trained in guerrilla tactics by the Cuban military. Its attack on the Palace of Justice in Bogotá and its subsequent violent suppression by the army were a shock to many Colombians, long accustomed to high levels of violence. The toll in lives was 115, including 11 Supreme Court justices. Another guerrilla group, the Popular Liberation Army (EPL), claimed to be agrarian by way of ideology and took Chinese Communist leader Mao Zedong as its hero and mentor.

All Colombian presidents since the Frente Nacional (National Front) coalition (1957–76) have attempted to negotiate with these guerrilla groups, with various levels of success. President Belisario Betancur (1982–86) succeeded in granting amnesty to many individual guerrillas who surrendered their arms and reintegrated

themselves peacefully into society. His successors, Virgilio Barco and eventually Cesar Gaviria, negotiated amnesty and reintegration agreements with the M–19, EPL, and Quintin Lamé indigenous rights guerrilla group, granting them generous monetary and political incentives. The FARC and ELN, however, used these cease-fire and amnesty periods to regroup and rearm themselves for increased violence after the offers expired.

During the early 1970s, informal criminal organizations began to coalesce around the increasingly profitable business of smuggling marijuana and cocaine into the United States. Several "cartels" were formed, the most notorious being that of Pablo Escobar and Rodrigo González Gacha, acting as insurance and logistics brokers for multiton shipments of cocaine to North America and Europe. Attempts to bring these criminals to justice led to a new phenomenon, that of narcoterrorism, as Escobar and his cohorts launched an indiscriminate bombing campaign in Colombia to dissuade the government in Bogotá from extraditing them to the United States for justice.[3] They preferred trial and jail in Colombia, where their incredible wealth could subvert the system in favor of low sentences and posh jails. The levels of violence escalated to the point at which three presidential candidates were assassinated prior to 1990. Escobar's death at the hands of a National Police special unit in 1993 ended the campaign of terror, although sporadic terrorist incidents have recurred whenever the issue of extradition is raised.

A recent description of the effects of terrorism on Colombia's society was given by a well-known journalist.

> Hundreds of thousands of families displaced. Tens of thousands of citizens kidnapped. Thousands of businessmen and their families fleeing the country because of the danger. Dozens of intellectuals assassinated or threatened. Dozens of human-rights activists dead and disappeared. Hundreds of journalists exiled, kidnapped and murdered. The internal armed conflict that Colombia is living through today destroys the country and its future. Citizens from all social classes feel in their own flesh the pain of war.[4]

Kidnappings today top 3,000 per year and represent a $700 million business (45 percent to the guerrillas and the rest to common criminals). About 6 percent of the kidnapping victims are killed during their detention, and government forces claim to rescue only about

20 percent.[5] The national murder toll is over 23,000 per year, including combat deaths, political assassinations, and criminal murder, in a population of only 38 million. Terrorist and guerrilla attacks by the FARC, ELN, and the Ejercito Popular Revolucionario (EPR) have resulted in the evacuation by government forces of more than 250 towns and municipalities.

Many Manifestations of Terrorism

There are many manifestations of any definition of *terrorism* in Colombia. *Fear* is a word used by all Colombians to express their primary concern: fear of not being able to leave their homes, fear of not making it safely through the day, and fear that their families will be kidnapped or killed at any time. One of Colombia's basic philosophical foundations, human dignity and respect for life, is gradually disappearing from society and the national discourse. The most visible causes of this fear are the Marxist insurgent groups: the FARC, ELN, and EPR. Their strategies and tactics involve many acts of terrorism in that they kill peasants suspected of colluding with the paramilitaries and they kidnap for ransom, preying on anyone suspected of possessing wealth beyond that prescribed by their communist dogma. They also use traditional military strategies and tactics and target the police and other symbols of government presence.

As with armed units in any other internal conflict, terrorists conduct military operations with specific strategic goals. The problem is that in Colombia these strategic goals include using the civil population as a "strategic tool" to achieve military advantage. Marxist guerrillas target the civilian population for kidnapping, extortion, and threats to safety in order to obtain resources to feed their military apparatus. Criminal behavior is justified in terms of "people's taxes" on the oligarchies, defined as anyone with enough income to pay them.

Armed private security groups, known as the right-wing paramilitaries, are loosely organized under Carlos Castano's United Self-Defense Forces of Colombia (AUC) and trace their origins to the legal self-defense groups of the 1980s. Their stated purpose is to fulfill the government's responsibility to defend the populace outside of the cities and rid the country of the scourge of Marxist guerrillas. Most of their tactics are considered to be acts of terrorism in that

they assassinate peasants accused or suspected of collusion with the guerrillas. These groups use murder as a mechanism to "clear" new territories of Marxist guerrillas and then impose their own control to dissuade the population from supporting the insurgents. Again, fear is their best ally.

These four groups—the FARC, ELN, EPR, and AUC—account for the majority of terrorist casualties in Colombia. However, a distinction must be made between the many acts of war they conduct against the armed forces of Colombia, or each other, and the acts of terrorism they conduct against the government or population in general. For instance, the massed troop attack by the FARC during November 1999 against the military posts at Puerto Inirida were an act of war; the destruction of electric pylons by the FARC and ELN in Antioquia Department during the same month were acts of terrorism in that they targeted the general population, not uniformed government forces. Ambushes of ELN columns by the AUC are acts of war, whereas AUC assassinations of peasants suspected of collaboration with the ELN are acts of terrorism calculated to intimidate the populace into refusing support to the Marxists.

Colombia also suffers from narcoterrorism, so called because the perpetrators are individuals or groups involved in the illegal drug business who carry out acts of terrorism to affect national policy related to drugs, such as the Treaty of Extradition with the United States. This phenomenon of using terrorism to affect national policy occurred with intensity during the late 1980s and early 1990s, when the U.S. government was pressuring the governments of Vigilio Barco and Cesar Gaviria to extradite known drug cartel leaders. A favorite weapon in this venue was the car bomb because of the indiscriminate way in which it spread fear. There have been recent manifestations of narcoterrorism, such as when President Andres Pastrana initially agreed to extradite several Colombian cocaine smugglers to the United States in December of 1999. With the dismantling of the cartels, this tactic may well be a phenomenon of the past. Public support of Pastrana helped solidify the policy, and the bombings stopped after the first offender was extradited.

Other aspects of terrorism manifested in Colombia could be described as economic terrorism, such as the practice of kidnapping wealthy individuals for ransom or forcing farmers in areas under guerrilla control to grow quotas of coca leaf. There is a new and increasing terrorism targeted against specific sectors of society, such as the selected assassination and intimidation of intellectuals or journalists who study or write about the war and security issues in general.

And, finally, one aspect of terrorism combines several elements of corruption, terrorism, narcoterrorism, and crime—all specifically targeted at the armed forces. There are many documented cases of FARC or ELN operatives targeting specific members of the military by attempting to blackmail them into criminal activity through force. This is the famous *plomo o plata* choice offered to many Colombian military or police personnel, consisting of an offer of *plata* (money) or some other reward balanced by the threat of a *plomo* (bullet) if the offer is not accepted. Sometimes the offer is money in exchange for intelligence or operational orders for the next week. Sometimes the offer is more aggressive, asking the victim to alter orders or leave certain areas of operation vacant for a period of time. Frequently, the threat is against the individual, and just as frequently it is against the family of the victim. This threat places members of the military in an untenable position, where they have to choose between loyalty to the country, the service, and their comrades in arms on the one hand and, on the other, their families, whom they cannot protect while out on operations. In a variation of the *plomo o plata* threat, the FARC has long offered a reward for the assassination of Air Force pilots, U.S. contract pilots conducting counterdrug fumigation operations, and, more recently, off-duty Colombian police and military personnel.

Acts of Terrorism, Acts of War

It is important to distinguish between acts of terrorism and acts of war because each has its own set of legal criteria under which government forces can act. Acts of war involve armed combatants and are dealt with primarily by political means, such as negotiations and amnesties, or through military action. Acts of terrorism, however, deal with unarmed civilians or military personnel and require a different set of legal criteria, which puts unique pressures on the national leaders involved.

Colombia has long dealt with Marxist insurgents as recognized political entities, which makes it difficult to refer to them as terrorists. The government deals with them through political negotiations, although they admittedly are involved in terrorist acts. Such terrorist acts can be dealt with by legal means at the national level (Colombian criminal law), international humanitarian law, or international human rights law. Unfortunately, Colombia does not have counterterrorism legislation, as its leaders prefer to use their constitutional and legal powers to dictate law or executive orders to resolve such crises in public order. An example is article 187 of Colombia's criminal code, which punishes terrorism as criminal conduct against public security.[6]

The confusing situation that results from defining terrorism from different points of view can be seen in the argument between the insurgents and the national forces over the placement of police stations within city limits. Where else should a police station be placed? Police forces exist to enforce national or local law in their areas of responsibility. Building a police station outside of the city limits would be ludicrous in that it increases reaction time to the point where the forces become useless in defending the population from criminals or terrorists. However, the FARC claims that this placement of a police station within a city is a violation of international norms because it creates collateral damage when the FARC attacks police (or military) stations. Collateral damage refers to the death or injury of innocent civilians who live or work near the police station. Basically, the FARC is asking the Colombian government to vacate the cities, towns, and municipalities so that the guerrillas can attack the police stations with minimum damage to neighboring areas. Of course, this would leave the towns defenseless against the FARC predators, something it wants but also something that violates the basic documents of governance in Colombia. However, the Colombian government has developed no strategy or public relations campaign to counter this argument because it assumes that the authority of a state to place police stations within the civil society for its protection is the normal thing to do. It assumes that normal practice does not need defending.

A differentiation made regarding the various actors in Colombian terrorism is the distinction between the political Left and Right. American assistance to Colombia is based on U.S. executive policy that prohibits assistance for counterinsurgency, thus proscribing military aid to fight the FARC, ELN, and EPR. However, assistance can be provided for (and is usually conditioned on) fighting the right-wing paramilitary groups. There is a recent move within the nongovernmental organization (NGO) human rights community to classify the paramilitaries as a terrorist group and to apply pressure on the United States to use its antidrug assistance against the paramilitaries for their terrorist acts. These same NGOs tend to oppose all U.S. assistance to the Colombian military on the grounds that it is corrupt and heavily involved in human rights violations. However, the NGOs offer no alternative plan for assistance to government forces, thus begging the question of who will impose the law and order they promote as a requirement for reducing such violations.

THREAT PERCEPTION

A major impact of the violence and terrorism in Colombia is the aggregate level of fear resulting from the unprecedented high level of instability and terror inflicted on society in general and governance specifically. All of these different elements produce a level of terror that each on its own could not produce, engendering other situations that impact the ability of society and the government to operate in a normal manner. As stated previously, violence has always been a part of Colombian politics, but the increasing level of lawlessness and near anarchy brought on by the FARC and ELN since 1985 has created an environment in which trust—in anyone—has almost disappeared.

This lack of trust now permeates society to the point where faith in the government's ability to deal with the security situation has almost evaporated. This situation is especially critical within the very forces entrusted to combat terrorism, increasing the compartmentalization of intelligence and information and reducing cooperation and joint action. The military and police have been forced to spend scarce resources and time investigating personnel and developing confidence-building measures within their institutions to overcome this result of terrorism. To date, this effort has met with a high degree of success. Evidence of the military and police's ability to overcome the lack of trust is to be found in the increasing popularity of their institutions with the population at large: the military ranks

much higher in popularity polls than the rest of the government and only slightly below such traditionally popular institutions as the Catholic Church and the press.

Crime levels are extremely high, and justice is extremely rare. The U.S. Department of State report on human rights for 1999 puts the level of impunity at 97 percent, which means that only 3 percent of all reported cases of crime result in a trial.[7] Furthermore, conviction rates are reportedly low. The net effect is severely negative, for criminals find that they can operate with impunity against a terrorized population in various forms, including kidnapping for profit (economic terrorism), forced labor (coca cultivation in FARC-controlled areas), extortion for protection (ELN threats to bomb the oil pipeline), kidnapping of minors who are forced to join the ranks of the guerrillas, and other copycat types of crime.

The effect of this terrorism is serious. Colombia is in its second year of economic recession, which is partially the result of the corruption of the Ernesto Samper administration but in great part because of the terrorism rampant throughout the country. One stated purpose of the terrorist acts conducted by the ELN is to scare away foreign investment from Colombia's natural resources. A recent study from Florida International University indicates that there has been a tremendous increase in foreign money entering banks in Miami, to the tune of $30.6 billion in foreign deposits in 2000, up from $12.4 billion in 1998.[8] A high percentage of that money comes from Colombia because of falling confidence in the economy of that country. Capital flight from Colombia reached $700 million in 1999 and has increased since the FARC announced a new policy of "taxing" national estates with more than $1 million in assets.

Threat Environment and Legal Framework

One complicated concept in Colombia's legal system is that of private dignity, an individual right embedded in the constitution. The basic concept is that of natural law, in which the foundation of individual rights emanates from the individual, not from the constitution or the state. People are considered to be rational individuals with an inherent essence that is unique and individual; from this essence emanates the natural rights of man. In other words, the law and its rights emanate from the individual, not vice versa. The impact of this concept on this essay is that Colombian law is based on the concept that acts of terrorism perpetrated against individuals violate the individual's inherent dignity. Terrorist acts, in effect, prevent individuals from maintaining and defending their dignity. Terrorist acts prevent the individual from exercising self-determination, thus violating his or her fundamental human rights.

The significance of this legal concept is that it can be used as a strategy to counter terrorism by providing the Colombian government with a juridical framework in which to combat the terrorists. Unfortunately, this framework of individual dignity has never been used at the national level. Despite having this underpinning of natural law and a highly specific delineation of national responsibilities in the constitution, the law has not been used to provide citizens with an environment in which they can exercise natural law. In fact, adherence to natural right without national-level support has resulted in individuals taking the law into their own hands and depending on themselves for their personal safety. The absence of a counterterrorism strategy developed by national leaders has forced a situation in which the basic foundation of the national charter (natural right) is ignored with impunity at all but individual levels. Of course, those individuals with anarchical or predatory tendencies can easily take advantage of such a situation, which they do. The narcotraffickers abuse the lack of law and order to ply their illegal trade, the guerrillas abuse the lack of government presence to impose their dogmas on the population, the criminal elements prey on the undefended populace, and the paramilitary groups take advantage of the anarchy to attack their perceived enemies. The only group in Colombia that does not adequately use the national principle of natural law is the government.

Thus, despite its elegant and sophisticated constitution, terrorism is rampant in Colombia. Human rights and international humanitarian law are continuously violated, although such crimes can be dealt with through the application of international law. Given that the government is not applying Colombian law, the next recourse is to use international humanitarian law to punish terrorist acts committed by the guerrillas and self-defense groups. International humanitarian law protects the civil population and noncombatants during an internal conflict. Specifically, article 33 of the Geneva Convention relates to the protection of civilians in time of war. It states that such protected persons may not be punished for offenses not personally committed and that collective penalties and acts of intimidation or terrorism are prohibited. Likewise, pillage and reprisals against protected persons or their property are prohibited. Other protocols in the convention include protocol II, which relates to the protection of victims of noninternational armed conflicts (adopted in 1977), and the Diplomatic Conference on the Reaffirmation and Development of International Humanitarian Law Applicable in Armed Conflicts.

Of course, the use of international law supposes a force sufficiently strong to apply it, something that currently does not exist in Colombia. This argument could be used in the future to advocate foreign intervention. But as yet no one has advocated such a strategy, and no foreign country has shown an interest in taking on Colombia's insecurity problems. Sixty-five percent of Colombians have shown an interest in this option, according to a 1999 poll responding to a question on the possibility of using U.S. troops to pacify the country.[9]

COUNTERTERRORISM STRATEGIES

This section will attempt to describe the many counterterrorism strategies used throughout Colombia by the various actors involved. The first strategy analyzed is a feature of all recent Colombian governments: none has developed or implemented a specific strategy. Obviously, this is a failed strategy in that it has engendered much of the instability in Colombia today and has led to a reliance on the U.S. government for strategic guidance. Other strategies include muddling through crisis decision making, changing labels to counter various groups in a policy vacuum, strategic dependence on one group of terrorists to counter others, reactive strategies, the on-again, off-again strategy of extradition, attempting to accommodate illegal practices (prohibiting the payment of ransom), changing labels as a military strategy, codependency on various groups, and negotiating settlements. A case study in accommodation, the experience of the Seventh-day Adventist (SDA) church in Colombia throughout the past decades of violence warrants special attention.

Colombia has debated and acted on counterterrorism strategies to the point of signing international agreements intended to stop specific types of terrorism. For instance, in 1963 Colombia signed the Convention on Offenses and Certain Other Acts on Board Aircraft, also known as the Tokyo Convention, which applies to actions by terrorists that affect the in-flight safety of passengers. In 1970, Colombia also signed the Convention for the Suppression of Unlawful Seizure of Aircraft, also known as the Hague Convention, which was drafted to stop the hijacking of aircraft. The third is the Convention for the Suppression of Unlawful Acts against the Safety of Civil Aviation, also known as the Montreal Convention, which applies to acts of aviation sabotage such as bombings or the armed takeover of aircraft in flight. More related to the terrorism commonly associated with Colombia, President Gaviria attempted throughout his administration to develop a national security policy on which to base strategy and tactics for combating terrorism and war. But his project failed to pass Congress and was abandoned by his successor.

As mentioned previously, one of the interesting aspects of studying how Colombians deal with high levels of violence is that until very recently few acknowledged that terrorism exists in the country. The society is so acculturated to violence that everyone talks about specific acts of terrorism but few treat the issue as a whole. Among academics, no one is considered an expert in terrorism, although there is a specific branch of sociology dedicated to the study of violence—*violentologia.* Specialists in this discipline acknowledge the political objectives of the perpetrators but hesitate to acknowledge that such acts meet the general definition of *terrorism.* The impact on government of this phenomenon is serious, as these academics have traditionally been called on to serve as presidential advisers for security issues. Because they do not recognize the problem as one of terrorism, they do not advise the government to develop counterterrorism strategies, preferring instead to recommend military solutions, negotiated settlements, or police strategies to deal with specific acts, such as kidnapping for ransom, bank robberies, or bombing campaigns conducted by drug mafias.

Society, in effect, has been left on its own, resulting in the development of various nongovernmental counterterrorism strategies, some of which cause serious security problems for the government.

Wealthy businessmen and members of the rural landowning elite, for instance, often take matters into their own hands, pooling resources to finance self-protection forces, known variously as self-defense groups under differing legal regimes, as right-wing militias, or as paramilitary death squads. Legitimate or not, these forces perform a basic function normally performed by government forces. In the absence of an effective government presence throughout most of the country, these groups are the primary defense against the depredations of the Marxist insurgent forces.

A second consideration relating to the development of counterterrorism strategies is the idealism of most of the actors. Most studies of Colombia's problems begin and end with statements relating to the need to develop an environment in which law and order exists, a genuine commitment from all the parties in the conflict to respect the human rights of the civilian population, or some such other idealistic scenario. None of these statements acknowledges the reality that Colombian society has become inured to or tolerant of high levels of violence and tolerant of terrorism as political dialogue. None considers that only those sectors of society concerned with respect for the rule of law are not part of the conflict but instead are the victims of terrorism. The warring parties (the Marxist guerrillas, the paramilitary groups, and select sectors of the government) have a definite objective in mind and use terrorism and the violence of war to achieve it. Law and order are the last things on their minds, unless law and order can reduce the risks that they take during combat operations.

Thus, the guerrillas and paramilitaries talk of negotiations, pacification, or humanization of the conflict and make promises to respect law and order while continuing the indiscriminate use of violence and terrorism. The government must take this fact into consideration when developing counterterrorism strategies to confront these groups.

Crisis Decision Making

A third consideration for developing a counterterrorism strategy is the way in which decisions are made in Colombia. Part of the reason for the lack of a comprehensive policy (security and otherwise) is the tendency among Colombian leaders to not formulate a plan before crises erupt. Thus, policy tends to be reactive and the decision makers are constantly overwhelmed by events. They end up reacting to crises, never getting far enough ahead to think through and plan objectives and the way to achieve them.

In the case of counterterrorism policy, the president has in place a bureaucratic apparatus to advise and assist him in enacting policy. According to the 1991 constitution, the president has at his disposal a crisis management committee to develop policy and guidance for governance. This committee consists of himself, the vice president, the minister of defense, and the military chief of staff. This group has historically been convened to deal with major security threats such as the war against the FARC and ELN; seldom, if ever, has the committee been convened to deal with terrorism per se or to develop a policy for countering terrorism. As a committee the group has no direct authority other than that given to its members in their individual offices. Moreover, the group is empowered to act only in an advisory capacity.

The decision-making methodology used in Colombia has been one of reacting to the intense pressures of the various actors in the conflict. For example, the severe level of violence used by Pablo Escobar in the early 1990s, which was aimed specifically at President Gaviria's efforts to extradite him to the United States, pressured Gaviria into changing his interpretation of the extradition law. Pressure by the United States then forced another change in the law, this time under President Samper, allowing the extradition. Remnants of this flip-flop were evident in 1999 when President Pastrana began extraditing drug smugglers to the United States under a new interpretation of the 1979 U.S.-Colombia Treaty of Extradition. This kind of situation results in a zero-sum game in which a gain for one side causes a loss to another, and also a loss to Colombia, no matter what the outcome.[10]

The constant changes in policy, each manifesting a bow to extreme pressure, represent a reactive strategy that attempts to cope with pressure from terrorists and other groups. The fact that the government changes its policy under pressure gives the terrorists hope that their objectives can be met and encourages more terrorism. The only way to escape this cycle is to find an effective leader capable of withstanding the pressure long enough to develop a coherent and stable policy and then demonstrate the strength to im-

plement it. Pastrana used this strategy when he hardened his position on extradition in the face of violence, ending the flip-flop cycle and providing Colombia with a rare example of a successful counterterrorism initiative. It must be recognized that Gaviria's defeat of Pablo Escobar and Samper's success in jailing members of the Cali cartel changed the level of power of the actors, leading to Pastrana's success.

Lack of a Cohesive Strategy

As stated previously, Colombia has never developed a coherent or coordinated counterterrorism strategy or policy at the national level. The only written national security policy I have been able to document was the 1932 law that united the state militias into one army to confront a Peruvian invasion (called the Leticia Incident). The next similar policy was the unwritten guidance provided to the military and police during La Violencia which basically stated that the military was to protect the cities and leave the rural areas to their own devices. President Gaviria initiated the next attempt in 1990 by creating a group of security advisers to develop what was called the National Strategy against Violence.[11] His plan was to force the political class in Colombia to assume responsibilities ignored for too long, to create a Ministry of Defense under a civilian minister, and to form a National Security Council, all in an effort to develop a strategy for planning the future pacification of Colombia. But bureaucratic inertia overtook this ambitious project, and the Escobar bombing campaign in response to his agreement to extradite drug traffickers to the United States effectively ended this unique attempt to end the cycle of violence.[12] Of note, Escobar's escape from prison (La Catedral) after bribing his police and military guards damaged this project as much as the bombing campaign did.

Offensive tactical successes have been achieved in specific instances, such as the destruction of the FARC's Casa Verde headquarters in 1990 (not altogether proven to have been a good idea) and the assault against M–19 terrorists who had taken over the Supreme Court building (not exactly considered a success, given the high number of casualties incurred). Several attempts have been made to develop such counterterrorism policies, although none has gained success at the strategic level. Most attempts at counterterrorism have been made at the tactical level and have resulted in poorly conceived and executed policy, with many overlapping responsibilities, missions, and authorities. The end result for most has been an uneven distribution of authority and budget allocation and a resulting disaster in terms of operations and successes. Few groups are formed with organic expertise, and thus there is a dependence on foreign or external sources for training, doctrine, and equipment.

As an example, President Samper attempted in 1996 to strengthen the ability of the judiciary to deal with terrorism, primarily by amending existing laws and creating new ones to protect prosecutors, judges, and witnesses from intimidation. The basic premise of this reform was to provide a measure of anonymity for the judiciary by permitting "faceless judges" to try high-profile cases in which there was a credible threat of intimidation or subversion by the accused. But these faceless judges were used for purposes other than the original intent, providing the judiciary with a venue susceptible to corruption and "business as usual." Such misuse of judicial power tends to cast doubt on the validity of judicial decisions and increases opposition from international groups.

Reactive Strategy

Current counterterrorism strategies tend to be based on reactions to specific cases rather than on a dispassionate analysis based on rational, long-range policy. As mentioned previously, Colombia is a signatory to three major international counterterrorism agreements, although all relate specifically to aircraft hijacking. There has been little dialogue in Bogotá on the subject of changing this system, and thus most strategies have evolved as a reaction to the increasing and ever-changing face of violence in the country. Examples of this are the independent courts established in 1991, the kidnapping law of 1996, the specialized judicial system of 1999, and the on-again, off-again nature of the extradition agreement being developed with the United States (analyzed elsewhere in this essay). Reacting to specific cases as a strategy may work in a country in which terrorism is infrequent, but in Colombia this is a failed strategy in that there is simply no chance of catching up to the point of preventing the crime.

One major component of the current Colombian government's strategy in countering the terrorism of the Marxist insurgents, illegal paramilitary groups, and various criminal factions inflicting terror is to substitute U.S. national policy for that of Colombia in exchange for American foreign aid. Early on, during the Pastrana administration, the military spoke in public of its principal mission of reducing the threat to national sovereignty of the FARC and ELN. After the first mention by Gen. Barry McCaffrey, director of the White House Office of National Drug Control Policy (ONDCP), of a possible U.S. aid package totaling more than a billion dollars, the U.S. Congress asked Pastrana for a coordinated plan for spending the assistance monies. Pastrana responded with Plan Colombia, a package cobbled together from elements of the U.S. Southern Command's military advice, the State Department's goals and objectives for Colombia, and part of his campaign platform (originally called Plan Colombia). That the program (now called Plan Colombia) was not completely Colombian was evident in the repeated calls received by the author of the plan from Colombian news reporters seeking a copy of the plan: apparently it was not available in Bogotá or in Spanish for at least six weeks after its publication! The plan has been amplified and expanded considerably since its initial publication, especially after the U.S. Congress approved a $1.3 billion aid package, as it forms the legal and practical basis for using this assistance.

After Plan Colombia was published, the military no longer referred to its role in countering the FARC and ELN but rather spoke of countering the threat from the narcotraffickers. Drugs became the overriding concern for reducing the threat from the Marxist guerrillas. And at first glance this concern makes a certain sense: the guerrillas are financed substantially by the illegal drug business; the United States promises aid if antidrug operations are increased; the principal source of income for the Marxist guerrillas is removed; and the guerrillas, starved for cash, sue for peace. But this approach ignores the reality that in more than four decades of fighting the war on drugs no one has made a significant dent in the availability or price of the drugs, the principal means of measuring successful antidrug operations.

Thus, it is evident that Colombia has sacrificed its own interests in favor of the $1.3 billion offered by the Clinton administration, ceding its national security interest (combating the guerrillas) to the interest of the United States (combating drug production). As a counterterrorism strategy, this one has yet to run its course, but given the lack of concern among the population for the drug problem, and given its real concern for the lack of security, it is doubtful that this strategy will outlast the term in office of its major Colombian proponent, President Pastrana. Combating the guerrillas is Colombia's most pressing security problem at this time, and any strategy that detracts from this concern also detracts from Colombia's security. Diverting troops and resources from this problem to serve the U.S. concern for stopping the flow of illegal drugs will only prolong the war. As such, then, Plan Colombia can be categorized as one of the many failed counterterrorism strategies that Colombia has adopted. Given the low price for which Colombia is getting this strategy ($1.3 billion), this could easily make it one of the worst practices Colombia has adopted.

Changing Labels as Strategy

Because the civilian government has not provided strategic guidance on which the military can base its doctrine and adequate intelligence collection plans, the military leadership has attempted to fill this gap by creating a national security policy and submitting it to the president for approval. This effort, generally developed in the National War College in Bogotá, has produced several counterterrorism strategies, all predicated on finding new or unique legal means of dealing with the insurgent groups. Several of the armed forces chiefs have worked to develop a definition of what the military calls *violence-provoking agents* in an effort to find a legal justification for carrying out the military mandates in the constitution. For example, during the early 1990s the FARC and ELN subversives were labeled common delinquents (criminals). This allowed the military to use its mandate to defend the constitutional order from the threat of common delinquency. This strategy also allowed the military to bend the rules of posse comitatus, the authority to arrest citizens. And so, for instance, the military resorted to "arresting" those captured during battle and holding them for interrogation prior to handing them over to the national penal system.

Many times throughout Colombia's history, and most recently during the 1980s, the government has authorized the formation of private self-defense groups to provide rural areas a measure of protection from the Marxist guerrillas. These were declared illegal by the 1991 constitution; at this point, the military variously labeled them delinquents, narcotraffickers, local militias, or paramilitary groups. Currently, the labeling strategy has returned to attempting to apply the "common delinquents with drug trafficking connections" label, to a great extent as a result of intense pressure from the human rights NGO community and the U.S. government. By using these various labels, the military hopes to bring into force various differing sections of Colombia's legal system and thus differing responsibilities for the military and police involved. For instance, political prisoners require a specific set of legal protections, such as the kind of penal uniforms they can be required to wear, the courts that have proper jurisdiction over them, and the length of time that they can be held before trial. Likewise, common criminals can be treated in various ways depending on the political situation: during "periods of exception" like states of siege, when civil liberties are restricted, criminals can be held incommunicado without being charged for a much longer period of time than is possible under peaceful conditions. Drug traffickers, under yet another part of Colombian law, are subject to extradition to the United States, a punishment that need not concern domestic terrorists.

This labeling process has varied according to the whim of the senior military officer and his particular philosophy of rule. But the efforts to change the labels and control legal authority were, in effect, attempts to fill the void of civilian leadership and in so doing find a way to carry out the constitutional mandate to provide security to the population. Thus far, none of the various legal regimes appealed to by military leaders as counterterrorism or counterinsurgency strategy has succeeded. But the failure is not the result of inaction by the military; it is directly attributable to the lack of support of the military by the rest of the government. Colombia has not yet witnessed the various parts of its government working in concert to defeat or at least reduce the terrorism, insurgency, and crime that increasingly make it impossible to live and prosper within its borders. Indeed, it could be argued, as do Heyman and Smart, that such efforts at labeling "criminal behavior" serve to coalesce resistance to the state's coercive measures and, furthermore, delegitimize the state by proving how inadequate is its ability to suppress illegal behavior.[13]

Strategic Reliance on the Paramilitaries

One strategy advanced by a renowned Colombian scholar of his country's violence, Dr. Eduardo Pizarro, is that of codependence on the illegal paramilitaries for strategic objectives.[14] According to this theory, the military is not directly linked to the paramilitaries in the fight against the Marxist insurgents in that there is no institutional link. There may be individuals in the military at all rank levels who have contact with members of the paramilitary groups, colluding with intelligence or operational and tactical orders, but it is doubtful that this contact rises to the level of collusion on an institutional level. Instead, the military tacitly relies on the presence of the paramilitaries to control certain areas of the country, thus saving scarce resources that can be used to fight the FARC and ELN elsewhere. The link may be strong in those areas in which many Colombian soldiers desert or leave the military and then return to their hometowns to join the paramilitaries. In that situation, the deserters maintain their knowledge of military tactics and operations. Thus, they can serve as a force multiplier for the local military commander, even without his knowledge or permission.

Given the Colombian use of the theory of natural law and the emphasis on the dignity of the individual, the use of self-defense groups throughout the many periods of instability makes a certain sense. In the absence of a government presence, individuals capable of defending themselves do so or band together to work for self-defense. Within this tradition, and in the absence of a specific policy to defend the rural population, it is natural for self-defense groups to form and seek advice or guidance from the local military groups. There was a long tradition of reliance on these groups as force multipliers for the military in the role of force augmentation or intelligence assets. When they were declared illegal, there was no provision for their replacement. It is understandable, then, that military commanders at all levels seek to use philosophical fellow travelers in their conflict with the Marxist rebels. As a military strategy, this approach is probably quite successful, as these illegal groups may provide intelligence on the FARC and ELN and carry out their own counterinsurgency operations. As a political strategy, however, it runs counter to the national leadership's orders and subverts the rule of law and the legal balance in civil-military relations.

Extradition

When it became apparent that the Colombian judicial system was incapable of bringing the cocaine cartels to justice, the U.S. government began pressuring Colombia to enforce the 1979 U.S.-Colombian Treaty of Extradition. As mentioned previously, the extreme pressure brought to bear by Escobar and his bombing campaign created a change in policy, with the Colombian Constituent Assembly finding the treaty unconstitutional and imposing a prohibition on extradition. Escobar's death ended the bombing campaign, but the Cali cartel took up his cause, primarily through a combination of bribery and selective assassination rather than a highly visible bombing campaign. In 1997, Congress again lifted the prohibition on extradition but pushed through a reform that made it not retroactive for crimes committed prior to 1997. The first extradition of a Colombian national took place in November 1999, effectively ending the pressure by the cartels to stop enforcement of the treaty. Again this procedure proved to be a difficult strategy to implement, but persistence and a significant change in personalities (the demise of the Medellin cartel and the jailing of members of the Cali cartel) helped end this extreme manifestation of terrorism. Extradition thus became a rare example of a successful counterterrorism strategy in Colombia.

The Anti-kidnapping Law: Making Ransom Illegal

One counterterrorism strategy attempted in the effort to curb kidnapping was a law passed to make payment of ransom illegal. As is the case with most Colombian law, it assumes that the country is in a state of peace and that kidnapping is an infrequent occurrence, although neither assumption has been true for decades. This law has proved to be unenforceable and was later declared unconstitutional, as few of the thousands of kidnapping cases are reported to law enforcement authorities. Public confidence in the latter's ability to deter kidnapping is low, and the probability of paying a ransom to keep kidnap victims alive is high. Few report a kidnapping incident to the authorities. With payment of ransom being illegal, fewer people still reported having paid one to obtain the release of family members. Statistics indicate that the National Police successfully resolve only 20 percent of reported kidnapping cases, too low a percentage for anyone to place much trust in the state forces. Thus, as a counterterrorism strategy this law proved to be an abysmal failure, ignored by most of those affected, and it was eventually discarded. The failure has also demonstrated that as a counterterrorism strategy the law has no deterrence effect on terrorists.

Coexistence as a Strategy

The following case is that of the Seventh-day Adventist church in Colombia, outlining the various strategies it used in coexisting with all the forces arrayed against it throughout Colombia's recent history. The principal strategy is one of accommodation—at times with the Catholic Church during the early 1900s, the Liberal bandits of the 1950s, and the FARC and ELN of more recent years. With few exceptions, the strategy worked well until 1998: no SDA minister had died at the hands of Catholic or Liberal bandits. Since then, reports indicate that all Protestant churches have suffered heavily, with a total of thirty-eight ministers killed between 1998 and 2000, dozens of churches closed throughout the country, and members left at the mercy of the terrorists.

Until the 1950s, Roman Catholicism had a privileged position in Colombia's legal system. Protestant religions had long sent missionaries to Colombia, however, under the guise of businessmen, educators, or health care workers. One such case was the SDA church, which began working first in the San Andres and Providencia Islands and then on the mainland, setting up schools and clinics throughout the country. Preachers, however, were forced to disguise their work because the Catholic Church and the government fiercely protected the legal religion's monopoly in spiritual matters, arresting and persecuting all Protestant ministers. The first strategy developed by the SDA (and this is a worldwide practice) was to avoid getting involved in political issues, a strategy that became critical during the period of La Violencia. A second

strategy was the use of disguises, with ministers passing themselves off as traveling businessmen, families on vacation, or refugees from the violence.

These strategies worked well during La Violencia, when the SDA preachers developed the reputation of being nonpartisan in the conflict. This reputation endured the transition from Liberal bandits to Marxist guerrillas; ministers caught at the *pescas milagrosas* or other roadblocks were encouraged by church leaders to show their credentials as ordained SDA ministers instead of the government-provided national identification card.[15] In one incident, a FARC leader recognized the SDA credential and interrupted the *pesca milagrosa* to lecture the captured bus passengers on the basic beliefs of the SDA church, concluding his remarks by pointing to the minister as someone who genuinely cared for the *campesinos* (peasants): "We fight to protect your political interests, and this man works to protect your spiritual interests."[16]

Until 1998, no SDA minister had been harmed by the Liberal bandits or any of their successor Marxist guerrilla groups, thus proving that the strategy of remaining politically neutral and using disguises can be successful. However, Colombian SDA leaders reported that in mid-1989 the FARC and ELN became much more intolerant of church activities, demanding a stop to all tithe collection and education activities for youth. Pastors were given strict geographical limitations, generally not to go beyond the town or village in which they lived, and church meetings and activities were severely curtailed. As a result, most SDA activity ceased outside of the major cities. One SDA minister who violated the FARC's orders was stopped on his way home from visiting a church member who lived out of town and was murdered for his infraction. A visiting colleague who accompanied him was told to spread the word that FARC rules were not to be violated. Church members have not been targeted specifically because of their religious affiliation, although youths are frequently lectured on the Marxist dogma of atheism.

The SDA is not alone in this latest change of strategies. All church personnel, Catholic and Protestant, have operated under similar conditions in rural Colombia since the FARC and ELN imposed their restrictions in mid-1989. Most have responded by yielding to the terrorism, retreating into the churches or deserting the rural areas completely, leaving their parishioners at the mercy of the guerrillas. It is interesting to note that the so-called paramilitary groups have demonstrated no interest in the religious activities of churches or individuals. The SDA reports that several members have been killed because their business activities appear to support the guerrillas (selling gasoline, for instance) but never because of their religious affiliation.

Reportedly, SDA leaders have attempted to meet in secret with leaders of the FARC and ELN insurgency movements, in order to present a view of church activities as a nonpolitical element in Colombian society. But such a strategy is fraught with danger in that any group perceived as lenient or deliberative with these groups is immediately targeted by the right-wing terrorist groups or the government for their complicity. In effect, the government and elements of society conspire to counter any counterterrorism strategy that involves dialogue with the insurgents. Thus, practically any effort by the church to protect its assets and personnel will create a new set of dangers, reducing the viability of the current counterterrorism strategy.

The SDA is not the only church affected by the lack of stability in Colombia. Recent analysis indicates that Marxist insurgents are increasing their attacks on churches throughout rural Colombia to the point of assassinating thirty-seven church leaders, thirty-six of them Protestant. Catholic priests have been expelled from the demilitarized zone in El Caguan, churches have been closed throughout the country, and many Protestant families have been forced to leave their homes for fear of persecution. The SDA strategy of coexistence has apparently failed since 1998 because the terrorists have changed the rules and now challenge the very presence of religious groups in areas under their control.

As a counterterrorism strategy, accommodation does not work in the long run, as demonstrated by this case study. True, there were no casualties for decades, but when the aggressor changed the rules no amount of accommodation could satisfy the new requirements. It follows that as a strategy for the rest of society or the government, accommodation of the FARC or ELN will not work either. The FARC's attitude toward the Pastrana government's efforts to negotiate a settlement to date seems to back up this assessment.

GOVERNMENT FORCES AND THEIR ROLES IN COUNTERTERRORISM

As mentioned previously, the president is charged in the constitution with being the primary authority in providing security to Colombia. On paper, there are plenty of forces and agencies provided for this role. But the key point here is that they exist mostly on paper: when they exist in reality, they are overwhelmed with the magnitude of the problem, and many are limited by law and practice in what they can accomplish.

Most of the actors involved are in the Ministry of Defense, including the military, the national police, and the intelligence community. Other players include the judiciary, the prosecutors, and some nongovernmental groups that actively play a part in the government's plans and programs for countering terrorism.[17]

The Intelligence Community

The Colombian intelligence community can trace its roots through the National Police to the 1941 Law 8, which created the police as a force dependent on the national executive and charged with investigating threats against life and liberty. Interestingly, however, few of the descriptive or founding documents mention terrorism except as it relates to international agreements or cooperation in combating international organized crime. None mentions terrorism in terms of domestic insecurity or the terrorist acts of the insurgents at both ends of the spectrum. This failure to mention terrorism is indicative of the mentality of Colombia's leadership even today, in that what is elsewhere defined as terrorism is considered either as a valid and accepted form of political dialogue or as a symptom of political warfare in Colombia.

The current intelligence community was reorganized in 1995 through Presidential Decree 2233 to more fully confront the various actors in the nation's violence. The primary agency is the National Intelligence System (known by its Spanish acronym, SINAI), basically an overarching committee comprised of the heads of the various specific agencies. Its function is to coordinate policy; strengthen cooperation; increase efficiency; and foster the planning, collection, analysis, and diffusion of intelligence. Its members include the intelligence directors of the Joint Staff, army, navy, air force, National Police, and Administrative Security Administration (DAS) organized into two basic directorates along functional and organizational lines. Both directorates perform similar coordination and planning tasks but do so at different levels. The National Intelligence Technical Council works at the national level, coordinating policy and objectives with the ministers of defense, justice, and interior and the various directors of national-level security forces. The Sectional Intelligence Technical Council operates at the state level, coordinating policy and objectives with governors, brigade commanders, and state police directors. The SINAI's involvement in countering terrorism relates more to policy objectives than operations in that it translates congressional or presidential directives into national policy on which the operational groups can base counterterrorism operations and tactics.

Military Intelligence

The Military Intelligence Service is comprised of the directors of intelligence of the various services and serves to coordinate policy and operations within the armed forces. All military intelligence entities function to provide usable information to their specific commanders so that they can carry out the objectives inherent in their mission: to defend national sovereignty, independence, territorial integrity, and constitutional order. The latter has traditionally been interpreted widely, which allows the military to operate against the Marxist insurgents, right-wing paramilitary groups, illegal drug traffickers, and other criminal elements involved in insurgent, criminal, or terrorist acts against the government or society. Intelligence-planning documents are reviewed annually by the National Technical Intelligence Council and are used to set the priorities of the various intelligence components of the military intelligence directorates (army, navy, and air force). Within the past eight years, these directorates have taken over greater responsibility for controlling the border regions and for fighting the subversive guerrilla movements.

Civilian Intelligence

The preeminent component of the National Intelligence Service, the DAS is directly responsible for state security, immigration, and emi-

gration. The primary divisions within the DAS are internal and external intelligence, analysis, operational archives, counterintelligence, and regional intelligence.

The National Police Intelligence Center (CIP) was formed to unify the various intelligence groups dealing with police intelligence. The primary operational groups include the operations, judicial police, intelligence analysis, counterdrug, special services, and anti-kidnapping and extortion directorates. These groups work together to provide the police with intelligence relating to specific issues.

Of note, in the CIP publication describing the national intelligence services of Colombia[18] counterterrorism is only mentioned twice: in terms of international cooperation with treaty organizations such as the International Criminal Police Organization (Interpol) and the Organization of American States (OAS); and in terms of bilateral relations with neighboring countries or the United States. The inference, again, is that there is no terrorism in Colombia, only violence. This seems to be a variation on the military's tactic of changing labels to find different legal regimes that can deal with the issue of terrorism.

Colombian National Police Integrated Counterterrorism Strategy

The national strategy to counter violence bounds the general action to confront the groups bent on inflicting terror on society. The strategy develops an integral framework of action that involves government leaders, the public forces, the state security forces, and the regional governments in the planning and operational phases of measures to combat the various destabilizing groups in the country.

The strategy involves policies involving the strengthening of the many institutions involved in all phases of governance: the administration of justice, public forces, human rights, social and economic rehabilitation, and the peace process. It also involves special measures to arrest the different factors altering the public order, such as drug trafficking, guerrilla forces, common and organized crime, paramilitary groups, and private justice.

Terrorism in Colombia is only one of the manifestations common to the different factors that alter the public order, one requiring a tactical approach involving the coordination and unification of the efforts of the judicial, penal, and operational aspects of the justice and security forces.

The National Defense and Security Council is responsible for articulating the different policies to be carried out in coordination with the Ministry of National Defense, involving thus the military and police forces. The Ministry of National Defense, through the military forces, develops the operations carried out and coordinated throughout the national territory against the terrorist groups, which in Colombia are primarily the guerrilla groups.

The national police develops strategies to be implemented by the various specialized units such as the National Police Intelligence Service, the Police Judicial and Investigation Center (DIJIN), and counterextortion and kidnapping groups (GAULA). These groups have specific missions to neutralize terrorist activity in Colombia.

Finally, in the framework of the National Intelligence System, the Colombian government has established a coordination system among the various intelligence agencies through the National Intelligence Plan to develop operations to neutralize and minimize the impact of terrorist activity throughout the country. (Policia Nacional Direccion de Inteligencia, *Reflexiones de Inteligencia #4*)

Police Forces

The principal method of dealing with the high level of kidnapping has been to create special anti-kidnapping groups, although more time seems to have been spent on organization and protection of turf and budgets than on reducing the level of kidnapping. The two primary groups formed were the National Anti-kidnapping Committee (CONASE) and the Joint Action Groups for Personal Freedom (GAULA).

CONASE

When President Samper developed the anti-kidnapping laws, he also included a special presidential force in response to the increase of kidnapping for ransom by the insurgents and criminal elements. All existing anti-kidnapping groups were disbanded, and the new groups were made dependent on the presidency through an anti-kidnapping czar. The czar was a cabinet-level appointee (ostensibly the head of the Procuraduria, or prosecutor general) with additional responsibilities as head of CONASE. Administratively, the personnel and maintenance of CONASE are handled through the Ministry of Justice, however.

The main action groups, known as the Anti-kidnapping and Antiextortion Groups (UNASE), are a continuation of the search groups of the same name founded under President Gaviria in 1990. They consist of a combination of forces drawn from among all the police and military services and formed into urban and rural counterterrorism forces with the primary function of hostage rescue. They are divided into four sections: intelligence, administration, analysis, and action. On paper, these groups seemed to provide an ideal method of dealing with the smugglers and terrorists, but in practice the attempts failed because of their lack of experience with joint operations. Service rivalries, inadequate funding sources, and the lack of an organic intelligence function virtually guaranteed failure. There were occasional and early successes at the tactical level, primarily involving antidrug intelligence collection, the capture of guerrilla leaders, and hostage rescue operations.

The most striking success of the UNASE groups was the dismantling of the Cali and Medellin cocaine cartels. The ability to work in small, disciplined groups within an environment of security (no leaks of information), coupled with a high level of technical ability (specifically, signals intelligence such as phone taps and radio monitoring), allowed these "search blocs" to close in on Pablo Escobar and kill him. This one operation succeeded in eliminating the motivating force behind the bombing campaign against the government's extradition policy and demonstrated to the other criminal groups that they were not secure either. It directly contributed to the dismantling of the Cali cartel by forcing its leaders to negotiate a surrender rather than face extradition or death at the hands of government forces.

GAULA

A more successful force is comprised of the GAULA groups, which also trace their origins to President Gaviria's UNASE. These include military, National Police, and civilian DAS intelligence personnel working closely with prosecutors to investigate and prevent kidnapping and to rescue hostages when necessary. Strategy and policy are coordinated by a high-level committee consisting of the president, the minister of defense, the commander of the armed forces, the director of the National Police, the president of the Criminal Chamber of the Superior Judicial Council, and the president of Pais Libre (an NGO created to counter the threat of kidnapping).

The GAULAs are divided, like the UNASE groups, into rural and urban units, with the National Police forming the urban units and the military operating in the rural areas where there is little police presence. Constant and perennial problems with the group's inefficiency include the lack of adequate funding, a dependence on other military or police units for intelligence, and a lack of adequate training for specialized jobs such as evidence handling. A high turnover rate is a serious problem under this system, especially in the military GAULA, which tends to reduce their effectiveness.

The primary strategy devised for the GAULA was that they could serve as crime-prevention groups, providing information to and depending for intelligence on a centralized data base. For this purpose, the basic structure consists of the following divisions: general secretariat, press officer, operations, strategic and tactical intelligence, kidnapping data base, extortion data base, national central data base, personnel, and electronics and communications. The operative units themselves are structured according to need: the elite GAULAs have more resources for more sophisticated operations, such as psychological operations, commandos, intelligence analysts, organic administrative personnel (for cover stories), "technical" groups for special weaponry, and public prosecutors to deal with captured criminals. Most groups, however, consist of a commando section dependent on a centralized administrative structure.

According to one military official, since 1995 the GAULAs have rescued 1,089 hostages and freed more than 100 persons under pressure (defined as forcing the kidnappers to flee and leave the hostages behind).[19] They have lost 262 hostages during thirty-nine failed rescue attempts. This means that the GAULAs have put a 20 percent dent in the 2,100 per year kidnapping industry, by no means a successful effort but a significant one nonetheless.

Military Forces

In the past two years, the Colombian military has created several organizations aimed specifically at countering terrorism. The army has organized and trained an antidrug battalion designed to support the National Police's efforts to stop the illegal drug trade, which fuels the terrorist and criminal elements in the country. More battalions are being trained for the same purpose. These battalions will in time be organized under an antidrug brigade.

An intelligence center has been created in Tres Esquinas to act as a joint intelligence collection, analysis, and dissemination entity to fuse tactically actionable information. This intelligence product can then be provided to action battalions such as the Marines' riverine combat elements (RCEs), the antidrug battalions, the National Police counterterrorism units, and the military's GAULA units. It will be some time before these fusion centers are operational, but the effort has begun and hopefully will soon begin producing results.

The army has created a rapid deployment force in the northern areas, based in Cundinamarca, which can operate against terrorists if provided with the proper intelligence and operational orders. The basic concept is to create and train forces capable of rapid response to any terrorist activity. Current forces include three army mobile brigades and a special forces brigade. When adequately equipped and trained, this could prove to be a credible force in countering terrorism in Colombia's northern regions. But, given the lack of available resources, these new assets will probably be used for counterinsurgency or antidrug operations, not for counterterrorism activities.

ANALYSIS

One of the major conclusions of this essay is that Colombia has a history of conducting peaceful negotiations with insurgent groups without accountability. At the end of each negotiation, the various actors agree to a general amnesty for all the combatants on both sides. The result has been leaving in place an incentive to continue or start new insurgent movements because there is no punishment attached to the many acts of terrorism inflicted on the society by the combatants. The solution would be to develop a comprehensive negotiation strategy that separates acts of war (or insurgency) from acts of terrorism and holds the latter to account while negotiating the former.

A second major conclusion is that Colombian leaders have not developed the national security strategy required for a national negotiation strategy. Absent such a strategy, leaders cannot call into play all the instruments of national power. Thus, the military, police, justice, treasury, interior, and development agencies cannot develop specific strategies to combat terrorism, insurgency, or even common crime. These elements of national power can only develop tactics for coping with the overwhelming threat to national sovereignty. Society, too, is left on its own to cope as best it can, sometimes following the government's lead, sometimes ignoring it in order to survive. Colombian *violentologo* scholar Eduardo Pizarro has described this phenomenon as a "partial collapse of the state" that has resulted in a kind of anarchy in which each individual is responsible for his or her own survival, a dangerous mix of violence, impunity, and lawlessness that has all the elements of a total collapse of the state.[20]

At a minimum, the Colombian government needs to recognize that, according to international norms, it is in a situation of internal conflict. This situation exists in the anarchy of Colombia's governance (or the lack of it), which makes it difficult to establish a distinction between ordinary crime, terrorism, and insurgency. The guerrillas pretend to be Robin Hoods, promising better government and more benefits for the citizenry, but in reality they are more akin to the Saudi terrorist Osama bin Laden, fully engaged in a conflict in which acts of terrorism are as prevalent as acts of war. This reality presents the Colombian government with two strategic options: use the label terrorism or use international humanitarian law to resolve the conflict. The first means to consider all the combatant groups to be terrorists and refuse to discuss or negotiate and thus accept the current situation as normal and let the killing continue. The second means to establish basic rules to protect the civilian population through international humanitarian law, creating ad hoc tribunals with international oversight or supervision to punish violations of the agreements.

Neither of these options would be easy. As always in Colombia, acts of terrorism are tied to huge economic profit. This link to profit, however, provides an indication of the solution based on the recognition that a purely military solution will not work. The solution requires fundamental changes in the workings of society and culture, not just imposition of the military will of one group over another. Society is, after all, the object of fear among all the combatant groups. Government forces are not yet a source of fear; they must work to protect society as a whole and citizens as individuals. Colombia must find a balance between the use of force against the combatants and guaranteeing the respect of law and human rights.

Many of the twelve counterterrorism strategies identified and analyzed in this essay are interrelated and cannot be acted upon in isolation. For instance, the strategy of having no national security policy is intimately linked with the facts that most policy decisions have been made in times of crisis and that one of the pressures on that system is the national security interest of the United States. This being an academic study, the various strategies will be listed in this section with a value judgment on how they have worked or failed in their objectives (if any).

The first strategy, and one with a long history in Colombia, was that of negotiating with the various actors involved in terrorism. Most studies of this aspect of Colombia's history present the ability to negotiate as a positive thing in terms of conflict resolution. But the fact remains that, despite this history of negotiating, the guerrillas and terrorists are stronger than ever in Colombia today. One negative impact of negotiations is the lesson left for others to follow: if a terrorist group becomes strong enough to make its mark felt, the government will negotiate an amnesty and peace treaty, freeing the group from all responsibility for the acts of terrorism or war carried out during its lifetime. Thus, while an amnesty worked in the short term to put an end to the M–19, the Quintin Lamé, and similar groups, others have formed or broken off to start their own movements. In the long term, amnesty reduces the accountability society normally demands of its members, allowing certain groups to live outside the law with impunity of action, and encourages others to do likewise. Additionally, this strategy has been used by the FARC several times as a venue for recovering from combat defeats and for rearming for future warfare. Thus, this strategy must be categorized as a failed one in terms of its success as a counterterrorism measure.

A second strategy used throughout Colombia is based on the constitutional philosophy of natural law, which gives everyone ultimate responsibility for his or her physical safety. Whether this philosophy is being invoked openly or tacitly is subject to debate, but it is the legal underpinning used to create self-defense groups at both ends of the political spectrum. The problem for the government and society comes when, as in 1991, the legal underpinning for overt self-defense groups is removed. The military grew accustomed to using such groups as a force multiplier against the Marxist insurgents. Such groups are difficult to manage and doubly so in a situation as inherently violent as that which exists in Colombia. Now the rules have changed, and the military has been given no replacement forces. Senior military leaders continue to rely on the self-defense forces (illegally) for intelligence and as strategic partners against a common enemy. Thus, this strategy has proved to be a mixed one for Colombia in that it allows for common defense for groups outside of the government's area of control but has proven to be a legal stumbling block both domestically and internationally because of these illegal groups' use of violence and terrorism.

The third strategy is one of omission. The lack of a security policy has been a serious detriment to Colombia, although it is difficult to argue that Colombian leaders adopt this strategy consciously. It is more likely that they adopt it through bureaucratic inertia and ignorance, in that few civilians understand the use of a state's power and its monopoly on the use of violence. In a country at peace, this is not such a bad strategy. However, this is not the case in Colombia. In adopting this strategy, Colombian civilian leaders force the military to play the charade of stringing together a series of tactics masquerading as strategy, hoping to keep the tactical inertia on their side. However, this is the strategy that most consistently fails in Colombia because in the absence of guidance from the civilian policymakers the military is not winning the war and frequently loses tactically also. The military is required to perform on the battlefield with no definition of what a victory is, an impossible task under any circumstances.

The fourth strategy is that of poor leadership. It is difficult to determine whether the lack of a cohesive strategy is a specific government strategy or the result of poor leadership and the government's inability to get ahead of the terrible circumstances of Colombian security issues. In past decades, presidents have spent most of their tenures attempting to react properly to a myriad of crises without taking the time or allowing for sufficient resources to plan ahead. The result has been a series of bad decisions designed to resolve short-term crises and never a planned, cohesive strategy. The impact of these two interrelated strategies (lack of strategy and reactive crisis decision making) is that the illegal Marxist guerrillas and right-wing paramilitary groups, having issued clearly defined strategies and objectives, have the upper hand in the conflict. Very little that the government does brings it nearer to a victory, while the illegal groups succeed merely by staying alive. Thus, as a counterterrorism strategy the lack of a cohesive policy, the continued use of crisis decision making, and reliance on a reactive policy fail significantly.

The fifth strategy, which is also related to the failed strategies, is the practice of relying on the United States. This strategy has tended to divert attention from the real problem by focusing the Colombian government forces on the symptoms of the problem (human rights violations and illegal drugs) rather than on the threat closest to home (the FARC and ELN). The result of this reliance will be to prolong the war, with the possibility of threatening the sovereignty of the state. In the case of Colombia, as a counterterrorism strategy, reliance on the United States is a policy failure. A more successful strategy would be that of Peru, where then-President Alberto Fujimori forced a resolution of the conflict and then tackled the symptoms of state weakness.

A sixth strategy being attempted as a result of increased U.S. pressure to counter the illegal drug business is for the Colombian military to begin to force coordination of the various intelligence organs of the state. While the emphasis is on antidrug operations in the Tres Esquinas area, the end result will be an improved ability to collect and analyze intelligence on the Marxist insurgents. Ironically, this kind of effort was the principal strategy used by President Fujimori in Peru to counter the Sendero Luminoso in 1991. As of now, this kind of coordination is insufficient in Colombia and responds primarily to U.S. interests, which results in a failed policy. But it has the potential to become a key strategy in resolving Colombia's terrorism problem if it is properly supported. Thus, as a counterterrorism strategy, increased coordination within the intelligence community has the potential to become a successful strategy.

A seventh strategy, employed by the military over the years, has been to change the labels it uses in describing the insurgents and paramilitary groups. As a strategy, this device has functioned to provide military strategy in the absence of national policy, thus allowing the military to use various legal regimes in dealing with the illegal militias. But in the end, because this use of various monikers and legal regimes has failed, and because it serves primarily to mask the lack of government policy, it does not allow the military to coordinate its actions with other government agencies or bodies. The lesson is that only the national level leaders of government can write policy, not a subordinate command with a vested interest in a specific result. Thus, as a counterterrorism strategy this practice is a policy failure.

The eighth strategy is the military's reliance on the now illegal paramilitary groups. This strategy may prove to be successful in the short run in that the paramilitaries may serve as a force multiplier. But it will prove to be a failure in the long run, as these groups do not share the values of law and order required of the government forces. The fact that they use terrorism as a primary strategy is proof enough that they have a different future in mind for Colombia. It does not matter that there is a long history of self-defense groups or that there is a hint of constitutional natural law in the formation and justification the paramilitaries use. The paramilitaries are terrorists themselves, at odds with government policy, and should not be factored in as part of the military's strategy. At the very least, international condemnation should be proof enough that this is a failed strategy.

A ninth strategy is the extradition of criminals from Colombia for trial in the United States, a measure used to counter the extreme terrorism these criminals occasionally impose in an attempt to retain the status quo. Colombia's history with extradition has not been a pleasant one, given the extremes to which Pablo Escobar and his cohorts were willing to resort. Certainly, extradition should be upheld when it is merited, that is, in cases of criminals sought in the United States for trial and punishment. But past attempts have been seen as admissions that Colombia's judicial system is incapable of trying and punishing criminals at home and as such represent a failed strategy from Colombia's point of view. A better strategy would be to strengthen the judicial system to the point at which such trials would be possible. Thus, although extradition may prove to be a successful strategy in the short term, it fails to satisfy domestic demands for security and law and order and fails as a long-term strategy to counter terrorism.

A tenth strategy is the attempt to legislate against terrorism by making the payment of ransom illegal. This strategy failed miserably for the same reason it was passed: kidnapping is too prevalent because the state does not have the ability to impose law and order. The population has too little confidence in the state's ability to protect it, and in the state's hostage rescue forces to perform effectively, and thus does not report incidents of kidnapping. As an attempt to counter terrorism, this strategy has proved to be an abysmal failure, with no deterrent value against either the criminals or the families of the victims who refuse to report the crime.

The eleventh strategy is that of the case study of the SDA church and its accommodation with its oppressors, which seemed to work for a long time. In the end, accommodation depends entirely on the goodwill of the aggressors, which left the church at the mercy of the terrorists. When the FARC changed the rules in 1998 and began closing churches and assassinating preachers, the SDA's vulnerability became apparent. Another strategy had to be developed, which involved closing churches and withdrawing from areas under terrorist control. Thus, as a counterterrorism strategy accommodation has proved to be a failure.

The twelfth strategy, the formation of military and police antiterrorism groups (UNASE and GAULA) that work in conjunction with the intelligence community, actually seems to have a positive record. The problem is that they are not supported well enough to show significant results. Lack of experience in joint operations, service rivalries, inadequate training, and low budget levels all work together to reduce the effectiveness of these groups. In essence, the GAULA and UNASE groups are overwhelmed by the magnitude of the problem and as a result are capable of handling successfully only about 20 percent of the cases reported. The victims generally lack the confidence in government forces to report all the incidents of kidnapping, so official statistics are probably low, which means that the percentage of victims rescued by the GAULA and UNASE groups is even lower than 20 percent. Yet their efforts represent one of the few examples of a successful counterterrorism strategy in Colombia, with the potential for even more success if they are properly supported.

CONCLUSION

Terrorism and violence are rampant in Colombia today, and have been for decades, because of a combination of reasons that almost defies comprehension. Some of these reasons are tied up in the historical forces involved in the foundation of the country, and others involve the basic formulation of society and its traditions. But this assertion need not be the final excuse for Colombia: historical precedents need not dictate the future. There are, however, several conclusions that can be deduced from the high levels of violence in Colombia, specifically conclusions relating to counterterrorism strategies. Perhaps the most important is that there is a complete lack of national consensus on just what constitutes terrorism in Colombia and what should be done about the current instability and lack of governance. There are perhaps as many solutions to the conflict as there are Colombians and certainly as many as there are separate and distinct sectors of Colombian society. Recent polling, for instance, indicates that upward of 60 percent of the population favors some kind of use of government force against the Marxist guerrillas.[21] Likewise, the numbers can be added up to indicate that upward of 50 percent favor some kind of negotiations with the same groups. But President Pastrana's strategy, embodied in Plan Colombia, shows no evidence of his having consulted the national will prior to its development.

This lack of national consensus has led to a lack of national strategy. Absent a clear mandate, or at least one that national leaders are willing to follow, the presidency has thus far not written a single, integrated plan that addresses the role of each of the elements of national power in confronting the violence and terrorism that are imposing such incredible levels of fear in Colombia. The military, for instance, is the element of government normally turned to in such situations, but there has been no definition of the armed forces' role in combating the FARC or ELN since their founding in 1967 and 1964, respectively. How Colombia hopes to win a war without telling its military to do so is hard to understand, but perhaps this appraisal explains the lack of success in attaining victory thus far.

Perhaps the most significant consequence of this lack of consensus and strategy is the lack of trust that it has engendered throughout society. The electorate mistrusts the politicians, the military mistrusts the civilian leadership it is sworn to uphold, and politicians mistrust the armed and police forces that protect them. Everyone mistrusts everyone else because the lack of consensus and strategy has resulted in governmental anarchy. And, of course, this lack of trust is the very thing terrorist organizations seek through their use of violence, to break down the bonds between individuals and political institutions and between leaders and society. This mistrust is as strong a weapon as dynamite, only it favors the elements within society that seek to break the country apart. Colombian leaders must work hard to regain that sense of trust, and they can only do so by finding a national consensus upon which they can develop a national strategy. Only then can Colombia develop effective strategies to combat the many factions seeking to impose terrorism as a means of attaining national power.

In the absence of an effective national leadership, two forces have stepped in to fill the vacuum—the Marxist insurgents and the paramilitary self-defense groups. Both use acts of terrorism to achieve their objectives. Government control has been reduced to such low levels that in the midst of negotiations with the FARC, guerrilla leaders have publicly announced their plans for a dual-track strategy (negotiations and conflict) and have promulgated "laws" that aim to tax the entire population. The paramilitary groups openly defy government policy, stating that they will not honor the demilitarized zone in the state of Bolivar declared by President Pastrana as a way to initiate negotiations with the ELN. Such open defiance of government authority is indicative of how badly counterterrorism strategies have failed.

Recommendations

One of Colombia's weak points in combating terrorism is the extreme violence of which its citizens are capable. President Gaviria was forced to yield to such an extreme in dealing with the drug cartel leaders (Gonzalez Gacha, Escobar, and the Ochoas) when they, calling themselves The Extraditables, initiated a severe campaign of bombings in Bogotá and Medellin. President Pastrana faced the beginnings of such a campaign when he announced the new arrangement for extraditing drug traffickers to the United States in 1999. Luckily, he stuck to his guns, and the bombings stopped. Granted, the drug traffickers Pastrana battled were not of the caliber of those his predecessor faced, but the same mix of conditions existed: extradition policy, terrorists, and bombing campaigns.

One way to achieve the balance between the need to wage war and guarantee law and order is to use the existing constitution's legal framework for rules of exception, such as the Declaration of Interior Emergency, localized use of the state of siege, or the Declaration of Interior Commotion. Such measures imply limiting the exercise of nonessential legal rights in specific geographic areas—rights such as assembly, association, mobilization, and the ownership of weapons. As it is currently configured, the Colombian state cannot guarantee even the most basic of human rights in most of the national territory—rights such as life, personal integrity, and freedom of thought. To consider the other rights mentioned as inviolable borders on the ludicrous. No one is suggesting that these restrictions become permanent but rather that temporary measures should be required in order for the government to restore the rule of law in areas where it has lost such control.

A second recommendation is to tackle the problem of illegal funds, which the terrorist organizations require to maintain their organizations. In most cases in Colombia, the combatants depend on the illegal drug business, kidnapping for ransom, or blackmail (protection money) to purchase weapons and equipment, pay its soldiers, and conduct psychological operations in the campaign for political support. There is ample evidence that the Marxist guerrillas meet a significant portion of their fiscal needs from the solicitation of ostensibly charitable, humanitarian, and philanthropic contributions, some of which are diverted to fund terrorist operations.

The lesson for Colombian leaders is clear. Waffling in making decisions about, or caving in to, terrorists leads to more terrorism; standing firm in policy and action succeeds in breaking the cycle. Yielding to the terrorists led to a temporary cessation of the bombing, but it increased the pressure from outside (specifically the United States) for Colombia to honor its legal agreements. And the terrorists were granted breathing room to continue their illegal acts. Thus, the primary recommendation resulting from this study is for Colombia to increase its ability to meet its obligations to its citizenry by combating the terrorism that so seriously affects it. The Colombian government must strengthen its resolve, policy, and forces to the point at which it can guarantee to its citizens the ability to live and act in safety and dignity, free from the lack of trust and high levels of impunity and terrorism that permeate the country today. In the long run, a strong and just state is the only successful counterterrorism strategy possible.

POSTSCRIPT

IT IS DOUBTFUL THAT the terrorist attack of September 11, 2001, had a significant impact on Colombia. Attitudes have changed, if only by deepening the population's dissatisfaction with the continuing insecurity and the government's approach to the terrorists. President George Bush's speech defining the role of the civilized world and its responsibility to fight terrorism, delineating those who are for us (law and order) and against us (terrorists or terrorist-sponsoring states), has raised hopes that there will be movement against the forces of terror. While this has not been translated into action in relation to U.S. policy toward the FARC and ELN, it has been interpreted by many as intimating the possibility of more international assistance to Colombia.

The FARC has not changed its attitude, however. In mid-January 2002, an unnamed field commander voiced the group's objectives: "Our goal is to take power, whatever the means. If that means by rifle, so be it. So, with or without the peace process, we shall continue with our plan." He estimated that the final offensive would be launched in a couple of years.[22] The context for this comment was one of international diplomatic scrambling to salvage the stalled peace negotiations between the Colombian government and the FARC. President Andres Pastrana, following the pattern of almost all his predecessors during the thirty-eight-year-old insurgent war, had declared his intent to stop talking and begin fighting—in the final year of his presidency after spending the past three years pushing an ill-conceived and poorly planned program of negotiations. On January 9, Pastrana suspended talks with the FARC, and ordered military action to recover the *zona de despeje* (the Switzerland-sized area vacated by the government and used as the location for the peace talks). He left the door open for further talks by giving the FARC time to meet his demands, which included a plan to declare a cease-fire.

Why all this flurry of activity to keep alive a project that few believe will produce results? Pastrana's proposal was greeted with optimism four years ago, as no one before had been willing to remove all possible objections (on the government's side) to allow talks to begin. But a careful analysis of Plan Colombia, as the process is called, showed deep flaws in the strategy. In fact, strategy, as the term is normally used, was almost totally absent from the plan. A major flaw, in relation to a counterterrorism strategy, is that the government continues to act as if the country is at peace. The legal regime employed is one based on the ideal of a country ruled by law, by peaceful coexistence, where differences are settled without resort to violence—this in a country with such an infamous reputation for illegal acts that it has spawned a branch of sociology dedicated to understanding it, *violentología*.

The national military's role in the war has not yet been defined: should it defeat the insurgents, or achieve a strategic balance? Government direction of the military has been accomplished by informal directive, a method that can change daily, removing from the military the ability to formulate long-range plans and strategies.

The Colombian government, having developed no strategy of its own, has adopted foreign ones in exchange for assistance. The worst case is the adoption of U.S. military strategy in exchange for $1.3 billion, which has subverted the priority of pacifying the nation to antidrug operations that offer little or no hope of producing peace. Another case is the subversion of counterinsurgency operations to nebulous peace plans in the hope of assistance from European nations that insist on dialogue with the insurgents. It is in light of this attitude that Colombia has welcomed the changes in world opinion that occurred after September 11. The logic runs thus: increased attention to terrorism translates into increased counterterrorism funding, Colombia has a major problem with groups recognized by the U.S. State Department as terrorists, and therefore these factors should translate into increased assistance to Colombia.

As has been stated throughout this essay, the primary problem is a lack of strategy on the part of the government as it confronts forces that have a strong strategic vision. As long as Colombia tolerates this lack of planning by its leaders, it will continue to experience the paralyzing effects of the war of terror imposed by the FARC, ELN, AUC, and other irregular forces. Evidence of such planned terror tactics abounds. The FARC is increasing in size and strength, as is the AUC. Coordinated attacks continue against the government forces, and there is evidence that the FARC is planning to take over any territory ceded by the ELN during its negotiations with the government. Furthermore, the FARC uses its strategy to shape future events and forces; it has repeatedly attempted to as-

sassinate the leading presidential candidate, Alvaro Uribe Vélez, whose platform on counterterrorism and counterinsurgency includes strengthening the national military forces, coordinating and increasing their efficiency in carrying the fight to the insurgents, and not negotiating from a position of weakness. Obviously, the FARC knows its enemies and works to ensure that they do not reach positions of power.

Unfortunately, it is painfully obvious that Colombia has no real plan for achieving peace any time soon, so any statement on its future involves more of the same, a hope for muddling through. Until politicians begin making the difficult decisions needed to unify the national effort to counter terrorism and insurgency, there will be no peace or security in Colombia.

Part II

Europe

SPAIN

Antonio Remiro Brotóns and Carlos Espósito

THE FIRST FEW MONTHS of the new millennium witnessed six dead victims of terrorism in Spain. After several months of false hope due to a rather long and deceiving cease-fire, ETA (Euskadi ta Askatasuna), the Basque Fatherland and Liberty terrorist group, resumed its outrages, killing Lt. Col. Pedro Antonio Blanco García on January 21, 2000, in Madrid. Then, a few days before the Spanish general elections of March 12, a powerful bomb killed Fernando Buesa, a Socialist Party member of the Basque Parliament, and his bodyguard in Vitoria (Alava). On May 7, José Luis López de la Calle, a journalist specializing in terrorism and a founder of a pacifist organization called the Forum of Ermua, was shot dead near his house in Andoain (Guipuzcoa). Jesús María Pedrosa Urquiza, councilor of the city of Durango (Vizcaya), received a mortal gunshot wound in the back of his neck on June 4, only because he was a town councilor of the Partido Popular, a conservative party that has governed Spain since 1996. Next, on July 15, 2000, ETA slaughtered José María Martín Carpena, another councilor of the Partido Popular, who was shot six times in the parking lot of his house in

Málaga (Andalucía) in front of his wife and daughter. These are just the latest, very sad examples of the persistence of terrorism in Spain after more than twenty years of democratic freedom, and it is also the cruel evidence that counterterrorist policies have not been successful thus far.

This essay presents the basic features of the counterterrorist policies adopted and enforced by Spain. The scope of the report is wide; however, we will underscore policies adopted against ETA's terrorism from the Spanish transition from dictatorship to democracy in 1975 to the present. Regarding the definition of *terrorism,* we assume that it is the deliberate employment of violence or the threat of violence by subnational groups and sovereign states to obtain radical strategic and political objectives by means of unlawful acts of intimidation.[1] The strategic goal of terrorism in carrying out these unlawful acts is also important because such acts are intended to create overwhelming fear in a target population larger than the civilian or military victims actually attacked or threatened.[2]

We will proceed by introducing the domestic sources of terrorism in Spain and giving a brief background history of ETA—its origins and evolution as a terrorist group. Next we identify the main counterterrorist governmental policies and evaluate them according to such criteria as efficacy, legality, and legitimacy. Finally, we address international cooperation, particularly the sometimes difficult relationship between Spain and France regarding ETA and its members. In addition, we include an overview of the legal instruments available to combat terrorism at the European level. The concluding remarks sum up the main points of the report.

SOURCES OF THE TERRORIST THREAT IN SPAIN

Spanish society is mainly concerned with domestic sources of terrorism—particularly with ETA, the most relevant one from any point of view. The governmental and public perception of other sources of terrorism, including global terrorism, as an actual threat to Spain is rather weak. There is no doubt that domestic terrorism has had and may still have connections with international terrorism, but these ties are rather fragile.[3] Therefore, the rest of this report focuses on domestic sources of terrorism, particularly ETA.

However, before the origins and evolution of ETA are described we must comment briefly on another terrorist group that has been important in recent times and is still active—Grupos Armados Antifascistas Primero de Octubre (GRAPO, Antifascist Armed Group of October First).[4]

The GRAPO operated particularly, but not exclusively, during the first part of the Spanish transition to democracy, which began around 1975. In fact, it took its name from the first act of terrorism of the group, which occurred in Madrid on October 1, 1976. The group stems from the Reconstituted Communist Party of Spain (PCER), which included an armed division that sought to undermine the perpetuation of Spanish dictatorship under Francisco Franco. The order to start violent activities came when the party was profoundly divided and was much alienated from the sympathies of the people.[5] While operative, the GRAPO killed eighty-three people and kidnapped three. The group lost some of its own members for several reasons: two died in a hunger strike, seventeen died as a consequence of fighting against security forces, five died because of the explosion of a bomb, one committed suicide, one was assassinated by the GRAPO itself, and two were assassinated by unknown people.

Let us return now to our central concern: ETA. The organization was set up in 1959 as a nationalist movement to resist the political oppression exercised over the Basque people since the end of the Spanish Civil War (1936–39).[6] A group of young and displeased people, known as EKIN (which in *Euskera,* the Basque language, means "to do"), began informal talks in the early 1950s to learn about and discuss nationalism and rediscover the Basque nationalist theories stated by Sabino Arana, who is recognized as the father of Basque nationalism.[7] Arana founded the Partido Nacionalista Vasco (Basque Nationalist Party) in 1892. In his writings, he favored a nationalism based on the Basque race and the idea that Euskadi (his chosen name for the Basque Land) is the fatherland of the Basques. The ETA did not follow Arana's ideology to the letter because the organization defended a nationalism grounded on the Basque language instead of giving essential importance to family names and race.[8] Consequently, the defense and promotion of the Euskera and Basque cultural manifestations were the main objectives of the group from the beginning. Of course, these objectives are inseparable from the more general aim of creating an independent homeland in the Basque region, that is, a Basque state.[9]

The ETA was born during difficult times for the Basque leaders of the Partido Nacionalista Vasco and the Basque people. Indeed, after the Spanish Civil War the Basque government was forced into exile. Its policy depended totally on its confidence in the Allied powers, which it supported and helped in many ways. After World War II, however, the Allies let the Basques down and recognized the dictatorship of Francisco Franco, particularly because it was anticommunist and the Cold War had become a principal concern of the United States. Franco's dictatorship prohibited Euskera from being spoken and some of Basque's cultural manifestations from being displayed. Moreover, according to Jáuregui, Franco realized one of the claims of Sabino Arana's nationalism that made possible the birth of ETA: the Spanish occupation of the Basque Land.[10]

Although ETA's members were nationalists, they differed from the traditional and conservative Basque nationalists of the Partido Nacionalista Vasco (PNV), particularly because they rejected calls for moderation and passivity. The members of the ETA were committed to *action*. In fact, they were determined to adopt violent measures several months before the death of Txabi Etxebarrieta, the first casualty of ETA, and the killing of Melitón Manzanas, the chief of the Political and Social Brigade of San Sebastián, in August 1968. The killing of Melitón Manzanas was followed by indiscriminate repression from Franco's government, which, added to the famous "Burgos trial" in 1970, created the image of ETA as a leftist political group fighting against Franco's dictatorship.[11] That somewhat benevolent vision of the band reached its peak with the assassination of the powerful prime minister Carrero Blanco in December 1973, causing tremendous damage to Franco's régime. Carrero Blanco's assassination revealed another important, lasting element of ETA: the military organization controls all other aspects of the revolutionary fight, political, social, and cultural. The superiority of the military over the political leadership has not always been easily accepted within ETA, as the internal leadership struggles of the organization show.

Ever since its formation, ETA has gone through many significant internal conflicts.[12] Now we have to underscore the important crisis that arose during the Sixth Assembly in 1974, which ended with the split of ETA into two factions: ETA/Political-Military and ETA-Military. The basis of this partition can be found in diverse political and strategic approaches and in ideological differences as well.[13] Nevertheless, the major basis of disagreement was over the use of armed force. Consequently, almost all the members of the political faction of ETA abandoned violence and formed a new political party known as Euskadiko Ezkerra or EE (Basque Left Wing). The military faction, which was the largest part of the organization, continued its strategy of violence. That strategy, however, has changed since the early 1970s. For instance, ETA brought into play new forms of violence such as abductions.[14] It also altered the range of the strategy of violence from a selective to an indiscriminate one. The explosion of a bomb in a popular coffee shop in Madrid in September 1974, which killed twelve people and injured seventy-two, provides evidence of that change. That strategy had its most horrible manifestation several years later, on June 19, 1987, with the explosion of a mighty bomb at the Catalonian supermarket Hipercor, which killed twenty-one people and injured almost fifty.

Another relevant development of the 1970s was the formation of Koordinadora Abertzale Socialista (KAS), which was created to coordinate the Basque National Liberation Movement (MLNV).[15] In 1976, a document called *KAS Alternative* became of fundamental importance as it established five conditions of negotiation with the Spanish government: amnesty, democratic liberties, expulsion from Euskadi of the state security forces, improvement of the living and working conditions of the working class, and a statute of autonomy that includes sovereignty for Euskadi. In fact, most of these conditions were fulfilled after the death of Franco in 1975. A new democracy based on the rule of law, with special concern for social rights, was established under the Spanish Constitution of 1978. The Statute of Autonomy of the Basque Country was adopted on October 25, 1979. Although this statute did not cover all the sovereign aspirations of the members of ETA, it marked a significant change for the Basque people since it granted a unique cluster of political powers to the Basque authorities. Moreover, a law of October 15, 1977, declared a general amnesty for all imprisoned persons guilty of crimes carried out before the initiation of the transition to democracy. Despite the fact that there were no ETA prisoners in Spanish jails in December 1977, ETA continued with the use of violence.[16]

It follows that ETA was not primarily an organization whose goal was to overthrow Franco's dictatorship. In reality, Franco was not the cause, but only a relevant condition, of ETA's violence.[17] As a matter of fact, ETA's violence increased dramatically after Franco's death, notwithstanding the broad political autonomy enjoyed by the Basque country, which has been governed by the PNV, either alone or in coalition with the Socialist Party, from the first democratic election carried out in the autonomous territory. Furthermore, Herri Batasuna, the political branch of ETA, which was created in 1978 and recognized as a legal political party, participated regularly in the political life of the Basque country, taking part in local and general elections.

In the 1980s and the 1990s, ETA had to cope with several organizational and ideological difficulties. The latter kinds of problems had their roots in the mediocrity of ETA's ideas, in its troubles with the political organization of the Basque National Liberation Movement, in its relationship with other Basque political parties, in the decline of Soviet Marxism as a viable social theory, and in other factors. Regarding the organizational and strategic obstacles, the Spanish and French police really hurt the terrorist band several times during those decades. For example, ETA experienced a crisis following Operation Sokoa of November 1986. Sokoa was a furniture store that actually served as ETA's nerve center in Hendaya (France). The operation, which was carried out by the French police in close collaboration with Spanish intelligence, concluded with the detention of the individuals responsible for the finances of ETA and the seizure of arms, money, and several important documents.[18] This was just one aspect of more general cooperation between France and Spain in terrorist matters.[19] Another important police operation that severely injured the terrorists involved the detention in Bidart in March 1992 of the heads of ETA: José Luis Alvarez Santacristina, Francisco Múgica Garmendia, and José Arregui Erostarbe. It took ETA a few months to recover from this police strike. However, somehow it has always survived, a situation that may be regarded as its sole but not trivial success.[20]

Two famous and dreadful abductions have been carried out by the ETA. The first was the kidnapping and lengthy incarceration of José Ortega Lara, a prison official who was kept in a horrendous cell from January 17, 1996, to July 1, 1997. The police (Guardia Civil) fortunately found him, and his liberation was celebrated in all sectors of Spanish society—except, of course, for the terrorist band, which was humiliated by the rescue. It immediately kidnapped Miguel Ángel Blanco Garrido, a twenty-nine-year-old councilor of the Partido Popular in Ermua. This abduction was particularly hideous because the terrorist organization tried to negotiate with Blanco's life the penitentiary policy of the Spanish government. The government was given a forty-eight-hour ultimatum, and after that time elapsed ETA assassinated Blanco. Thousands of people expressed indignation over this act and came out of their homes to display a profound repulsion for this crime. The atmosphere created by this spontaneous, silent, and broad protest of civil society is known as the "spirit of Ermua."[21] This reaction by civil society, either organized in nongovernmental organizations or simply in an individual capacity, should be emphasized. Indeed, this kind of spontaneous demonstration is rather new in Spain, given the fact that most of the preceding protests against violence were coordinated by political parties. As a matter of fact, the reaction of civil society may be seen as a rejoinder both to violence and to the failure of democratic parties to deal with terrorism after the end of the Ajuría Enea Pact and the establishment of the Lizarra Pact.[22]

The strength of ETA today varies depending on the criteria and the moment that one chooses to judge it. Of course, the people who are actually willing to kill or kidnap are few in number, but the band has considerable support in the Basque region. This help has been essential to the endurance of ETA.[23] As we indicated, the social backing of terrorist activities has been declining in recent years; however, from the results of Herri Batasuna in elections throughout its history we can conclude that 10 to 15 percent of the Basque population is inclined to support and collaborate in different ways with ETA.

EVALUATION OF GOVERNMENTAL POLICIES

In order to evaluate governmental policies and actions in combating both domestic and international terrorism, one should first present the main antiterrorist policies adopted by Spain. However, let us start with a brief statement of some fundamentals of these policies from a theoretical point of view. Except for the military element, which is excluded from most European counterterrorism policies, we can share the view of Yonah Alexander, who affirms that those fundamentals should consist of the following elements.[24]

> First, the development of coherent, high-priority antiterrorism policies at the highest levels of government. Second, an efficient organizational structure for dealing with terrorist acts. Third, enhancing global intelligence efforts and operations. Fourth, a strong law enforcement commitment to combating terrorism. Fifth, a fair but just governmental system. Sixth, the development of appropriate covert military responses. Seventh, an active public awareness program, and eighth, unilateral and multilateral coordination of responses to terrorism.[25]

In the case of Spain, the description of antiterrorist policy includes police and judicial action, negotiation, a program of integration for the members of ETA, dispersion of prisoners among several facilities, and international cooperation. We will return to these issues in a moment; however, we should state that there are many voices that would deny the existence of a serious antiterrorist policy in Spain in the broad sense of the concept. For example, Santiago Sánchez maintains that Spain lacks "a true anti-terrorist policy," that is, a serious, long-term plan designed with the most scrupulous respect for the law to fight terrorism.[26] To support his thesis, he points to the futile hopes that ETA would put an end to its terrorist activities after the establishment of a democracy in Spain and that the end of ETA terrorism would have occurred when the Socialist Party won the 1982 elections. He notes that until the 1980s France did not change its sanctuary policy, permitting ETA members to find refuge in their country. Having said that, we can nevertheless assume that the basic counterterrorist strategies in Spain are those mentioned previously—that is, police and judicial action, negotiation, integration of terrorists, dispersion of prisoners, and international cooperation.

Police action has been a primary concern of every government.[27] The recent history of Spain has seen many ups and downs in the record of the police fight against terrorism. We can only give here a few facts concerning the normative structure of the system, which was marked by opposition from remnants of Franco's regime that remained in the emerging democratic organization and its pro-

cedures. Nevertheless, the police structure to fight terrorism experienced many reforms after the restoration of democracy as a result of the consensus of the main political parties. For instance, the limitation of military jurisdiction began with a law of 1978 regulating the police. But the truth was that the police were not well coordinated in the implementation of their counterterrorist policies. In fact, violent acts rose to astonishing levels between 1978 and 1980.[28] That reality led the minister of the interior, Juan José Rosón, to make structural changes in the ministry and to implement a much more efficacious policy to combat terrorism than the one Spain had been following. For example, a single command for the fight against terrorism was set up (Mando Único para la Lucha Antiterrorista), and some special groups were created by the Guardia Civil to fight rural terrorism. After the adoption of the 1978 Constitution, police counterterrorist activity was governed by several laws that permitted certain special procedures to be used in cases of terrorism under the theoretical permission of article 55(2) CE, such as long bans on communication for arrested suspects.[29] Under the socialist government, a comprehensive policy to fight terrorism was intended with the so-called ZEN (Zona Especial Norte, or North Special Zone) plan, which tried to connect police responses to political and economic measures intended to change the conditions that made possible the persistence of terrorism.[30] In addition to these national reforms, we have to take into account that a new autonomous Basque police, the Ertzaintza, was created in the early 1980s. The Ertzaintza introduced an element of ambiguity to police action against terrorism, although most doubts about its effectiveness were removed in April 1990, when the Basque police arrested four members of ETA.

Regarding negotiation, we should begin by admitting that to negotiate with a terrorist group is very difficult for many reasons.[31] At the outset, we should say that the process of negotiation with a terrorist group lacks transparency and may entrap constitutional authorities under a mere continuation of violence by other means. The goals of a terrorist organization are not always explicit and may even change constantly. In addition, terrorist goals are framed in a very radical way only to perpetuate the terrorist organization. This kind of consideration leads some analysts to maintain that negotiation is a mistake. Santiago Sánchez, for example, asks harsh questions concerning negotiation, such as: who negotiates, what do we negotiate, who benefits from negotiation, and why? He affirms that negotiation is only another tactic used by the terrorists to achieve their goals. Furthermore, in 1996 Sánchez anticipated our current situation when he wrote the following:

> Negotiation over the past twenty years has been a halting and repetitive procedure, an unfinished tale of frustration for each Government. Over the next few years we shall watch as the farce continues, feeding both ETA's image and antiterrorist policy: the former will offer a cease-fire; the Nationalist Basque Party (PNV) will say that it has always been prepared to talk; the Government will insist that it will not negotiate politically with those who are not legitimate representatives of the people; ETA will continue to kill; and, in the back room, obscure police officers and one of the terrorist leaders at the time will sit down to discuss the terms of "social reintegration" for ETA terrorists who are fed up with being in gaol.[32]

Spanish governments, however, have usually maintained a double discourse. To the public the message is that the one and only policy in relation to ETA is police action, but they have also kept the back door open for negotiation with ETA.[33] Examples of this approach are the Algiers negotiations and the Zurich talks. The Algiers negotiations between representatives of the Socialist government and ETA began in April 1986, but they ended without result in February 1988 after the death of ETA's main negotiator, Txomin Iturbe, as a result of a domestic accident. Although he was replaced by another member, on February 25, 1988, ETA kidnapped Emiliano Revilla, a businessman from Madrid, and consequently frustrated any further contacts with the government. The Zurich talks involved the conservative government of the Partido Popular and representatives of ETA during the cease-fire of 1998–99. These talks were a total failure, and the policy of the present government of the Partido Popular seems to be based on the rejection of negotiations.[34]

The Spanish government has also tried to undermine the internal cohesion of the terrorist group by offering pardons, separating terrorist prisoners, and promising a reintegration of the prisoner into society if he or she collaborates with the Justice Department.[35] Of course, all of these policies have inherent problems. For example, general amnesties are in principle prohibited by the Constitution.[36] Pardons always come after a sentence of a judicial court, which is a hurdle in the application of this antiterrorist policy, particularly because of the different responsibilities of the police and the courts in the enforcement of the law governing terrorism vis-à-vis the discretional powers of the executive.[37] A further concern about reintegration policy appears if one considers the fact that it may have the opposite effect because it reduces the cost of participation in a terrorist band.[38]

Other kinds of problems with reintegration of terrorists into society as a policy lie within the terrorist organization, which reacts to reintegration in a hostile way. The best Spanish example of this is the assassination of Dolores González Catarain (known as Yoyes). She agreed to reintegration but was killed by her former comrades on August 10, 1986, while taking a stroll with her baby in her hometown Ordizia.

The dispersion of prisoners, which consists basically of separating ETA members by sending them to different prisons, began around 1988. It was a decision of Minister of the Interior Enrique Múgica, himself a Basque and member of the Socialist Party.[39] The main objective of that measure was to attack the internal cohesion of the members of ETA because most were concentrated in three prisons, a situation that benefited their communication and organization. The policy of dispersion is particularly problematic now because the prisoners are away from members of their families, who must travel many kilometers to visit them. The families, therefore, develop a sense of resentment against the central authorities. That resentment has bred sympathy for the basic demands of the terrorist group.

Let us now evaluate the efficacy of these policies.

1. First, has there been a reduction in the number of terrorist incidents?[40] The figures needed to provide a proper answer to this question should be put in a historical context. However, as a general approach one can affirm that the number of ETA terrorist incidents has decreased since the peak that Spain experienced during the late 1970s and early 1980s. We are referring to incidents perpetrated by ETA directly because there is a rather problematic practice of low-intensity disturbance by young radicals or groups supporting ETA in the Basque country (table 1 shows the importance of these latter groups). These groups create a sense of insecurity in Basque society

because their members attack pacifist expressions; burn various items, from bank machines to city busses, destroy public furniture and sculpture; and so on.

2. The same kind of consideration is in order if one intends to investigate whether there has been a reduction in the number of killings in terrorist incidents. There have been about eight hundred killings due to ETA terrorism since the beginning of its violent activities in the late 1960s. However, the number of killings has constantly decreased since the early 1980s. It killed ninety-six people in 1980, but between 1993 and 1997 the average number of fatal casualties was between ten and eleven per year (see table 2). The lack of killings in 1999 was due to a cease-fire declared by ETA from mid-1998 to December 3, 1999, which was instituted to support a dialogue after the Lizarra Pact involving all the nationalist political parties of the Basque country and also the Basque branch of the national left-wing party Izquierda Unida.

As noted previously, violent terrorist strategies in Spain varied over time. However, from table 3, one can conclude that ETA has attacked people across the entire spectrum of Spanish society: for example, civilians, politicians, military, police officials, and public prosecutors. A particularly shocking violent strategy consisted of killing notable people such as politicians, judges, and professors. For example, in February 1994 a terrorist got into the School of Law of the Autonomous University of Madrid and shot one of our most respected and prestigious professors of law, Francisco Tomás y

TABLE 1. Terrorist Incidents of ETA Support Groups

	Number
1987	130
1988	150
1989	300
1990	270
1991	300
1992	550
1993	400
1994	287
1995	924
1996	1,202
1997	970
1998	489
1999	302

TABLE 2. Number of ETA Murders (by year)

	Deaths
1968	2
1969	1
1970	0
1971	0
1972	1
1973	6
1974	19
1975	16
1976	17
1977	11
1978	68
1979	80
1980	96
1981	31
1982	40
1983	40
1984	33
1985	37
1986	40
1987	52
1988	19
1989	19
1990	25
1991	46
1992	26
1993	14
1994	12
1995	15
1996	5
1997	13
1998	6
1999	0
2000	6
Total	796

TABLE 3. Number of Mortally Wounded Victims of the ETA by Profession (1968–99)

	Victims
Civilians	294
Guardia Civil	199
Police	146
Military	94
Municipal police	23
Elected officials	22
Ertzaintza (Basque Autonomous Police)	9
Jail guards	5
Judiciary	4

Valiente, a former president of the Constitutional Court. But the band also kills common people just because they belong to the governing party or a national political party. For example, nine councilors of the Partido Popular were assassinated between January 23, 1995, and July 15, 2000. As table 4 shows, although the Basque Land is the location that bears the heaviest number of casualties, ETA operates throughout Spain and also in France.

3. For several reasons, it is difficult to affirm that Spain has experienced a reduction in the costs resulting from terrorist incidents, even during ETA's last cease-fire from September 1998 to December 1999. As a matter of fact, there are no comprehensive statistics on costs. One should take into account that there are many possible sources of damage from terrorist activities, such as those of the grave site destruction campaigns of Jarrai (the youth branch of the Basque National Liberation Movement) and the Taldes Y's repulsive *kale borroka* or street-fighting campaigns. Nevertheless, it may be helpful to combine the sources of information that we describe in the commentary that follows and in table 2.

TABLE 4. Number of ETA Killings by Location

	Killings
Alava	41
Alicante	3
Barcelona	50
Cádiz	1
Cantabría	4
Castellón	1
Córdoba	1
Granada	2
Guipuzcoa	299
La Rioja	4
León	1
Madrid	115
Málaga	1
Navarra	38
Salamanca	1
Sevilla	6
Valencia	3
Vizcaya	207
Zaragoza	13
Total killings in Euskadi (Basque Land)	547
Total killings in the rest of Spain	244
Killings in France	5

Spain has legislation providing for compensation by the national administration for victims of terrorism, that is, those physically or psychologically injured as a consequence of terrorist activities. The Annex of the Solidarity with the Victims of Terrorism Act of October 8, 1999, establishes the following amounts as compensation for victims of terrorism: 23 million pesetas in case of death, 65 million in case of major disability, 16 million in case of total permanent disability, and 6 million pesetas in case of partial permanent disability.[41] Of course, the calculation is an easy task in the case of death victims, but it is much more difficult with injured victims. Table 5 shows the number of persons injured as a result of ETA activities.

4. As to the number of ETA terrorists convicted, we have not found official information as to the number of prisoners who are either members or collaborators of the band. Unofficial sources report approximately five hundred prisoners related to ETA. In contrast, there is precise information as to the detentions made by the police in Spain and France (see table 6).

From a total of 6,914 detentions in Spain, 4,742 persons were arrested by the National Police Corps, 2,042 by the Guardia Civil, and 138 by the Basque Autonomous Police.

5. As to the preservation of basic national structures and policies (e.g., the rule of law, democracy, civil rights, and civil liberties), there has been a certain lack of public trust in the effectiveness of counterterrorist policies by democratic institutions because of excesses committed in the past by paramilitary groups, that is, the Grupos Antiterroristas de Liberación.[42] The GAL has its roots in groups that were active in the mid-1970s, such as the Batallón Vasco Español or the Antiterrorismo ETA (ATE). The GAL was a clandestine organization created to combat ETA through the use of ETA methods, such as murder and other illegal actions. The GAL operated between 1983 and 1986, and reportedly killed twenty-seven people. In the beginning, GAL activities were directed at undermining ETA's organizational structure in France. Its actions were intended as a remedy to the sanctuary policy that France had in relation to ETA members living in the South of France but also as a way "to export the Basque problem to French territory."[43] The GAL based its actions on a sort of "eye for an eye" principle: every victim of ETA would be avenged.

We cannot go into each and every detail of the GAL criminal record. However, we should give an account of two famous cases: Lasa/Zabala and Marey. The first refers to the first criminal action of the GAL, which consisted of kidnapping and killing two refugees from Bayone, José Antonio Lasa Arostegui and José Ignacio Zabala Artano, who disappeared in October 1983 and whose dead bodies

TABLE 5. Persons Injured by ETA Activities (1961–99)

	Number of Terrorist Activities	Injured Persons
1961	1	0
1962	0	0
1963	0	0
1964	1	0
1965	0	0
1966	0	0
1967	10	0
1968	30	0
1969	26	1
1970	17	0
1971	20	2
1972	76	6
1973	3	9
1974	83	74
1975	88	4
1976	74	12
1977	106	12
1978	199	96
1979	290	88
1980	173	73
1981	170	58
1982	232	46
1983	176	71
1984	175	69
1985	147	73
1986	137	173
1987	79	221
1988	95	93
1989	112	38
1990	118	136
1991	141	219
1992	54	62
1993	47	71
1994	42	49
1995	7	21
1996	77	55
1997	68	21
1998	13	2
1999	1	0
Total	3,127	1,855

were found in January 1985. Their identities were confirmed only in 1995, using DNA tests. The second case is also infamous. It consisted of a disgraceful abduction by the GAL that took place on December 4, 1983, when it kidnapped Segundo Marey in Hendaya by mistake. After noting the error, the GAL tried to justify its actions, alleging that Marey was an ETA collaborator.

The crucial point for our discussion of respect for the rule of law is the outcome of these crimes. Indeed, both were judged and condemned severely. In the Marey case, the Supreme Court confirmed the punishment imposed by the Audiencia Nacional on several politicians, including a former minister of the interior and other officials of the Ministry of the Interior of the Socialist government.[44] In the case of Lasa and Zabala, Gen. Enrique Rodríguez Galindo, the most relevant person in the fight against terrorism for several years, was held responsible for their murders along with four members of the Guardia Civil.[45]

TABLE 6. Detentions of Members of ETA, Members of Other Basque Terrorist Organizations, and Collaborators

	Spain	France	Total for Both Countries
1977	105	0	105
1978	214	0	214
1979	430	0	430
1980	576	0	576
1981	802	2	804
1982	767	70	837
1983	448	0	448
1984	728	22	750
1985	519	3	522
1986	597	33	630
1987	531	115	646
1988	108	134	242
1989	129	108	237
1990	107	82	189
1991	124	86	210
1992	181	152	333
1993	92	83	175
1994	103	116	219
1995	78	71	149
1996	76	143	219
1997	61	68	129
1998	122	39	161
1999	16	30	46
Total	6,914	1,357	8,271

International cooperation against terrorism is relatively new for Spain.[46] Indeed, the most important acts of international cooperation against ETA began in the early 1980s when the French and Spanish governments began to talk and exchange information on terrorism. In 1983, they finally established a sort of permanent system of informal consultations and a ministerial seminar every six months. Note that the importance of this cooperation is striking when one takes into account the former French policy toward terrorism in Spain, in which France provided a sanctuary for terrorists such as the members of ETA.[47] This French policy was understood as a form of implicit agreement with violent groups: French police or authorities would not prosecute them as long as they did not engage in terrorist acts within the French frontiers. However, the policy was also reflected in two other factors. One is the fact that Spain had an authoritarian regime for about forty years. The other is the poor record of supplying information on terrorism aimed at foreign countries that Spanish governments had during the transition to democracy.[48] The last point is relevant to the importance of a good system of information about terrorists that can be shared with the rest of the world and particularly with allied democracies.

The relationship between Spain and France is key to understanding the nature of terrorist cooperation problems in the case of ETA. Earlier we mentioned the context and facts that led some countries to develop a sympathetic image of ETA as a fighter against Franco's authoritarian regime. France had this view for many years and consequently granted refugee status to the members of ETA. In addition, French authorities systematically denied Spanish applications to extradite members of ETA. In some way, for Spain the extradition issue became offensive, given that Franco died in 1975 and Spain became a constitutional democracy in the late 1970s. The sanctuary policy toward ETA members only changed in December 1983 when French president François Mitterand accepted the possibility of granting extradition applications and rejecting refugee status for members of ETA. In 1984, France and Spain's relationship changed substantially because that year witnessed the revision of France's negotiating attitude toward the admission of Spain to the European Community and also toward the

end of the refugee policy for the Basques. The latter was a consequence of the Agreements of the Castellana, of June 14, 1984, negotiated by ministers José Barrionuevo of Spain and Gaston Deferre of France.[49]

Spanish prime minister Felipe González suggested to French prime minister Pierre Mauroy the adoption of various policies against ETA: control the terrorists living in France, confine the most dangerous members of ETA in the northern regions, expel them to third countries, and extradite to Spain suspects of assassinations in Spain. The French government launched an aggressive campaign against ETA a few days later, with detentions, confinements, and deportations to Latin America. Cooperation in the fight against terrorism has ruled relations between Spain and France ever since and has permitted the performance of crucial operations against ETA, Iparretarrak (a separatist group of the French Basque Land), and other supporters of terrorism, as the previously mentioned Sokoa operation and Bidart detentions demonstrate.[50]

Regarding the normative dimension of international cooperation in the field of counterterrorist policies from a Spanish point of view, we have to take into account the international and European contexts. International law concerning terrorism has been the object of many studies, and we will only say that Spain is a party to the main treaties governing the subject.[51] Of course, the limitations of these agreements are publicly known. Just to mention the most important limitations, we can say that only a few states have ratified most of these treaties, that there is much controversy about the definition of political offenses and terrorist acts, and that the treaties have poor mechanisms of enforcement.

At the general European level, the European Convention on the Suppression of Terrorism, adopted in 1977 by the Council of Europe, should be mentioned.[52] This convention is relevant because it limits the definition of political crimes that are not extraditable. France, for instance, ratified this convention in 1986 and amended its Penal Code to admit that the fact of being part of an armed band may no longer be a political crime. In other words, the European Convention on Extradition may become applicable to the members of armed bands.[53]

One of the most encouraging new developments in European cooperation is the police and judicial cooperation in criminal matters under the European Union Treaty.[54] Cooperation on police and home affairs has been an issue for the ministries of the member states of the European Community since the creation of the so-called Trevi Group, composed of the ministers of the interior, which not only permitted but also fostered intergovernmental cooperation in these fields. The Treaty of Maastricht institutionalized this form of cooperation under Title VI of the European Union Treaty (also known as the third pillar of the European Union [EU]), and the Treaty of Amsterdam continued that evolution by creating a new area of freedom, security, and justice and clarifying the objectives of the European Union within the third pillar.[55]

The aim of the European Union under Title VI is "to provide citizens with a high level of safety within an area of freedom, security and justice by developing common action among the Member States in the fields of police and judicial cooperation in criminal matters and by preventing and combating racism and xenophobia."[56] This provision implies a specialization of the third pillar, which now only deals with police and judicial cooperation in criminal matters after the transfer of all the other subjects to the first pillar.[57]

In order to complete the description of European Union law that may affect counterterrorist policies, it can be added that in addition to the conditions mentioned, Article 35 talks about more general limitations that are difficult to define in precise terms. This article stipulates that the European Court "shall have no jurisdiction to review the validity or proportionality of operations carried out by the police or other law enforcement services of a Member State or the exercise of the responsibilities incumbent upon Member States with regard to the maintenance of law and order and the safeguarding of internal security." In our view, this provision excludes counterterrorism policies from the jurisdiction of the European Court of Justice.

Some specific measures adopted under the third pillar on the subject of counterterrorism are the following.

1. The Convention on the Simplified Extradition Procedure, concerning the extradition of consenting persons, drawn up by the council and signed by all member states on March 10, 1995.[58]
2. The joint action of October 15, 1996, adopted by the council on the basis of former Article K.3 of the Treaty on European Union

concerning the creation and maintenance of a directory of specialized counterterrorist competencies, skills, and expertise to facilitate counterterrorist cooperation between the member states of the European Union.[59]

3. The Convention Relating to Extradition between the Member States of the European Union drawn up by the council and signed by all member states on September 27, 1996.[60] This convention supplements and facilitates the application, among others, of the European Convention on the Suppression of Terrorism. Many aspects of this convention are relevant to the fight against terrorism; however, Articles 3 and 5 must be underlined. Article 3, on "conspiracy and association to commit offenses," provides an exception to the rule of dual incrimination, derogating from Article 2 (1) of this convention and from the corresponding Article 2 of the European Convention on Extradition and Article 2 of the Benelux Treaty. Article 5, on "political offenses," provides, on the one hand, that no offense may be regarded as political for the purpose of extradition, and, on the other hand, rejects the possibility of making a reservation derogating from the said principle in cases of terrorist offenses.
4. The Council Decision of December 3, 1998, instructing the European Police (Europol) to deal with crimes committed or likely to be committed in the course of terrorist activities against life, limb, personal freedom or property.[61] Article 1 of that decision provides that "As from the date of taking up its activities in accordance with Article 45(4) of the Europol Convention, Europol shall have the authority to deal with crimes committed or likely to be committed in the course of terrorist activities against life, limb, personal freedom or property."
5. The Council Recommendation of December 9, 1999, on cooperation in combating the financing of terrorist groups.[62]

Of course, the third pillar opens a new dimension for international cooperation, but it also creates new problems of control and accountability within its structure.[63] Besides, there may be an overlapping problem if one considers that the third pillar has rules governing terrorism only within the internal frontiers of Europe and not beyond those borders, a matter that falls under the second pillar.[64]

To sum up, many factors have influenced the Spanish government's willingness and ability to cooperate with other nations in combating terrorism. However, two issues have been essential: first, a general one that we can describe as the search for a new identity as a democratic country vis-à-vis the world and especially the European Community; and, second, the more specific one that was the urgent need of help from the French government in order to combat ETA's terrorism effectively.

CONCLUDING REMARKS ON COUNTERTERRORISM

We have already asserted the view that counterterrorist policies in the case of Spain have not been fully successful from a general perspective. Some authors, however, would defend the efficacy of specific policies, such as the dispersion of prisoners, which, according to them, has done great harm to the cohesion of ETA.[65] In any case, a clear lesson for the Spanish government and for Spain as a democracy is that terrorism should never be fought with illegal forces or methods and that the democratic authorities should neither tolerate nor support groups such as the GAL. In other words, the rule of law should always be respected in combating terrorism. We are convinced that Spain has reacted in a proper manner to the deviations from the rule of law, as the judgments of the Audiencia Nacional and the Supreme Court have evidenced.[66]

Another lesson of the Spanish experience is not to be ingenuous and assume that a transition to democracy will change the radical demands of a terrorist group. In fact, the Basque people have achieved a unique degree of self-government within Spain, so participation, recognition, and access to the democratic system are already available to Basque citizens. Therefore, it is suitable to conclude that national separatist groups such as ETA have a very destructive understanding of the principle of self-determination. Indeed, national separatism has nothing to do with the fight for individual rights and liberties or the democratic regulation of states. National separatist groups approve of liberties just to undermine the fundamental values of the democratic society.

POSTSCRIPT

THE HORRIBLE EVENTS OF September 11 have already had a substantial impact on the general strategy of Spain in combating terrorism. In this brief postscript, we draw attention to a few relevant facts

that indicate the enormous influence those terrorist acts have had on Spanish policies. In particular, we underline the international and European significance of the Spanish condemnation of the terrorist attack and the new consensus against terrorism. The scope and limits of the solidarity expressed by the Spanish government to the U.S. authorities are also mentioned.

Spain strongly condemned the terrorist attack perpetrated against the United States on September 11, 2001. The Spanish government, individually and also as a member of the European Union (EU), clearly stated that it was an attack on the international community as a whole and expressed its solidarity with the American people and its full support of U.S. policies against terrorism.[67] This support is grounded both in the rejection of the terrorist acts of September 11 and in the plea for reciprocity to fight ETA's terrorism within Spain. Indeed, while the Spanish government sincerely deplored the terrorist attack, it also found an opportunity to advance its counterterrorist policies throughout the world, especially in the EU.

At the international level, Spain has defended the United Nations decisions against terrorism and particularly welcomed Security Council Resolutions 1368 and 1373. The first one condemned the terrorist attacks in the strongest terms and described those acts as a threat to international peace and security, recognizing an inherent right of individual or collective self-defense in accordance with the United Nations Charter. The second resolution, of September 28, on Threats to International Peace and Security Caused by Terrorist Acts, is even more important for Spain because it declares that all states should prevent and suppress the financing of terrorism and should take a number of other important measures. Among them, apart from the creation of the committee and the monitoring system, it is essential for Spain that the resolution appeals to all states to "take appropriate measures in conformity with the relevant provisions of national and international law before granting refugee status, including international standards of human rights, for the purpose of ensuring that the asylum-seeker has not planned, facilitated or participated in the commission of terrorist acts."

The terrorist attack also provided an effective stimulus to cooperation among EU members on instituting a new common strategy against terrorism. Spain has been struggling for a clear response against terrorism in order to combat ETA within Spain but also throughout the EU territory. In other words, since the attack counterterrorism policies have become an EU priority objective. The consequences of that impulse have already been significant. Indeed, the terrorist acts have led the EU to foster the so-called third pillar, speeding up the process of creating an area of freedom, security, and justice, and to step up cooperation with its partners, especially the United States. For example, the director of Europol has received instructions to negotiate an agreement with the United States that would provide for an exchange of liaison officers between Europol and U.S. police agencies. Within the EU, the Laeken European Council on December 14–15 adopted the Framework Decision on the European Arrest Warrant and the Surrender Procedures between the Member States. The Framework Decision establishes "the rules under which a Member State shall execute in its territory a European arrest warrant issued by a judicial authority in another Member State." It is fair to say that this framework decision, which implies the mutual recognition of court judgments among EU members, is a qualitative step forward in the fight against terrorism for both Spain and the EU.

As noted, Spanish support of the United States is, in principle, unconditional. However, one should take into account the fact that Spain is under the obligation to respect the rule of law. Consequently, it is not in a position to accept certain initiatives that the United States is trying to implement, such as the one contained in the Presidential Executive Order of November 13, 2001, dealing with "Detention, Treatment, and Trial of Certain Non-Citizens in the War Against Terrorism." This executive order is contrary to Spanish constitutional law (especially Article 24) and the European and international laws of human rights. Furthermore, the treaty governing extradition between Spain and the United States (May 29, 1970) expressly excludes persons subject to possible capital punishment (Article 7) and special courts (Article 4) from extradition.

Terence Taylor

TERRORISM COMES IN MANY different forms. Britain's experience of terrorism has been mainly domestic and overseas terrorism associated with independence movements in the dying days of empire. In view of this experience, this essay focuses mainly on "Irish terrorism," although it does address the British approach to, and experience with, modern international terrorism and seeks to contrast the two in an analysis of the lessons that can be learned. The experience of independence-related terrorism is largely ignored.

NATIONAL STRUCTURES

Legislation and Definitions

Britain's counterterrorism legislation has evolved in response to the perceived threat of terrorism, as seen in the context of prevailing views on how acts of terrorism should be considered and the existing governmental structures used for dealing with those types of acts. The principal perceived threat was Irish Republicanism.

Indeed, it was only in the wake of the 1974 Birmingham bombing that the Prevention of Terrorism Act was drafted to supplement the 1920 Emergency Powers Act (Northern Ireland). Later international terrorism was added to the list of perceived threats, but until 2000 (non-Irish) domestic terrorism was specifically excluded. Thus, terrorism was defined as either Irish or international terrorism. The law allowed for no other domestic terrorism.

The prevailing view at the time of the 1974 Prevention of Terrorism Act was that terrorism is a criminal, not a political, act. This view persisted until 2001. The principal governmental structures for dealing with criminal acts are the United Kingdom's fifty or so police forces and the criminal justice system.

Until July 2000, the principal legislative measures governing terrorism in Britain were the following.

The Prevention of Terrorism (Temporary Provisions) Act (PTA) of 1989 (c. 4), applicable only in Great Britain

The Northern Ireland (Emergency Provisions) Act (EPA) of 1996 (c. 22), applicable only in Northern Ireland (amended in 1998)

Sections 1–4 of the Criminal Justice (Terrorism and Conspiracy) Act (CJT & CA) of 1998 (c. 40)

In addition, the government had recourse to the Emergency Powers Act of 1920 to provide the authorities with "such power and duties as His Majesty may deem necessary for the preservation of peace, for securing and regulating the supply and distribution of food, water, fuel or light, and other necessities, for maintaining the means of transit or locomotion, and for any other purposes essential to the public safety and life of the community."[1]

This legislative slate provided various means to prevent terrorism and investigate and prosecute acts of terrorism. Essentially, these measures fell into three categories.

Power for the home secretary to proscribe terrorist organizations and the definition of various offenses connected with such organizations (e.g., membership in and fund-raising for the organization)

The creation of specific offenses connected with terrorism, such as fund-raising or training in the use of firearms for a terrorist act

Police powers to prevent and investigate terrorist acts, such as powers of investigation, arrest, stop and search, and detention

The definition of *terrorism* applied was "the use of violence for political ends, and includes any use of violence for the purpose of putting the public or any section of the public in fear,"[2] but it was applied only to Irish and international terrorism.

A notable feature of Britain's terrorism legislation prior to 2000 was that it was all temporary. This was because it evolved in response to Irish terrorism and later to international terrorism, both of which were originally viewed as transient problems. Furthermore, the powers created under terrorist legislation were similar to those envisaged under the Emergency Powers Act of 1920. Any powers granted under this act were temporary in order to ensure that they would not become regularized and hence infringe upon basic civil rights. Powers granted under the Emergency Powers Act had to be reviewed by Parliament within five days of proclamation and renewed each month, specifically to protect against abuse and extension of emergency powers. As a natural extension of these civil rights protection concerns, Britain's counterterrorist laws had to be renewed on an annual basis.

There was a substantive change in the situation when the Terrorism Act of 2000 was passed by Parliament on July 10. This act addressed the omission of non-Irish domestic terrorism from the earlier legislation and made most of its provisions permanent. The main provisions are as follows.

The act represents permanent nationwide antiterrorist legislation (to replace the existing separate, temporary legislation for Northern Ireland and Great Britain).

The definition of *terrorism* will for the first time apply to so-called domestic terrorism as well as international terrorism and terrorism connected with the affairs of Northern Ireland.

The police will retain the powers that they have under the current legislation to stop and search and take other actions to combat terrorism and will have strengthened powers to tackle terrorist financing and seek forfeiture of terrorist assets.

A judge (rather than a minister) will consider police applications for extensions of detention under the terrorist power of arrest.

The act includes additional temporary measures that apply to Northern Ireland only.

The act replaces the PTA and the EPA and will be reviewed on an annual basis. The British government intended for the act to be fully implemented early in 2001. However, the Northern Ireland provisions—extending the life of the EPA for a limited period—went into effect immediately. The 1996 EPA would otherwise have repealed itself on August 24, 2000.

Organizations and Responsibilities

In the United Kingdom, the home secretary is responsible for all security and counterterrorism issues. While the Foreign and Commonwealth Office (FCO) leads in negotiating international treaties dealing with terrorism, the passage of enabling legislation and the implementation of these treaties within the United Kingdom are ultimately the responsibility of the home secretary. Likewise, there is partial devolution of police powers in that both Scotland and Northern Ireland have independent police forces but they are subordinate to the home secretary on terrorism policy.

Within the Home Office, responsibility for terrorism policy falls under the Organized and International Crime Directorate. Within this directorate is the Terrorism Protection Unit (TPU), which is itself split into different sections dealing with, inter alia, Irish terrorism, international terrorism, contingency planning, and domestic terrorism (issues such as animal rights activists).

In line with Britain's consideration of terrorism as a criminal act, responsibility on the ground for responding to a terrorist act within the United Kingdom falls to the chief constable of the relevant fifty or so police authorities. The police may then call in whatever additional resources they deem necessary, be it fire department, ambulance, hospital, local and national government, intelligence, scientific, or military. However, any decision to launch an assault against terrorists requires ministerial approval. Consequently, for any protracted terrorist incident a Cabinet Office Briefing Room (COBR) is established and acts as the crisis management center. COBR comprises relevant ministers and senior officials. Its link to the scene of the

crime is the government liaison officer (GLO), a senior Home Office civil servant, who is sent to the scene of the incident. The GLO takes a team with him or her, comprising (if it is an incident of international terrorism) an official from the FCO, a Security Service officer, and a press officer, who in turn will cooperate with the police spokesperson dealing with the incident and the Home Office director of public relations, who will be located with the home secretary in the COBR. Any request for military assistance, be it for an assault or, say, to call on the government's expertise in chemical, biological, or nuclear weapons, passes from the police through the GLO.

COUNTERTERRORISM MEASURES

Deterrence

Knowing the terrorist's mind can greatly assist in the development of counterterrorism measures. A domestic political terrorist organization cannot afford to alienate the citizens whose sympathies it is trying to win, as the Irish Republican Army (IRA) found when it kidnapped and killed William Best in Derry in May 1972.[3] In its later years, the IRA consequently was forced to focus more of its attacks on military, political, and economic targets and take measures to limit collateral civilian damage (e.g., telephone warnings with identifying passwords to alert the authorities that the call was genuine).[4] Foreign religious or ideological terrorists are unlikely to be so constrained vis-à-vis the citizenry of the country attacked, but they also have their target audiences to consider.

In short, terrorists are not irrational: they aim to maximize attention to their cause. While some will see value in the martyrdom associated with suicide attacks, for the most part terrorists, while going for the prestige target, will opt for targets that are less well protected. By increasing preparedness, responding rapidly, and vigorously prosecuting those who perpetrate terrorism, the United Kingdom hopes to deter or divert terrorist activity from its shores. Deterrence cannot eliminate terrorism, but it can minimize its occurrence by raising the terrorist's perception of the costs, be they political, financial, or human.

There are three elements to deterrence.

Taking a tough stance that threatens severe consequences to would-be attackers

Giving credence to that stance through one's actions

Publicizing the deterrence policy

The United Kingdom has consistently held a position of no negotiation with terrorists. It is stated policy that anyone who takes a hostage in the United Kingdom will not be given free passage out of the country in return for the release of the hostage, nor will ransoms be paid for hostages taken outside the country. It is also stated policy that perpetrators of terrorism will be tracked down and prosecuted to the fullest extent of the law.

These policies have been borne out by the United Kingdom's actions. The government has not paid ransoms, nor allowed them to be paid by others, for its citizens taken hostage overseas. It has besieged hostage takers, most notably at the Iranian embassy siege (April 30–May 5, 1980), the Libyan embassy siege (April 17–27, 1984), and the Stansted Airport hijacking (August 26–27, 1986). While the case of the Libyan embassy was complicated by diplomatic status considerations, the terrorists in the other incidents were either killed or arrested and prosecuted by the security forces. Indeed, the Iranian embassy siege added greatly to the United Kingdom's terrorism deterrence by creating a myth, understandably not confirmed by the government, that it was British policy in such cases to kill all but one of the hostage takers, leaving that one alive for debriefing to provide information that would help improve further counterterrorism procedures. Finally, the British government frequently publicizes its strong antiterrorism stance through statements made at all levels of government, from the head of state (the monarch) and the prime minister (as head of government) on down.

Preparedness

Contingency

Based on its experience over the years, the Home Office's TPU has, in consultation with the various police and other relevant authorities, drawn up a series of contingency plans. There are contingency plans for bomb attacks (both before and after the bomb goes off), hostage taking, chemical and biological weapons attacks, nuclear incidents, attacks on oil rigs, and breaches of public order (covering, inter alia, disturbances of the peace related to animal rights, anarchy, and genetically modified crops).

Single Set of Standard Operating Procedures

Key to the effectiveness of responding to terrorist incidents is adherence to a single set of standard operating procedures (SOPs). Police authorities throughout the United Kingdom use the same set, as do the emergency services (hospitals, ambulances, and fire departments), government ministries, the military, and the security services. This established set of procedures minimizes errors due to "learning on the job" or confusion. It enables a rapid, coordinated response of different government departments and other agencies.

Training

Training plays a major role in ensuring that the SOPs are adhered to and that contingency plans can be implemented smoothly. Each year, there are twenty one-day desktop training exercises, coordinated by the TPU, whereby the police authorities run through the SOPs and the relevant contingency plan so that the appropriate staff members will know what to do in the event of a real incident.

In addition, there are three live exercises a year. These exercises last from thirty-six to forty-eight hours and are held over a weekend. They involve setting up all the apparatus of a real response. The COBR is convened, under the home secretary, in the Cabinet Office. The GLO convenes his or her team, and they travel to the site of the "incident." All the relevant authorities (police, hospitals, fire, ambulance, and local authorities) and utilities (electricity, water, gas, and telecommunications) at the site of the incident run through the procedures and contingency plans. This exercise may include calling in staff persons to bring them up to emergency response levels, cordoning off areas around the incident, having "casualties" who have to be taken to hospitals, coordinating the distribution of casualties among hospitals, and running through all medical emergency procedures. Similarly, these exercises test the liaison function of the GLO's team, the policy- and decision-making abilities of the COBR, and public relations handling.

At the technical level, a great deal of training takes place. Staff persons at ports, airports, and railway stations are trained to look for items of unattended luggage in public places since luggage may contain terrorist bombs. At this level, calling the police to cordon off the area around the item (or evacuate the building) and, if necessary, to call in a bomb disposal unit are well-established procedures given the United Kingdom's experience with IRA bombing campaigns. Likewise, security staff at airports are routinely trained to operate bomb detection equipment. Specialist branches of the police and military are trained in bomb disposal, forensic sciences associated with terrorist bombings, sharpshooting, siege tactics, siege assaults, and siege and hostage negotiations, to provide the technical skills needed to react to a terrorist incident.

Equipment

These specialist units have, over the years, also developed specialized equipment to facilitate their tasks. Hostage negotiators are assisted by being able to listen in on the terrorists with sensitive microphones or even observe their movements through cameras placed in drill holes in the walls of the building in which the hostages are being held. Siege assault teams are assisted with stun grenades and special ties that enable them quickly to bind anyone found in an assault, hostage or terrorist, thereby disabling that individual. Bomb disposal teams have developed remote controlled robot vehicles to investigate and disable suspicious packages or unattended luggage.

Assessing and Minimizing the Threat

The British government has had a long history of having to deal with terrorist threats, be it from Irish terrorism, independence groups, or international groups that object to Britain's foreign policy stance. Consequently, government and military installations, particularly those overseas, have long-established procedures to assess the terrorist threat on a regular basis and to design and implement measures and procedures to minimize the threat. Examples are:

Design of government offices. In the light of experience, some high-risk offices are built with a blast resistant ground floor—that is, this floor is empty. In addition, the overall building structure is designed to withstand an attack involving a car bomb driven into the building.

Office layout. Desks are arranged away from exterior windows so that the official's back is to the window. In this way, if a bomb

goes off outside, injuries due to flying glass will be minimized. Similarly, high-risk office buildings are equipped with blast resistant curtains (to catch flying glass) or with special glass.

Controlled access. Access to these buildings is tightly controlled. Visitors are required to submit to searches to ensure that they are not carrying bombs or weapons. In addition, visitors must wear access authorization at all times when in the building.

Security procedures. Mail room staff and officials are taught how to identify suspicious mail for letter and parcel bombs and how to follow the procedures should there be a suspicious mail item. Likewise, the staff and officials are taught how to respond to the presence of an unauthorized person (or an unaccompanied authorized visitor) in a restricted area.

These measures are designed both to make the office a less attractive terrorist target and to minimize the consequences of a terrorist attack should one be launched against it.

At times of heightened terrorist threat levels, these lessons were passed on to the utilities and infrastructure providers. For example, trash cans were removed from streets, airports, railway stations, and underground stations in the wake of a spate of IRA bombs placed in trash cans in public thoroughfares.

In the wake of the Bishopsgate attack, the Home Office decided that the lessons of threat assessment and reduction learned by the government should be made available to the business community. In 1994, the Home Office published a handbook for managers: *Bombs: Protecting People and Property.* This handbook walks managers through the process of assessing the threat to their businesses and evaluating their particular vulnerability. It talks them through five contingency plans covering mail bombs, incendiary devices, a bomb in the building, a bomb outside the building, and telephoned bomb threats. An appendix details the actions to be taken, the questions to be asked, and the information to be recorded by staff should a telephone bomb threat be received.

The handbook also explains deterrence and detection, addressing in detail issues such as doors, access routes, windows, intruder alarms, closed-circuit television, lighting, general security SOPs, and vigilance. It also addresses building evacuation plans, bomb shelters, and how to go about reoccupying the building after the initial threat has passed, bearing in mind the possibility of secondary devices and the potential dangers of structural damage, such as to a gas pipe. In this connection, it also explains how a business can develop a plan to search the premises for unexpected or foreign items prior to reoccupation.

A separate handbook for managers—*Maximising Business Resilience to Terrorist Bombings*—was published by the Home Office in the wake of the Manchester bombing of 1996. It uses both the Bishopsgate and Manchester bombings as case studies for how the authorities and businesses should respond to a bombing attack in a business district, breaking the study down into initial action, recovery, and lessons learned. It then walks managers through recovery planning. In this regard, it shows managers how to recover business in the aftermath of a catastrophic terrorist attack by taking precautionary measures (such as backing up data, adopting clear desk policies, and holding key information at another site), response measures, and measures for the continuity stage.

Early Warning: Intelligence

Clearly, a major tool in minimizing or diverting either generic or specific terrorist threats is to be forewarned with intelligence. Both the Security Service and the Secret Intelligence Service, respectively Britain's internal and external security intelligence services, expend a great many of their resources in analyzing and picking up terrorist threats.[5] The resources of these services are deployed at all stages. Assessments of, and intelligence about, terrorist threats are made routinely or before a rumored specific incident. The expertise of the services is available, through the GLO, to the relevant police authority during any ongoing terrorist incident, and their resources are available to assist police investigations following an incident.

Reaction

Powers

As noted in the preceding section on legislation, the police (and, at borders, immigration and customs officers) have far-reaching powers to arrest, detain, stop and search, seize assets, and cordon off areas in relation to suspicions of terrorist activities. These powers are available to them to prevent terrorist incidents, contain an ongoing incident, and investigate an incident.

Speed

The preparation of contingency plans and the delegation within the United Kingdom of control of a terrorist incident to the local police authority, under the overall responsibility of the home secretary, allow for both rapid response and centralized control and, hence, consistency of approach. For instance, in the case of Bishopsgate, within two minutes of the vehicle being primed and abandoned by terrorists, a local policeman had identified the vehicle carrying the terrorist bomb as being suspicious, even before the phone call from the Provisional IRA was received warning of its imminent detonation. Within minutes, police were taping off a cordoned area and implementing an existing evacuation plan developed with area businesses beforehand. By calling designated key holders at various businesses, using loud-hailers and their vehicles' public address systems, the police were able, with the few officers close to the scene, to evacuate almost entirely a very large area within minutes, before the device exploded. The fact that within twenty minutes staff at a bank had followed their contingency plan and sought refuge in the basement is a testament to the value of the contingency plans that the Home Office encourages businesses to develop.

Coordination: No Turf Wars or Egos

The most outstanding feature of the United Kingdom's machinery for dealing with terrorist incidents is that, while it is centrally planned, it allows for genuine delegation of responsibility for a rapid response to the unexpected. Those responsible for each part understand precisely their roles and functions. There are no conflicting or overlapping jurisdictions. Consequently, there are no turf wars or ego considerations in responding to incidents. This, together with the regular training exercises, contributes considerably to the speed and effectiveness of the response to terrorist acts.

Actions

The first priority in a terrorist incident is to secure and contain the site. As noted previously, this is the responsibility of the local police authority under the leadership of its chief constable. While this is ongoing, the police call upon such additional expertise as may be required, such as the bomb squad, fire and ambulance services, forensic or negotiation experts, and (through the GLO) military, intelligence, or diplomatic teams. They can stand hospitals on alert to receive casualties and bring in local authorities and utilities providers to assist them as required.

Investigation

Investigations start with the securing of the site and the preservation of evidence. They proceed from there along normal police enquiry lines, with witness interviews, accumulation of forensic evidence, and follow-ups of any leads. Should the police require it, the assistance of the security services is available to them, both within the United Kingdom and internationally, particularly in tracing movements of personnel, finance, and weaponry and in following links between various organizations.

Prosecution

The United Kingdom's policy is to prosecute cases of terrorism to the full extent of the law. In doing this, normal criminal justice procedures are followed in implementing counterterrorism legislation.

INTERNATIONAL STRUCTURES

Legislation

The United Kingdom places much importance on putting an international legislative framework in place to combat international terrorism. It strongly supports and is actively involved in the negotiation of international conventions banning various aspects of terrorism. There are currently twelve United Nations (UN) international terrorism conventions, all of which the United Kingdom has ratified or intends to ratify.

Organizations and Responsibilities

The United Kingdom views the UN as the most appropriate international forum within which to deal with terrorism issues. While there are consultations among the G-8 countries (the Group of Eight leading democracies: Britain, Canada, France, Germany, Italy, Japan, Russia, and the United States), the North Atlantic Treaty Organization

(NATO), the European Union, and technical institutions, such as Interpol, that may become involved in combating terrorism, the United Kingdom considers the UN the best forum for deliberation and negotiation of international treaties on terrorism. This approach also includes the use of UN technical organs (such as the International Maritime Organization or International Air Transport Association) as the best forums in which to coordinate policies and actions.

Within the United Kingdom, it is the FCO and its Counter Terrorism Policy Department that have the lead role on international aspects of terrorism. They negotiate terrorism treaties on the country's behalf and deal with incidents of terrorism affecting British interests outside British jurisdiction. However, once it becomes a domestic matter (e.g., the domestic implementation of an international treaty or a hijacked aircraft leaves international and enters British airspace) the lead role passes from the FCO to the Home Office.

Foreign and Bilateral Assistance

The United Kingdom has no formal international aid program with regard to terrorism. However, given its experience and success in developing countermeasures, it does seek to share its experiences with countries that express an interest.

One way of doing so is to visit other countries to explain the United Kingdom's "best practices" in confronting terrorism and taking countermeasures. Another is to send or receive observers on training exercises. Occasionally, officials from other countries will be invited to attend British training sessions on specific aspects of counterterrorism (be it policing or judicial processes). Occasionally, the expertise of the Special Air Service (SAS) has been made available to advise on how to end a siege with an assault (as in the hijacking of the Lufthansa aircraft to Mogadishu in October 1977).

THE UNITED KINGDOM'S EXPERIENCE OF TERRORISM

Terrorist Incidents in the United Kingdom

Domestic Groups against U.K. Targets

Northern Ireland. The bulk of terrorism in the United Kingdom since World War II has been Irish terrorism in Northern Ireland.

Modern terrorism in Northern Ireland—that is, that starting in 1969 and known as the "Troubles"—began as an adjunct to a civil rights movement launched by activists in the minority Catholic community to redress discriminatory practices against it. Sympathies in the Catholic community had historically lain with independence from the United Kingdom through union with the Republic of Ireland. It was a natural step that many in a movement to obtain full civil rights for the Catholic minority, even when the rights were realized, would also sympathize with the goal of secession from Britain and union with the Republic.

Very early on in the "Troubles," security officials were warning that there could be no purely military solution.[6] Indeed, the need for political solutions was recognized all along. The Northern Ireland government of the time, led by Terence O'Neill and his successor James Chichester-Clark, was following a policy of reform, liberal Unionism, and gradualist friendship with the Republic of Ireland. And, in the wake of the Battle of Bogside in August 1969, the British government moved swiftly to guarantee publicly that all the reforms sought by the Northern Ireland Civil Rights Association (NICRA)—the civil rights movement—would be granted. While the majority of the Catholic community would probably have been satisfied with this if it had been properly implemented, many Unionists saw no need to compromise, and indeed were threatened by the thought of it and so sought to bring down the reformist government (and succeeded). On the other side, fervent nationalists did not want a solution to the civil rights issues that left Ulster a part of the United Kingdom. Consequently, extremists on both sides had common cause in heightening tension between the Protestant and Roman Catholic communities and undermining efforts at nonsectarian reform.

A full chronology of the "Troubles" is not possible here.[7] Tables 1–3 illustrate the extent and breadth of terrorism in the province. Abbreviations used are as follows.

RUC	Royal Ulster Constabulary
RUC "R"	Royal Ulster Constabulary Reserves
Army	British Army
UDR	Ulster Defence Regiment[8]
RIR	Royal Irish Rangers, later merged with the UDR to become the Royal Irish Regiment

Great Britain. Irish terrorism in Great Britain (mainland Britain comprising England, Scotland, and Wales) began on October 31, 1971, with the bombing of the restaurant at the top of the London Post Office Tower. This was followed in February 1972 by the bombing of a public house in Aldershot—a garrison town in the south of England—frequented by soldiers. Seven people were killed and 19 injured. These incidents generated massive publicity and attention for the IRA cause (not surprisingly, much of it negative in Britain). It was more than a year until the next bomb in Britain. Then, in March 1973, two bombs were set off in London, one outside the Old Bailey,

TABLE 1. Deaths in Northern Ireland Due to Irish Terrorism

	RUC	RUC "R"	Army	UDR/RIR	Civilian	Total
1969	1				13	14
1970	2				23	25
1971	11		43	5	115	174
1972	14	3	105	26	322	470
1973	10	3	58	8	173	252
1974	12	3	30	7	168	220
1975	7	4	14	6	216	247
1976	13	10	14	15	245	297
1977	8	6	15	14	69	112
1978	4	6	14	7	50	81
1979	9	5	38	10	51	113
1980	3	6	8	9	50	76
1981	13	8	10	13	57	101
1982	8	4	21	7	57	97
1983	9	9	5	10	44	77
1984	7	2	9	10	36	64
1985	14	9	2	4	26	55
1986	10	2	4	8	37	61
1987	9	7	3	8	68	95
1988	4	2	21	12	55	94
1989	7	2	12	2	39	62
1990	7	5	7	8	49	76
1991	5	1	5	8	75	94
1992	2	1	4	2	76	85
1993	3	3	6	2	70	84
1994	3		1	2	56	62
1995	1				8	9
1996			1		14	15
1997	3	1	1		17	22
1998	1		1		53	55
1999					7	7
2000					1	1
Total	200	102	452	203	2,340	3,297

Source: Data from Statistics and Research Agency, Royal Ulster Constabulary.
Note: Figures include the Royal Irish Regiment (Home Service Battalions).

the main criminal court in London, killing 1 and injuring 243; two other bombs were defused. It is believed that these bombs were planted to protest the referendum on the status of Northern Ireland, in which the Protestant majority in favor of remaining in the Union prevailed. Two days later, a bomb went off in a hall in Glasgow at an event organized by Protestants supporting the continuation of the Union. By the end of 1973, there had been some seventy IRA terrorist incidents in Great Britain broken into two campaigns. More than forty bombings were carried out in the six weeks from August 18 to September 28, 1973, and a further twenty in London from December 17 to December 26, 1973, in retaliation for the jailing of the Irish ter-

TABLE 2. Terrorist Incidents in Northern Ireland

	Shootings	Bombs	Armed Robberies
1969	73	10	
1970	213	170	
1971	1,756	1,515	489
1972	10,631	1,853	1,931
1973	5,019	1,520	1,317
1974	3,208	1,113	1,353
1975	1,803	635	1,325
1976	1,908	1,192	889
1977	1,081	535	676
1978	755	633	493
1979	728	564	504
1980	642	400	467
1981	1,142	529	689
1982	547	332	693
1983	424	367	718
1984	334	248	710
1985	238	215	542
1986	392	254	839
1987	674	384	955
1988	538	458	742
1989	566	420	604
1990	557	286	492
1991	499	368	607
1992	506	371	739
1993	476	289	643
1994	348	222	555
1995	50	2	421
1996	125	25	405
1997	225	93	401
1998	211	243	369
1999	125	100	431
2000 (up to January 31)	4	5	50
Total	35,798	15,351	21,049

Source: Data from Statistics and Research Agency, Royal Ulster Constabulary.

rorists who had attacked the Old Bailey in March. These campaigns included a letter bomb sent to the home of the prime minister (10 Downing Street); a parcel bomb sent to the headquarters of the governing Conservative Party; and bombs at the Baker Street Underground station, the London Stock Exchange, the House of Commons, the Bank of England, various other banks, Euston and Kings Cross railway stations, shops, hotels, and the home of a prominent British general. The December campaign also saw a new tactic—a car bomb outside a government building. In total, Irish terrorism in Great Britain in 1973 resulted in some 15 dead and 109 injured.

TABLE 3. Firearms and Explosive Finds

	Firearms	Explosives (kgs)
1969	14	102
1970	324	305
1971	716	1,246
1972	1,259	18,819
1973	1,313	17,426
1974	1,236	11,848
1975	820	4,996
1976	736	9,849
1977	563	1,728
1978	393	956
1979	300	905
1980	203	821
1981	357	6,419
1982	288	2,298
1983	166	1,706
1984	187	3,871
1985	173	3,344
1986	174	2,443
1987	206	5,885
1988	489	4,728
1989	246	1,377
1990	179	1,969
1991	164	4,167
1992	194	2,167
1993	196	3,944
1994	178	1,285
1995	118	5
1996	98	1,677
1997	105	1,258
1998	88	883
1999	113	89
2000 (to January 31)	9	<1
Total	11,605	115,517

Source: Data from Statistics and Research Agency, Royal Ulster Constabulary.

The year 1974 saw no letup. Forty-one terrorist incidents saw 56 dead and 442 injured. Incidents included a campaign of letter bombs sent to the homes of those opposed to the IRA; armed robberies; bombs at a newspaper office, at a defense college, on an army bus transporting military personnel, at pubs and clubs frequented by military personnel, at telephone exchanges, and at prominent shops (Harrods and Selfridges in London); an attack on an army base in the north of England; individual shootings of soldiers and businessmen in Great Britain; large bombs at a Heathrow Airport car park, at the Tower of London, at Westminster Hall in the center of London, and in the center of Manchester, Bristol, and Birmingham; and another new tactic—bombs placed in mail boxes and garbage cans on the sides of public streets.

Despite an official cease-fire with the IRA in the early part of the year, 1975 was another bloody year. Splinter groups within the IRA breached the cease-fire in August, and the hunger strike undertaken by IRA prisoners in the Maze Prison in Northern Ireland, who were seeking recognition as political prisoners and hence special treatment, sparked a new round of terror from September onward. All in all, some twenty-nine incidents resulted in 11 deaths and 217 injuries. There were more bombs in shopping centers in London and Manchester; more assassinations of individuals; and more bomb attacks on pubs, underground stations, and hotels. New tactics included drive-by shootings, drive-by bombings (tossing a nail bomb out of the window of a speeding car), and bomb attacks on restaurants.

Irish terrorism in Great Britain dropped off significantly in 1976. While eleven incidents resulted in one death and some ninety injuries, the bulk of the damage resulted from a single bomb at the Olympia Ideal Home Exhibition in London in April of that year, which injured some eighty people.

From 1977 onward, Irish terrorism within Great Britain, as shown in tables 1 and 2, slowed significantly. There were still spectacular and bloody incidents, such as the nail bomb at the Chelsea Barracks in October 1991, which killed two and injured thirty-eight. But the bad years became the exception—years like 1982 (in which there were eleven deaths and fifty-one injuries from bomb attacks at Hyde Park and the Regent's Park bandstand), 1989 (eleven deaths in one attack on an army barracks), 1992 (six deaths and ninety-two injured, mainly

from one bomb attack on the Baltic Exchange, a Warrington shopping mall in Lancashire, and another at Bishopsgate in the City of London).

In addition to Irish terrorism, there have been numerous incidents of social unrest and violent campaigns that have bordered on terrorism, which, because of the legal definition of *terrorism* used in the United Kingdom until the new act was introduced, were not classified as such. For instance, at least one animal rights group action has resulted in a human death. Damage to property has been incurred by the antihunting lobby, antifur demonstrators, demonstrators against genetically modified food, and anarchists. Several recent anarchist demonstrations, sometimes characterized as anticapitalist and antiglobalization, have deteriorated into riots, resulting in injuries and extensive property damage. While this kind of demonstration appears to be a growing phenomenon with an international dimension (and as such merits further study), this essay will not expand on this issue further.[9]

Domestic Groups against Foreign Targets

There have been two reported incidents of Irish terrorism directed against foreign targets in the United Kingdom, both of which occurred in Northern Ireland. The United States was the target of an incident in March 1974 when IRA terrorists attempted to break into the U.S. Naval Communications Center in Londonderry, Northern Ireland, to steal weapons. The attempt failed. In December 1973, the German honorary consul in Northern Ireland, a businessman, was kidnapped, presumably by the IRA, and was later found dead. Possible motives included ransom or discouraging foreign investment in Northern Ireland.

In October 1975, a bomb went off under a car in which Carolyn Kennedy, daughter of the late president John F. Kennedy, was to be a passenger. It killed one and injured seven. It was initially thought that she might have been the target, but this was later discounted. The car was owned by a Conservative member of Parliament, Hugh Fraser, and he was the intended victim.

Foreign Groups against U.K. Targets

Most of the foreign terrorist incidents in the United Kingdom have been connected with the situation in the Middle East. However, even these have been few and far between.

On April 17, 1984, a shot was fired from the Libyan embassy in London into a crowd of demonstrators on the pavement outside, killing a British policewoman. This resulted in a week-long siege of the embassy until the British government agreed to allow the gunman and other embassy staff to leave the country.

On December 21, 1988, Pan American Flight 103 from Frankfurt to New York exploded over Lockerbie, Scotland, killing all 259 passengers and crew on board and 11 persons on the ground. While this was obviously an attack on an American target launched out of Frankfurt, it occurred in British airspace and hence has been pursued diligently by British authorities. The trial of two Libyan secret service agents got under way in 1999 in the Netherlands, under Scottish jurisdiction, as part of a negotiated deal between the United States and the United Kingdom on the one hand and Libya on the other. It was brokered by the United Nations in return for the lifting of UN-imposed sanctions against Libya.

A car bomb was set off outside Balfour House in London, home to a Jewish charity, on July 27, 1994. It was presumed that an Arab terrorist group had carried out this attack. Five people were injured.

Finally, in the spring of 1998 there were intelligence reports that Iraq had sponsored biological weapons terrorism against U.K. targets, using duty-free bottles of perfume and alcohol to smuggle the biological agent into the country. Public warnings were disseminated on the radio and television about the risk, but no incidents were reported.

Foreign Groups against Foreign Targets

In December 1970, the terrorist group Black September killed the Jordanian ambassador in London in retaliation for Jordanian attacks on Palestinian camps in Jordan. In September 1972, a Palestinian terrorist sent a letter bomb to the Israeli embassy in London, which killed one person there. In August 1978, the Popular Liberation Front of Palestine (PFLP) ambushed an El Al stewardess in London, killing her. In June 1982, the Abu Nidal group killed the Israeli ambassador in London. The Israeli embassy came under attack again in July 1994, with a car bomb detonated just outside, which injured fourteen. Arab terrorists were presumed responsible, as they were for a letter bomb attack against the *al Hayat* newspaper in London in January 1997, which injured two people. This attack

was part of an international campaign against *al Hayat* offices around the world, including those in Washington, D.C., and the UN Headquarters in New York.

London did not escape the wave of Sikh terrorism of the mid-1990s. In January 1995, a bomb went off at a Sikh newspaper office in London, killing the editor. London has also been the scene of a number of foreign political assassinations, notably those of Yemeni officials in the late 1970s and of a Bulgarian defector, Georgi Markov, in 1984. In these cases, it was presumed that the assassinations were undertaken on behalf of the victims' own governments.

Finally, London saw another hijacking in February 2000 when an Afghani airliner hijacked in Pakistan was finally diverted to Stansted Airport. After a lengthy siege and much negotiation, all the passengers were freed and eighteen people were taken into custody. The main motivation of the hijackers appears to have been to escape from Afghanistan and seek asylum in the West.

Terrorist Incidents against U.K. Assets Abroad

Domestic Groups against U.K. Overseas Assets

The only reported incidents of this nature have been acts by Irish terrorists. The first was the firebombing of the British embassy in Dublin in February 1972, which resulted in no injuries. In 1973, the IRA launched a campaign of letter bombings against British targets, including two overseas embassies. Bombs were received at diplomatic missions in Washington, D.C., and Paris in August; in Gibraltar, Zaire, Lisbon, and Brussels in September; and in two British Army of the Rhine (BAOR) bases in Germany, also in September. In total, two people were injured in these incidents.

The next such incident was the bombing of the car of the British ambassador to Dublin in July 1976, which killed the ambassador and injured two other people. In August 1978, there were eight more attacks on BAOR bases, causing several deaths. In March 1979, an IRA terrorist killed the British ambassador to The Hague in his car, together with his Dutch driver, and the same night the same terrorist mistakenly killed a Belgian citizen while attempting to kill a British diplomat assigned to NATO. In August 1979, the IRA pulled off one of its highest profile assassinations when it blew up Lord Mountbatten's boat in the Republic of Ireland. Two other people were killed along with Mountbatten. The same day, a bomb went off in the Grand Palais in Brussels, moments before a British Army band was due to perform there, injuring eighteen people. In December 1979, Irish terrorists mailed various letter bombs from Belgium to prominent people in Britain. One of these bombs exploded prematurely in a Brussels post office, wounding two.

March 1980 saw a resumption of bomb attacks on BAOR bases. Six attacks resulted in four injuries. Again, in December 1980, terrorists shot at a British commissioner to the European Community, with no injury. February 1981 saw one of the more adventurous attacks on British overseas assets, with the takeover of a British coal ship moored off the coast of Donegal in the Republic of Ireland. The terrorists threatened all British shipping in Irish waters. The next month, a British businessman was shot and injured in Dublin in a further attempt to discourage British commercial activity in Ireland.

The last overseas incident occurred in June 1996, with a mortar attack on another BAOR base. No casualties resulted.

Domestic Groups against Foreign Overseas Assets

The principal attacks have been related to Irish terrorism, with most directed against the Republic of Ireland. The first incident in the Republic was an armed robbery in April 1970 in Dublin. This was followed by a bomb in Dublin in October 1970, which killed one person. Another IRA bomb went off in Dublin in December 1971, also killing one. The year 1972 saw two further bombs in the Irish Republic, in June and December, resulting in two deaths and two injuries. In November 1975, bombs exploded at Shannon Airport, killing one and injuring seven.

The year 1975 saw the beginning of Protestant terrorism in the Republic. A total of four bombs in Dublin killed twenty-six people on May 17, 1975. June 1975 saw the killing of a Saor Eire member in Cork. There were eighteen firebomb attacks in Dublin in 1976 (in February and August), resulting in no injuries, and a train robbery in Dublin. In November 1977, an IRA armed robbery at a supermarket went wrong, resulting in a siege, which lasted twelve hours but resulted in no injuries. In October 1978, an IRA bomb was set off on a train in Dublin. The Belfast-Dublin train was again the target of two IRA bombings in 1979 (April and September) and one in May 1980. In January 1980, a bank manager and his two daughters were kidnapped by the IRA for ransom. They were released unharmed once $60,000 ransom was paid. Thereafter, Irish terrorism in the Republic ended.

There have been very few incidents of Irish terrorism against other targets. In September 1971, the IRA threatened the U.S. embassy in Dublin, claiming that war would be declared on the United States if a noted IRA leader were not released from a U.S. prison. This threat turned out to be baseless. Discouragement of foreign investment in Ireland lay behind both the letter bomb sent to a Canadian company, Alcan, in Dublin shortly after it had announced plans for a major investment in the Republic in September 1975 and the kidnapping of a Dutch businessman in Dublin in October 1975.

Foreign Groups Based in the United Kingdom against Foreign Overseas Assets

While there have been no reported cases of terrorism being launched against foreign targets overseas by foreign groups based in the United Kingdom, there is a growing concern that this may happen. The new Terrorism Act will allow the home secretary to ban any such groups. To date, concerns have centered on Yemeni fundamentalist Muslim clerics encouraging youngsters to join terrorist camps in Yemen and Afghanistan and on Egyptian, Saudi, and Sikh dissidents.

Foreign Groups against U.K. Overseas Assets

Incidents involving foreign attacks on British assets overseas fall into four categories: attacks perpetrated by independence movements, hijackings of British aircraft and ships, targeted kidnappings of British personnel, and more indiscriminate kidnappings of Western rather than British tourists.

The first instance of a foreign terrorist attack against British interests where Britain was no longer a colonial power was the hijacking of a British Overseas Airways Corporation aircraft by Palestinians in Jordan on September 6, 1970. On the same day, Swiss and German aircraft were also successfully hijacked at the same airfield, and an El Al flight only escaped hijacking because security personnel overpowered the would-be hijackers. In this instance, Britain, along with Switzerland and Germany, released terrorists held in their prisons in order to secure the release of the hostages.

The only other hijacking of a British aircraft occurred in Dubai in 1974 where the Palestinian Rejectionist Front took over a DC-10. In this instance, the aircraft was flown to Tunisia, and a German passenger was killed before the hijacking was over.

Kidnapping of British diplomats began in October 1970 with the kidnapping of the British trade commissioner in Quebec. On January 8, 1971, the British ambassador to Uruguay was kidnapped by that country's Tupamoros terrorists and held for eight months before being released. In 1984, the British ambassador in Lebanon was visiting the American embassy when it was the target of a truck bomb. He was slightly injured.

Lebanon saw the majority of targeted kidnappings of British personnel. On April 14, 1986, a British television journalist, John McCarthy, was kidnapped in Beirut. On January 10, 1987, while trying to negotiate the release of McCarthy and several Americans who had been kidnapped, Terry Waite, the special envoy of the archbishop of Canterbury, was also kidnapped. Then, on May 12, 1989, Jackie Mann, a British UN aid worker, was also kidnapped. All were released, respectively, in August, November, and September 1991 after UN intervention on behalf of all the hostages held in Lebanon.

The 1990s saw British tourists caught up in domestic disorder and terrorism in other countries. On October 21, 1992, a British citizen was killed in Egypt when gunmen opened up on a group of tourists. A similar incident in 1999 resulted in the deaths of three Britons. British subjects were also killed in Cambodia on July 26, 1994, when Khmer Rouge guerrillas attacked an international group of tourists. In 1995 and 1997, British tourists were taken hostage and killed by guerrillas in Indian-held Kashmir. On December 28, 1998, four tourists (including two Britons) were killed in Yemen when security forces there attempted to liberate them from their kidnappers. Also in 1998, two British telecommunications workers were kidnapped in Chechnya, along with a New Zealander and an American. After a failed rescue attempt by local security forces, their captors beheaded them. In 1999, two British aid workers, also in Chechnya, were held captive for several months by Chechen separatists. It is not clear whether these acts were committed purely for financial gain or as part of the conflict with the Russian government. In June 2000, the November 17 group murdered the British military attaché in Athens, allegedly because of the United Kingdom's prominent role in the military campaign against Yugoslavia over Kosovo.

In the thirty years from 1970 to 2000, there have been fourteen incidents of foreign terrorism overseas involving British persons or assets that cannot be linked directly to efforts by a country to gain independence from the United Kingdom. As a consequence of these incidents, seventeen Britons have been killed and one has been injured.

Independence-Related Actions against U.K. Overseas Assets

As a colonial power, the United Kingdom experienced a number of terror campaigns aimed at gaining independence for the colony in which the acts were committed. The first such campaign, post–World War II, was conducted by Zionist groups agitating for the creation of an Israeli state in the Palestine Mandate. Between November 27, 1945 and December 29, 1947, some 118 British soldiers and policemen were killed in Palestine by the group Irgun. Similar campaigns against Britain conducted by groups other than Zionists were, inter alia, in Malaya (late 1940s to early 1960s), Cyprus (1955–60), Kenya (1955–59), and Aden (1964–67). The most recent incident occurred in Quebec in October 1970 when the British trade commissioner was kidnapped by Quebecois separatists. He was released unharmed.

PRESENT THREAT ASSESSMENT

For domestic terrorism, the Northern Ireland peace process notwithstanding, by far the largest perceived threat remains that of Irish terrorism. There is a growing tendency in official circles to view disturbances of the peace and violent demonstrations or campaigns (such as those conducted by anarchists and activists involved with animal rights, genetically modified food, fur, and hunting) as terrorism. While the threat and occurrence of such disturbances are indeed on the increase, the general public's perception of them does not yet equate them with acts in the mold of Irish terrorism. Indeed, given that (with the exception of the anarchists) the aim of these demonstrations and campaigns is to convince the public of the benevolence of the activists' views, the violence of the campaigns and demonstrations is likely to remain at low levels.

The threat of international terrorism within the United Kingdom's borders is viewed as being minimal. Of the five incidents treated as international terrorism within the United Kingdom in the last thirty years, only the Iranian embassy siege might meet consensus as a terrorist incident. The Stansted Airport hijacking cases were both more truly asylum cases. The Kurdish takeover of the Greek consulate in 1999 was more of a political demonstration that was treated as terrorism because of the hostage-taking element. The Libyan embassy siege had more to do with strained international relations than traditional views of terrorism. The killings of Yemeni and Bulgarian dissidents in London in the late 1970s and early 1980s was really state-sponsored assassination.

If there is a perception of the threat of international terrorism within Britain's shores currently, it has more to do with the launching of domestic terrorism elsewhere by foreign groups located in Britain than against Britain itself. In particular, Egyptian and Yemeni groups have been identified as causes for concern. The Terrorism Act has addressed this issue by giving the home secretary powers to ban foreign terrorist groups located within the United Kingdom, not just Irish terrorist organizations.

Because of Britain's close alignment with the United States, a constant threat to British assets remains overseas. An example is the assassination of the British military attaché in Athens by the November 17 group in June 2000. Attacks sponsored or inspired by the Saudi dissident Osama bin Laden or by Iraq currently pose the greatest perceived risks.

PUBLIC PERCEPTIONS AND AWARENESS

Informing the Public: Policy

As will be discussed, terrorism issues attract a great deal of publicity in the British media. Government officials can rely on extensive press, television, and radio coverage for pronouncements on government policy. For example, the introduction of the Terrorism Bill (now Act) into Parliament received large spreads in the British broadsheets and much coverage by serious news programs.

On a day-to-day level, the public becomes aware of policy as terrorist incidents unfold. Britain's reaction to the taking of a citizen hostage overseas will almost always be reported within the context of its overall policy of dealing with hostage taking. Similarly, reporting of sieges will also include the British government's policy and SOPs for dealing with such incidents.

As noted previously, the Home Office has an active policy of informing the business community of terrorism policy and best practices. And the public becomes aware of best practices through going about their daily lives.

General Awareness of Best Practices

Since Irish terrorism spilled over into Great Britain in the 1970s, the British public has been extremely aware of the terrorist threat and, increasingly as time went on, of best practices in countering terrorism. Anyone visiting a British airport will have heard the frequent announcements over the public address system warning persons to report to airport security personnel any unattended luggage that they see. This carries over into the public's awareness of unattended packages in other public thoroughfares or transport, such as on subway trains or in railway stations. Local authorities and transport companies removed public trash cans from streets and stations when the IRA began placing nail bombs in them. The delegation of responsibility for local contingency plans to police authorities ensures that they will develop contingency plans for each major business area within their patch.

Media Coverage

The British media covers terrorism, both within the United Kingdom and internationally, very thoroughly. Hostage-taking incidents in Yemen or Chechnya, political terrorism in Algeria or Colombia, or piracy in Thai waters are reported in depth. Terrorist incidents within the United Kingdom are front-page news.

Analysis of Counterterrorism Strategies and Tactics: Benefits and Social Consequences

If any proof were needed, the experience of the United Kingdom shows that international and domestic terrorism are very different beasts. The same powers are available to British authorities to counter both international and domestic terrorism. International terrorism within the United Kingdom is virtually nil. Irish terrorism, despite the massive efforts to beat it head on, while much reduced in its intensity, could not be completely eliminated by counterterrorist measures. At best, it was contained within limits, a development that made political negotiation a profitable option for the nationalists.

A key difference, of course, is the degree of sympathy that the terrorist can expect to inspire in the local population and hence the amount of assistance (both overt and tacit) he or she might be rendered in attacking or evading the security forces. No matter how just, a foreign terrorist cause is unlikely to attract the widespread support among the local population necessary for a prolonged campaign. With domestic terror, the opposite may be true: the source of the terrorist's grievance may well give him or her ready access to a pool of sympathizers who share the same grievances, even if those persons do not initially agree with terrorism as a tool. Clearly, terrorist organizations benefit when they have continual recruitment of new members unknown to the security forces or when the base of their sympathizers and supporters is so wide that the security forces simply cannot detain or intern all of them. Conversely, when the security forces are able to arrest active members faster than the terrorist organization can recruit them and are able to sustain that record, the terrorist organization's days are numbered.

The troubles in Northern Ireland show how, even with the best of technical counterterrorist measures in place, the fight against terrorism could not be won permanently without a political process effective enough to resolve differences between the communities. Perhaps the principal lessons from Northern Ireland are that identifying and committing to good policies is insufficient for resolving fundamental disputes: the implementation and perceptions of the policies and those implementing them are equally important. It was perhaps on these last two parameters, rather than the former, that British efforts in Northern Ireland suffered their most serious setbacks.

Policies

The "Troubles" started as a civil rights movement aimed at rectifying evident inequalities between the majority Protestant and mi-

nority Catholic communities. Within a year of the Troubles, and before the IRA had begun to exploit them effectively, the British government had conceded in principle that all the civil rights movement's demands should be met.[10] Specifically, British and Northern Ireland ministers acted to make access to housing, education, employment, and government more fair. They reformed the RUC and disarmed it to address Catholic concerns about its Protestant bias. They established a Police Authority of Northern Ireland to hold the RUC accountable and allowed for Catholic representation on it. Electoral reform was pushed through to ensure one person, one vote, ending the company votes that favored Protestants. There were plans for power sharing and committee systems to enable the structural minority (the Catholics) to have a say and influence in a "first past the post" majority system of government that assured that the Protestant Unionists would always be the party of government within the province. Even that Protestant government was committed to the platform of reforms and friendship with the Republic. And the British government went so far as to say that if reformists in Stormont (the seat of Northern Ireland government) were defeated (by Protestant extremists who opposed reforms benefiting the Catholics) direct rule would be established whereby Northern Ireland would be ruled from Westminster in order to push those reforms through.

That should have eviscerated the basis for protest, other than protests based on republicanism (the desire to withdraw Ulster from the United Kingdom and seek unity with the Republic of Ireland) and hence should have seen the end of the mass demonstrations and rioting. However, extremist Unionists succeeded in bringing down the reformist Stormont government. Even when direct rule was imposed in March 1972 as a result, through obstruction, noncooperation, and strike actions they managed to thwart Westminster's efforts to impose reforms and reconcile the two communities. Thus, the extremist Unionists effectively obtained a veto on the reforms that could have ended the Troubles, even at times when they may not have had an absolute majority of the vote in Northern Ireland. The ever-present threat of large-scale disruption and violent action by the large loyalist majority and its paramilitaries severely limited the British sphere of action in responding to the perceived grievances of the nationalist sympathizers.

Political

Power sharing did not survive long in Northern Ireland. Certain Unionists disrupted meetings, refused to participate, or simply used the machinery of government to ensure that it could not work. The committee system was never implemented. Catholics, too, thwarted some of the efforts to implement reforms and obtain more say for their community. They boycotted the border poll, a census aimed at establishing the relative sizes of the Catholic and Protestant communities, and hence for a while the statistics used for power-sharing purposes underrepresented them. For its part, Westminster did try repeatedly to foster talks between the two communities to end the Troubles, although some criticized the vigor with which these efforts were pursued and the willingness of the British government to pressure or override the Protestants.[11]

Westminster did not always help, either. In May 1970, local government reforms effectively reduced the power of local councils to "bins, bogs, and burials," taking away the major portfolios of housing and education and giving them to the Protestant-dominated Northern Ireland government. This left Catholic communities feeling even more disenfranchised than before. In October 1970, local elections were postponed because of the Troubles (they were not held until October 1973), leaving them further disenfranchised.

In such a state of perceived disenfranchisement, the right to peaceful demonstration becomes more important. But here both the Northern Ireland and British governments, faced with the potential for large-scale public protest and violence, appeared to discriminate against the Catholic community. Out of public order concerns, the police could ban marches. Thus, whenever the Catholic community organized a march the Protestants could veto it by organizing a march at the same time and place, thereby ensuring rioting and that both marches would be banned. To rub salt into the wound, at one point all marches except traditional ones (i.e., Protestant Orange Order marches) were banned, giving the Protestants the right to march but denying it to the Catholics. Those participating in an illegal march risked arrest and imprisonment.

The major difficulty here was the inability of the enforcement agencies—the RUC and later the British Army and its UDR—to gain the trust and respect of both communities as impartial protectors. By 1969, the RUC had come to be seen by the Catholic community as Protestant dominated, used as a tool against them and not as a nonsectarian body bent on unbiased enforcement of the rule of law. In particular, the armed B Specials branch was detested by the Catholics. Additionally, the failure of the RUC to protect the People's Democracy March in January 1969 from Loyalist attacks fixed in the minds of many Catholics the idea that the RUC served only the Protestant community. Reforms were prompt, and the new RUC was in place within the year. These reforms disbanded the B Specials, replacing them with the RUC Reserves. Disarmed, the RUC sought to increase recruitment of Catholics into its ranks and established a civilian board, the Northern Ireland Police Authority (PANI) to hold the RUC accountable to the public.

But almost immediately these reforms failed. Nationalists refused to participate in the PANI. Recruitment into the RUC of Catholics never neared proportional representation, and in time it became an almost exclusively Protestant organization. The RUC never gained the trust of the Catholic community, and in response to the violence they had to rearm themselves.

The British Army initially was seen as more impartial, and there were hopes among the Catholic community initially that it would serve to protect them against the more aggressive Unionists. One of its first acts was to establish the Peace Line, separating the clashing Protestant and Catholic communities by setting up no-go areas. This did initially reduce the vulnerability of Catholic communities to being evicted from their homes by Unionist intimidation or firebombing.

However, by March 1970 the army was clashing regularly with Catholic youths and using water cannon, tear agents (C.S. gas), and baton charges to disperse them. "Snatch squads" were developed to arrest instigators, and the army warned that it might have to shoot to kill in order to defend itself from attacks with firebombs and bricks.

Throughout 1970, Catholic trust in the army diminished. On June 27, when Unionists attacked the Catholic Short Strand enclave in

East Belfast, the army was noticeable by its absence. A small number of IRA gunmen opened fire on the attackers, making them instant heroes among the Catholic community and establishing the perception among Catholics that without them their enclave would have been defenseless. Then, just one week later, on July 3, 1970, the army imposed a twenty-four-hour curfew in the Catholic Falls Road area of Belfast, conducting (in the minds of some) unnecessarily intrusive house searches for weapons caches. While the searches were a tactical success, uncovering many weapons, they caused alienation of the security forces among both communities. In particular, encouraged by the paramilitary organizations, they destroyed much of the trust the Catholic community may have had left in the army.

Matters would only get worse with the accidental shooting of a Catholic civilian by the army on July 31, 1970. The interrogation techniques used were initially deemed by the European Court of Human Rights to be "torture," but this was later revised to "inhumane."[12] But the incident that turned the army into the "enemy" was Bloody Sunday. A demonstration on January 30, 1972, organized by NICRA, became a riot when the army used snatch squad tactics to make arrests. From there, it disintegrated into a major shooting incident as soldiers fired at what they thought were snipers. The result was that the army killed thirteen apparently unarmed Catholics. Faith in the British government was hard hit when the official inquiry in April 1972 exonerated the soldiers, even though no one else that day, including top journalists, had heard any gunshots before the army commenced firing. As part of the current peace process, a new inquiry began in April 2000 to attempt to allay concerns about earlier investigations.

Faith in the institutions of law and order was further undermined when the British and Northern Ireland governments failed to investigate killings of Catholic civilians by the security forces. Even when procedures for complaint handling were set up, the minute number of complaints that resulted in any form of public reprimand for members of the security forces involved, be it RUC or army, undermined Catholic faith in the system of accountability, too. Even the army's positive achievements were turned against them. The no-go areas became a haven for IRA activity and, when the Unionists began to set up their own no-go areas in July 1972, the army had to remove all no-go areas (in Operation Motorman, conducted on July

31, 1972). This operation was successful in assuring access to all areas by the security forces and local government officials.[13]

Legal Institutions

Perhaps the one single measure that turned Catholics against their government more than any other was internment. This policy was introduced on August 9, 1971, in response to Unionist agitation within the Stormont government to do more about public disorder and the riots. Internment allowed security forces to hold and interrogate people without pressing charges. That night, 342 Catholics were interned. That they viewed this measure as anti-Catholic is hardly surprising, for over the three years of its existence 1,981 Catholics were interned while only 107 Protestants suffered the same fate. While internment may have been introduced as a measure to combat the IRA more effectively, it undoubtedly played into its hands, increasing sympathy and boosting recruitment.

Other legal measures also discredited the system in Catholic eyes. As a means of shielding juries from intimidation and hence allowing the justice system to operate effectively, the British accepted a recommendation from an enquiry by Lord Diplock that security-related trials be held in front of a single judge with no jury. In fact, this opened the "Diplock courts" to the charge of arbitrariness, undermining public faith in the court system. The fact that 75 to 80 percent of convictions in Diplock courts were obtained on the basis of confessions and that later the uncorroborated evidence of paid informants would be used to obtain convictions eroded their credibility. However, given the IRA campaign to intimidate witnesses, the British government had few alternatives if a court system was to operate at all.

One British success in this arena was the negotiation of extradition treaties with the United States and the Republic of Ireland that allowed those accused of terrorism in Northern Ireland to be extradited to the United Kingdom for trial rather than be treated as political dissidents and be granted asylum in the United States. Further, the British government was able, at least until the hunger strike, to maintain the position internationally that the Northern Ireland conflict was an internal affair and there should be no external interference from the United States, the Republic of Ireland, or the United Nations. This position was held until the time was more propitious to promote the peace process, involving the United States, that resulted in the 1999 Good Friday Agreement endorsed by referenda in the Irish Republic and Northern Ireland.

Perceptions

Regardless of the validity of its actions and policies, or even of how well objectively the political, security, and judicial systems performed in implementing them, the perception of the nationalist community was what was paramount if support for the IRA were to be undermined to the point of eliminating it and terrorism or public disorder as a normal part of life in Northern Ireland. With actions by the paramilitaries on all sides denying effective operation of the jury system, in particular, the British government had little alternative but to follow the course it took in relation to the criminal justice system and direct rule. Another obstacle to progress in peace processes is the vested interest in continuing a campaign of violence not so much for political reasons as for economic ones, particularly when a terrorist campaign continues over decades.

CONCLUSION

The sad fact is that, where age-old societal wounds exist as was the case in Northern Ireland and for many parts of the world, it is easier for extremists to derail reform or peace processes than it is for the vested powers to hold society together. However, there is little doubt that the success of security forces in reducing the effectiveness of terrorist organizations is an essential element in allowing governments to maintain and develop democratic and equitable political and legal processes. This interaction between security forces and government is evident from the Northern Ireland peace process, despite halting progress, where the communities are steadily distancing themselves from paramilitary action as means of achieving their objectives. This case also demonstrates that international cooperation can be essential to stemming terrorist violence and, where appropriate, in helping to mediate a political end to violence. With regard to the defense against international terrorism, U.K. government policies and counterterrorism operations have enjoyed

particular success in limiting its impact on British citizens and, in certain cases, the citizens of other countries. As the Northern Ireland case demonstrates, concessions may have to be made to complete a peace process but only in a context in which the parties concerned have stopped using terrorism as the principal means of achieving their objectives.

POSTSCRIPT

SINCE THIS ESSAY WAS written, as in a number of other countries, legislative action and counterterrorism policy have developed rapidly in the United Kingdom and continue to do so. Even before the September 11, 2001, attacks in the United States the United Kingdom introduced the Terrorism Act 2000, which entered into force in February 2001. One of the principal features of this act was to extend the powers of the courts to deal with those who are alleged to have conducted terrorist attacks outside the United Kingdom. This was an important territorial extension of the investigatory powers of the police as well as the courts. In direct response to the September 11 attacks, Parliament rapidly passed the Anti-terrorism, Crime and Security Act, which received royal assent on December 14, 2001. The act is a package of measures aimed at strengthening the government's power to detect and prosecute terrorists and undermine terrorist and criminal networks. It complements and builds on the Terrorism Act 2000.

The December 2001 act includes measures to cut off terrorists from their funds by ensuring better information sharing between intelligence and security agencies; preventing terrorists from abusing immigration and asylum laws; tightening security in relation to aviation, at civil nuclear sites, and at laboratories holding stocks of dangerous substances; and enabling prompt action to implement measures agreed on by all European Union member countries to tackle terrorism and directly related crimes. Among the measures to achieve these objectives are

- Enabling law enforcement agencies to target and track terrorists by requiring carriers to supply information about passengers and freight.

- Requiring communications service providers to retain data (such as billing details)—not content—and make them available for terrorist and criminal investigations.
- Removing people's right to unreasonably refuse to assist the police in identifying them by allowing the police to require the removal of hand and face coverings (such as masks).
- Removing legal barriers that prevent customs and revenue officers from sharing information with other law enforcement agencies.
- Introducing penalties for those who willingly choose to withhold information from the authorities that could help to prevent future terrorist attacks.
- Introducing penalties for crimes of corruption committed by U.K. citizens and companies abroad and foreign nationals in the country that undermine good governance.
- Preventing terrorists from abusing immigration and asylum procedures.
- Allowing extended detention for suspected international terrorists who threaten national security and for whom there is no immediate prospect of removal. These provisions will lapse after five years unless renewed by primary legislation.
- Enabling retention of certain fingerprints taken in immigration and asylum cases for ten years to help prevent people from reapplying for asylum so as to create multiple identities that could be used for criminal ends.
- Allowing immediate and unilateral U.K. action to freeze the assets of overseas individuals or groups that carry out or support terrorist acts.
- Granting the power to freeze assets at the start of an investigation, reducing the risk that funds will be used or moved.
- Strengthening current legislation related to chemical, nuclear, and biological weapons and ensuring the protection and security of aviation and civil nuclear sites.
- Improving the enforcement of aviation security, including new powers enabling the removal and arrest of people in restricted areas, the detention of aircraft for security reasons, and making it an offense to falsely claim to be an approved air cargo agent.
- Allowing officers to stop, detain, question, and search people traveling or believed to be traveling by aircraft within Great Britain and within Northern Ireland.
- Making it an offense to aid or abet the overseas use or development of chemical, nuclear, biological, or radiological weapons.

- Ensuring that laboratories holding stocks of potentially dangerous disease pathogens adhere to the highest standards of security.

In order to help allay concerns over possible restrictions on civil liberties, the act creates a review committee of privy councillors who will report to Parliament within two years on its operation. If the committee highlights an issue of concern, it will be fully debated in Parliament. The government attempted to include in the 2001 act a provision to make incitement of religious hatred a crime, but this failed to make its way through the parliamentary process as granted powers that many legislators thought could be unfairly exploited. The September 11 events were the impetus for moving U.K. legislation and policy in relation to terrorism further from purely domestic concerns, principally with terrorism related to Ulster, to a broader basis with an international dimension as well as directly linking the issue to organized crime. The much reduced public tolerance for terrorist acts, quite apart from perceptions of the justice of the cause they seek to promote, is likely to push the peace process in Northern Ireland nearer its goal.

Part III

Middle East

ISRAEL

Shlomo Gazit

THIS ESSAY ATTEMPTS TO survey the Israeli experience in countering and coping with terrorism. The challenge Israel faces vis-à-vis Arab-Palestinian terrorism is not a new one. It dates back some eighty years to the time when Jews began settling in Israel in the early part of the last century, three decades before the establishment of the state in 1948. We will deal here with the conclusions and lessons that Israel has drawn in more than three decades—the period following the Six Day War of June 1967 between Israel and the rest of the Arab world. At the end of the war, Israel found itself controlling the entire territory of the former British Mandate period (1922–48) in Palestine and administering military rule over a large Arab-Palestinian population.

NATURE OF THE TERRORIST THREAT AGAINST ISRAEL

The source of the main (and almost only) terrorist threat against Israel is Palestinian elements (which are occasionally joined by other

Arab and radical Islamic elements, primarily Iranians) that refuse to recognize and come to terms with the existence of an independent Jewish political entity in the heart of "their" Middle East. This terrorism operates against Israeli targets with a clear, dual purpose: on the one hand, the desire to harm, hurt, and wear down Israel as much as possible; and, on the other hand, the desire to achieve a strategic Palestinian objective—the advancement of an escalation process intended to bring about an open and direct all-Arab war that will defeat Israel militarily and enable the establishment of a Palestinian state in place of the Jewish entity. This is political terrorism. Under existing conditions, even if the losses in Israeli lives and property are relatively limited, Israel regards this terrorism as a dangerous strategic threat, particularly because of the painful psychological ramifications that impact on the Israeli public.

This Arab terrorist activity is focused on Israel in the area of the pre-1967 borders; in the territories Israel occupied during the war of June 1967; against Israeli targets outside of Israel such as political and economic missions; upon the various forms of civil transportation to and from Israel; upon Israeli citizens abroad; against Jewish targets in various locales around the world; and, in exceptional cases, even against third-party targets such as international aviation, embassies, and political figures (as in the assassination of Robert Kennedy).

The great advantage of Palestinian terrorist activity is the extensive support it enjoys from Arab and Muslim countries either bordering or near Israel. This support finds expression in the physical refuge given to terrorists, both before and after their attacks, and in the freedom furnished to terrorists to organize themselves, draft operatives, and train for their missions. It extends to supplying arms and materials, financing, diplomatic immunity, and documentation, enabling terrorists to transfer arms and supplies from country to country without fear.

THE CHALLENGE OF PALESTINIAN TERRORISM

Israel is coping, almost simultaneously, with three different sources of Arab-Palestinian terrorism: private individuals, organizations, and militias.

The first type is the most primitive and least dangerous from the standpoint of its military and political ramifications: individual acts of terrorism. It involves an individual Arab-Palestinian setting out on his or her own initiative and attacking the first Israeli(s) to come along.

Typically, the first characteristic of this type of terrorist is that the individual neither operates for nor is controlled by any organized terrorism movement. He or she simply acts on the basis of feelings of hatred and/or retribution against Israel. The second characteristic is the type of weapon used, "cold" ones that can easily be obtained: knives, hatchets, iron pipes, and sometimes simply a can of gasoline and box of matches for setting fire to Israeli forests and fields. The only weapons that resemble "hot" arms (e.g., guns, bombs, and hand grenades) are Molotov cocktails, which are easily prepared at home in the most primitive manner. The third characteristic is the absence of the ability to obtain advance intelligence about such actions. And the fourth and last characteristic is the willingness of the terrorist to refuse to plan a getaway. In most cases, if the individual terrorist is not killed on the spot Israeli citizens in the vicinity will catch him or her.

Organizations

The second type of terrorism against Israel consists of acts of organized terrorism. This type of action most often involves several people backed by an existing operations system. Typically, organized Arab-Palestinian terrorism is hardly ever planned and carried out in the manner of a military operation, which is characterized by the following.

- Defining the objective of the attack
- Establishing the date and time for executing it
- Planning the action and obtaining approval from a superior and central command
- Aggregating special weapons and employing them for the training of the operations team in advance of the action
- Planning media coverage of the action

Another characteristic of organized terrorism is the potential for Israeli intelligence to penetrate these organizations, leading to possible forewarning about impending planned operations. Nonetheless, advance intelligence is rarely so detailed or precise as to enable Israelis to foil the planned actions. Organized terrorist actions include shooting at civilians and/or Israeli forces, planting mines and bombs, attacking vehicles in Israeli territory, and penetrating Israeli population centers with booby-trapped cars.

In recent years, organized Palestinian terrorism has been almost exclusively initiated by organizations identifying with the extremist Islamic fundamentalist movement (primarily Hamas and the Palestinian Islamic Jihad). These organizations have introduced a new form of organized terrorist attacks, including suicide bombers on passenger-filled buses or in any other place filled with Israeli civilians.

Such attacks are particularly troubling for two reasons: The first derives from the fact that it is almost impossible to deter the fanatical suicide bomber from carrying out his or her mission. The second is the inadequacy of our security inspection systems for pinpointing such a bomber before that individual reaches a target. Between April 1993 and January 2000, about forty fanatical suicide bombers carried out thirty-six such attacks. The 147 Israelis killed by them accounted for more than half of all Israeli terrorism victims during this period.

A fairly large and complex organization stands behind and supports even a single suicide bomber, and it follows the operation every step of the way. This organization commences its actions by first seeking out young men who are open to being influenced into undertaking a suicide mission. Once such an individual agrees, there is a need to escort the suicide bomber through the complex process of preparing him and his mission. First comes the intensive psychological, ideological, and religious preparation and brainwashing. Then it must provide the explosives and move them to a hiding place near the target, where they will be fitted into a "living bomb." After these measures have been taken, the bomber is brought to the targeted vicinity and videotaped by his commanders prior to embarking upon his mission. Last, but not least, media coverage of the terrorist act is planned, including the broadcast and distribution of the tape, which shows the extreme devotion of the suicide bomber and gives credit to the organization.

Such terrorist actions are also executed outside the borders of Israel. These include attacks against air transportation to Israel, official and commercial Israeli representations around the world, Israelis traveling abroad, and even Jewish institutions. The most extreme example of such an attack was the killing of eleven Israeli athletes at the Munich Olympics in September 1972.

Militias

The third form of terrorism involves armed and organized militias located across Israel's borders. Since no country with a strong central government willingly permits the existence, let alone the activities, of hostile armed militias within its borders, the only such threat currently is from Lebanese territory. From the 1970s through the early 1980s, these militias in Lebanon consisted of Palestinians who were equipped with heavy ordnance, including artillery and Katyusha rockets. Their activities across the border led to serious military confrontations, the height of which was the Lebanon War of 1982 in which Israel invaded and occupied southern Lebanon and forced the Palestinian forces to leave the country. Over the past decade, almost all Lebanese militias have been comprised of Shi'ite Muslim Hizbullah forces.

Such militias and other terrorist organizations have the following features in common.

The objectives of their actions involve a total lack of distinction between harming military/defense forces and innocent civilians.

Even when living and operating in a friendly country, the vast majority of these militias do not maintain a standard military framework of units, camps, installations, uniforms, and the like. Quite the contrary, they choose to mingle with the civilian population because of the concealment this provides and the refuge they can find among civilians.

Almost without exception, these organizations operate simultaneously in a military fashion and a framework that allows them to initiate regular terrorist actions. The "expertise" of Hizbullah in this context is to penetrate Israel for terrorist actions using individuals who appear to be innocent tourists and to attack Jewish institutions around the world.

Unlike the Palestinian militias, whose goal is to establish a Palestinian state, the common denominator among members of Hizbullah is religious extremism. This feature is what makes it particularly difficult for Israeli intelligence operatives to penetrate the Hizbullah.

The key weakness of these terrorist units derives from their dependence on the goodwill of the host country that permits their operations. The moment the government changes its policy, the militia loses its right to exist, leaving it with the difficult choice of either embarking on a life and death military confrontation with the state's authorities (and, in the case of Lebanon, also with Syrian military forces) or accepting the verdict and ceasing its terrorist activities or even closing down its organization. Indeed, the Israeli withdrawal from its security zone in South Lebanon (May 2000) has forced Lebanon, Hizbullah, and Syria to reassess their strategy of attacking Israeli military targets there as well as along the border.

PRINCIPLES OF ISRAELI STRATEGY

Comparisons between the terrorist threats extant in Israel and those in any other country are often deceptive. It is important to understand and remember that terrorism in all other countries is usually directed only against the governing authority. Such terrorism does not aspire to destroy both the state and its people. This is not the case in Israel, where the objective of terrorism is the physical eradication of the Jewish state, country, and people. At the same time, in many respects, Israel cannot make a distinction between the comprehensive struggle for its right to exist in the Middle East—a struggle conducted with the neighboring Arab states that surround it—and the struggle against terrorism.

Palestinian terrorism derives from the specific conditions in which the Palestinians and Israelis find themselves, and the proper response to it is to be sought in the immediate environs. As long as the Israeli-Arab conflict continues, and as long as this conflict is sufficiently severe, there will be terrorist actions. Without ignoring the importance of the external support from Arab states that Palestinian terrorism enjoys, that support has no influence on the basic fact of the continuation of the terrorist phenomenon. Support for terrorist actions by the Arab states or any other third party simply contributes to the intensity of these actions and, to some degree, to the capacity for terrorists to achieve their objectives.

There is no doubt that a political solution between Israel and the Arab elements with which it is in conflict is inescapable. Such a political agreement, once achieved and implemented, will also lead to the gradual decline and ultimate disappearance of such terrorism.

At the same time, this fundamental assumption about the relationship between a political agreement and the reduction or disappearance of terrorism should not be taken to mean that Israel has in any way surrendered to the inevitability of peace or is passive about potential terrorist threats. On the contrary: Israel maintains that it will not be possible to reach a political agreement unless the leadership of the Arab terrorist organizations comes to recognize and acknowledge that Israel cannot be defeated and the organizations cannot achieve their goals without negotiations and the appropriate political compromises.

The unequivocal conclusion is that Israel must intensify its struggle against terror, using every means at its disposal. Only such a consistent, energetic, and uncompromising struggle will accomplish this objective. In the framework of this effort, Israel aspires to achieve three goals.

1. Maintain its position of strength. Precisely because Israel has revealed that its ultimate objective is a political solution, under no circumstances must it allow itself to be dragged to the negotiating table and a peace agreement in a state of defeat, failure, weakness, or battle fatigue.
2. Maintain pressure vis-à-vis the terrorist organizations and limit the freedom of action of terrorists and their potential for success. In fact, Israel aspires to maneuver the Palestinian terrorist organizations into a position of defensiveness and in so doing extinguish any hope that they might achieve a resounding victory.
3. Not only come to the negotiating table from a position of strength but cause the terrorist organizations to do so in a weakened state. It must be borne in mind that sooner or later military confrontation will be replaced with negotiations and yesterday's enemy will become

tomorrow's neighbor and perhaps even a future ally. Thus, it is extremely important to avoid taking steps that might serve as future obstacles to the ultimate process of making peace.

Israel's strategy is aimed at depriving Palestinian terrorists of the natural solidarity and support of the local population for the Palestinian struggle against Israel. The Arab-Palestinian population is a "sea" on which the terrorist depends for both shelter and survival, just like a fish depends on water. Israeli policy has tried to walk a tightrope in this area, balancing between fighting the terrorists and not wishing to stir up the population or create a natural incubator from which new terrorists can be drafted. Similarly, Israel has sought to discourage the Palestinian population from identifying with its own "freedom fighters" in any field.

Moshe Dayan, the Israeli minister of defense from 1967 to 1974, was responsible for formulating and implementing Israeli policy in the occupied territories during the seven years following the Six Day War. Based on his assumption that no people wants to live under the regime of a conquering army, Dayan took care to shape a policy geared toward easing and limiting, insofar as possible, the unavoidable implications of foreign rule. This policy prevailed for the seven years that Dayan served as minister, and a certain momentum carried it through the next five years, albeit with less attentiveness to its letter and spirit.

Starting in the late 1970s, after the Likud Party rose to power in Israel, this policy was turned almost upside down. Dayan's policy of minimizing the visibility of the Israeli presence was replaced with a policy of high exposure in all conceivable areas of public life. The attention paid to fair treatment and demonstrating respect for the residents of the territories disappeared. Worse than that, the opposite behavior quickly became prevalent, with demonstrations of domination, patronization, and humiliation for their own sake. What's more, in the course of time all of the characteristics that typify military occupation came to be evidenced by the Israeli army, including acts of corruption.

Added to this mix, of course, was the new Israeli settlement policy in Judaea and Samaria (the West Bank) and the Gaza Strip. This policy necessitated expropriating uncultivated Arab-owned land. Irrespective of whether this land was privately or state owned, it was

the only reserve of land remaining to the Palestinian residents for future expansion and development.[1] The *settlement* process (*hityashvut,* a special word in Hebrew pertaining to settling in the biblical land of Israel, as promised according to the Old Testament by God to Abraham) had forced Israel to take control of local water sources, to pave wide roads, and to establish communities that stood out in the landscape for miles around, amplifying the resentment of the indigenous population.

In December 1987, the spontaneous popular uprising of the Arab population, which came to be known as the *intifada,* erupted. This was an explosion that occurred without warning. Although the handwriting on the wall had been clear for many years and many had warned that the situation on the ground was on the verge of eruption, there was no major figure within the Israeli political system to stand up and say that the extant policy was flawed. No one dared suggest the "preventive medicine" of drastically and meaningfully altering it.

ISRAELI INTELLIGENCE ORGANIZATIONS

The primary responsibility for the war against terrorism is placed on one of the three branches of Israeli intelligence: the General Security Service (GSS, also known by it's Hebrew acronym, SHABAK); the Israeli Defense Forces Intelligence Branch; and the Mossad, the Israeli intelligence agency.[2] The GSS came to have primary responsibility for fighting terrorism via a gradual process, which started immediately following the Six Day War. The GSS was assigned the task of establishing a HUMINT (human intelligence) network of agents in the West Bank and Gaza covering both the political mood of Palestinians and possible efforts aimed at organizing terrorist actions. When the commands of the terrorist organizations moved across the borders into various Arab countries, the GSS began operating outside of Israel as well in its effort to recruit operatives. At a later stage, when Israel began developing a widespread defense network (primarily in connection with air transport security) both within its borders and around the world, the mission was assigned to the GSS, whose professional staff was responsible for implementation and supervision. The other two intelligence agencies also continued to deal with terrorism, each in its respective areas of responsibility.

Subsequent to the murder of the Israeli athletes at the Munich Olympics in 1972, a new position was created: the prime minister's adviser on terrorism. This adviser has no operational responsibility (and does not supplant the authority of the three intelligence organizations); rather, the adviser's primary role is to recommend policy and coordinate the activities of the various elements that have operative responsibility for dealing with terrorism.

ARAB HOST COUNTRY RESPONSIBILITY FOR THE WAR AGAINST TERRORISM

Immediately after the first Palestinian attempts to organize for terrorism were quashed in the occupied territories, the terrorists moved their headquarters and bases across the border—mostly into Jordan and its East Bank. Israeli policy on this point has been uniform: it is inconceivable that an adjacent Arab country should permit terrorists to operate freely within and across its borders against Israel and expect to enjoy "immunity" from Israeli responses. If terrorists are permitted to cross such a border into Israeli territory, then Israeli forces will do the same in the opposite direction.

This policy eventually, if not immediately, bore fruit. It took Jordan three years to understand the grim options it faced: either take action to rein in and put an end to the activities of Palestinian organizations within its territory or risk losing both control and sovereignty. When a confrontation between Jordan and the Palestinian organizations finally took place during "Black September" in 1970, the terrorists were both repressed and expelled.[3]

Syria was the next in line, since it permited the activities of almost all of the Palestinian organizations within its territory, including offices and training facilities. The strong and centralized government in Damascus was quick, however, to establish that these terrorist organizations were not to operate directly against Israel from within Syrian borders or the Golan Heights and that any action undertaken was to be fully coordinated with and supervised by Damascus.

The transfer of the Palestinian headquarters from Jordan to

Beirut in 1971 created a new problem. The Lebanese government was in tatters because of conflicts derived from the delicate balance between the country's various ethnic communities. It was incapable of taking vigorous action against the Palestinian organizations in Beirut, which launched operations against Israel in every possible manner. With the outbreak of civil war in Lebanon in 1975, the authorities had far more serious problems than restraining the Palestinians. Palestinian operations emanating from Lebanon led, however, to Israel's decision to enter Lebanese territory in 1982 in an effort to accomplish this mission itself.

By 1993, the PLO was clearly in a weakened state. Adding to its failures along the length of Israel's borders and the expulsion of its operatives to Tunis in 1982, the stand that the PLO had taken as the only supporter of the policies of Iraq's leader Saddam Hussein in Kuwait and during the Gulf War (1991) served to isolate it from the permanent support it had enjoyed from the other Arab states. This crisis deprived it of both political and financial support, and it even lost the freedom to use the territories of those countries for concealment or sanctuary, let alone for offices, training, or staging grounds for operations.

From Israel's standpoint, this was the ideal time to embark on negotiations with the organization, which was at the nadir of its weakness. The negotiations, which were conducted in parallel in Washington and Oslo in 1993, led to a Declaration of Principles (DOP) in Oslo, including an agreement that assigned administrative authority for the lives of the Palestinian population in the occupied territories to an elected Palestinian Authority (PA).

Thus were created the conditions that, to the greatest possible extent, eased the war against terrorism within Israel's borders and in the territories under its control. The PA not only became a partner in suppressing terror without being hated by its own people but it succeeded in persuading the majority of its people that terrorist activity does not serve their best interests—it only postpones the attainment of a final and comprehensive settlement with Israel. Indeed, during the seven years following the DOP we witnessed the dramatic results of the PA's intervention in the territories under its control. The number of Palestinian terrorist attacks within Israel and the Palestinian territories dropped from 3,143 in 1993 to 242 in 1999 (see table 1).

Further, since Oslo, the Islamic organizations have regulated their own activities on the basis of the prevailing political mood. As progress has been evidenced in the peace process and the local population shows relative satisfaction with it, the Islamic organizations have stopped—or at least limited—their terrorist activities. When either a crisis in relations occurs between Palestinians and Israelis or an atmosphere of economic distress appears in Palestinian areas, the organizations use the opportunity to renew attacks, knowing that they can count on popular support from their members.

THE ISRAELI MODUS OPERANDI

In its war against terrorism, Israel has defined four strategic objectives.

1. A comprehensive strategic concept presenting a multidimensional front for the ongoing battle rather than an ad hoc operation comprising only tactical and fragmented actions. Israel has not always been consistent in hewing to this objective, having been dragged more than once into responding to terrorist attacks that had been carried out more to influence Israeli public opinion than to challenge Israel's long-range ability to cope with terrorism.
2. Combining offensive and defensive operations and psychological and political elements. While the claim that there is no strictly military solution to the problem of terrorism is valid, it is important to note Israel's unequivocal policy, which claims that there is no strictly political solution. What's more, it is imperative to initiate operations, which will debilitate the terrorist organizations in every possible manner.

TABLE 1. Terrorist Attacks within Israel and the Palestinian Territories

	Hot Weapons[a]	Cold Weapons[b]	Total Attacks
1993	1,257	1,886	3,143
1994	505	1,693	2,198
1995	138	422	560
1996	95	216	311
1997	79	398	477
1998	73	355	428
1999	31	211	242

Source: Data provided by Israeli Ministry of Defense.
[a]Hot weapons include gunfire, explosives, and hand grenades.
[b]Cold weapons include Molotov cocktails, arson, and stabbing.

3. The most important weapons in this long war are patience, determination, and cunning and not necessarily firepower, military prowess, or operational and tactical daring. Within this strategic objective, Israel should also have included restraint and the ability to absorb blows. In this regard, there is a complex reciprocal relationship in Israel between the security leadership responsible for implementation and the political leadership responsible for decision making and approvals. More than once, the security leadership has pressured for immediate military reprisal, fearing that if it is not approved by the government while the memory of a given terrorist outrage is still tangible there will be no response at all. Of Israel's various leaders, one who is fondly remembered as being exceptional is Levi Eshkol, who served as prime minister during the 1960s. In response to proposals for a military response to a terrorist incident, he coined the phrase: "The ledger is open, and the hand is writing!" What a pity that Levi Eshkol was the only leader with this attitude.
4. Finally, cooperation among all the "players" is imperative in this complex war. First among these is, of course, cooperation among the defense forces, the political system, the general public, and—on a special level of importance—the mass media.[4]

DEFENSIVE VERSUS OFFENSIVE STRATEGY

It is highly doubtful whether there is any other form of warfare wherein Israel finds that the ratio between the energy invested in offense is so clearly favorable compared to the investment in defensive action. The more Israel invested in defense and security the more it served the terrorists' interests and objectives. This was typical in cases of terrorist acts launched from across the Jordanian, and later the Lebanese, borders. In some extreme cases, the terrorists were able to achieve their goals without doing a thing.[5] On the other hand, based on the clear assumption that the terrorists' resources are always quite limited, the more the Palestinian terrorists were pursued, finding themselves fleeing in search of hiding places and sanctuary, the more their operational capability was affected. This was due to the fact that they consequently found it difficult to recruit new members to their ranks, properly organize them, train their people, and find new resources.

The first pillar supporting Israel's war against Palestinian terrorism is intelligence. While it plays an important role in any form of warfare, it is in the war against terrorism that this role is unique and distinctive.

1. Intelligence in the service of the war against terrorism is very much like that needed by the police in their dealings with criminals. Intelligence has to be extremely specific (providing names, addresses, vehicles, routines, modus operandi, and so on). It has to be perfectly accurate, detailed, and up-to-date. Israel has learned time and again that the shelf life of any piece of information dealing with terrorist activities is extremely short lived.

2. We have learned that, in order to serve an operational purpose, intelligence has to be almost exclusively of a tactical nature. While it has always been of interest to learn about the political goals of the various Palestinian terrorist organizations, their ideological differences, and their ties to and cooperation with neighboring Arab countries, such information has served only very limited immediate operational needs, if any.

3. Israel's most important intelligence source has always been HUMINT. Because of strict compartmentalization among terrorists, and particularly because of the strict ideological and fanatic character of the Islamic extremist organizations, we have found it extremely difficult to penetrate each and every terrorist cell and recruit their members as our sources. What's more, the data gleaned from such sources have always been extremely limited in scope.

It is widely known that the life expectancy of any intelligence source is quite short. In the case of a HUMINT source, it is extremely short. In most instances, the source completes its life expectancy after it has provided its first piece of operational information.

4. A rich source of intelligence, based on the long and ongoing Israeli experience, is the apprehended terrorist. We have learned that it is extremely important to capture terrorists alive. We have had constant conflict between our intelligence agencies—which wanted the terrorist alive, considering him or her to be one of our best potential sources of information—and the Israel Defense Forces (IDF) commanders and troops or the police who, motivated by strong feelings of hatred and vengeance, only wish to see him or her dead.

Experience has taught us that such an interrogation should be conducted as soon as possible in order to deal with two urgent matters. The first is, of course, the compelling need to learn of a pending terrorist act that might be prevented through timely action. The second, and no less important, is the information that might be gleaned and assist in the arrest of members of the group before they have the time to disperse.

One cannot expect terrorists to volunteer crucial information. Our experience has shown, however, that they may be more cooperative under the following circumstances.

a. If they are interrogated immediately, while still in shock over having been apprehended (in some cases, perhaps also in pain from injuries sustained).
b. If they are interrogated before it becomes known that they have been taken alive. On the other hand, if they know they do not face a death sentence, they see no reason to "play the hero."
c. In some cases, mild physical pressure may be extremely effective, especially when there is an element of urgency, such as looking for a "ticking bomb."[6]

5. While we normally extract intelligence from live terrorists, those killed in action are no less important. Identifying the dead, their families, and their villages has, in many cases, led us to the arrest of other members of the same terrorist group.

Israeli intelligence failed in one important area: coping with the infrastructure that raises funds to finance the activities of the Palestinian terrorism organizations. We knew very well of the monies being transferred from around the world and being deposited in various accounts in the banking system. Although Israel knew this routine, however, it did not have the tools for legally accessing these accounts and monies, something that a democratic country such as Israel could not assail.

Another area in which Israel was somewhat lax was in its efforts against the Islamic extremist Palestinian Hamas movement. This organization exploited the permission given to it to establish and operate a legitimate system of educational, health, and welfare institutions (mosques, clinics, preschools, and the like) by turning them into an infrastructure for terrorist activity.

Pinpoint Defense

Pinpoint defense—the use of precise protective measures—is meant to provide a response to intelligence about a specific potential attack. Such information should give us all, or at least some, of the following elements about the expected attack: the location selected for the attack (the precise point or at least the general area), the staging point from which the terrorists will depart, their route to the target, the means of transportation between points, the type of ordnance, and the plan of action. Whenever we have had such specific information, the investment in taking defensive measures, in spite of the heavy burden involved, was always worthwhile in terms of the successful results it yielded.

Israel's greatest and most impressive achievement has been the thwarting of Palestinian terrorism against air traffic to and from Israel. Though large in scale, it falls under the rubric of pinpoint defense. The first terrorist incident of this nature took place in July 1968, when an El Al flight from Rome to Israel was hijacked. The plane was diverted to Algeria, where both the passengers and the airliner were held as hostages for sixteen Palestinian terrorist prisoners.

In the wake of this incident, the Israeli defense establishment quickly devised and deployed a comprehensive security system. This included placing experienced security agents on every El Al flight and instituting meticulous security checks of all passengers and their luggage at every terminal from which the airline departed. This vigilant system has foiled every hijacking attempt from the day it was implemented.

The other side of this coin is the heavy burden these measures place on the country's budget, the traveling public, and the security apparatus. Coldly weighing the financial burden against the horrible price of a passenger plane blown up in midair with all its passengers, the balance was objectively and justifiably tipped for the institution of these security precautions. Still, after more than thirty years of taking such precautions, and with terrorist attempts against Israel's air transport having entirely disappeared, it is appropriate to consider whether the time hasn't come to significantly reduce Israel's huge investment in such defense and prevention.[7]

In contrast to situations wherein specific intelligence has facilitated pinpoint defense, Israel has found itself more than once with information that was insufficient to inhibit attacks or take the necessary protective measures. In such cases, it has had to take general and comprehensive precautionary steps.

Information of a general nature might be about the intention to kidnap a soldier or civilian as a hostage for bargaining, to conduct a suicide bombing mission on a passenger bus, or to plant a bomb where there are throngs of people. Such warnings have been very general for the most part, with no information about when the attempts might take place except something to the effect of "around the holiday period." Similarly, they generally are not specific about the location. In the best case, we have to be satisfied with knowing that the targeted area might be in "the center of the country" or "the Sharon area."

In such cases, Israel has taken four types of steps.

1. The intelligence and security services of the Palestinian Authority are alerted immediately in the hope that it will act in every possible way to inhibit or short-circuit the potential attack. Indeed, for better than five years we have been seeing close coordination between the two sides on the operations level. Both have been working together to prevent heavy and painful incidents that might undermine relations between Israel and the PA and the prospects for advancing the peace process (table 1).
2. A proactive step is taken, in almost all cases of a generalized warning of this nature, in imposing either a general closure or a limited one controlling movements to a specific area (if the information available enables and justifies this step). Such a closure prevents free entry of Palestinians from the administered territories into Israeli territory.[8] In parallel, large military and police forces are immediately deployed to establish roadblocks for monitoring vehicular traffic from the territories into Israel. If slightly more detailed information is available, defense forces are deployed at bus stations and even on the buses themselves, at soldiers' transportation stations, or at the entrances to busy shopping centers.
3. Most important, the general public is asked to be particularly alert and contact the police immediately about any instance that raises suspicion. The special system that has been established in Israel for such circumstances has earned the highest level of appreciation

from the public. This appreciation is in dramatic contrast to the severe criticism the public otherwise levels at the ways in which the police deal with "regular" civilian crimes.

4. Inspections are conducted at the entrances to public buildings. In contrast to the effective precautions detailed previously, note should be taken of a procedure whose benefits are highly dubious. After a terrorist attempt at a Jerusalem movie theater thirty-two years ago, Israel established a huge system of "security wardens" at the entrance to every place of entertainment in Israel. Then, following an attack at a Jerusalem grocery store, another layer of inspectors was posted at the entrances of all the malls and shopping centers in the country.

Thus, for more than thirty years we have had what has become a multibranched system operating with a "small army" of perhaps forty thousand men and women employed daily in this security activity. Throughout these years, there hasn't been a single case in which this army has succeeded in preventing a terrorist act. During this time, however, no one has so much as raised a question as to their effectiveness and the continued need for them at a level established decades ago and at a time when there was a critical threat that demanded an immediate response to a new challenge. Today, looking at the situation soberly and knowing, as we do, how these security checks are conducted in practice, there is great doubt as to whether they might be effective in exposing even the most primitive attempt at a terrorist attack.[9]

What is most worrisome about this deployment of guards or wardens—which now encompasses even preschools and all other schools, colleges, and universities—is the absence of a mechanism for regularly examining and assessing the existing security systems and procedures and taking decisions to modify them in any way (whether reducing, expanding, or eliminating them). The basic responsibility for such assessments rests with the prime minister's adviser on antiterrorism. Under the present circumstances, it would be more appropriate to assign the responsibility to those on the decision-making, rather than advisory, level.

The weakness of Israel's political system is to blame for this. There is no single person responsible for the establishment of security systems nor for their ongoing functioning. This array of security systems developed over the course of years, not by virtue of a one-time decision but as the result of a series of "small decisions" based on situational exigencies. What's more, their applied operations and even their budgets are scattered among different government offices. The Ministry of Transport is responsible for operating security systems at airports, train stations, and on airplanes; the Ministry of Education for security at educational institutions and places of entertainment; the Ministry of Health for security at the entrances to medical centers; the Ministry of Industry and Trade for selecting which large businesses will be guarded; and so on, and so forth. And each and every one of them annually fights the Ministry of the Treasury for its appropriate share of the national budget.

Almost without exception, all of these security measures, together with the huge army of "security wardens," were initiated in response to a painful terrorist act. Their purpose had been twofold: first and foremost, to minimize the threat of a similar terrorist act in the future; and, second, to convince the Israeli public that the "authorities" have reacted properly with the introduction of effective security measures.

While these measures have no doubt served as a deterrent to the potential terrorist (save, of course, the "suicide bomber"), the real cost effectiveness has been very limited. With the exception of high-security installations, where there are both the conditions and the time to perform a comprehensive check (including with metal detectors), in all other places the inspections have been far from satisfying. There is a need to allow masses of people to enter the sites, and because the wardens are not trained or qualified for their task their inspections are very superficial. Furthermore, little flexibility has been shown in the operation of this "army" of wardens, which could increase deterrence by means of random checks.

PREVENTIVE AND OFFENSIVE ACTIVITY

I have indicated the great importance that Israel assigns to its offense strategy in countering Arab terrorism. These offensive actions are meant to put pressure on the terrorist organization to compartmentalize its activities, to hide and frequently change bases of operations, to constantly reequip itself with new weapons and equipment to replace those destroyed by Israeli actions, and—

perhaps most severe of all—to create an ongoing concern and suspicion of traitors and informers who might be cooperating with Israel's security services.

The key to these preventive and offensive activities depends, of course, on the availability of precise and updated intelligence. There is no practical difference between a standard offensive operation against terrorists and an attempt to intercept and foil a specific terrorist act based on advance intelligence. One should bear in mind that any offensive operation against terrorists is always also serving the preventive goal. In the past, and continuing through the present, Israel has had to carry out such actions in four different areas.

1. Activities in the areas exclusively under Israel's legal and military responsibility (i.e., in Israel proper and in the occupied territories wholly under the control of the Israeli military administration or where Israel has ultimate responsibility for security). As is to be expected, terrorist activity is compartmentalized, necessitating that Israel take the following steps.
   a. Preventive detentions, including the arrest and interrogation of suspicious individuals
   b. Seizing weapons, storage facilities, and laboratories for the production of explosives and weapons or counterfeiting documents
   c. Exercising extreme caution not to harm innocent Arab citizens in the vicinity of the target
   d. Taking the appropriate steps to protect the identities of the intelligence sources that facilitated the offensive action
2. Attacking and inhibiting terrorist activity in areas controlled by the Palestinian Authority. The dominant Israeli consideration, with regard to such actions, is political—that is, Israel's relations with the PA political leadership and those heading the Palestinian intelligence and security efforts.[10]
3. Cross-border attacks against terrorist targets in neighboring Arab countries. Again, in consideration of political sensitivity, Israel constrains itself from carrying out direct military operations in these neighboring countries since such open acts could lead to escalation and even outright war.[11]
4. In addition to vigorous and extensive diplomatic activities, whereby Israel tries to engage various elements to persuade the authorities in those Arab countries to prevent terrorist organizations from op-

erating freely, Israel occasionally initiates direct covert actions. Clearly, in carrying out such attacks care is taken not to leave "an Israeli calling card." And, even when all evidence suggests that Israel was behind an action of this sort, it will never make pronouncements or acknowledge its responsibility. Nonetheless, intentions are one thing and reality another.[12]

5. Attacks against individuals and terrorist infrastructures in neutral countries. In these cases as well, almost no one doubts the Israeli responsibility for such actions, but compartmentalization and secrecy make it difficult to unequivocally lay direct blame on Israel.[13]

Targeting Terrorist Leaders

Israeli offensive operations against terrorists have placed particular emphasis on creating the impression that nothing escapes the attention of Israeli intelligence and no terrorist can successfully hide or escape punishment. This is the essence of Israel's psychological warfare. We work hard to intimate that:

1. There have been numerous traitors among the Palestinian terrorists.
2. The loyalty and credibility of key terrorist figures is to be doubted, and these individuals are directly responsible for many failures.
3. Numerous terrorist groups have sought dialogue with Israel for the sake of negotiated agreement and compromise.

Israel has to cope with a serious question, however, as to the degree to which it is worth attempting to eliminate senior Arab terrorism leaders. The starting assumption for examining this issue is that Israel will not be able to conceal its involvement in and responsibility for any given operation. The implications of this fact demand that Israel examine and weigh the following questions before taking a decision for such action.

1. What the chances are for a "clean" operation, with little risk of complications during its execution?
2. What is the status of the leader or commander targeted for elimination? What are the assessments of the potential outcome in terms of the effect his absence would have on the operational capability of the organization he heads?

3. What is the intelligence assessment as to the nature, timing, and place of potential retaliatory attacks in the wake of a successful Israeli operation?
4. Finally, and not insignificantly, what might the effect be on Israeli public opinion?

The Israeli security services are almost exclusively responsible for making the first three of these determinations. Although the ultimate decision (and responsibility, of course) falls to the decision-making level of government—be it the prime minister alone or a ministerial committee appointed to grant such approvals—it does not have its own tools for assessing and judging these three elements, whether pro or con. Consequently, the functional decision is in the hands of the security system, for assessment of the chances of a "clean" operation is exclusively the domain of the service that would carry it out—the head of the Mossad, the head of the GSS, or the IDF chief of staff. All three, however, usually excuse themselves from weighing the political considerations involved in any given operation based on the claim (unquestionably justified from a formal standpoint) that it is not their business or responsibility to do so. Thus, in making their presentations they will knowingly tend to diminish the likelihood of the failure of an operation and what types of complications Israel and those carrying out the operation might encounter.[14]

Whenever a terrorism commander targeted for elimination belongs to a large organization, it is less likely that his elimination will meaningfully affect the operational capacity of that group. Moreover, there would be no effect whatsoever if the individual's functional status is political rather than operational. In such a case, there is a clear gap between the political-psychological repercussions of the liquidation and the functional benefits.[15]

Such is not the case with regard to the leader of a small and intimate terrorism organization. In such a case, the elimination of a senior operational figure can paralyze the organization's ability to function for a relatively long time and sometimes even cause it to disappear entirely. A successful example of such an experience was the killing in Malta in October 1995 of Fat'hi Shkaki, head of the Palestinian Islamic Jihad. In the more than five years that have passed since then, the organization has been unable to recover from the blow it suffered.

Both military and political Israeli decision makers prefer the "elimination" of top (political) leaders of Palestinian terrorist organizations. Their expectation is that once these well-known figures are killed in a spectacular operation it may serve Israel by deterring other terrorists as well as having a positive impact on Israeli public opinion.

On the other hand, there is hardly any chance of concealing Israel's responsibility and direct involvement in such acts. This often generates painful terrorist reprisals, and furthermore, as the operational benefit of the assassination is negligible, the terrorists have no difficulty in finding a replacement.

We have learned, however, that the elimination of terrorist leaders on the lower (operational) level is more effective in most cases. It is easier to hide Israel's involvement in the act; thus, there are good reasons not to expect terrorist vengeance and reprisals and the immediate operational results are better guaranteed.

It is up to the security services (the shared responsibility of the heads of the Mossad, GSS, and IDF intelligence branch) to present this dilemma to the appropriate leaders who have to take such decisions in advance of the decision-making process.[16] This consideration has to do with the third factor, which calls for examination of the likelihood of retaliation and the type of political reactions—especially the terrorist factor—that can be expected in the wake of an operation of this nature. Such an assessment does not, of course, have a foundation in solid facts, but the heads of Israel's security services can present the decision maker with realistic assessments of what can be expected. Israel has experienced painful attacks directed against Jewish institutions around the world. In these attacks, terrorist organizations chose the easiest targets for retaliation—targets that would cause distress to Israel while entailing almost no operational risks for the terrorists carrying out the attack.

An example of a particularly painful retaliation of a different nature was the attacks by Palestinian suicide bombers in February through March 1996. They dealt Israel an extremely hard blow, which forced the government to halt all scheduled steps according to the Oslo agreement, essentially tipping the political balance and ultimately causing the failure of the Labor Party in general and the personal failure of Shimon Peres in particular, several months later.

The fourth issue, as noted, is entirely within the realm of the judgment of the government. In this area, it is hard to imagine that a politician would willingly forgo the chance to garner a fairly easy prestigious achievement in an area that troubles the public as much as the war against terrorism. And the more complex the military operation the more it lends—whether directly or via reflected glory—a can-do, creative air to the leader who took the decision and authorized the operation, thereby handing him a political achievement. Only rarely will public opinion blame the resulting fallout or political repercussions on the decision maker who approved the operation.

Many—if not most—Israelis have found it difficult to reconcile the vast difference between the political, legal, and moral limitations placed on a country founded on the rule of law, with a society and state that see themselves as part of the civilized and developed world, and the almost total lack of restraint or limitations of a terrorist organization, which is unaccountable to anyone.

If one is to summarize the Israeli experience in this area, the greater portion of these actions—even when they were spectacular from an operations standpoint—have contributed only marginally to Israel's efforts against terrorism. The political fallout from operations that failed (such as the killing of Busheiki in Lillehammer and the attempt against Mashal in Amman) and the painful repercussions that ensued cast a heavy shadow on Israel's judgment in this area. And, as noted, these clearly were the products of the different considerations employed by the operations and security level versus the governmental level.

ISRAELI PUNITIVE MEASURES

In spite of the fact that Israeli law permits death sentences for terrorism, Israel took the conscious decision, from the first day of its military administration over the Arab-Palestinian populace in the territories occupied in the 1967 war, not to invoke this option. The fundamental assumption underlying this decision was that the harm that would result from carrying out death sentences would be greater than any benefits that would accrue to the struggle against terrorism. This policy had been adopted in spite of the fact that a large portion of the Israeli public continually calls for retaliatory punishment. This policy takes into account the following.

The terrorist who embarks on an attack (and all the more so in the case of a suicide attack) is not deterred by the threat of a death sentence.

Carrying out death sentences would trigger severe reactions in the international political sphere, severe and painful retaliations by the terrorists themselves, and upheaval in the domestic moral arena within Israel itself.[17]

The death sentence would deprive Israel of an important future negotiating tool in the give-and-take framework of expected agreements between Israel and the Palestinians.

An executed terrorist would be regarded as a *shahid*—an Islamic martyr whose reward is his or her place in paradise—encouraging other young Palestinians to do the same.

Finally, although we do not have direct proof of this supposition, it is likely that a terrorist who knows he faces a possible death sentence in any event will be more determined not to be taken alive. If captured and imprisoned, he or she would likely be inclined to take a rigid stance during interrogation and imprisonment, not revealing the intelligence that is so vital to us.

The assortment of punitive measures at the disposal of the Israeli authorities is rich and varied and based on the emergency security regulations established by the British Mandatory Government in 1945.

- Administrative detention of a suspect whom, for various reasons, cannot be put on trial by Israel.
- Imprisonment of terrorists per sentences imposed by an Israeli military tribunal. Such sentences are the most severe, with the majority being life terms (or even multiple life sentences).
- Demolition of homes or dwellings of terrorists either caught or killed during the course of a terrorist action. The main function of this punishment is to serve as a deterrent to other residents of the territories from offering any form of shelter or assistance to terrorists.
- Initially, Israel expelled key political figures, primarily those who were active on the national level or actively inciting on the local level for various acts of resistance. For a long period, such expulsions served as the most severe punishment and greatest

deterrence of all those in the repertoire of punishments that Israel could mete out.

- Such expulsions could be carried out only if they came as a surprise in order to preclude Jordanian and Lebanese authorities from blocking entry of the deportees into their territories. With the passage of time, the terrorist organizations began to turn immediately to Israel's High Court of Justice, which, without exception, would allow the potential deportee to present his or her case before a special appeals committee. In turn, this gave Jordan and Lebanon sufficient time to prevent the entry of such individuals to their territories. Later, after Israel signed a peace treaty with Jordan, only the Lebanese option remained.[18]

Following a severe terrorist action, Israel would initiate a number of security measures. Although the purpose of these measures was related to security—they were intended to facilitate the search for terrorists or to foil additional attacks—their by-product also proved to be a certain level of punishment from which the collective Palestinian public suffered. The steps usually taken included the following.

- A curfew is immediately imposed in the vicinity of the attack. This is for the sake of two security interests: to immediately calm emotions in the vicinity of the attack and to limit the escape routes of the perpetrator(s).
- A "closure" is usually imposed on the occupied territories in the wake of a severe attack within Israeli territory for the purpose of preventing the entry of residents of the Arab territories into Israel. The punishment imposed by a curfew or closure has proven itself, over the years, to be of very limited operational efficiency. The main purpose of this measure has been to mollify Israeli public opinion, which has had difficulty in coming to terms with the fact that neither the government nor the security services have any effective means of dealing with the terrorist threat.
- Various tactical security measures are frequently taken for the sake of hampering the ability of terrorists to initiate sundry actions and in order to consolidate Israeli control and command on the ground.

TERRORISM AND THE MEDIA

The ways in which the modern communications media operate; the presence of journalists, cameras, and television crews in almost every potential hot spot; and their ability to report from the scene in real time, using both words and pictures, have made the media the natural allies of the Arab terrorist organizations operating against Israel.

The Palestinians quickly learned how to exploit the media for their purposes, as follows.

1. Immediate reporting from the site of a terrorist attack brings the horrors of the act into the living rooms of every home and family in Israel.
2. The international media broadcast and distribute pictures from the site of the incident, thus supplying a platform, resonance, and free propaganda to the terrorist cause against Israel.
3. The media also convey a picture of the heavy hand Israel's defense forces employ. These pictures have a negative impact on Israel's political efforts in the neutral and international arena.
4. Finally, the Palestinian media assist in building the myth of the courage of the Palestinian "freedom fighters," the Islamic martyrs who sacrifice their lives for the Palestinian homeland.

At the same time, the media also have a negative role that harms the terrorist organizations and their activities. Foremost among these is the fact that the extensive coverage engenders greater public discussion of the threat and pushes the authorities to accelerate the search for solutions. Perhaps most important of all, media coverage arouses international public opinion against terrorism and this impels governments to take direct action against terrorism and to cooperate with other governments in their war against it.

The negative reactions among the world media to certain types of attacks have had the effect of causing the Palestinian terrorist organizations to stop conducting them. Notable among these is the cessation of airplane hijackings and attacks against Israeli passengers at air terminals around the world. Nor is it by chance that no attempts have been made to take over cruise ships and hold their passengers hostage since the time Palestinian terrorists overran the *Achille Lauro* in October 1985.

On balance, Israel's achievements in this area are far from ideal. The following are three recommendations made by a top Israeli journalist with rich experience in issues relating to security.

1. First, the media must exercise self-restraint in their reporting. Stop the endless recycling of pictures of the horror and attendant headlines, cease the hysterical style of writing and reporting so as to avoid exacerbating the trauma, and avoid the creation of myths with regard to Palestinian heroism.
2. Politicians must not exploit the terrorist attacks to advance their political and personal interests.
3. An objective and focused discussion should be initiated—perhaps together with academic and legal authorities—about the concepts of "freedom of expression" and "the public's right to know" in dealing with terrorism and terrorist attacks.[19]

More than four years have passed since these suggestions were made. To date, nothing has been done in Israel to advance any of these recommendations. On the contrary, Israel finds itself mired in the incremental and methodical process of growing irresponsibility that prevails in this area. One of the reasons for this is the absolute lassitude of Israel's military censorship, which has progressively lost its teeth over the years.

SUMMING UP THE ISRAELI EXPERIENCE

Palestinian terrorism does not comprise a threat to Israel's existence. Moreover, the strategic goals vis-à-vis Israel that the Palestinian-Arab entities have established as a national objective negate in advance any likelihood that Israel will ever surrender to terrorist pressure. Such a capitulation, in Israel's case, would be tantamount to agreeing that the country and nation should cease to exist. Nonetheless, Israel made a mistake when it assumed that it could address terrorism strictly as a tactical problem. It has been shown, and continues to be evidenced, that it also has strategic ramifications.

The summary of Israel's war against Arab terrorism since the Six Day War, when Israel occupied the territories densely populated with Arab-Palestinians hostile to both it and its rule, is quite encouraging. Notwithstanding Israel's tremendous efforts and investments, the achievements in four particular areas are worthy of special note.

Israel's economy has developed and flourished, and terrorism has had no affect on it.[20]

Israel's population not only grew but doubled during this period, thanks to the massive immigration of Jews who were not deterred by terrorism.

The success of Israel's struggle against the terrorist organizations (along with other developments in the international and regional spheres) is what motivated the main Palestinian terrorist organizations—the PLO and Fatah—to first abandon terrorist activities in the international arena and then—for seven years, now—to abandon it entirely.

The greatest failure of the Palestinians has been their inability to stop Israel's settlement efforts in the Palestinian territories.

These successes were achieved despite the fact that Israel refrained from instituting repressive measures or draconian punishments, which might have discouraged the vast majority of the Palestinian populace from supporting terrorism. Internal Israeli moral and political-international considerations prevented this. These successes also accrued in spite of the failure (which could have been foreseen) of the policy of the Israeli military administration, which was not sufficiently positive and attractive to obtain the genuine cooperation of the Palestinian residents.

The Israeli experience in its war against terrorism has unique characteristics that prevent most other countries from copying and applying it. At the same time, in the post–World War II period of modern political and military history, it is doubtful whether any other country has acquired such rich experience and myriad lessons—both good and bad—in this grim and difficult war. In this regard, the Israeli experience serves as an important primer for every country and society that is called upon to fight the threat of terrorism.

POSTSCRIPT

THIS ESSAY, WHICH DESCRIBES Israel's experience in its war against terrorism, was written about a year and a half before the outbreak of the Palestinian uprising known as the Al-Aqsa Intifada. The problems Israel faces today are radically different from the threat that confronted it prior to that date. The new terrorist reality more closely resembles a war between two states and two peoples, a war in which political and moral considerations restrict Israel's military freedom of action.

The threat of Palestinian terrorism has changed in almost every way. It is no longer carried out by individual terrorists forced to operate in isolation and hiding. Today Israel faces tens of thousands of Palestinian fighters: police and soldiers whose salaries are paid by the Palestinian Authority as well as militias linked politically to the authority or radical Islamic groups. They use firearms without constraint: various kinds of light weaponry, light mortars and rockets, and large amounts of explosives.

The characteristics of this new terrorism, in addition to those previously familiar, are:

Frequent gunfire attacks and explosives aimed at Israeli civilian vehicles

Unbridled gunfire attacks in dense Israeli population centers

Terrorist incursions into Israeli army bases and civilian settlements to carry out indiscriminate killings

Lately, specific attempts to kill high-ranking Israeli politicians and security officials[21]

The goal of Palestinian terrorism has remained the same. Only its scope, its intensity, the nature of its operations, and the number of casualties have changed. For internal political reasons, Israel has failed to reassess its position in the face of this new security challenge and maintains a completely inflexible approach: absolute refusal to withdraw from isolated settlements or military facilities, which could significantly ease the burden of defense.

The increased scope of terrorist operations has obliged Israel to develop, and especially to expand, its modes of warfare. As a chief priority, bowing to Israeli public opinion, civilian security efforts have been greatly expanded. This includes the following steps.

Forming a large-scale defensive security system, manned by military personnel, in all small, isolated settlements in the occupied territories, including both defense of transportation routes in these areas and on the spot defense of Israeli vehicles at all times.

Constructing a system of defensive fences, both normal and electronic, and other fortifications around settlements at risk.

Shielding civilian vehicles on these routes to withstand gunfire.

Distributing personal protection equipment (such as bulletproof vests) to soldiers and civilians at risk.

Deploying large numbers of security guards in public areas inside Israel (bus stations, markets, malls, entertainment venues, and so on). This security force is financed partly by the Ministry of Defense and partly by other relevant government offices and private employers.

Since most terrorist activity originates in areas controlled by the Palestinian Authority, Israel attaches great importance to steps aimed at protecting its territory from infiltration. To prevent uncontrolled entry, Israel has imposed a total closure between its area and Palestinian territories. This closure has been extremely damaging to the local Palestinian population (barring them from working in Israel, severely harming trade, and creating an acute sense of siege in the territories). In the offensive field, Israel has adopted a policy of incursion into PA areas. The claim, which Israel repeats whenever the Israel Defense Force penetrates PA territory to carry out arrests and other punitive actions, is that "since the Palestinian Authority fails to prevent terrorists from operating against Israel, we are left with no choice but to take this task upon ourselves."

Israel has provided the Palestinians with lists of operatives involved in instigating, organizing, and carrying out terrorist activities. Because the PA does not hinder or detain these wanted terrorists, Israel undertakes focused operations with the aim of arresting or killing key operatives. This depends on the possession of reliable, precise, and up-to-date intelligence, which enables Israel to carry out helicopter attacks against houses and vehicles belonging to such persons or to rig their vehicles with explosives.

In the first months of the *intifada*, Israel carried out punitive actions from the air against Palestinian government and military facilities. In order to avoid Palestinian civilian casualties, either the targets chosen were isolated, unoccupied facilities or the attacks took place at times when such casualties would not ensue. It was soon realized that these operations were futile and very damaging to public relations, and they ceased.

Indeed, another aspect of this new type of conflict is dealing with the media and public relations. Beyond the desire to cause Israel maximum damage and casualties, the Palestinian leadership has two goals. One is to undermine the morale of the Israeli people so that they will tire of the constant war of attrition and pressure their leaders to adopt a more flexible position vis-à-vis the Palestinians. The other goal is to enlist the support of world opinion and neutral governments in the hope that they will compel Israel to accept an international peacekeeping force or observers to "protect Palestinians" or adopt other anti-Israeli decisions.

In terms of the country's goals vis-à-vis the Palestinians, Israel hopes that severe economic pressure and the large number of casualties will break the Palestinian fighting spirit and cause the leadership to effect a cease-fire and return to the negotiation table. Israel is conducting a considerably successful global public relations campaign to prevent massive international support for the Palestinian position.

The terrorist attacks by Islamic extremists in New York and Washington last September had a political effect on the Israeli struggle against Arab terrorism. The United States, wishing to assemble a coalition that would include most of the world's Muslim and Arab states, lacked the freedom of action to classify groups acting against Israel as "terrorist organizations" and states supporting such groups as "states that support terrorism"—designations that can, and should, be used to cast those states out of the international community.

The chairman of the PA, Yasser Arafat, has learned the lesson of his mistake in 1991, when he supported Iraqi president Saddam Hussein in the Gulf War. This time he immediately declared his support for the United States, though making very clear the damage he could cause to the coalition by stirring crowds in Arab capitals into demonstrating in favor of Osama bin Laden. Similar considerations prevented the United States from condemning Iran, Syria, and Lebanon as states that support terrorism (despite their backing of fanatical Islamic groups such as Hamas, Hizbullah, and the Islamic Jihad).

At the time of writing, we do not yet know the outcome of the campaign in Afghanistan against bin Laden. We do not know where and to what end the coalition will next direct its antiterrorist ef-

forts. In any case, as long as Iran, Syria, Lebanon, and the PA are not declared to be states that support terrorism, and as long as Israel is asked to refrain from excessive actions that would force Arafat into making good his threat to break up the coalition, one can expect no significant change in the Israeli struggle against terrorism.

TURKEY

Gunduz S. Aktan and Ali M. Koknar

JUST AS IT DID in the violence-ridden twentieth century, Turkey bears the dubious distinction of having to fight perhaps the most varied medley of outlaws bent on destroying its way of life in the new millennium. These terrorists target not only the Turkish state but ordinary Turkish citizens. Even teachers, Muslim clergymen, technicians, and local administrators (village headmen) have been targeted, as they were perceived by the terrorists to be agents of the government.[1]

In this environment, there are remnants of Cold War era terrorism as well as adherents of more contemporary political movements at work. The latter groups pursue a variety of causes, each claiming to be representative of various grievances, including the repression of an ethnic minority, of a social class, of the entire nation by the "oligarchy," of the entire nation by the secular establishment, of an ethnic minority by another terrorist group, of Muslims by the "global Zionist conspiracy," and so on and so forth. While fragmented in purpose, these terrorists have caused substantial damage to Turkey: thirty-five thousand Turkish citizens lost their lives between 1984 and 2000 as a result of terrorism.[2]

BACKGROUND

The first wave of modern political terrorism hit Turkey in the late 1960s with Marxist students taking up arms to fight the regime. A spate of kidnappings, robberies, and murders went on for three years and subsided in 1971 after the military cracked down on the terrorists. Most of the terrorist leaders were either killed, arrested, or left the country for Europe or other parts of the Middle East.

The second wave of terrorism began in 1974, when most of the terrorist leaders convicted after the 1971 crackdown were released from prison due to a politically motivated amnesty granted by the government of the day. These terrorists soon went back to work and set up bigger and more resourceful groups, which unleashed urban terrorism the likes of which Turks had never seen. As Marxist terrorists targeted law enforcement personnel, conservative politicians, businessmen, and "uncooperative" citizens, ultranationalist groups also armed themselves and began attacking the Marxists as well as those suspected of aiding them. In the meantime, a terrorist group from Lebanon called the Armenian Secret Army for the Liberation of Armenia (ASALA) was assassinating Turkish diplomats all over the world and attacking targets inside Turkey at random.[3] This spiral of terror led to a chaotic situation by 1980 when the daily body count was sometimes in the dozens, totaling around five thousand for the period between 1975 and 1980. Turkish armed forces seized power in a bloodless coup on September 12, 1980, and restored order with countrywide martial law. Thereafter things remained more or less calm for the next three years.

As a result of the December 1983 general elections, a civilian government came to power, shortly after which the third wave of terrorism began. On August 15, 1984, almost eight months after Turkey returned to democracy, a small group of Kurdish separatists began attacking military outposts in the southeastern part of the country, announcing the commencement of a new form of terrorism in Turkey, the ethnically nationalist, rural low-intensity conflict (LIC). For the next fifteen years, Turkish authorities found themselves fighting this new form of terrorism as well as the more traditional urban Marxist type and the new Islamic fundamentalist terrorists. With the arrests of major Kurdish separatist terrorist leaders in 1999 and a series of successful operations against the Marxists and Islamic fundamentalists, the third wave of terror also seems to have reached its end. In the coming years, Turkey may find itself in the unavoidable position of having to fight a fourth wave of terrorism as a result of the circumstances this essay attempts to explore.

THE CULPRITS: ROGUES' GALLERY

The following terrorist organizations share responsibility for most of the terrorism that takes place in Turkey today.

Ethnically Inspired: Fighting the "Colonialists"

Partiya Karkaren Kurdistan
(Kurdistan Workers' Party, or PKK)

Led by Abdullah Ocalan (known as Apo—currently on death row in Turkey) between 1984 and 2000, the PKK posed the major terrorist threat in Turkey. This Maoist organization, which claims to pursue the rights of Turkey's Kurds, is undergoing a process of transformation at present.[4]

Communists: Fighting the "Capitalist Oligarchs"

Devrimci Halk Kurtulus Partisi/Cephesi-Devrimci Sol
(Revolutionary People's Liberation Party/Front-Revolutionary Left, or DHKP/C-DEVSOL)

A Marxist-Leninist nonethnic organization, it is better known for its urban activity and attacks against American nationals and interests in Turkey, but currently it is working hard to gain a foothold in the countryside as well. Dursun Karatas, who is currently at large in Western Europe, mostly in Belgium, leads DEVSOL. A direct descendant of one of Turkey's deadliest Marxist terrorist organizations in the 1970s, the infamous Turkiye Halk Kurtulus Partisi-Cephesi

(THKP-C), DEVSOL continues to target individual Turkish law enforcement and intelligence officers.

Turkiye Komunist Partisi/Marksist Leninist-Turkiye Isci Koylu Kurtulus Ordusu (Turkish Communist Party/Marxist-Leninist-Turkish Workers and Peasants Liberation Army, or TKP/ML-TIKKO)

This is a Maoist organization with a religious twist (most members belong to Turkey's Alawite Muslim sect) active in both urban and rural areas. Advocating class (peasantry) warfare against the system, TIKKO also traces its roots to the 1970s and, although nonracial in philosophy, recruits heavily from among Turkey's Kurds.

Marksist Leninist Komunist Partisi/Kurulus (Marxist-Leninist Communist Party/Foundation) (MLKP/K)

An emerging Marxist-Leninist organization that is nonethnic and homogeneous in its membership, this group is well armed and organized in its operations. So far it has been confined to Turkey's metropolitan centers since it became operational in 1994.

Islamic Fundamentalists: Fighting the "Secular Infidels"

Fundamentalist subversive and terrorist activity in Turkey began in the 1960s. As early as 1967 and 1973, the leaders of Hizb-ul-Tahrir (Islamic Liberation Party) were imprisoned for attempting to bring the Islamic State Constitution (Sharia) to Turkey.[5] Islamic Jihad appeared as a real terrorist threat in the 1980s after a series of assassinations of Jordanian, Saudi, and Iraqi diplomats. In the 1990s, however, a new breed of terrorist appeared.

Hizbullah (Party of God)

Not to be confused with its Lebanese namesake, this Islamic fundamentalist organization comprises an exclusively Kurdish membership and aims at setting up an Islamic Kurdish state in Turkey. Hizbullah started out as a proestablishment reactionary movement against the PKK in the Kurdish-populated eastern and southeastern parts of Turkey. One of the most controversial terrorist activities of Hizbullah in southeastern Turkey has been the liquidation of dozens of pro-PKK activists, journalists, intellectuals, and politicians—a development that began in the fall of 1991 and continued throughout 1992 and 1993. The Hizbullah regards the PKK as Islam's enemy and has accused it of "trying to create an atheist community, supporting the communist system, trying to divide the people through chauvinist activities and directing pressure on the Muslim people."[6]

Some Turkish experts argue that Hizbullah's goal is the establishment of an Islamic state in Turkey that will not necessarily be confined to the Kurdish areas of the country but will use these areas as springboards.[7] Turkish authorities believe that Hizbullah came under Iranian control in 1993 and turned its efforts against the Turkish state. Hizbullah is now organized in western Turkey as well.[8] Despite a recent crackdown, which resulted in the killing of its leader, Huseyin Velioglu, and arrests of hundreds of its members and supporters, it still enjoys a support base among Turkey's ultrareligious Kurds. Even after the arrest of almost two hundred of its members, authorities estimate that around five hundred armed Hizbullah members are still at large. As of October 2000, Hizbullah's remaining members were known to have opened negotiations with other Turkish Islamic fundamentalist terrorist groups in order to consolidate their forces.[9]

Islami Buyuk Dogu Akincilari-Cephesi (Islamic Great Orient Raiders Front, or IBDA-C)

This relatively new organization recruited approximately two hundred former Marxists and Islamic fundamentalists alike, creating a highly educated, dynamic, and determined cadre of militants bent on destroying the system in Turkey and replacing it with a socialist, Islamic fundamentalist one.[10] Its members also profess very strong patriotic sentiments, a position that contradicts Islamic teaching, which underplays nationalism. Its leader, Salih Izzet Erdis (also known as Salih Mirzabeyoglu), is currently incarcerated in Istanbul. It is responsible for a number of assassinations and attacks against targets deemed un-Islamic by the organization.

Islami Hareket (Islamic Movement)

A fundamentalist organization, Islamic Movement is inspired by Iran and has been responsible for a spate of assassinations and other attacks against secular intellectuals and Jewish targets in Turkey since 1983. Some members once belonged to the Turkish Is-

lamic Jihad of the 1980s.[11] Irfan Cagrici is widely believed to have led this organization, which murdered a number of secular Turkish intellectuals and Iranian dissidents in Turkey. Some former Islamic Movement members went on to start Hizbullah.[12]

In addition to these major players, a number of smaller Kurdish, Marxist, and Islamic fundamentalist terrorist groups exist and operate in Turkey. Although the smaller Kurdish and Marxist groups are not very significant in the terrorist threat they pose, it is worth noting that smaller Islamic fundamentalist groups, such as the Army of Quds (Jerusalem), are responsible for a spate of assassinations of secular Turkish intellectuals and for bomb attacks against Israeli and American targets. These groups are believed to be sponsored by Iranian sources, while an expatriate Turkish group of fundamentalists in Germany calling itself the Federated Islamic State of Anatolia also has ties to Iran.

INTERNATIONAL TERRORIST ACTIVITY IN TURKEY

Al Qaeda (the Base)

Turkish terrorists not only travel abroad, but it appears that they also invite other terrorists into Turkey. In the past, Palestinian and Iranian elements have attacked Israeli and Turkish Jewish targets such as diplomats, community leaders, businessmen, and synagogues in Turkey. Turkish authorities have divulged information that Osama bin Laden's Al Qaeda members have been using Turkey as a transit point. Throughout 1999, there were numerous reports of Al Qaeda members of Algerian, Iranian, Uzbek, Libyan, and Egyptian origin infiltrating Turkey to attack the Organization for Security and Cooperation in Europe (OSCE) summit held in Istanbul in November, which was attended by President Bill Clinton and many other heads of government. In December of the same year, Turks arrested an IBDA C member who admitted connections with Al Qaeda. In October 2000, American security agents began tracking three Al Qaeda operatives who had entered Turkey but subsequently lost them and were forced to alert Turkish authorities, fearing that they might attack the American consulate in Istanbul. These three individuals, two Yemenis and an Algerian associated with Osama bin Laden, were believed to have remained in Turkey until December 2000. In December 2000, Turkey also extradited to Italy a Tunisian national, Mahraz Hamdouni, whom the Italian authorities believed worked in Western Europe for Al Qaeda. Hamdouni had been arrested in Istanbul by the Turkish police acting on an international warrant.

Lebanese Hizbullah

Moral as well as limited financial support is rendered to Lebanese Hizbullah and Palestinian Hamas by sympathizers in Turkey. Some fundamentalist-controlled town councils held public fund-raisers for these organizations, especially during 1996 and 1997. In November 1997, Israeli Shin Beth security agents in Tel Aviv arrested a German man, Steven Smyrek, who had arrived there from Istanbul to conduct a reconnaissance for a suicide bombing by the Lebanese Hizbullah.

Front Islamique du Salut (Islamic Salvation Front, or FIS)

In August 1998, Turkish police in Izmir detained and then deported Mr. Rabah al-Kabir, European coordinator of the radical Algerian terrorist organization FIS. Al Kabir, a resident of Germany, was reportedly trying to make contact with supporters in Turkey at the time.

In February 1998, following a determination by the Turkish military's Milli Askeri Stratejik Konsept (National Military Strategic Concept, or MASK) study stating that the Islamic fundamentalist threat to Turkish national security was surpassing the separatist and Marxist ones, the powerful Milli Guvenlik Konseyi (National Security Council, or MGK) cracked down on fundamentalist organizations all over the country. The MASK had stipulated the need for suppression of fundamentalist subversive activity by military force if necessary. Unlike the United States, where the military is denied domestic law enforcement powers by the Posse Comitatus Act (Title 18, "Use of Army and Air Force as Posse Comitatus," United States Code, sec. 1385), by law the Turkish military is responsible for internal defense as well as protection of the country against foreign threats.

But who are the members of these organizations? What motivates a Turkish citizen to join one and partake in its illegal acts? Over the years, Turkish authorities and scientists have undertaken a number of studies to answer these questions. The common denominators they have discovered are as follows. The ordinary Turkish terrorist is of average intelligence, not very perceptive of his environment, an introvert, and easily manipulated. Contrary to some popular thinking, these people are not outgoing, psychotic types prone to violence. What is interesting about these results is that the convicted terrorists among whom the research was undertaken included adherents of all the different political ideologies mentioned previously.[13] Dire economic conditions, religious sensitivities (including denominational differences, such as the one between Turkey's majority Sunnis and minority Alawites that led to bloody incidents in the late 1970s), ethnic consciousness, and pressure from the feudal social structures all push young Turkish people into the arms of terrorist organizations. In a survey undertaken between 1994 and 1996 that studied 2,355 convicted PKK terrorists, it was revealed that most came from the countryside and were single, undereducated, and poor speakers of Turkish.[14]

TERRORISTS' AIMS

According to the PKK's party program, "Kurdistan" (the lands where the PKK hopes to set up an independent state in the future) is divided by four "colonizers," namely, Turkey, Iraq, Iran, and Syria, which are also "clients of imperialism" themselves. The largest part of Kurdistan is in Turkey, and the so-called Turkish Kurdistan is nominated to lead the "revolution." The character of the revolution is "national" (decolonization and independence) and "democratic" (liquidation of the medieval feudal structures). The minimum aim is to destroy colonization and establish an independent, democratic, and united Kurdish state. The ultimate aim is to establish a state based on communism.[15]

In the face of its military defeat by Turkish security forces, the

PKK has somewhat changed its rhetoric from pursuit of independence to recognition of the Kurdish identity and limited autonomy. The Marxists and Islamic fundamentalists are less modest and advocate the destruction of the existing Turkish state, which they wish to replace with Marxist-Leninist and Islamic fundamentalist regimes, respectively.

Deterring terrorism and prosecuting terrorists, however, may be insufficient to end terrorism, especially when a large population supports the terrorist cause.[16] In the absence of legal or other forms of discrimination against Turkish citizens of Kurdish origin who have enjoyed full political rights under the Turkish constitution, access to the system has never really been an issue. In this regard, Turkish Kurds have risen to high levels of government in both elected and appointed positions.

SUPPORT FOR TERRORISTS

There are four types of external support rendered to terrorists. These are moral, political, resource, and sanctuary.[17] Unfortunately Turkey's terrorists enjoyed, and to an extent continue to enjoy, all four types of support from various sources.

Moral

The acknowledgment of the terrorists' cause as just and admirable is rendered to most Turkish terrorist organizations from abroad. The governments of Greece and southern Cyprus have made public statements in the past blessing PKK's struggle. That organization is known to enjoy close working relationships with terrorist organizations such as Sri Lanka's Liberation Tigers of Tamil Eelam (LTTE), the German Red Army Faction (and its successors), Spanish Euskadi Ta Askatasuna (Basque Fatherland and Liberty, or ETA), and the Lebanese Hizbullah.[18] Most Turkish terrorist organizations have political, logistical and moral relationships with foreign and domestic terrorists as well as with some state sponsors of terrorism. While much has been written about foreign relationships, of more tactical value is the nature of the relationships these terrorists have with one another inside the country. A good example is the deal PKK

worked out in the 1990s with DEVSOL and TIKKO in order to increase its urban activity. The former was somewhat successful in transforming its preexisting relationship into a practical working one inside Turkey by which DEVSOL and TIKKO cadres in the cities launched attacks as PKK's subcontractors and also helped it expand into Turkey's northern and southern coastal regions where it lacked a support base. All three groups shared training and supply facilities in Lebanon's Bekaa Valley, in Greece, and in southern Cyprus.

Political

The second form of external support rendered to terrorists, which involves the active promotion of the terrorists' strategic goals in international forums, is political. To that end, members of Parliament and diplomats from Greece, the United Kingdom, the United States, France, Germany, Italy, Russia, The Netherlands, Norway, and South Africa have directly or indirectly assisted Turkish terrorists in making their case in their respective capitals and in the international arena.

Resources

The third form of external support is resources, including money, weapons, food, advisers, and training. According to Turkish intelligence sources, Iran is a good example for this type of support, which it renders to the PKK and Islamic fundamentalist terrorists in Turkey. Ocalan's younger brother, Osman, is reportedly seeking more Iranian funds, weapons, and logistics. He visited Iran in October 2000 for meetings with Iranian intelligence officials, and he asked them to intervene on behalf of PKK to persuade the Iranian-backed Iraqi Kurdish group Patriotic Union of Kurdistan (PUK) to stop attacking PKK fighters in its territory in northern Iraq. Marxist and PKK terrorists have received similar support from Greece and Syria in the past.

Sanctuary

The fourth type of support is sanctuary for secure training and operational and logistical bases. This type of support was rendered to the PKK in the 1980s and 1990s by Syria and continues to be rendered to it by Iran. Turkish authorities believe that Iran allows safe passage to PKK terrorists, who also receive medical attention in that country. They also claim that Syria and Armenia continue to allow PKK to recruit new members in those countries. According to Turkish intelligence sources, a PKK leader, Cemil Bayik, is in contact with Syrian president Bashar Assad, in violation of the 1998 Adana Accord that Syria signed with Turkey by which it pledged to cease and desist its aid to PKK.

GOVERNMENT POLICY AND HUMAN RIGHTS

A Question of Law and Order

From the beginning of the PKK activities, Turkey considered the incidents a law and order question. The people's war rhetoric of Ocalan did not impress Turkish authorities, for they were quite familiar with it from their decades-long struggle against the Turkish Marxists. During its fight against terrorism, Turkey made a point of not complying with terrorist demands, most of which have been irreconcilable with the democratic system under the Turkish constitution. One demand that both the PKK and the Marxist terrorists have in common is a general amnesty for all imprisoned terrorists.[19] From death row, PKK leader Ocalan has offered a deal by which PKK members will lay down their arms if the Turkish government pardons all convicted terrorists. This so-called peace project has been ignored by the Turkish government so far.

Human Rights Problems

Civil Liberties

In countering the brutal terrorist campaign of the late 1970s, Turkey was forced to limit civil rights and liberties in order to restore law and order by declaring martial law in 1980. Martial law only lasted three years. With the transfer of power to civilian hands, other legal methods were put to use to better fight terrorism. While practices such as evacuation of villages, incommunicado detention of suspects, state security courts that featured military judges alongside civilian ones until 1999, and administrative orders closing newspapers and banning public meetings in the area under emergency rule have been criticized, these were permissible under the Turkish constitution and legal recourse was available to the people affected by them.

Nonviolent Political Crime

The Turkish law on antiterrorism has an article that stipulates imprisonment for "every kind of propaganda" that contributes to terrorism. The lack of clarity in this article gave the prosecutors and judges too much discretion, a development that prompted criticism in Western human rights circles. However, according to the Turkish reasoning, so long as there is an armed group fighting a guerrilla war in the mountains, the views that are expressed orally or in writing to support the declared political objectives of this group inevitably help justify its terrorism, even without directly inciting violence.

Detention without Trial

In Turkey, the period of time during which a detainee can be held before being arraigned, while longer than in the United States, is in line with European standards. The European Court of Human Rights allows a maximum of four days of detention. The court did not qualify this decision according to circumstances. For instance, the existence of a public emergency does not warrant longer detention periods. For some time, Turkey applied fifteen days of detention for terrorist suspects and thirty days in the emergency area. Later these periods were reduced by half to the current seven days, during the first four days of which the detainee may not be contacted by his or her legal counsel if the authorities so order. This practice subjected Turkey to international criticism and to lawsuits at the European Court of Human Rights.[20]

Legal Reform

Turkish criminal procedure law was revised in the 1990s, making it more liberal and in line with internationally accepted human rights norms such as right to counsel during detention and shorter detention periods prior to arraignment. The lifting of the ban on communist and religiously oriented speech weakened the terrorists' argument. Turkey has signed all the major international conventions on the protection of human rights and abides by its obligations as a result of its accession to these conventions. Turkish citizens have access to the European Court of Human Rights should they feel that their grievances were not addressed after they exhausted the remedies provided by Turkish justice.

Cultural Rights

As far as cultural rights are concerned, the relaxation of restrictions on the public use of the Kurdish language is often erroneously interpreted as a concession on the part of the Turkish government. In fact, the restrictions had originally been imposed by the military while the country was under martial law in the early 1980s. As part of a democratization effort that included the abolition of legislation banning communism and religious fundamentalism in a nonviolent context, Kurdish language restrictions were lifted in 1991.[21]

TERRORIST GOALS COUNTERED

Terrorist goals may include recognition, coercion, provocation, intimidation, and insurgency support.[22] Various terrorists in Turkey had all or some of these goals. The following are some of the tools that the Turkish government used to respond to terrorism. Many of these options were pursued simultaneously.[23]

Deterrence

Governments can use their coercive capacity to make terrorism too costly for those who seek to use it. They can do this by means of military strikes against terrorist bases, assassinations of key leaders, collective punishment, or other methods.[24] With the creation of a no-fly zone above the thirty-sixth parallel after the Gulf War, the PKK found a safe haven in northern Iraq, where a power vacuum existed in the absence of the Iraqi military. Turkey launched air strikes and cross-border operations against PKK targets in northern Iraq and Iran on numerous occasions, destroying bases and training camps and forcing PKK units to more remote mountainous areas far from major roads, making their supply lines long and arduous.

Negotiations

Turkish counterterrorism policy's backbone is a no compromise/no negotiations approach. However, after Ocalan's incarceration, Western pressure on the Turkish government to enter into negotiations with the PKK has increased. Martha Crenshaw, a political scientist at Wesleyan University, proposes negotiations as the only possible way to resolve some long-standing disputes and suggests that governments can elect to enter into negotiations with terrorist groups and make concessions in exchange for the groups' renunciation of violence.[25] The governments of Colombia and Spain entered into negotiations with their respective terrorist adversaries, the unfortunate results of which are still being revealed on television screens today. Fortunately, Turkey did not make this fateful decision, thanks in part to its military success and in part to the political determination of its successive governments.

Special Criminal Justice Tools

Governments can treat terrorism primarily as a crime and therefore pursue the extradition, prosecution, and incarceration of suspects. One drawback to this approach is that the prosecution of terrorists in a court of law can compromise government efforts to gather intelligence on terrorist organizations.[26]

Repentance Law

The Turkish government made good use of the "repentance law," passed in the 1980s, which allows terrorists to turn themselves in to the criminal justice system. Under this law, more than two thousand four hundred terrorists surrendered to security forces in order to qualify for reduced sentences. Many repentant terrorists were "turned" into informers and actively participated in counterterrorist operations, yielding positive results. Crenshaw suggests that such peace overtures must be well timed. Ideally, they should come at a time when the government is strong and the terrorist organization is undergoing a period of introspection.[27] Immediately after Ocalan's arrest in 1999, Prime Minister Bulent Ecevit issued a call to all PKK members to take advantage of the repentance law.

Southeastern Turkey, the part of the country most affected by terrorism, has been under emergency rule since 1987. This status has allowed the administrative and security authorities in the area to cooperate more efficiently while expanding the powers of the security agencies. Emergency rule now covers four provinces in eastern and southeastern Turkey, down from thirteen provinces in 1990.

State Security Courts

Special criminal courts called "state security courts" were established that handle all criminal cases in which the offenses are deemed to threaten national security. These courts do not have caseloads as heavy as the regular criminal courts and are able to hear cases rapidly.

COUNTERTERRORISM TACTICS IMPLEMENTED

Military Tactics

Village Guard Militia

Crenshaw suggests that governments can make targets hard to attack. As targets are strengthened, however, some terrorist groups may shift their sights to softer targets.[28] A law passed in 1985 made it possible for the security forces to train and arm volunteer Village Guards from among the very same Kurdish population that PKK recruited its cadres. The creation of this progovernment militia force contributed a great deal to the security forces' tactical success in the field. The volunteer Village Guards, numbering close to ninety-five thousand, made it hard for the PKK to find "soft" targets, unprotected remote hamlets that can provide supplies and fresh recruits.[29] In the high-unemployment environment of southeastern Turkey, Village Guard wages were often the only source of income for entire progovernment Kurdish families. But PKK leader Ocalan put into practice a new strategy intended to crush Village Guards. He declared them and their clans "traitors-collaborators" and ordered punitive strikes against villages protected by them. These strikes earned Ocalan the nickname "baby killer," as PKK terrorists often wiped out entire Village Guard families in those raids. More than twelve hundred Village Guards have been killed in action against the PKK since the inception of this program.

Proxy Forces

Turkey entered into agreements with Iraqi Kurdish groups, especially the Iraqi Kurdistan Democratic Party (IKDP) of Masood Barzani, and in the summer of 2000 with Jalal Talabani's PUK, by which IKDP's and PUK's own fighters (*pashmarga*) participate in Turkish cross-border operations against PKK bases in northern Iraq and deny sanctuary to PKK terrorists in their zones of control. The PKK has used northern Iraq as a base for its attacks in Turkey's southeast, and many of its forces retreated to the mountainous region after the 1999 capture of Ocalan. As of mid-2000, more than forty-five hundred PKK terrorists had sought sanctuary in PUK's zone of control in northern Iraq. Turkey also armed and trained a small group of ethnically Turkish Turcoman residents of northern Iraq with a view to deploying them in a similar fashion. These efforts, akin to Israel's creation of a buffer zone in southern Lebanon and Israel's relationship with the South Lebanese Army, caused the PKK to lose some of its freedom of movement in northern Iraq.

Special Warfare Training

Realizing in the late 1990s that they were not prepared for LIC, Turkish security forces, both military and civilian, launched an effort to adapt their training and equipment to this new type of warfare. Turkish antiterrorism specialists conduct joint training exercises with North Atlantic Treaty Organization (NATO) allies such as the United States, Great Britain, and Germany as well as other friendly nations such as Israel. All branches of the Turkish security services created and/or enhanced their special operations departments, recruiting, training, and equipping operators capable of conducting unconventional counterinsurgency (COIN) operations. The Turkish National Police, responsible for urban law enforcement, formed a new Special Operations Department numbering no less than sixty-two hundred officers. The Turkish military created a professional enlisted corps, which filled the gap between career noncommissioned officers and draftee enlisted men who are discharged after eighteen months of service.

In the mountainous Turkish southeast, helicopter gunships, mostly American Bell AH–1 Cobras, turned out to be deadly effective—so much so that when Turkey ordered additional units in 1995 the PKK went on a campaign via its sympathizers in Washington and successfully pressed the U.S. State Department to disallow the sale. The Turkish utility helicopter fleet was expanded with European and American utility helicopters, boosting the security forces' airlift capacity tremendously. Especially in mountainous southeastern Turkey, heliborne operations proved to be very useful. But they were also risky. In the spring of 1997, the PKK shot down two Turkish Army helicopters using SA7 surface to air missiles (SAMs), which prompted the Turkish Army to invest in an extensive retrofit program to equip its helicopter fleet with passive SAM defense systems.

Both law enforcement agencies and military units acquired second- and third-generation night vision devices as well as thermal imaging equipment, enabling them to conduct surveillance and proactive operations under low light conditions. The military made use of light and heavy mortars, mobile and stationary, as well as medium- and heavy-caliber artillery pieces, some of which were airlifted to remote mountaintop firebases. This suppressive fire capability aided the small unit infantry operations against rural terrorists.

The PKK conducted mine warfare, which the Turkish security forces countered by utilizing mine-resistant wheeled and tracked armored personnel carriers and acquiring modern mine detection and clearance equipment. Yet PKK's heavy use of antipersonnel land mines took a toll on Turkish security forces as well as the local civilian population. The unconventional methods practiced by the terrorists also motivated Turkish security forces to come up with innovative solutions, in pursuit of which they evaluated modern technology but also went back to their armories. Counterinsurgency units efficiently used 60 mm patrol mortars and 57 mm recoilless rifles that the Turkish military had previously mothballed. Modern small arms better suited for COIN missions, body armor, nonlethal weapons, and canine units were also acquired by Turkish security forces.

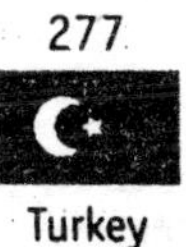

Draining the Swamp

In the meantime, defensive tactics were also employed to preempt the terrorists' own tactics. Remote villages and hamlets, often the target of terrorist attacks, were evacuated and their residents encouraged to relocate to safer zones, especially in the early 1990s. This tactic degraded the terrorists' logistical resources and curbed their ability to conduct propaganda and recruitment activities. Human rights circles in the West condemned this tactic, alleging that 3 million people had been forcibly removed, thus changing the demographic composition of the region. In reality, the objective of evacuations was to save these vulnerable people living in remote areas from the constant PKK demands for supplies, recruits, and shelter. The entire population of the emergency region is approximately 6 million people, half of whom live in urban areas. Another 3 million occupy 18,500 villages and hamlets. Only about 300,000 people (i.e., 5 percent of the region's total population), who occupied approximately 2,000 villages and hamlets, were evacuated. The Turkish government is investing millions of dollars in rebuilding villages destroyed by the PKK, the inhabitants of which were relocated to safer zones. So far, more than 32,000 inhabitants of more than 330 villages and hamlets have returned to their homes after security was restored.[30]

The Turkish military was especially effective in cordon and search operations at the battalion level during COIN. After these operations, cleared areas were saturated with security elements to deter the PKK from returning in the future, effectively "draining the swamp."[31] Turkey deployed a combined force of more than 300,000 in the emergency area. This number included 150,000 army troops, 10,000 from the air force, 50,000 Gendarmerie (the military rural police force), 40,000 police officers, and 95,000 Village Guards. Since 1993, the primary counterterrorism enforcement authority in the emergency area lies with the military, organized under three corps commands (two army and one Gendarmerie corps).

Intelligence

Turks also boosted their intelligence capability to better fight terrorism. This measure meant improving both their human intelligence (HUMINT) and signals intelligence (SIGINT) capabilities. Innovative new methods, such as satellite imagery obtained from NATO allies and Israel as well as aerial imagery obtained by Turkish Air Force reconnaissance flights over the emergency area and northern Iraq, proved useful.[32]

Turkish intelligence operators performed several successful snatch missions abroad, the most famous of which is the arrest of PKK leader Ocalan in Kenya.[33] High-level PKK officials were captured in and extradited from Iraq, Libya, Moldova, and Rumania. As a result, many terrorists who felt safe abroad are now more careful and subdued in their actions than they used to be. A case in point is Fehriye Erdal, a DEVSOL member wanted for murder in Turkey who found sanctuary in Belgium recently. As much as the Belgian authorities hoped to ship Erdal to a third country, they had no luck finding a willing host from among the forty-four countries they contacted, most of them in Latin America and Africa.

Some Turkish special operations units conducted pseudo-operations.[34] During these clandestine intelligence-gathering missions, conducted in the tradition of the Israeli Sayeret Duvedevan and Rhodesian Selous Scouts, Turkish intelligence operators, among whom were sometimes "turned" former terrorists,[35] disguised themselves as guerrillas and approached suspected terrorist sympathizers, gathering valuable intelligence from them.

Psychological operations were also conducted on multiple fronts. While the military conducted its own "winning hearts and minds" campaign in eastern and southeastern Turkey, providing mobile health clinics and assisting schools in Kurdish-populated areas, the General Staff set up a civil cooperation bureau that liaised with the Turkish press and also utilized the Muslim clergy in spreading its antiterrorist messages. The Turkish military even set up and operated a local television station that broadcast in Kurdish. The arrest of PKK leaders was used by the authorities to showcase the government's treatment of captured terrorists in an effort to encourage terrorists at large to turn themselves in to the authorities.[36]

INTERNATIONAL COOPERATION

Turkish security agencies cooperated closely with their counterparts abroad, especially in the United States, Germany, and Israel.

Turkish intelligence also conducted its own HUMINT collection missions in neighboring countries and Europe, where Turkish terrorist organizations are most active. These covert missions often helped detect early warning signals of planned terrorist attacks in Turkey such as suicide bombings. This cooperation is motivated by the fact that the threat posed by terrorists is often common to all countries involved. For example, DEVSOL targets both Turkish and American interests.[37]

Listings

On the diplomatic front, Turkey scored a legal success when the PKK and DEVSOL were listed as terrorist organizations by the U.S. Department of State and were prohibited from collecting material support in the United States. The American listing also gave Turkey's counterterrorism effort the moral and political backing of the world's only superpower. The PKK was also banned in Germany, making its operations there illegal, although in practice this ban was not as effective as the American one. In France, Belgium, and the Netherlands, Turkey has not been able to repeat the diplomatic success it achieved in persuading German authorities to ban the PKK. Turkish Marxists, especially DEVSOL, continue to have a very strong presence in these countries.

Resistance to International Intervention

Especially in the first half of the 1990s, there was international pressure on Turkey to apply the Geneva Conventions, which govern the laws of war. Had Turkey yielded to these pressures to conduct its security operations under the international laws of war, it would have had to accord prisoner of war status to captured PKK terrorists, opening the door for international organizations, such as the International Committee of the Red Cross or the United Nations (UN) High Commission on Refugees, to interfere in its counterterrorism effort, which it considers a domestic issue. Turkish authorities were concerned that the application of the Geneva Conventions could pave the way to the international recognition of the PKK as a political party to the conflict. The international human rights community focused on the alleged human rights violations by Turkish security forces while almost totally ignoring atrocious terrorist acts of the PKK on the assumption that human rights are violated only by states.

Diplomatic Relations

Turkey maintained diplomatic relations with countries that supported or tolerated terrorist groups on their territory while pursuing various methods in dealing with the problem. In the case of Syria, the prime backer of the PKK, an outright military threat that Turkey issued in 1998 was an appropriate response to Syrian hostility. In the case of Italy and the Republic of South Africa, economic boycotts were utilized.

Turkey's anticipated European Union (EU) membership is also having an impact on its fight with terrorism. Membership means a high standard of government conduct and tough scrutiny of civil liberties and human rights. Turkey's application for full membership in the EU did not please everybody. Some in Europe considered Turkey to be a country with a culture and religion that differs from the European norm and as such not appropriate for European integration. They thought that excessive human rights criticism would deter Turkey from insisting on full membership. These circles also pointed to the European Parliament resolutions condemning Turkey and condoning PKK terrorism.[38]

SHORTCOMINGS OF THE TURKISH COUNTERTERRORISM EFFORT

Some of the tactics the Turkish government applied in its counterterrorism efforts did not yield the desired results and exposed severe shortcomings in certain areas. These shortcomings included the lack of coordination among the various Turkish intelligence services, the failure of the correctional system, the inability to apply capital punishment, corruption among security personnel, and an inadequate government response to new forms of violence.

Lack of Coordination among Intelligence Services

Coordination and information sharing among the various intelligence and security services in Turkey, especially in the 1980s and early 1990s, were far from satisfactory, resulting in a duplication of effort and setbacks for the common cause. In the 1980s, Milli Istihbarat Teskilati (MIT, the National Intelligence Organization, a civilian agency that reports directly to the prime minister) lacked HUMINT assets in the rural southeast, where the PKK operated. This void led to the creation of Jandarma Istihbarat ve Terorle Mucadele (JITEM, the Gendarmerie Intelligence and Counterterrorism, the Turkish military rural police intelligence department's own counterterrorism wing). However, MIT gathered valuable intelligence across the border in Syria, Iran, Iraq, and Greece and other European countries. Currently, MIT shares the intelligence-gathering responsibility with the Turkish General Staff's intelligence branch, JITEM, and the Turkish National Police intelligence branch.

Failure of the Correctional System

Captured and incarcerated terrorists, far from being rehabilitated, could not even be properly supervised while in jail. Turkish prisons are notoriously "run by their inmates." Incarcerated terrorists live in wards that they turn into terrorist training academies and give instruction not only in ideology but in practical matters such as close combat, bomb making, and other terrorist tactics. Armed groups such as DEVSOL and IBDA-C hold sway in many of Turkey's large, overcrowded prison dormitories. A current project to transfer hard core terrorists from these wards to maximum security cells in newly built prisons has been met with great resistance from terrorist supporters and so-called human rights advocates on the outside. The transfers are aimed at breaking the inmate grip on the jails. In December 2000, Turkish authorities stormed twenty prisons around the country and forcibly removed the majority of DEVSOL and TIKKO inmates, who resisted with firearms and makeshift incendiary devices, resulting in the deaths of thirty inmates and two Turkish Gendarmerie troopers. While no less humane than similar maximum security facilities in the West and certainly less restrictive than American SuperMax prisons, the transfers are being portrayed by terrorist supporters as human rights violations. One cannot help but draw a comparison between conditions in Turkish and Peruvian jails, where once terrorists also ruled. Experts agree that regaining control of the jails helped Peruvian authorities' overall efforts against the Shining Path (once Peru's major terrorist organization), ultimately contributing to that organization's demise.

Capital Punishment

While the death sentence remains on Turkey's statute books, no executions have been carried out since 1984. In the fight against terrorism, the deterrence factor of capital punishment is a serious card Turkey has not been able to play. Furthermore, there is public debate about abolishing capital punishment altogether so that Turkey will be in line with the European human rights norms.

Corruption

Turkey has not been very successful in curbing the underground economy and money laundering by criminals. On account of their involvement in trafficking narcotics, terrorist groups such as the PKK and DEVSOL have been able to launder their profits and transfer funds in and out of Turkey. A degree of corruption occurred among the security forces engaged in the fight against terrorism mainly because of the narcotics involved. In hindsight, it can be said that some security force members assumed that they possessed extralegal powers and exercised those for personal gain, committing acts of extortion, murder, robbery, and assistance to drug runners. The Turkish judiciary has cracked down on such corruption and racketeering since 1998.

Response to New Forms of Terrorist Violence

During the 1980s and the 1990s, Turkey encountered forms of violence that it had not experienced before. The phenomenon of suicide bombings emerged in the late 1990s in a desperate attempt by the PKK to make up for the ground it had lost in the rural areas and to export terrorism to urban centers. Both Marxists and Islamic fundamentalists successfully utilized bombs (including car bombs) to assassinate bureaucrats, security officials, and intellectuals. Security forces often fell victim to terrorist ambushes, especially in rural areas but also in the cities, as Marxist terrorists acquired heavy firepower, for example, antitank rockets, military grade explosives such as C4, and command-detonated bomb-making capability.

Hizbullah introduced kidnapping to Turkey as a terrorist tool. This organization kidnapped hundreds of civilians, almost all of them of Kurdish origin, to obtain money and intelligence. Most of Hizbullah's victims were eventually tortured to death. Turkish security officials recovered the bodies of perhaps less than half the people Hizbullah kidnapped in the late 1990s. As of late 2000, thirteen alleged leaders of Hizbullah faced the death penalty on charges of murdering more than 150 people and attempting the violent overthrow of Turkey's secular order. The PKK also massively resorted to kidnapping children as young as fifteen years old from the villages and hamlets in the southeast and deploying them as "child soldiers," especially in the first half of the 1990s.

Both the PKK and Hizbullah established a network of sympathizers—civilians who provided sanctuary, supplies, and funds to terrorists. The PKK often acknowledged that its operations would not have been so successful without the participation of this militia, which is called Koma Gel in Kurdish. It is thought to number around fifty thousand with another three hundred thousand sympathizers.[39] The PKK and TIKKO recruited foreigners to serve in their armed formations. Citizens of Iraq, Iran, Syria, Armenia, Lebanon, Greece, and Germany are known to have participated in PKK attacks against Turkey, while TIKKO fielded Swiss nationals in the early 1990s.[40]

ACCOUNTING FOR THE COUNTERTERRORIST STRUGGLE

As the terrorist threat continues in Turkey, the struggle against it has yielded both pluses and minuses. On the plus side, Turkey has gained the relative safety of its citizens, especially in the southeastern and eastern parts of the country. It also gained the respect of its allies and friends in the world when it came out on the winning side of the counterterrorist fight. Even during the early 1990s, at the height of the terrorist campaign in Turkey, free and fair elections continued to be held and the percentage of voters going to the polls remained above North American and European percentages. On the minus side, many young lives were lost, not only among the security forces and civilians but also on the terrorist side. When taking stock, Turks are aware that the terrorists who met their fate fighting the state were also Turkish citizens who might have led peaceful and productive lives had they not been subverted by the terrorist organizations. Moreover, the country's image abroad has been tarnished by allegations of human rights abuses by the security forces.

Despite more than thirty-five years of brutal urban and rural terrorism, which became an LIC, Turkey has managed to preserve its Western-style parliamentary democracy and the rule of law under its constitution without making significant compromises from its way of life. But it has done so at a hefty price.

Number of Incidents

In 1984, the year PKK began its open armed struggle against the Turkish government, the total number of terrorist incidents attributable to it was 160.[41] Thereafter, the numbers changed as shown in table 1.

Casualties

Along with the variations in the number of incidents, the number of casualties as a result of terrorist attacks also changed. From about

TABLE 1. Terrorist Incidents in Turkey

	Number of Incidents
1985	489
1994	6,400[a]
1995	4,000[b]
1996	1,500
1997	900
2000	500[c]

[a]At the height of PKK's campaign.

[b]Thereafter the number of incidents began to decline rapidly, although the PKK was still attacking Turkish military outposts along the Iraqi border with 122 mm Katyusha rockets.

[c]Back to the level of terrorist activity in 1985 when the PKK was in its armed propaganda stage.

130 in 1984 (including military, law enforcement, and civilians killed and wounded by terrorists), it rose to a high of 5,500 in 1994, after which the numbers declined drastically.[42]

During the first ten months of 2000, 570 PKK members were taken out of action (350 killed and 220 captured). Nearly 600 supporters were arrested for aiding and abetting the terrorists. Also during the first ten months of 2000, 66 people were killed by PKK terrorists (27 security force members and 39 civilians), mostly as a result of land mines and other unexploded ordnance incidents.[43] In other words, 350 terrorists were killed for the loss of 27 security force members. The 1:13 kill ratio in favor of the security forces during the first ten months of 2000 may be compared with the 1:3 ratio in 1994 and the dismal 1:2 in 1992 when the PKK enjoyed a balance of power with the security forces in certain zones in the emergency area. The kill ratio for the period between 1984 and 2000 was close to 1:6. As far as LICs are concerned, experts agree that the 1:10 ratio is a healthy indicator of a professional and seasoned COIN force getting the job done. Since 1984, the Turkish military bore the brunt of the casualties, with nearly 4,000 officers, noncommissioned officers, and enlisted men killed in counterterrorism operations. The National Police lost almost 200 officers.

Economic Damage Inflicted by Terrorists

The national economy has been seriously impacted by the cost of fighting terrorism. Since 1984, Turkey has spent almost $100 billion on fighting terrorism and injecting capital to kick start the local economy in the southeastern part of the country, where only 10 percent of the population lives. The low per capita income in the southeast (10 percent of the per capita income in western Turkey) is attributed to the lack of natural resources except for limited oil reserves (100 percent of Turkey's domestic oil production comes from the emergency area; the PKK has specifically targeted oil wells, pipelines, and pump stations) and rich water sources, the remoteness of the region from commercial centers, and the mountainous, nonarable nature of the land. In its heyday (the late 1980s and early 1990s), the PKK deliberately destroyed the economy of southeastern Turkey by attacking economic assets and infrastructure. Construction sites were abandoned. Mines were closed. Unemployment skyrocketed. The entire southeastern region was turned into a desolate land where fear reigned.[44]

The Turkish government invests many times more than what it collects in taxes in southeastern Turkey, the region most affected by terrorism.[45] It invests more money in infrastructure and quality of life projects in southeastern Turkey than in other parts of the country. The Guneydogu Anadolu Projesi (Southeastern Anatolia Project, or GAP), a massive irrigation and hydroelectric generation project nearing completion, is estimated to cost the Turkish government $32 billion and is expected to create 3.3 million new jobs.[46] It is interesting to note that captured terrorists in 1998 revealed Syrian plans in which PKK cadres would be sent to sabotage components of this project.

LESSONS LEARNED

From these experiences, Turks were able to draw some lessons that might be applicable to similar situations elsewhere.

Determination Is the Key

Even when the PKK was at the height of its campaign during the mid-1990s, the Turkish government did not consider entering into negotiations with it. This determination paid off later, as the terrorists' strength was diminished.

Complacency Is a Cardinal Sin

When the PKK first struck in 1984, the authorities in Ankara dismissed its adherents as common bandits without developing so much as a curiosity about their leadership, bases, and supporters. Some experts claim that Turkey made its first major mistake in its counterterrorism strategy when in 1987 most of eastern and southeastern Turkey was transferred from martial law to emergency rule, effectively handing administrative power from the military to civilians. The civilian authorities were clearly unprepared to handle such a responsibility in an LIC environment before securing the efficient cooperation of the Turkish military.[47] Even the military, which fought the terrorists on a daily basis, took no less than seven years to realize the seriousness of the threat it faced.

Mission, Enemy, Terrain and Weather, and Troops and Resources Available, Time and Political Considerations (METT-TP): Analysis Is a Useful Tool

The METT-T model is an analytical tool routinely used by military commanders for planning and mission analysis. However, in an LIC environment political objectives drive military decisions at every level, from strategic to tactical, and the traditional METT-T factors are expanded to include *P*, for political factors.[48] In 1991, the Turkish General Staff under the chairman of the Joint Chiefs, Gen. Dogan Gures, conducted a METT-TP analysis (Vazife-Dusman-Arazi-Kuvvet Analizi, or VDAK, in Turkish military jargon.)[49] In that analysis, the Internal Defense and Development (IDAD) strategy model, per U.S. Army's Field Manual FM 100–20, 2–8, was probably followed. The result of the METT-TP analysis marked a turning point in the Turkish struggle against terrorism both rural and urban. Turkey adopted a preemptive COIN strategy. Presumably, that the Turkish General Staff's METT-TP findings alone did not result in the change of tactics in 1991, but they were probably supported by a decision of the Turkish government to deal with the terrorism problem before it destroyed the regime.[50]

CONCLUSIONS

PKK's Disintegration?

Leadership

Terrorists disillusioned with Ocalan's leadership and the PKK's failure are increasingly leaving the organization. These terrorists are likely to start their own spin-off organizations, which may launch attacks in Turkey independent of PKK command and control. Crenshaw suggests splitting pragmatists from radical rejectionists. Such efforts can diminish public support for the terrorists and deny them a strong base from which to operate.[51] Until he was arrested and brought to Turkey in 1999, PKK's leader Abdullah Ocalan ruled the organization with an iron fist. Despite convening its general assembly and electing a leadership team, Ocalan made all the decisions no matter how trivial the issues. The membership still regards him as the leader, although he is now in prison, while most day-to-day decisions are made by a temporary leadership council composed of his lieutenants—Osman Ocalan, Cemil Bayik, Nizamettin Tas, Murat Karayilan, Duran Kalkan, and Mustafa Karasu—who do not enjoy popular support among the cadres. This arrangement has contributed to divisions within the PKK. Nevertheless, should the PKK's political expectations not be fulfilled, it can be expected to revert to armed attacks supported by Palestinian *intifada*-type uprisings (called *serhildan* in Kurdish), which it attempted once before in the 1992–93 period in Kurdish-populated areas.

Internal Dynamics

The organization's internal dynamics are very volatile, its members torn between Kurdish nationalism, tribal loyalties, religious conviction, Marxist idealism, the concern of individuals for their well-being, and a desire to join the greater Turkish society into which most of their fellow Kurds have been integrated. In the light of these dynamics, it might be easier to appreciate the fact that more and more PKK members are leaving the organization. These internal divisions are not new. Disappointed with Ocalan's dictatorial rule, a group of PKK members split off in 1998. As these new members were attempting to form a new organization, which they called PKK Vejin (Resurrection), they were promptly assassinated in Damascus, Syria, by Ocalan's hardliners. Ocalan's arrest and his conciliatory rhetoric on death row sparked a new wave of departures from the organization. As of January 2001, PKK was keeping nearly two hundred of its dissident cadres at a special prison camp in northern Iraq.

Recent Clashes

While the authorities attribute the reduced number of terrorist incidents to COIN operations, skeptics interpret the data differently. They claim that PKK's tactical withdrawal from Turkey into northern Iraq and Iran, under Ocalan's orders, is the reason for fewer armed clashes between terrorists and security forces. Experts point out that the clashes during 2000 were mostly instances in which individual PKK units in the field were ambushed by security forces, as opposed to the more common type of clashes that occurred a few years ago when the PKK would ambush security forces on patrol or attack military camps. Yet, as of October 2000, PKK units continued to engage Turkish security forces near the border areas close to Iran and Iraq. Nevertheless, Turkish military commanders announced in October 2000 that for the first time since 1993, when the military was given the lead in fighting the PKK in the emergency area, they were ready to hand the lead back to the law enforcement authorities—a sign that the PKK threat is perceived as diminished.[52] There are also those who suggest that the PKK will use this respite to regroup and reorganize its armed militants while reserving the option to launch a new campaign of terror should Ocalan's so-called peace initiative fail and if the PKK does not succeed in transforming itself into a legitimate political movement. Turkish intelligence commented that approximately 500 to 1,000 dissident terrorists were no longer obeying Ocalan's lieutenants and were operating independently inside Turkey and northern Iraq, where they were preparing to establish themselves in their own bases for the winter. This group, in addition to the 4,500 to 5,000 PKK terrorists across the border in northern Iraq, continues to pose a threat to Turkey.[53] This is probably why the Turkish Army sent approximately 10,000 troops along with tanks and artillery into northern Iraq in January 2001.

Jihad Alumni

Many Turkish Islamic fundamentalists have volunteered in *jihad* (Islamic holy war) type struggles in places such as Afghanistan, Kashmir, Bosnia, Kosovo, Tajikistan, and Chechnya. Some of these veterans have returned to Turkey but maintain their contacts with their fellow *mujaheddeen* (Islamic holy warriors) abroad. The IBDA-C sports some of these veterans among its members.[54] In essence, fundamentalist terrorist organizations, such as Hizbullah and IBDA-C, have sported charismatic leaders who were reluctant to share authority with their cohorts. With IBDA-C's leader incarcerated and Hizbullah's dead, these organizations will be working to reorganize in the near future. As they do so, Turkish authorities, who received valuable support from the Israeli intelligence agency,

Mossad, in the first few months of 2000, will continue to pursue Hizbullah terrorists, having conducted more than 720 operations against this organization in 2000 alone, arresting 2,700 suspected terrorists, 1,700 of whom were later indicted.[55] Nevertheless, in January 2001 terrorists widely suspected to be members of Hizbullah assassinated the police chief of Diyarbakir Province in southeastern Turkey along with his five bodyguards in a military-style ambush, sending a clear message to the authorities that the organization is still alive and kicking.

In the wake of new violence and acts of terrorism in Israel and elsewhere in the Middle East, American and Israeli assets in Turkey are under increased risk of attack from Islamic fundamentalist and Marxist terrorists. Marginal Turkish leftist parties known for their sympathies for organizations such as the PKK and DEVSOL, as well as fundamentalists, including IBDA-C sympathizers, have demonstrated against not only Israel but also the United States, which they blame for the violence in Palestine.[56]

Marxist Uproar

In 2000, Marxist terrorist organizations maintained their lowest level of operations, but this will no longer be the case in 2001. Ambushing cruisers and sniping at security buildings and vehicles, DEVSOL and TIKKO are attacking the Turkish police to avenge the deaths of thirty of their members during the prison takeovers in December 2000. In a gruesome turn of events, DEVSOL borrowed a tactic from the PKK, sending a suicide bomber to a police station in Istanbul in an attempt to kill the local police chief.

Narcoterrorism as an Emerging Threat

Collusion between Terrorism and Organized Crime

The PKK, DEVSOL, and to an extent Hizbullah have engaged in narcotics and arms trafficking as well as smuggling illegal aliens into Western Europe.[57] These activities have grown to be a very profitable business and an important source of income by means of which the terrorist groups finance their organizations.[58] The PKK works hard to increase the number of its supporters in Europe by using the loopholes in asylum laws. The rise in the level of profits,[59]

especially from narcotics, means that trafficking is likely to continue regardless of the political developments that affect these organizations' causes. Apart from voluntary contributions from the Kurdish diaspora, whose inhabitants support the PKK, the main source of financing is drug trafficking.[60] In this huge enterprise, the PKK cooperates in concert with criminal Kurdish clans in a manner similar to that of the Sicilian Mafia families. Between 1984 and 1993, fourteen of the forty-two tons of heroin, or 33 percent of the total, that reached Europe were seized from Turkish citizens, 95 percent of whom were affiliated with the PKK.[61]

A Creeping "Colombian Syndrome"

Throughout the 1970s, Turkey's major terrorist problem was with the Marxists. In the 1980s, it was the Kurdish separatists. In the 1990s, Islamic fundamentalists gained prominence among other terrorist groups. In the twenty-first century, the greater danger may be from gangsters in league with terrorists, with a likely effect of narcoterrorism in the worst Colombian fashion. In 1993, Turkey's top investigative journalist, Ugur Mumcu, was assassinated in a car bombing. Mumcu had written hundreds of articles and dozens of books detailing the intricate relationships between Turkey's terrorist organizations, drug runners, and arms traffickers. Although suspicion first fell on Islami Hareket terrorists, who murdered other secular Turkish intellectuals before and after the Mumcu assassination, some experts speculated that Islami Hareket was acting as a subcontractor for one of Turkey's top drug barons, Behcet Canturk, an ethnic Kurd tied to the PKK's main man in Western Europe, Yasar Kaya. Canturk was rumored to have paid Islami Hareket $25,000 to assassinate Mumcu, who had published a book detailing Canturk's illegal activities in Turkey and Europe.[62] Before he himself was killed in 1994, Canturk was a key figure in the PKK's relationship with drug runners, a relationship similar to the Colombian Cali cartel's relationship with Colombia's major terrorist group, the Revolutionary Armed Forces of Colombia (FARC).[63]

Government Response

In October 2000, the Turkish minister of the interior, Sadettin Tantan, a former police chief himself, underscored the emergence of corruption and racketeering as the primary threat to Turkish national security, surpassing Kurdish separatist, Marxist, and Islamic fundamentalist terrorism.[64] Concerned commentators are already calling for the Turkish National Security Council to undertake a threat analysis similar to the 1991 study, this time targeting the drug runners, money launderers, and racketeers.[65] The Turkish military has expressed interest in the subject, and an effort is reportedly under way to include corruption and racketeering in the National Military Strategic Concept document.[66] This is thought to be a major threat to Turkish national security that needs to be countered.[67]

In the past three decades, the Republic of Turkey has endured much hardship because of terrorism.[68] However, the Turkish government's determination not to give in to the demands of the terrorists, who wish to change the Turkish regime, has prevailed. Owing to its location at the crossroads of the East and the West, Turkey will continue to be targeted by terrorists in an attempt to bring it under the influence of one global political power or another. But the Turkish nation's firm commitment to a democratic and secular way of life, as proven by the many sons and daughters it has sacrificed in the struggle against terrorism, will prevent these efforts in the twenty-first century as well.

POSTSCRIPT

WHILE THE WORLD WAS watching the news in the aftermath of the terror attacks in New York and Washington, D.C., on September 11, 2001, domestic terror incidents continued to take place in Turkey. During the two months following the September 11 attacks, fifteen terrorists who belonged to the PKK, the Turkish Hizbullah, TIKKO, and DEVSOL were killed in various incidents in which eight Turkish security force members and a civilian also lost their lives.

The Turkish security forces engaged the PKK terrorists in southeastern Turkey in sporadic clashes and conducted two major cross-border operations against PKK bases in northern Iraq in the fall of 2001. Meanwhile, the PKK went forward with its efforts to "politicize" its "struggle" by creating new front organizations to engage in open political activity and to recruit new members in Belgium.

Turkey's foremost Marxist terrorist organization, DEVSOL, also

worked harder on its own kind of public relations campaign, ordering dozens of its members in prison and outside to starve themselves to death and set themselves on fire in order to protest the transfer of their imprisoned leaders and hardcore cadres to new, maximum security prisons. As hunger strikers died in scores, with their sympathizers turning the dreadful events into macabre shows of defiance on television, other DEVSOL members became suicide bombers and attacked the Turkish police, killing officers and civilians alike in deadly attacks in Istanbul.

The Turkish Hizbullah, with most of its leaders killed, arrested, or on the run, continued to launch retaliatory attacks against the Turkish security forces and expanded from its power base in southeastern Turkey into western Turkish cities in search of new members. Hizbullah, with a long tradition of being shrouded in silence and mystery, also launched a public relations campaign, claiming responsibility for its attacks, and tried to demonstrate that it had not yet been broken while not forgetting to voice its approval of the September 11 attacks.

A fundamentalist Islamic organization, the so-called Federated Islamic State of Anatolia (FISA, also known as the Caliphate State), operating under the legal title of the Union of Islamic Societies and Communities from its base in Cologne, Germany, enjoyed support among the Turkish immigrant workers in that country. Although it is believed to have only about one thousand active members and with its leader, Metin Kaplan, serving the first year of a four-year prison term for being an accessory to murder, the FISA poses a legitimate terrorist threat to Turkey.

A Turkish Connection with September 11?

The somewhat cultish FISA provided traces of the connections between Turkish Islamic fundamentalists and the Al Qaeda network. In October 1998, several FISA members were arrested in Turkey while they prepared to launch a suicide attack against the mausoleum of Mustafa Kemal Ataturk, founder of the modern secular Turkish state, using a single engine Cessna aircraft loaded with a large amount of explosives. The mausoleum, a national shrine to modern Turkey's Western secular tradition, would have been the perfect target for the Islamic fundamentalists, who hate what it symbolizes as much as the

September 11 attackers hated the Twin Towers and the Pentagon for what they symbolized. German intelligence also believes that Kaplan's followers met with Al Qaeda operatives in Afghanistan on several occasions after 1996 and negotiated an alliance. Shortly after September 11, one of Kaplan's top lieutenants was arrested while trying to board a flight from Germany to Iran with terrorist training manuals and a chemical-protective suit in his luggage. American attorney general John Ashcroft declared that the man, who had also been charged for the botched 1998 suicide attack in Ankara, was a sleeper agent for Osama bin Laden. The fact that the leader of the September 11 suicide team, Mohammad Atta, while studying in Hamburg, Germany, had befriended a Turkish woman and traveled to Turkey on several occasions also raised some questions.

In light of this, it is not surprising that the American authorities have detained no less than fifty Turkish citizens along with thousands of other Muslims from the Middle Eastern countries and elsewhere. Turkish Islamic fundamentalist organizations such as IBDA-C and FISA have been working to cross-pollinate the small Turkish American community in the United States for the past few years, and the U.S. authorities were aware of the fact that several Turks participated in the activities of certain above-board Islamic organizations, mostly charities, active in the United States. Some of these charities were closed, and the U.S. government, which found them to be associated with Al Qaeda after September 11, froze their accounts. While none of the detained Turks was implicated in the attacks or held for immigration irregularities, just three weeks after the attacks the German authorities arrested a Turk along with two Yemenis for planning terrorist attacks in Germany.

As the U.S. authorities began releasing lists of individuals and companies believed to be part of the complex web of finances that supported the Al Qaeda network, some Turkish businessmen and companies appeared on the lists as well. Furthermore, as the American-assisted anti-Taliban forces advanced in Afghanistan in November 2001, some Turkish volunteers who had been fighting alongside the Taliban and Al Qaeda forces crawled out of the woodwork, and some even found themselves arrested while trying to sneak out of Afghanistan. Though very small in number, the Turkish volunteers point to the direct links between Al Qaeda and Islamic fundamentalist terrorists in Turkey.

The government of Turkey, on the other hand, has readily joined the U.S. war on terrorism. Taking advantage of its excellent relations with Pakistan, the Turkish president and ministers visited Gen. Pervez Musharraf, president of Pakistan, encouraging him to render his support to the antiterrorist coalition alongside the United States.

Turkey has had a long history of training Afghan officials in both Afghanistan and Turkey since the 1920s. Thousands of Afghan students have attended Turkish schools. On the strength of its historic and ethnic ties to Afghanistan, Turkey maintained a presence in the country even during the civil war of the 1990s. The Turkish government gave military aid to the ethnic Uzbek general Abdurrashid Dostum of the anti-Taliban Northern Alliance, which made it possible to develop intelligence resources in the country. For humanitarian reasons, Turkey also built and operated hospitals and schools in the Taliban-controlled parts of Afghanistan. These resources were useful to the coalition when the U.S. operation in Afghanistan began in October 2001.

Turkey also relied on its working experience and amicable relations in Central Asian countries such as Uzbekistan, where it has been assisting the government for the last two years in its own antiterrorism campaign against Islamic fundamentalists of the Islamic Movement of Uzbekistan, an Al Qaeda affiliate. The Turkish Air Force helped revamp Soviet era airbases in Uzbekistan and Tajikistan for use by coalition aircraft. Turkey readied a company of its elite Special Forces, with extensive experience in counterinsurgency operations in the mountainous Turkish southeast and northern Iraq, for duty with the Northern Alliance when the U.S. antiterrorism campaign began in October 2001. But only one squad from this company was deployed with General Dostum's forces by the end of the year. Turkey also earmarked a navy frigate for patrol duty in the Indian Ocean and two thousand troops to participate in an international peacekeeping force in Afghanistan. Inside Turkey, two thousand other Turkish soldiers, airmen, and sailors worked exclusively on coalition operations, using eight different facilities, including the joint U.S.-Turkish Incirlik airbase in southern Turkey and the joint Turkish-NATO Combined Air Operations Center (CAOC) in Eskisehir in northwestern Turkey. Wary of the Al Qaeda assassination of

Northern Alliance commander Ahmad Shah Massood days before the September 11 attacks; Turkish police trained the bodyguards of the head of Afghanistan's Northern Alliance, Burhanuddin Rabbani. Turkish police also shared their experience in fighting Islamic fundamentalist terrorists such as the Turkish Hizbullah with the American Federal Bureau of Investigation.

The Impact of September 11 on Turkey's Terrorism Problem

For years, the U.S. government has best understood and appreciated the Turkish counterterrorism effort. Unfortunately, this sentiment was not fully shared by Turkey's European allies. Save for a symbolic ban in Germany, Turkish terrorist organizations such as the PKK and DEVSOL continue to operate unimpeded in Western Europe. Turkey has requested that its European allies blacklist these organizations, as well as Islamic fundamentalist groups such as the Turkish Hizbullah, FISA, and others, just as the United States has been doing, and freeze their funds. After September 11, the U.S. State Department added the Turkish Hizbullah to its terrorist exclusion list, which already included PKK and DEVSOL. Several European Union states with large Kurdish immigrant communities are reluctant to see the PKK on such a list, to the dismay of NATO ally Turkey. While the EU listed the PKK as a terrorist organization, it omitted the PKK's political wing, the Eniya Rizgariya Netewa Kurdistan (ERNK, or National Liberation Front of Kurdistan), DEVSOL, Turkish Hizbullah, and FISA. Turkey wanted the following organizations to be banned in Europe: PKK-ERNK, IBDA-C, FISA, Hizbullah, DEVSOL, TIKKO, MLKP, and another Islamic fundamentalist organization known as Islamic Society–National View, which Turks believed FISA had sprouted from in the early 1980s. The PKK-ERNK continues to operate as a legal party in the Netherlands and has a television station based in Great Britain. Some European governments remain paralyzed by a fear that their large Kurdish and Muslim fundamentalist populations may become restive and violent unless they go some way toward accommodating their demands. In Germany alone, there are an estimated eight hundred members of Hizbullah and many more PKK activists and sympathizers. The most visible impact of September 11 on Turkey's terrorism problem occurred when Germany, under pressure from the United States, finally banned FISA and froze its assets in December 2001, citing FISA's violation of German laws. German authorities also indicated to Turkey that they might extradite FISA's incarcerated leader, Metin Kaplan, to Turkey after the completion of his sentence in Germany, provided that Turkey promises not to execute him.

What the Future May Bring

The PKK makes about $10 million from donations, extortion, and drug running in Europe every year. The Islamic fundamentalist organizations also collect millions of dollars from Turkish immigrant worker communities in Western Europe under the guise of Islamic investment schemes, from which they divert funds to terrorist activities. Turkey has advised its NATO allies that the PKK uses bank accounts in Switzerland, Jersey Island, Sweden, Belgium, Denmark, and southern Cyprus to launder its money, while the Islamic fundamentalists rely on couriers who carry cash by hand. This flow of money also feeds underground economic activities in Turkey, compounding the spiral of corruption and lawlessness. In order to better combat this problem, Turkey has passed new legislation, in accordance with the UN Treaty for the Prevention of the Financing of Terrorism, allowing it to compensate the victims of terrorism out of the frozen funds of the terrorists. The Turkish Treasury also cooperated closely with the United States to go after the funds and front companies affiliated with the Al Qaeda organization that operated in Turkey.

With its German activities curbed, FISA was expected to shift its operations to the Netherlands, where it has invested around $13 million of the funds collected from its thirty thousand supporters. In Austria, Turkish Hizbullah and FISA members were already using the same locations for their meetings. The combination of FISA's finances and Hizbullah's military capabilities presented the perfect combination to attack Western, especially American, targets inside Turkey, such as the Incirlik airbase, which bin Laden had reportedly ordered his followers to prepare to attack. Allied aircraft have used Incirlik since the end of the Gulf War in 1991 to enforce the northern no-fly zone in Iraq. It would probably be one of the nerve centers in the event of an expansion of the American war on terrorism to Iraq.

Such a possible development worries Turkish officials due to the fact that it would further burden the already struggling Turkish economy, which has suffered a great deal due to the loss of trade with Iraq under UN sanctions and the loss of oil pipeline revenues from that country. Any operations against Iraq would also damage the tourism industry in Turkey, one of the few lifesavers in the ongoing economic crisis. Thus, by the end of 2001 Turkey and EU states were opposing military action against Iraq unless it is proved Baghdad had a hand in the suicide airliner or anthrax attacks on the United States.

As the Turkish Hizbullah, with its new leader, Isa Altsoy, who is believed to be hiding in Germany under an assumed name with an Iranian passport, worked to recruit new members and replenish its arsenal, and as the worsening clashes between Israel and the Palestinians further antagonized Muslim sentiment toward the West, by the end of 2001 it became clear that the fight against terrorism, and particularly against Islamic fundamentalist terrorism, will be a long-term process.

Asia

Ved Marwah

TERRORISM HAS CLAIMED MORE lives in India than anywhere else in the world. More than one hundred thousand persons have fallen victim to terrorism in various parts of the country. It continues to cause large-scale death and destruction in states like Jammu and Kashmir, Tripura, Manipur, Nagaland, and Assam. Terrorism in its contemporary phase claimed its first victim in Punjab in 1978, although communal and ethnic violence has been a part of the Indian scene since independence in 1947. One of the notable features of terrorism in India is that the country's neighbor, Pakistan, has been assisting every terrorist group in India.

In a large pluralist country like India, the problems of internal security management are enormous. Relatively minor incidents can snowball into major conflagrations. India is a multireligious, multiethnic, and multicultural society with a history of communal and ethnic violence among various groups. It is not difficult to stir up trouble by pitting one group against the other. The rise of contentious politics between different groups based on confessional, ethnic, racial, linguistic, and other divisive criteria is the root cause of many secessionist movements now flourishing in India.

Heterogeneous assemblages of contending ethno-political groups are, no doubt, at the base of the ethnic conflict problem, but the uneven process of development and the pace of change in India have also contributed to these conflicts. Intergroup shifts in relative power and prosperity have often provoked violent reactions by groups who see themselves as losing out to the others or by groups who see an opportunity to improve their lot at the expense of their rivals. But many of these conflicts have been sustained by logistical assistance and sanctuaries provided by India's neighbors, particularly Pakistan. Once an open conflict begins between a minority group and the state, foreign assistance that enhances the group's fighting capacity becomes a crucial element. Logistics assistance includes military training, transport, supply of arms and explosives, advisers, and on the ground support of combat units and cross-border raids. Availability of sanctuaries in the neighboring areas provides an important strategic advantage for the armed rebels. The dispersion of people across international boundaries has also profoundly influenced the shape of political conflict in the border states.

Pakistan's involvement in sponsoring and supporting terrorism in India is both overt and covert. Pakistan has become the biggest center for spreading international terrorism. The most notorious terrorist organizations, such as the Harakat ul-Mujahideen, Al Badr, and Lashkar-e-Toiba, are openly operating from Pakistan with direct support from the Pakistani government. Harakat ul-Mujahideen is an Islamic fundamentalist organization, a duplicate of the notorious Harakat ul-Ansar. It is affiliated with Pakistan's Jamaat-i-Islami and is tightly controlled by Pakistan's Inter-Services Intelligence (ISI).[1] It has been very active in Kashmir. Al Badr is an ISI-sponsored Kashmiri terrorist group based in Muzaffarabad in Pakistan-occupied Kashmir.[2] Lashkar-e-Toiba is another "well-armed militia and a large ISI-sponsored force actively fighting in Indian Kashmir."[3] Sponsoring terrorism in India has become an essential component of Pakistan's internal and external policies.

The diffusion of small arms in this region, following the U.S. intervention in Afghanistan in the 1980s in response to the Soviet occupation of that country, ensured a regular supply of arms to the ter-

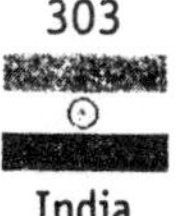

rorist groups. As the Washington-based Human Rights Watch said in its report of September 1994, *India: Arms and Abuses in Indian Punjab and Kashmir,* the massive proliferation of small arms and light weapons in South Asia is directly linked to the U.S. intervention in Afghanistan.[4] The United States pumped in a huge supply of small arms to the Afghan *mujahedeens* (those who wage jihad—Islam's holy warriors) through Pakistan's ISI agency. Since then, these arms have found their way into the hands of the many terrorist groups operating in the region. The smuggling of arms into India has been facilitated by the thriving arms bazaars at Dara Adamkhel, Landikotal, and Miran Shah on the Pakistan-Afghanistan border.

First treating terrorism as a minor law and order problem, and then reacting in panic when the situation showed signs of deterioration, both the central and state governments in India have responded to terrorism in an inconsistent manner. At times, their inconsistent response, driven more by the compulsions of electoral politics, has been counterproductive. Terrorist movements actually gained public support whenever government overreacted or underreacted. It was a mistake to treat terrorism in the initial stages as a mere law and order problem and leave it to the law enforcement agencies to handle it on their own. This mistake was committed in Punjab and then repeated in Jammu and Kashmir. If terrorism had been tackled more comprehensively before it took root, maybe the situation in both Punjab and Jammu and Kashmir would not have taken such an ugly turn. Both the central and the state governments underestimated the problem far too long and then overreacted, which was also a mistake.

Under the Indian Constitution, powers are divided between the central and state governments. India has a federal system of government. Law and order is a state subject. Therefore, law enforcement agencies are under the control of the state governments. While the responsibility for controlling terrorism primarily rests with state governments, the central government also provides assistance to the states in tackling terrorism. The armed forces are under the control of the central government. The central government has constituted a number of paramilitary forces, like the Border Security Force (BSF), the Indo-Tibetan Border Police (ITBP), and the Central Reserve Police Force (CRPF). The paramilitary forces were constituted with a specific aim to discourage, as far as possible, the deployment of the army for dealing with internal and border security. Their training and equipment are on the military pattern, but not entirely. In spite of their military training, they are more like the armed police, but better trained and equipped. They are under the control of the Ministry of Home Affairs and not the Ministry of Defense as in the case of the army. The BSF, ITBP, and CRPF are officered by police officers and not army officers. The central government has also under its control central intelligence agencies, internal and external. The central government has, therefore, a crucial role to play in tackling terrorism. It has also a vital role in dealing with political, economic, and social causes that are at the root of the terrorist problem.

Different factors are responsible for the rise of terrorism in different states. It is a mix of economic, political, ideological, religious, and ethnic factors. The many terrorist movements operating in the country have not followed a uniform pattern. Therefore, statewise analysis of the movements will be helpful in understanding the growth of this menace and the death and destruction it has caused. But other factors, such as left-wing extremism and drugs, need to be considered, too. For a more focused analysis, events that transpired before India's independence in 1947 have been excluded from this study.

PUNJAB

Terrorism in Punjab has its roots in state politics. The Akali Dal, one of the main political parties in the state, has been fighting for political power by espousing the cause of the Sikh religion. According to the Akali Dal, there is no separation between the Sikh religion and Sikh politics. The Sikhs have carried a sense of grievance ever since the partition of British India into two countries—India and Pakistan—in 1947.[5] India's partition was based primarily on the number of Hindus and Muslims living in different parts of the country. Other religious groups, like the Sikhs, whose numbers were much smaller, did not figure in the scheme of the partition. The consequences of the partition have been unfair to the Sikhs. Approximately 2.5 million Sikhs were forced to migrate from West Punjab in Pakistan to East Punjab, Delhi, and Uttar Pradesh in India. Sikhs lost their fertile land, the privileges they had enjoyed under British rule, and political clout. Despite making some noise about a separate Sikh state at the time of independence, the Sikhs never seriously made the demand until much later.

Jarnail Singh Bhindranwale, a Sikh religious leader, humiliated when his followers were killed in a clash with the Nirankaris, a deviant sect, in 1978, joined hands with the Akali Dal leadership, itself humiliated by its defeat in the 1980 parliamentary elections, to launch a terrorist movement in the state. Having lost power in what they considered an arbitrary dismissal of the state government because they still commanded a majority in the legislature, the Akali Dal leaders lost hope of regaining power by democratic means. Reminding the Sikhs of their militant tradition, Bhindranwale justified the violent twist in his movement and openly warned of the elimination of anyone who opposed his demands. The movement soon transformed itself into a terrorist group fighting for a separate Sikh state.

The initial response by the state and central governments was muddled. The well-known rivalry between Punjab chief minister Darbara Singh and union home minister Giani Zail Singh created further complications. Bhindranwale publicly exhorted his followers to commit violent acts, but the governments in both New Delhi and Punjab were hesitant to take action against him for fear of adverse political fallout. He successfully challenged the Indian state and exposed its weaknesses.

A series of assassinations of prominent Nirankari and Hindu leaders followed. Bhindranwale made a clever tactical move and shifted his headquarters to the Golden Temple complex at Amritsar, the most sacred Sikh temple. He commanded the terrorist movement from there. Thirteen persons were killed in terrorist acts in 1982 (for data on terrorism in Punjab, see table 1). The number rose to seventy-five in 1983; most alarming was the fact that the dead included twenty policemen.[c] Nothing gave terrorism a bigger boost and demoralized the Punjab police more than the mishandling of the murder of its deputy inspector general (DIG) of police, A. S. Atwal, within the precincts of the Golden Temple. The body of the DIG could not even be removed from the temple for a long time because the state government was hesitant to send the police inside for fear of offending Sikh religious sentiments. The police took no action to investigate the murder and arrest the culprits.

Pakistan got actively involved in supporting terrorism in the state in 1983 when it began supplying AK–47 rifles to the terrorist groups there. The introduction of assault rifles resulted in a dramatic increase in the number of casualties, giving the terrorists a definite edge over the Punjab police. The Punjab police officers were their favorite targets. In October 1983, the terrorists hijacked a bus in Amritsar and selectively shot dead the Hindu passengers. These selective killings created a furor all over the country. The killing of the bus passengers was not a daring act, nor could it have been easily prevented. This reality, however, did not prevent the central government from putting the blame on the state. The central government panicked under strong public criticism and dismissed the popularly elected Darbara Singh government. The central government then brought the state government under the direct rule of the central government by invoking the emergency provision of the Indian Constitution and imposed president's rule in Punjab. Under president's rule, all executive authority is exercised by the state governor under the direct supervision of the central government. This was a terrible blunder. With the dismissal of the

TABLE 1. Terrorism in Punjab

	Number Killed
1981	13
1982	13
1983	75
1984	359
1985	63
1986	520
1987	901
1988	1,949
1989	1,168
1990	2,467
1991	2,586
1992	1,461
1993	n/a
1994	n/a
1995	n/a
1996	n/a
1997	54
1998	0
1999	14

Source: Ministry of Home Affairs, government of India; government of Punjab.

state government, the buffer between the central government and the terrorist groups was removed. Bhindranwale now directly confronted the central government. Unfortunately, even at this stage the central government treated terrorism as merely a law and order problem.

Yet another failure of the central government was its inability to appreciate the need for strengthening the Punjab police, which was at that time in a state of confusion and demoralization. Instead of taking measures to strengthen the Punjab police, the central government reacted by dispatching almost one hundred companies (a company comprises around ninety men) of paramilitary forces after the promulgation of president's rule. The central government's inability to appreciate the crucial role of the Punjab police in the fight against terrorism was no less a mistake than the dismissal of the Darbara Singh government.

A sharp increase in the number of terrorist acts and the number of persons killed was noticeable after the imposition of president's rule. The central paramilitary forces lacked local knowledge and had little information about the terrorists, their hideouts, and their plans. They were never trained to fight terrorism. For the newly inducted forces, terrorism was like any other law and order problem, such as organized crime, and these forces initially tried to tackle it merely through a greater show of force. This misplaced faith in the military forces further marginalized and demoralized the Punjab police. Feeling humiliated, a section of the demoralized police empathized with the terrorists instead of fighting them.

Pakistan's support of the terrorism in Punjab made it easier for the terrorist groups to smuggle sophisticated weapons across the border. As the ISI of Pakistan got more directly involved with the terrorist movement, it began to provide sanctuary and training to the terrorist groups operating in Punjab.

In 1983-84, when the terrorists began fortifying the Golden Temple in full public view, both the central and state governments chose to turn a blind eye for fear of precipitating a more difficult situation. If action for the demolition of the fortifications had been taken in time, the situation could have been contained without too much bloodshed. The situation was allowed to drift until it became too serious to ignore. The drift and indecision of the governments set the stage for attempting a military solution to the problem of the Golden

Temple. The task of flushing out the terrorists was handed over to the army, which was ignorant of the nature and complexity of the problem with which they were dealing. The 1984 Blue Star operation by the army in the Golden Temple resulted in the deaths of more than four thousand innocent persons and the destruction of the Akal Takht inside the Golden Temple, one of the most sacred places of the Sikhs. The entire Sikh community reacted very strongly against the assault on the Golden Temple complex. For them, this was an assault on the Sikh religion. Large numbers of Sikhs became alienated from India. What Bhindranwale had not so far demanded openly, a separate Sikh state, now became the main demand of the Sikhs. They demanded Khalistan, the recognition of a separate Sikh state outside the Indian union. The moderate Sikh leadership became irrelevant. The short-sighted, ill-planned, and poorly executed Operation Blue Star laid a solid foundation for terrorism in Punjab. The Sikhs swore vengeance, and a large number of their youths began joining the terrorist ranks.

Prime Minister Indira Gandhi fell victim to the bullets of a Sikh assassin on October 31, 1984. Her own Sikh security guard killed her. As if the assassination of Mrs. Gandhi was not tragic enough, it was followed by anti-Sikh riots in Delhi, Kanpur, and other parts of the country. A large number of Sikhs were brutally killed, most of them burned alive, and their property, which was worth hundreds of millions of rupees, was destroyed. In the capital city of Delhi alone, more than three thousand Sikhs were burned alive in the most gruesome manner, with the Delhi police playing a most shameful passive role.

The terrorist movement reached new heights after the 1984 riots. Many young Sikhs joined the terrorist ranks to settle scores with the perpetrators of the 1984 riots. After a brief lull in 1985, the number of those killed rose to 520 in 1986. The number includes 42 policemen killed.[7]

After the tragic events in 1984, the central government made belated attempts to reach a political accord with the Akali Dal. On July 24, 1985, an accord was signed between Prime Minister Rajiv Gandhi and the Akali Dal president Harchand Singh Longowal. Within a month of the accord, however, Longowal was shot dead inside the precincts of a Sikh temple in his own village. The state assembly elections followed in September 1985, and the Longowal faction of the

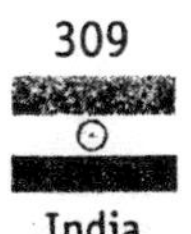

Akali Dal was swept into power. The central government repeated its earlier mistake and dismissed the Akali Dal government in 1987 when it came under public criticism for failing to control the situation. President's rule was once again imposed in Punjab in May 1987.

The security forces sent to Punjab were neither organized nor trained to effectively counter terrorist attacks. The terrorists were moving around in groups of one or two, rather than as a large unit, to avoid detection, and they were attacking both soft and hard targets. The Punjab terrorists succeeded in spreading their network and engaged in an increasing number of daring bank robberies and shootouts. They began committing terrorist acts as far away as Delhi, Bombay, Ahmedabad, and Calcutta. Exploiting the weak government response, the terrorists once again made the Golden Temple their operational headquarters. Undeterred by their ouster from the temple in 1984, the terrorists again began fortifying it in full public view. This time, the central government gave the task of flushing the terrorists from the Golden Temple to the National Security Guard (NSG), a professional composite force of commandos. Unlike the case of Operation Blue Star in 1984, this time the task was completed by the NSG without undue loss of life. Not a single civilian was killed in the well-executed operation, named Operation Black Thunder. This was perhaps one of the most successful antiterrorism operations anywhere in the world. The *Economist* in London said this in so many words in its issue of May 1988.[8] The most important difference between Operation Blue Star and Operation Black Thunder was that, while the former was conceived in haste, underestimating terrorist strength, the latter was meticulously planned.

The situation improved for some time after the successful completion of Operation Black Thunder. However, it soon deteriorated because of the central government's failure to take effective follow-up action. Taking advantage of the central government's policy of drift, the militants once again struck back in a big way. The next few years witnessed a significant increase in terrorist acts. The number of terrorist incidents rose to 2,116 in 1990. A total of 2,467 persons, including 493 policemen, were killed in these incidents.[9] Terrorists especially targeted police and judicial officers, leading to an almost total collapse of the criminal justice system. There was also an increase in the use of explosives in the state in 1990.

The next couple of years saw the worst phase of terrorism in

Punjab. With increasing pressure from the Punjab police, the terrorists retaliated by targeting the family members of the Punjab police officers, including women and children. The Punjab police displayed much grit and courage in not buckling under pressure from the terrorists.

The decision to revive the political process and hold state assembly elections in 1992 proved decisive in the battle against terrorism. Beant Singh, the newly elected chief minister, gave his unstinted support to the Punjab police in fighting terrorism. He turned the tide of public opinion against the terrorists. In 1991, the number of persons killed in terrorist-related violence rose to 2,586. The situation improved in 1992 when the number of those killed was 1,461. The situation showed dramatic improvement in the next few years, although the level of terrorist violence continued to be high. The end of terrorism in the state came in 1995.

JAMMU AND KASHMIR

Jammu and Kashmir is strategically an important state because of its geographical location. It has been a subject of dispute between India and Pakistan since partition in 1947. Pakistan claims it because the majority of the population in the state is Muslim. India, on the other hand, does not accept the Pakistani claim. Under the Indian Independence Act 1947, it was for the maharajah, the princely ruler of the state, to decide whether to accede to India or Pakistan or become independent. He decided to accede to India, but Pakistan refuses to accept the legal accession. It has been doing everything possible, including waging war, to annex the state. After 1947, India and Pakistan fought three more wars in 1965, 1971, and 1999, but the dispute remains unresolved.

Hostility between India and Pakistan was not only caused by the Kashmir dispute but has much deeper historical and ideological roots. The Indian partition was the bloodiest in human history. India is a secular state where all religious groups have equal rights, while Pakistan is a theocratic state where Islam is the state religion and all minorities are second-class citizens. India has never accepted the two-nation theory that Hindus and Muslims cannot live peacefully together.

Having failed in its effort to persuade Maharajah Hari Singh, the princely ruler of Jammu and Kashmir, to accede to Pakistan, that country's fifteen-day-old government tried to forcibly annex the state by sending in raiders—"tribal Pathans"—armed and transported by the Pakistani government and backed by its regular troops in civilian clothes on October 22, 1947. Ever since, Pakistani rulers have been trying to annex the state by all sorts of overt and covert military means. Interestingly, it repeated the 1947 raid tactics in the 1999 Kargil conflict in which the intrusion across the Line of Control (LoC) was spearheaded by the so-called *mujahedeens*.

It would be a mistake to treat Kashmir as a mere territorial dispute. For India, Jammu and Kashmir represents the essential character of the secular Indian state. It cannot afford to give it up because that would mean giving in to communal forces. India cannot afford to do that. It does not accept the Pakistani claim on the basis of the religious divide between Hindus and Muslims. An admission of this divide would mean opening afresh the wounds of the partition in 1947 when millions of innocent men and women were slaughtered in the communal riots that followed the partition. It needs to be highlighted that secular India today has more Muslims than does the Islamic state of Pakistan. The logic of partition on religious grounds is no longer valid in any case.

Terrorism in its present form appeared in the state around 1988. Unfortunately, the initial state government response was indifferent and inadequate. Instead of dealing with the terrorists firmly under the law, the Farooq Abdullah government, which had come to power in the state after an accord with the Congress Party in 1986, blew hot and cold and generally followed a policy of drift. In the process, it lost both effectiveness and legitimacy. The state police, which earlier had tried to deal with the problem with courage and determination at great personal risk, was not given adequate political support. The mishandling of the hostage case of Rubaiya Sayeed (the daughter of the then union home minister) in December 1989 confirmed the common perception that neither the state nor the central government had the necessary political will and determination to stand up to the terrorist movement. The state government under pressure from the central government conceded to all the terrorist demands and released six hard-core terrorists to secure the release of the hostage.

In October 1989, thirty-nine persons were injured in forty-nine explosions (for data on terrorism in Jammu and Kashmir see table 2).[10] Firearms were used in fifteen incidents. The situation in the state deteriorated to such an extent that no judicial officer was willing to pass an order against a terrorist. The elected state government and the criminal justice system virtually collapsed under the pressure of the militants.

A turning point could have come in 1991, when the situation showed some improvement, if the state government had not given in rather tamely to the terrorist demands by repeating its earlier mistake. It released twelve terrorists to secure the release of a hostage, an Indian Oil Company executive, K. Doraiswamy, who had been kidnapped.

In the first two weeks of January 1992, 202 incidents of terrorism took place in the state, which included 173 armed attacks, 17 cases of arson, and 4 bomb explosions. In these incidents, seventy-six persons, including seven members of the security forces, were killed.[11] The spurt in militant activity in the valley extended to the Jammu region in August 1992. In 1993, there was an upsurge of terrorism in the Doda region also.

The infiltration of foreign terrorists into the state began in 1992. Early that year the presence of a few Afghan terrorists was noticed in Pakistan Occupied Kashmir (POK). Since then, the number of foreign infiltrators has kept increasing. Terrorism in the state today is

TABLE 2. Terrorism in Jammu and Kashmir

	Number of Incidents	Number Killed
1988	390	31
1989	2,154	92
1990	3,905	1,177
1991	3,122	1,393
1992	4,971	1,909
1993	4,457	2,567
1994	4,584	2,899
1995	4,479	2,796
1996	4,224	3,122
1997	3,004	2,477
1998	2,993	2,327
1999	2,938	2,632

Source: Ministry of Home Affairs, government of India; government of Jammu and Kashmir.

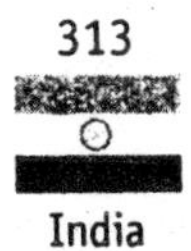

being sustained mostly by the terrorists from outside. Most are from Afghanistan and Pakistan. The local component has been shrinking for some years. Hizbul Mujahideen, a Kashmir-based pro-Pakistan group, and Al Badr, Harakat ul-Jihad-Islami, and Harakat ul-Mujahideen were the main groups involved in bringing in foreign mercenaries in the early years. At the end of 1993, the number of terrorists in Jammu and Kashmir was estimated at about twelve hundred. Today the number has risen to ten thousand, and many more terrorist outfits based in Afghanistan and Pakistan have joined in to train and send terrorists into the state.

The situation in the state further deteriorated in 1994. During that year, more than twenty-five hundred persons were killed in terrorist-related violence, which included 370 cases of kidnapping, 2,000 cases of bomb attacks, and more than 500 incidents of arson. In as many as 85 incidents, rockets were used. The year 1995 opened with multiple blasts at Maulana Azad Stadium in Jammu during the Republic Day Parade, which almost killed the governor, Gen. K. V. Krishna Rao. It also saw an increase in the use of remote-controlled devices to detonate explosives. The burning down of the shrine of the much-revered Sufi (a liberal sect) saint, Nooruddin Noorani (known as Chirar-e-Sherif) near Srinagar in December 1995 was a victory of sorts for the terrorists. Another sensational incident, the kidnapping of five foreign tourists by a terrorist group calling itself Al Faran, also took place in 1995.

In 1996, more than three thousand persons were killed in 4,224 incidents of terrorism. The electoral process was revived in 1996. Parliamentary elections in the state were held in 1996, followed by the state assembly elections later in the year. National Conference, a regional political party under the leadership of Farooq Abdullah, won a thumping victory in the assembly polls. Farooq Abdullah returned as the state chief minister. The state participated in the parliamentary elections again in 1998 and 1999.

The number of incidents dropped in 1997, 1998, and 1999, although the number of persons killed continues to be high. The use of high explosives (such as RDX, or Cyclomethylenetrinitramine) was the main reason for the high casualty rate. The situation, which had been showing some signs of improvement, deteriorated after the Kargil war was started by Pakistan's intrusion in 1999.

The situation continues to be difficult. The people in the state are sick and tired of violence. They are disillusioned with Pakistan, and accession to Pakistan is no longer a popular demand. Successful holding of the parliamentary and then state assembly elections has completely transformed the political scene. The militants are under pressure from the security forces, but the level of violence is still quite high. The terrorist movement is today dominated by foreign terrorist groups like the Harakat ul-Ansar, Al Badr, and Laskar-e-Toiba. In the post-Kargil scenario, terrorist violence has increased due to infiltration of a large number of Pakistanis and Afghani *mujahedeens* into the state since June 1999. They are specifically targeting the security forces.

Religion, bigotry, and fanaticism are not the only factors responsible for the rise of terrorism in the state. According to a study undertaken by Brigadier Arjun Ray, a senior Indian army officer, the average Kashmiri militant is driven by economic and political frustration rather than religious fanaticism.[12] The secessionist movement is being sustained not so much by ideology as by frustration and anger over poor governance.

The rise of terrorism can be attributed also to some ineffective policies of the state and national governments. Some notable mistakes were the dismissal of the Farooq Abdullah government in 1984, the mishandling of the Rubaiya Sayeed kidnapping case in 1989, the dissolution of the state assembly in 1990, and the release of twelve hard-core terrorists in 1991 in the Doraiswamy kidnapping case. Unfortunately, the tendency of each successive government has been to put the blame on the predecessor governments and then start playing musical chairs with the top bureaucrats. This practice has done a lot of damage to the state administration's credibility and has reduced its effectiveness.

THE NORTHEAST

The Northeast is a strategically vulnerable region. It is hemmed in on three sides by China, Myanmar (formerly Burma), Bhutan, and Bangladesh (formerly East Pakistan). It is linked to the rest of India by a narrow twenty-kilometer-wide strip near Siliguri, a northern town in West Bengal. Politically, the region is divided into seven states—Assam, Nagaland, Manipur, Tripura, Meghalaya, Arunachal

Pradesh, and Mizoram. Terrorism continues to take its toll in Assam, Nagaland, Manipur, and Tripura, although the situation is relatively peaceful in Mizoram, Meghalaya, and Arunachal Pradesh. At one time, the situation in Mizoram was also very serious, but conditions improved following a political accord reached in 1986.

Terrorism has thrived in the region because of its geographical location, physical remoteness, economic backwardness, and the political alienation of a large portion of the population. The inhabitants of this region, dominated by different tribes, are an ethnically distinct people. Physiographical constraints, geographical isolation, difficult communications, long years of neglect, and a sense of pride in assertion of the identity of the people who live there have created an explosive mix. Taking advantage of this situation, hostile external forces have been encouraging and helping the forces of subversion in the region since independence in 1947. Their aim is to divide India on ethnic and religious lines. A number of terrorist groups find support and easy sanctuaries in the neighboring countries of Bangladesh, Nepal, Myanmar, and Bhutan. The terrain has also helped the spread of terrorism: it is mostly hilly. The hilly terrain, carpeted with thick forests and unprotected international boundaries, provides an ideal environment for the breeding of secessionist and terrorist forces in the region. It is eminently suited for committing terrorist acts. The steep terrain and jungle roads provide easy traps for attacks on the moving convoys of the security forces. The dispersion of ethnic groups across the international borders has further compounded the problem.

Paradoxically, the growth of democracy in this region has helped the terrorist forces. There is a known and well-established link between terrorism and electoral politics. Politicians have been exploiting the many grievances of the people in this far-flung region for electoral gains. Admittedly, partition of the country has hurt this region more than any other part of the country. The region has since become landlocked. Its main rail, road, and water links to the rest of the country were broken, as they passed through East Pakistan (now Bangladesh). High transport costs have made even essential commodities much more expensive compared to costs in the rest of the country.

All seven states in the Northeast are facing serious political and economic problems. That separatism and its inevitable offspring, terrorism, can be highly contagious has been repeatedly demonstrated there. The proliferation of arms and the anger and frustration of unemployed youth have created an environment favorable to the spread of terrorism. An alarming increase in the number of drug addiction cases among the educated unemployed in the Northeast is one of the consequences of this vicious circle of increasing unemployment and spread of terrorism. Disillusioned with corrupt politicians and seeing no future for themselves, youths are joining the terrorist ranks. Political instability and a stagnant economy have allowed the situation to drift. Out of the seven states in the Northeast, terrorism is most rampant in Nagaland, Manipur, Assam, and Tripura.

Nagaland

With a population of about 1.5 million and an area covering 16,579 square kilometers, Nagaland is inhabited mostly by the tribal people known as Nagas. But an estimated 550,000 Nagas also live outside Nagaland in the neighboring states of Manipur, Assam, and Arunachal Pradesh and in the Somra Tract along the international border with Myanmar. There are sixteen major and twenty minor Naga tribes.

Insurgency in the Naga Hills surfaced almost immediately after Indian independence in 1947. In the initial years, the insurgency movement received moral and diplomatic support from the British, the erstwhile colonial rulers, because they were sympathetic to the Naga militants for their role during World War II. Material support came from Pakistan in the form of arms and ammunition. In the first few years, all the weaponry of the secessionist forces was supplied by Pakistan's intelligence agency through East Pakistan. The secessionists, who were ideologically committed to the Left, also received material support from insurgent groups in Burma and later from the Communist government of China. By 1953, the movement had gathered momentum and since then the number of terrorist acts has kept increasing. The most active secessionist groups are the Naga National Council (NNC) and the National Socialist Council of Nagaland (NSCN).

With his army background, Z. A. Phizo, the leader of the secessionist force, went about organizing terrorism in a military fashion.

He formed two separate wings: one armed and the other political. He announced the formation of a parallel government in 1956 and initiated the forcible collection of "taxes," a form of extortion. Well versed in jungle warfare, his armed wing fully exploited the hilly terrain and the forest area to hit the security forces. The basic strategy was to lay ambushes, attack security outposts, and kill as many security personnel and dissenting Naga leaders as possible.

Unfamiliar with the local customs and language, the security forces found it extremely difficult to distinguish between a terrorist and an ordinary inhabitant. In search operations, the security forces sometimes harassed innocent villagers. This harassment resulted in further alienation of the local people. Because of this sense of grievance, the terrorists could set up operational bases in remote areas that were almost inaccessible to the security forces. The result was that while the terrorist groups received advance intelligence about the movements of the security forces the forces knew very little about the movements of the terrorists.

Phizo maintained close links with the Pakistani and Chinese intelligence agencies. With their support, he was able to establish bases outside the country—in the Chittagong Hill Tracts in East Pakistan and the Arakan Hill Tracts in Burma. The Pakistani intelligence agency was actively involved in supporting the terrorist movement right from the beginning. The Chinese jumped into the fray only in 1967 after the 1962 India-China War. The external factor played a crucial role in sustaining the terrorist movement in Nagaland. The Pakistani support, however, weakened after the 1971 Indo-Pakistan War, which ended in Pakistan's defeat by the Indian forces and the separation of its eastern half into an independent Bangladesh. In recent years, Pakistan's support has again increased, and its ISI is actively engaged in supporting terrorism in Nagaland.

Terrorism in the state has experienced many ups and downs. After Pakistan's defeat in 1971, there was a lull for some years. Negotiations between the NSCN and the central government had been going on for some years, but they made more headway after 1971. The negotiations were successfully concluded with the signing of what is known as the Shillong Accord on November 11, 1975. According to this accord, the underground Nagas were to surrender their arms and begin to participate in the electoral process. However, a number of underground Nagas who had gone to China for training and were under Communist influence, repudiated the accord and refused to surrender. They shifted their base to the North Burma Hills under the leadership of Isac Swu and Th. Muivah, the two leaders of the NSCN. The 1975 accord was also repudiated by Phizo.

In a parallel development, a group of moderate Naga leaders took part in the 1974 state assembly elections. But it was not long before political power corrupted the newly elected leaders, and an ugly process of defection and counterdefection ensued. In this free for all, there was an increase in violent crime and acts of terrorism. Preoccupied with tackling terrorism, the state government could pay little attention to the task of economic development in Nagaland.

The NSCN split into two factions in 1988: the Khaplang faction, or NSCN(K), and the Isac-Muivah faction, NSCN(IM). Both factions have managed to extend their areas of influence in the region. Lack of coordination among the security forces and the civilian state government and active support from Pakistan's ISI have created a difficult situation. A cease-fire agreement was signed with the NSCN(IM) in 1997, but protracted negotiations have not resulted in a settlement. The situation in the state continues to be difficult. For data on terrorism in Nagaland, see table 3.

Manipur

Manipur has a population of 1,837,000 and an area of 22,327 square kilometers. It can be divided into two distinct parts: the valley and the hills. The predominant inhabitants of the state, known as Meiteis, dominate the valley. The hill districts are inhabited mainly by the Naga, Kuki, Paite, and Zomi tribes.

TABLE 3. Terrorism in the States of Nagaland, Manipur, Assam, and Tripura

	1996		1997		1998		1999	
	Incidents	Killed	Incidents	Killed	Incidents	Killed	Incidents	Killed
Nagaland	261	191	380	135	202	46	294	30
Manipur	417	241	691	628	345	251	284	169
Assam	396	589	427	380	735	794	447	341
Tripura	391	178	303	270	568	251	614	282

Source: Ministry of Home Affairs, government of India, and the governments of Nagaland, Manipur, Assam, and Tripura.

Manipur has a history of leftist extremism. Economic unrest among Meitei youths was an important factor for the rise of terrorism. The aim of extremist violence in the valley was initially to highlight social and economic discrimination against the Meiteis. It turned secessionist as the violence increased. The violence began in the 1960s but it took a more serious turn only in the late 1970s. Terrorist acts, such as assassinations, ambushes of security forces personnel, looting of banks and treasuries, and extortion of money from government departments, traders, and transporters, increased later in the 1970s.

Being a border state, Manipur is vulnerable to terrorism. The hilly terrain is helpful in laying ambushes against the security forces. Manipur has a thinly guarded international border with Myanmar that is 350 kilometers long. This situation makes monitoring infiltration and the smuggling of arms difficult. Terrorists move quite freely in and out of Manipur from Myanmar. The NSCN(K) and the NSCN(IM) have sanctuaries in Myanmar.

Peace returned to Manipur for a brief period after the creation of Bangladesh in 1971, but terrorism returned in a more virulent form within a couple of years. More than one terrorist group has been active in the state. The United National Liberation Front, the People's Liberation Army, the People's Revolutionary Party of Kangleipak, the Kangleipak Communist Party, and the Kanglei Yawol Kanna Lup mostly operate in the valley. The NSCN(IM), the NSCN(K), the Kuki National Army, and the Kuki National Front operate mostly in the hill districts. Over the years, terrorism in Manipur has degenerated into organized crime, and most of the terrorist acts are not committed to pursue an ideological goal but to extort money.

Two factors have contributed most to the worsening of the situation: corruption and maladministration. Political and administrative structures have become corrupt and weak. This situation has adversely affected economic development. The state of the infrastructure is extremely poor. People do not have even such basic necessities as water and power; road transport is in poor shape. People suffer from a psychological and physical sense of deprivation and remoteness. Disillusionment with democracy has in fact pushed the people toward terrorism. Except for government jobs, which have reached a saturation point, there are few other sources of employment.

The demand for a Greater Nagaland by the NSCN(IM), which includes the Naga-dominated hill districts in Manipur, and the peace talks between the government of India and the NSCN(IM) since 1997 have created suspicion in the minds of the Meiteis in the valley that the hill districts may be separated from the state under pressure from the Nagas. This suspicion has created some misgivings and sympathy for the valley terrorists among the Meiteis. The people in Manipur are generally tired of the unending violence, but the level of terrorist violence in the state continues to be high because of conflict among the main ethnic groups. For data on terrorism in Manipur, see table 3.

Assam

The terrorist movement in Assam arose around one main issue: the influx of outsiders into the state. Agitation for the deportation of illegal immigrants took a more serious turn in 1980. Until 1979, the movement against the outsiders relied mainly on demonstrations and agitations. Having failed in their efforts to pressure the central government to expel illegal immigrants, the movement became violent and took to terrorism. The demand to secede from India came much later.

The United Liberation Front of Assam (ULFA), the main terrorist group, was formed in 1979 under the leadership of Paresh Baruah, a student leader from Assam. It has been causing disruption of communications, hitting economic targets, and committing selected kidnappings and killings to create terror. The ULFA has also developed links to Naga and Kachin—a Myanmar-based tribe—terrorist groups in the region. Recently it has developed links to the ISI of Pakistan. The Assam police have sufficient evidence to prove that the ISI has been actively involved in fomenting violence and terrorism in the state. In addition to creating and promoting terrorist outfits along ethnic and communal lines, the ISI has been supplying arms and explosives to these groups. The ISI's hand is visible in recent cases of the sabotage of oil pipelines, communications lines, railway lines, roads, bridges, and other vital installations. These are vulnerable targets. It is difficult to effectively patrol and protect these installations, which are spread over large areas.[13]

The situation did improve for a while after a political accord was reached with the All Assam Students' Union (AASU) in 1985. This brought peace for a few years. In the elections that followed the accord, the Asom Gana Parishad (AGP), the new political party formed by the AASU, swept into power. Its leader, Prafulla Kumar Mohanta, became the youngest chief minister in the country. Unfortunately, internal squabbles in the AGP and accusations of corruption tarnished the image of the new state government, which had come to power with so much goodwill. One of the factions of AASU opposing Mohanta began openly supporting the ULFA.

Terrorist violence reached new heights in 1990, when there were reports that the ULFA had developed links to the Liberation Tigers of Tamil Eelam (LTTE), a terrorist group operating in Sri Lanka. Widespread extortion disrupted economic life in the state. The army was asked to take over antiterrorism operations in 1991. The army operations did have an impact for a few months, but the situation soon worsened as public support for the ULFA increased in reaction to the complaints of human rights violations against the army. Since then, the terrorist movement has had many ups and downs. Today, terrorism in the state has lost much of its idealism; it has degenerated into an extortion industry. The ULFA has built sanctuaries in the border areas in Bangladesh and Bhutan. For data on terrorism in Assam, see table 3.

Tripura

The spread of terrorism in Tripura also has its origin in fears among the indigenous population due to the entry of a large migrant population from the neighboring states. It all started with the migration of Hindu Bengali refugees from East Pakistan after the partition in 1947. The problem has since worsened with a further influx of Muslim migrants into the state from Bangladesh, not on grounds of religious persecution, as in the case of the Hindu refugees, but as an escape from economic hardship. This migration has further tilted the demographic balance in Tripura against the local tribes, causing serious misgivings among them as they have been reduced to minority status in their own land.

The Tripura Upjati Juva Samiti was formed in 1967 to protect the rights of the local tribes. It later formed an armed wing known as Tripura National Volunteers (TNV) to terrorize the immigrant population into leaving Tripura. The ideology of TNV is built around ethnic identity and socialism. Its avowed goal is to drive nontribal peoples from Tripura. It began committing terrorist acts in 1980 and has built sanctuaries in Bangladesh. Cox's Bazar in Bangladesh has become a major center for the supply of arms and explosives to the terrorist groups in the Northeast, particularly Tripura. These consignments of arms are smuggled in trawlers from Chittagong in Bangladesh and unloaded in Dholai in South Tripura.

After a comparative lull in the late 1980s and early 1990s, the situation has been deteriorating since 1996. The National Liberation Front of Tripura (NLFT) is responsible for most of the terrorist acts perpetrated in the last few years. It has been targeting nontribal groups and government officials. The number of terrorist incidents increased from 391 in 1996 to 614 in 1999. The NLFT was responsible for 313 of those incidents in 1999, more than half the total. The other major protribal group operating in the state is the All Tripura Tribal Force (ATTF). Internecine clashes between the NLFT and ATTF for supremacy among the tribal groups are also responsible for a number of terrorist acts.

The ethnic divide between the Bengalis from Bangladesh and the indigenous tribal groups has led to the formation of a counterterrorist organization called the United Bengali Liberation Front, which targets tribal groups. The possibility of large-scale ethnic violence between the Bengali population and the tribal groups cannot be ruled out, and such a development will further complicate the situation. The recent elections to the Tripura Tribal Area Autonomous District Council have further polarized the population along ethnic lines. Electoral politics are a negative factor in the deteriorating situation in the state.

The state police have been accused of partisan behavior. Tripura's experience shows that such deeply rooted ethnic conflict can flare up again unless it is dealt with effectively on a continuous basis. Politicization of the local police and its partisan behavior have made the police less effective in tackling terrorism. The state is increasingly dependent on the paramilitary forces for even the routine maintenance of law and order. The state government has now asked the central government to send in the army to deal with terrorism. For data on terrorism in Tripura, see table 3.

The leftist extremist movements in India had their beginnings as rural-based movements protesting feudal oppression and exploitation, but they have since spread their influence in the urban areas, also with the backing of some left-leaning urban intellectuals. Their base has remained largely among the peasants and tribal groups, spread spatially over large tracts of central, southcentral, and eastern India. Basically, leftist extremism is a have-not movement that still believes in ushering in a revolution through the barrel of a gun. Extreme poverty, social and economic exploitation, and a new political awareness among the marginalized and dispossessed are the root cause of this type of revolutionary terrorism.

The most active groups indulging in terrorist acts in India are the People's War Group (PWG) in Andhra Pradesh and Maoist Communist Centre (MCC) in Bihar. The leftist extremist movement in India is fragmented into about forty groups, but it is very active in Bihar and Andhra Pradesh and to a lesser degree in Madhya Pradesh, Orissa, Maharashtra, and eastern Uttar Pradesh. The PWG, the MCC, and Communist Party of India (Marxist-Leninist), or CPI(ML), are responsible for committing terrorist acts in various parts of the country. For data on leftist extremist terrorism, see table 4.

The paradox is that the worst-affected state—Bihar—has been ruled by a political party, the Rashtriya Janata Dal, representing the economically deprived and socially backward sectors of the society for many years. This fact only shows that political empowerment alone does not provide a solution to the type of terrorism prevalent

TABLE 4. Left-Wing Terrorism

	1996		1997		1998		1999	
	Incidents	Killed	Incidents	Killed	Incidents	Killed	Incidents	Killed
Andhra Pradesh	933	186	863	234	736	205	602	151
Bihar	564	320	470	325	373	206	481	378
Madhya Pradesh	113	23	102	14	179	59	95	47
Maharashtra	39	11	35	9	43	13	40	15
Orissa	23	n/a	24	n/a	11	5	5	n/a
West Bengal	8	1	2	1	3	1	4	3
Other states	11	n/a	5	1	6	n/a	19	4
Total	1,691	541	1,501	584	1,351	489	1,246	598

Source: Ministry of Home Affairs, government of India; state governments, as listed.

in Bihar. Leftist extremism in India was born out of social and economic exploitation, and as long as this exploitation does not end the terrorism will also continue. The growth of private armies along caste lines in Bihar has added another dimension to this problem. At times, it is difficult to distinguish between caste violence and the terrorist acts committed by leftist extremist groups. The two are becoming intertwined in the vicious and vindictive environment in Bihar. This development has led to gruesome cases of massacres of innocent civilians at regular intervals.

The record of the central as well as of the state governments in dealing with the problem of terrorism has been uneven. The general tendency has been to treat it as a mere law and order problem, something for the police to handle. This approach has not succeeded. Paradoxically, as democracy has taken deeper root in India it has also created a new awareness among the poor and deprived. The problem is embodied in socioeconomic and political structures. It has to be addressed with great sensitivity. The afflicted areas are located in the most underdeveloped pockets of India. The central issue in all these areas is social oppression, desperate poverty, and abdication of an economic development role by the state. This type of terrorism cannot be effectively tackled without fostering economic and social development and ending the exploitation of the poor.

SPECIAL ANTITERRORISM LAWS

The criminal justice system was one of the first casualties in the affected states of Punjab, Jammu, and Kashmir, and the Northeast region. Victims, witnesses, investigating officers, prosecutors, judicial officers, and prison officials were terrorized to such an extent that no one was willing to complain, depose, or take any action against the terrorists. In such an environment, a special antiterrorism law, the Terrorist and Disruptive Activities Act (TADA), was enacted in 1986. Unfortunately, it was grossly misused, not as much in the afflicted areas as in states like Gujarat and Maharashtra, where terrorism did not pose a major problem. Faced with so much public criticism, the central government allowed the TADA to lapse in 1995. The central government has still to come up with alternative legislation with adequate legal safeguards against its misuse.

It is in this context that the legal framework in which the security forces have to operate assumes great importance. Normal functioning of the criminal justice system becomes difficult in affected areas. The police and judicial officers are generally afraid of taking action against the terrorists. The situation in which the security forces have to operate has become very difficult. The Indian experience shows that there is no point in legislating ideal laws that cannot be enforced. Unfortunately, the practice of turning a blind eye to blatant illegalities perpetrated by the security forces while demanding the abrogation of special laws like the TADA needs to be exposed. It is more prudent to have less than ideal laws that take into consideration the situation on the ground, the difficulties faced by the security forces, and the need to strengthen the criminal justice system than to insist on normal laws and procedures that the state has no intention of implementing due to "practical" considerations. Under no circumstances should the misuse of any law, special or normal, be tolerated. The special laws, however, need to be constantly reviewed and should not remain on the statute books a day longer than necessary. Those guilty of misusing the special laws should be given prompt and exemplary punishment, and suitable safeguards should be provided to ensure that they cannot be easily misused. A more comprehensive view of terrorism laws will have to be taken if the problem of terrorism and insurgencies in India is to be dealt with effectively.

Experts on terrorism have expressed concern over the abysmally low rate of conviction for terrorist crimes in India. The country's criminal justice system needs to have the requisite deterrent effect to tackle the menace. The weakness of the Indian system was rightly identified by a well-known expert on terrorism, Paul Wilkinson, during a visit to India. He stated that "democracies cannot afford any dilution of the rule of law. There should be laws on terrorism and a professional approach is required to the criminal justice system." He rightly observed that "India needs an effective and pro-active criminal justice system supplemented by an elaborate intelligence network."[14]

Another factor that plays an important role in sustaining terrorism in India is the narcolink. The link between drug smugglers from Pakistan and the Punjab terrorists is a well-known fact. Some of the most notorious Punjab terrorists began their careers as drug smugglers. In the Northeast also, profits from drug traffic have been used to finance terrorism. The NSCN has been accused of waging a violent campaign against the Kukis, a tribe in Manipur, primarily to gain control over the drug-smuggling trade route from Moreh in Manipur, which has been traditionally controlled by the Kukis. The ISI of Pakistan is known to recruit drug smugglers to sneak arms and explosives into India. The ISI's links with organized crime are well known. It makes use of the organized crime network to commit terrorist acts in India. The Bombay blasts in 1993, which killed more than three hundred persons and injured many more, were the handiwork of "mafia dons" operating out of Karachi in Pakistan. Some top politicians and government officials in Pakistan are reported to have direct links to the drug trade. Similar networks are also operating in India. Huge amounts of funds generated by drug smuggling are being laundered through these networks. They are used to finance the smuggling of arms and explosives into India.

SUCCESSES AND FAILURES: LESSONS FROM THE INDIAN EXPERIENCE

In fighting terrorism, India's experience has been mixed. While India has succeeded in controlling terrorism in Punjab and Mizoram, it has so far failed to do so in Jammu and Kashmir and the northeastern states of Assam, Nagaland, Manipur, and Tripura. Nor have the state governments been able to deal effectively with the terrorism of leftist extremist groups.

In Punjab, where terrorism raged for about eighteen years, the situation has been brought under control. Today Punjab is one of the more peaceful states in the country, with hardly any incidents of terrorism. It is another matter that the terrorism problem could perhaps have been controlled earlier if it had been handled more competently. The counterterrorism strategy pursued in Punjab has many lessons, some positive and some negative.

The Blue Star operation of 1984 was a disaster, as it alienated the entire Sikh community. It directly contributed to an increase in recruitment to terrorist ranks. Seething with anger and driven by an overpowering desire to wreak vengeance for the ill-conceived operation, young Sikh boys and girls joined the terrorist ranks in large numbers. Terrorism took a more brutal form in the state from that time onward. Instead of taking an integrated view of the problem and tackling the root causes of terrorism, the central and the state governments concentrated exclusively on the military aspect. Another big blunder made by the central government was the dismissal of the popularly elected government and the imposition of president's rule in 1983 and 1987.

The credit for improvement in the situation goes to the revival of the political process. The situation made a dramatic turnaround after the return of the popularly elected state government under Beant Singh in 1991. The success in Punjab was the result of a combination of factors, the most important being the successful political initiative to restore democracy and the resurgence of the Punjab police. With the general public becoming disenchanted with the aims and methods of terrorism, it did not take long for the security forces to expose the seamy side of terrorism. The resurgent Punjab police were able to pick up important terrorist leaders one by one. This development was a serious blow to the terrorist movement in Punjab. Once the leadership was neutralized, the whole organizational structure of the various terrorist groups operating in the state collapsed. The number of arrests and killings of terrorists rose considerably in the following years until 1996, when the movement began to decline. The vital role played by the political leadership needs to be specially highlighted. The state government under Beant Singh was very clear and categorical in its opposition to terrorism. Though Singh was later assassinated, it was primarily his efforts that set the stage for the defeat of terrorism in the state.

Intelligence about the hiding places and plans of terrorists started pouring in, and people gained confidence in the bona fides of the newly elected state government. The police were able to neutralize terrorists because of the availability of this newfound intelligence. The image of invincibility of terrorists disappeared very soon, and whatever support they had also waned. *Terrorism* today is a dirty word in Punjab. The political parties and leaders who found it convenient to support terrorism now swear by the democratic process and openly condemn it. Terrorism is the antithesis of democracy because it substitutes rule by the few for rule by the majority. Democratic institutions are the biggest hurdle in the way of terrorism. Nothing should be done to weaken them, although terrorism puts much strain on their effective functioning.

Lack of economic development and employment opportunities no doubt pushed youth toward terrorist groups. However, it is also true that economic development became a casualty once terrorism took root. The vicious circle could only be broken by a comprehensive counterterrorism strategy that combined the enforcement of the rule of law with imaginative political initiatives and concrete steps for economic development.

However, even in this victory the state government failed to deal adequately with one very important factor: the strengthening of the criminal justice system. In its anxiety to deal with terrorism effectively, it gave a free hand to the Punjab police to suppress it. There were serious allegations of police excesses. The judicial system became a casualty. Already under threat from terrorists, it crumbled further. The judicial officers took the easy way out by not issuing injunctions against the accused terrorists, and they ignored public complaints of police excesses. The consequences of this short-sighted policy have been grave. The state has paid a heavy price in terms of the violation of human rights and the rule of law. It has taken some time for the criminal justice system to be put back on track.

Another lesson that clearly comes through is that without the active participation of the local police it is very difficult for the army or the paramilitary forces to succeed against the terrorists. It is generally the local police who receive intelligence about terrorists. Local background is an essential component of an effective counterterrorism strategy. An outside force that has no local knowledge finds it extremely difficult to deal with the problem of terrorism. More human rights violations take place when the counterterrorism strategy is dominated by the army or the paramilitary forces. Terrorism no doubt thrives when the government is weak and floundering, but the paradox is that it also gains when the gov-

ernment overreacts and takes recourse to shortcut measures. Many young men joined the terrorist ranks not because they believed in terrorist ideology but because they wanted to take vengeance on the security forces for their alleged excesses. Brutal methods of some of the most notorious Punjab police officers actually strengthened, rather than weakened, the terrorist movement.

By making undue political and economic concessions to the Sikh extremists, the government did not succeed in defeating terrorism. Giving in to unjustified demands only encouraged more demands, and the process of making demands became endless. As long as the terrorists were in command of the situation, they were not interested in finding a political solution. It was only when they were under pressure and retreating that they expressed their willingness to discuss their demands. Otherwise, they found ways to abort the negotiations by making impossible demands.

It is a fact that a few sensational incidents brought the Indian government more into disrepute than did less sensational cases of terrorism. Terrorism thrived on publicity, and sensational killings gave them that advantage. The Punjab experience shows that instead of anticipating this sense of public outrage and dealing with it in a cool and calculated manner the central government succumbed too easily to public criticism. It derailed the political process twice in 1983 and 1987 by dismissing the popularly elected state governments because they could not prevent the killing of bus passengers who belonged to the minority community. In its anxiety to placate the public, it ignored the fact that the passengers were soft targets and the killings were not easily preventable.

As regards Mizoram, once the security forces gained an upper hand the terrorist groups became demoralized. The loss of sanctuaries in the Chittagong Hills Tract in Bangladesh was a serious setback. But the situation took a dramatic turn for the better only after a political accord with the Mizo National Front was reached in 1986. The front was swept into power in the assembly elections that followed the accord.

In the case of Jammu and Kashmir, while there are some similarities with the Punjab experience, there are also vital differences. In the case of both Punjab and Jammu and Kashmir, the ideological base of terrorism was built around religion: to create a divide between the Hindus and the Sikhs in Punjab and the Hindus and the

Muslims in Jammu and Kashmir. There is, however, a big difference. In the case of Punjab, while Pakistan did jump into the fray and assisted the terrorist groups in Punjab, it did so in a covert manner because Pakistan at no time had any territorial dispute with India over Punjab. On the other hand, in the case of Jammu and Kashmir, Pakistan has been more directly involved. Since 1947, it has been trying to annex Jammu and Kashmir because it considers annexation to be the unfinished task of the partition. There is no doubt an internal dimension also, but the terrorist movement is being sustained entirely by external forces, most notably the support it receives from Pakistan. The movement in Jammu and Kashmir could not have been sustained without Pakistani support. This external dimension makes the task of finding an internal political solution to the problem difficult. The dispersal of some of the Kashmiri population across the Line of Control makes the task even more complicated. However, the situation would not have deteriorated to the extent it did if the state government had paid more attention to public grievances against the state administrative and political machinery.

In the case of the Northeast, the short-sighted approach to the problem that advocates a policy of "faster integration into the mainstream" is to some extent responsible for the alienation of the local people and the growth of terrorism. Lack of understanding about what hurts the people and lack of support for economic and security policies followed by the government have only succeeded in alienating the people. Lack of social and economic development has created a fertile environment for the spread of terrorism. More attention needs to be paid to creating job opportunities and improving the infrastructure, such as roads and electrical power.

By twisting historical facts and religious folklore, terrorist movements have been able to develop an ideology and rhetoric of their own. Ideology and rhetoric are heard with hope and reverence by their supporters. Fired by religious fervor and revolutionary ideology, the young recruits have no hesitation in ruthlessly attacking the decayed political and moral order of what they perceive to be hedonistic societies. But the fact also remains that terrorism in all the states grew out of the people's anger against the ruling political elite. The orations in places of worship of Sikhs, the *gurdwaras* in Punjab, and the mosques in Jammu and Kashmir against the prevailing moral decadence played the most crucial role in mobilizing the people behind the terrorists.

The Indian experience clearly shows that the terrorists' main aim was to acquire political power and wealth. Extortion, therefore, has become an essential component of the terrorist strategy, especially in the Northeast. Ideology has taken a back seat. The ideologies of some groups have also undergone major changes. In the initial stages, most of the movements demanded only political and economic justice and autonomy in the existing political system. Movements like that of the Bodos, a tribal group in Assam, and the Sikhs in Punjab began making secessionist demands as the movements gained momentum. The People's War Group in Andhra Pradesh and Bihar is concerned with economic and political justice for the deprived sectors of the society. This they seek to secure by replacing the existing political structure, which according to them is unfair and serves only vested interests. So far they have not demanded secession and independence from the Indian union.

It has been part of the terrorist strategy to provoke the government to respond to the acts not only of terrorists but of those who are sympathetic to terrorist causes. Repression, in fact, increases popular disaffection and generates popular support for terrorist demands. It justifies terrorist methods to settle scores with government and security forces. Some terrorist acts are deliberately committed to provoke a vicious cycle of violence and counter-violence. Caught in the cross fire, the victims generally blame the security forces, not the terrorists, for their miseries.

The Indian experience in different states underlines the need to reduce ethnic and social inequalities, narrow disparities in educational and employment opportunities, and create an effective machinery for the redress of public grievances. Steps to reduce economic deprivation can erode the base of public support on which extremist movements thrive. Improved opportunities for raising individuals' economic status can take the sting out of extremist movements. Most people are more concerned with their daily lives than with supporting a terrorist movement. It is easier to find solutions to seemingly intractable political problems in an environment in which people are by and large satisfied with the functioning of the government than in an environment of popular dissatisfaction.

The fact that successive governments in Jammu and Kashmir were dominated by a few families sent a wrong message to the people. These governments were seen as corrupt and self-seeking and an imposition by the central government. The people in the state blamed the central government for their miseries and for imposing corrupt governments on them. The imposition of the government of Bakshi Gulam Mohammed, the removal of Bakshi, the appointment of G. M. Sadiq as the chief minister, the dismissal of Farooq Abdullah, and then his return after the much maligned pact between the Congress Party and the National Conference were all perceived by the people in the valley as part of the conspiracy to deprive them of their fundamental, political, and economic rights. This perception is deeply embedded in their consciousness, making them a vulnerable target for terrorism and anti-India forces. This impression needs to be changed. The democratic process should be allowed to function without antidemocratic pressure or hindrance. While the authorities need to send a clear signal to the terrorists that they have the capability and determination to prevent and punish terrorist acts, the use of force need not be indiscriminate and vindictive.

Long-term solutions can be found only by reducing the alienation of the people. This goai can be achieved by displaying greater sensitivity to the people's separate identities and taking concrete steps toward fulfilling their political and economic aspirations. Encroachment on tribal land by immigrants has to be stopped and land that has been misappropriated restored to the indigenous tribal groups. The remoteness of the region can be reduced by reestablishing the old links—road, rail, and water—through Bangladesh to facilitate trade and traffic.

CONCLUSION

A more comprehensive security policy that addresses both national and international concerns has to be developed. Pakistan does not appear to be in a mood to reverse its policy of aiding and abetting terrorism in India in the near future. Without giving up the hope for improved relations with Pakistan, or for a concerted international action against terrorism, India will have to fight the

battle against terrorism and insurgency by relying on its own strength and resources.

India will be more than willing to cooperate with the international community to control terrorism. It has signed a number of bilateral agreements with countries like Egypt and is taking an active role in building a consensus against terrorism in the United Nations. It is against countries providing sanctuary to terrorist groups on religious or ideological grounds. India today does not give sanctuary to any external terrorist group, but it expects its neighbors to do the same.

Foreign-sponsored terrorism cannot make much headway if the internal environment in the country does not support it. A sense of insecurity among the minorities provides terrorism an opening in which to take root. It is important to win the confidence of minority groups. But more than anything else it is economic policies that will determine the future of these movements. A thriving economy, which gives hope to people, is more likely to defeat all types of extremist movements than any other strategy. Violent extremist movements grow more easily under conditions of poverty and misrule. Corruption and nepotism have provided the bedrock for the growth of terrorist movements in India. This has been true of all the affected areas in the country—Jammu and Kashmir, Punjab, the Northeast, Bihar, and Andhra Pradesh.

The need for a well-coordinated security apparatus can hardly be overemphasized. The police, paramilitary forces, army, and intelligence agencies have to coordinate their efforts if they are to win the battle against subversive forces. For as long as possible, dealing with extremist violence should be entirely the responsibility of the police and paramilitary forces. The army should not normally be entrusted with the task of dealing with internal security problems. But it has to undertake this role when the police or the paramilitary forces are unable to cope with the situation on their own. There may not be any alternative to deploying the army in proxy war situations when the police are unable to cope with terrorism. A composite force, including the police, paramilitaries, and the army, organized along the lines of the NSG has proved to be most effective in dealing with terrorism, as it demands a different type of expertise than what is available at present with separate institutions operating independently.

POSTSCRIPT

THE TRAGIC SEPTEMBER 11, 2001, terrorist attacks on the United States in New York and Washington and the two suicide attacks in India—one against the State Legislative Assembly in Srinagar on October 1, 2001, and the other on the Indian Parliament on December 13, 2001—have shocked the nation as never before. These dramatic events have brought the issue of national security and terrorism to the forefront of the national agenda. Even though India has been a victim of terrorism from Pakistan and Afghanistan for many years, no one had seriously believed that the terrorists could go to such extremes. India has been repeatedly warning the international community about the grave threat international terrorism poses to world peace, but its warnings were not taken seriously. It is now slowly sinking in that the fanatic terrorists can go to any extreme, including the use of weapons of mass destruction.

Even before these incidents, there was enough evidence available to suggest that Osama bin Laden and his Al Qaeda network were behind many of the terrorist incidents in Jammu and Kashmir. Terrorism feeds on pathological hatred, and combined with religious fanaticism it is a deadly mixture. The Pakistani and Islamic fundamentalist hatred of the Hindus and India has to be seen in the context of India's partition in 1947. It is not a coincidence that the Taliban drew much of its inspiration from the Deoband School of Islam, which is located in India not far from Delhi. All evidence points to the fact that after being pushed out of Afghanistan Osama bin Laden, his network, and these self-proclaimed protectors of Islam may have moved into the tribal area of the North West Frontier Province and Pakistan Occupied Kashmir, where already a number of terrorist training camps sponsored by the ISI and the Al Qaeda network are functioning. The October 1 incident in Srinagar and the December 13 incident in Delhi point to the fact that the terrorist movement, at least in the short run, could be intensified by Pakistan. The remnants of defeated Taliban from Afghanistan are likely to move into Jammu and Kashmir. The fact that since September 11 there has been an escalation of terrorism in Jammu and Kashmir gives credence to this belief.

Indian policymakers have no option but to confront this menace squarely. These incidents have proved that appeasement only in-

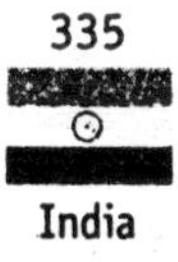

creases the terrorists' appetite for more blood. Suicide terrorists are brought up and sustained on uninterrupted hatred for a people belonging to another religion or ethnic group. In their zeal to impose their type of Islam and settle scores with the Hindu community, India is an obvious target. The ruling establishment in Pakistan, which is dominated by the army, survives on this hatred of what it calls "Hindu India." Of course, its members conveniently forget the fact that in the world today India has the second-largest population of Muslims (after Indonesia).

The terrorist outfits that are active in India, especially in Jammu and Kashmir, like Jaish-e-Mohammad, Lashker-e-Toiba, and Hizbul Mujahideen have their roots in Pakistan and are closely linked to the Al Qaeda network. They have joint training camps and common sources of huge funds. Since the roots of crossborder terrorism against India lie in Pakistan and Afghanistan, Indian policymakers have naturally approached the international community to take note of it and act before it is too late. The defeat of the Taliban is not going to end terrorism. Various terrorist networks are likely to regroup and commit more daring and sensational acts. The use of weapons of mass destruction—biological, chemical, and nuclear—cannot be ruled out. Pakistan can provide them with the necessary expertise and equipment to produce these weapons. Pakistan is part of the problem and will become a part of the solution only if the West mounts strong pressure on the Pakistani establishment to give up this double game of making a distinction between acts of terrorism by the so-called freedom fighters and those by the terrorist groups.

With the changing nature and intensity of the threat, a reassessment of India's response at various levels of organizational structure and preparation to respond to major terrorist incidents is under way. There is tremendous pressure by an enraged public to respond effectively against the cross-border terrorism that has been waged by Pakistan for the last twenty years. It wants India to raise the cost of terrorism to the sponsoring country. Available policy options range from diplomacy to covert action, physical security enhancement, and military force. India has enacted a new law against terrorism. The Prevention of Terrorism Act has already been enacted, although its passage in the two houses of Parliament involved a lot of controversy. All the major political parties are unanimous, however, that there is a need to strengthen the legal mechanisms that deal with terrorism. An intensive campaign has been launched to plug the various channels of funding to the terrorist groups. The recovery of rupees 50 lakhs (equivalent to about one hundred thousand dollars) from a vehicle in Srinagar in Jammu and Kashmir in November 2001 and rupees 35 lakhs from Delhi in January 2002 are one result of the intensification of this drive. Efforts are also under way to build a political consensus in the country to deal with religious fundamentalism and extremism.

The Kashmiri conflict between India and Pakistan is not a territorial dispute but an important part of the Islamic Jihad being waged by Islamic fundamentalists operating from countries like Pakistan, Saudi Arabia, and Afghanistan during the Taliban occupation. Security experts have warned of an activation of Pakistani, Taliban, and Al Qaeda combined sleeper cells dormant in India. The root of the terrorist scourge in India is not the Lashker-e-Toiba or Jaish-e-Mohammad but their common father—the hardliner religious fanatics in the Pakistani military. Without reform of the Pakistani power structure, there will be no end to terrorism in this region.

JAPAN

Isao Itabashi and Masamichi Ogawara,
with David Leheny

TOKYO HAS FOR MOST of the postwar period enjoyed a reputation as one of the safest and most secure metropolitan areas in the world. Perhaps it was this reputation that made the March 20, 1995, attack on the Tokyo subway system by Aum Shinrikyo (hereafter, Aum) such a shock to domestic and international audiences alike. Releasing packages of sarin gas on different subway trains converging on Kasumigaseki Station, the subway stop for Japan's major bureaucratic organs, the religious cult fortunately managed to kill only 12 people. Roughly 5,500 were injured, however, with many of them still suffering from the effects of the gas attack years after the incident. This was not the first time that Aum had engaged in an attack with chemical weapons. On June 27, 1994, the group used sarin in Matsumoto City in Nagano Prefecture (north of Tokyo) in an incident that killed 7 and injured nearly 150. At the time, police had been mystified by the incident and had not blamed Aum.[1] Nor did the group plan to stop its attacks. After the subway incident, police investigators found that the cult had developed other chemical agents, such as VX gas, tabun, and soman, and had also grown biological agents like the anthrax bacillus and *Clostridium botulinum*.

The attacks could have turned out to be much worse than they ultimately were. After all, Aum was prepared to kill indiscriminately and had the means to do so. The subway incident has forced Japanese law enforcement authorities to reevaluate the nation's preparedness against terrorism, a problem that had until then seemed largely irrelevant on Japanese soil. Moreover, the attack has clearly served as a catalyst to encourage a rethinking of security policies in other nations, including the United States. After all, the lessons of the Aum experience were not limited to Japan, nor can we assume that counterterrorism specialists were the only ones paying attention. Groups with an inclination to develop weapons of mass destruction for terrorist violence must also have watched the developments in the Aum case with great interest.

Japan's apparently lax stance toward terrorism was further challenged less than two years later when a left-wing Peruvian organization, the Tupac Amaru Revolutionary Movement (MRTA), raided the Japanese ambassador's residence in Lima during a party to celebrate the Japanese emperor's birthday. Taking nearly seven hundred hostages, including prominent officials from Japan, Peru, and other nations, the group made four principal demands to the Peruvian government: the release of all MRTA colleagues held in Peruvian jails, safe transport to the central Amazon region, changes in economic policy, and payment of a war tax. The MRTA captors released hostages in stages but still held key personnel for 127 days. Then, on April 22, 1997, Peruvian forces raided the compound, freeing the seventy-one remaining hostages and killing all of the MRTA rebels. One hostage and two members of the rescue party were killed in the attack. The MRTA's demands did not focus on Japan. Instead, the group took advantage of the close ties between Japan and Peru and the relatively light security surrounding the party in order to capture hostages that might make the Peruvian government blink. Even so, the crisis convinced the Japanese government of the need to improve its security and counterterrorism measures for Japanese nationals and Japanese interests overseas. In spite of Japan's economic importance, its low political profile had evidently lulled the government into a more easygoing security stance than was required; the Peruvian case has now forced the Japanese government to reevaluate its stance.

Even armed with this incentive, however, the Japanese government's steps toward counterterrorism policy have been tightly constrained by institutional legacies, political disputes, and constitutional restraints. Because of the strict limits on police and military power in postwar Japan, the government can shift policy even on such an important topic as terrorism only incrementally. In this essay, we examine the nature of these constraints, documenting as well the nature of the terrorist attacks that have provoked revisions in the government's approach to domestic and international terrorism.[2] Although Japan's counterterrorist capacities are still nowhere near as extensive as those in the United States, for example, the country has made some changes that—even if they are subtle and minor when viewed from overseas—demonstrate a dramatic rethinking of the problem among key policymakers in the Japanese context. Moreover, the organizational structure displays another, potentially more serious problem: because of the way in which security and police roles are limited, terrorism is not treated as a discrete political issue requiring a response but rather as a subset of other types of crises, which include natural disasters and accidents. As a result, some of the main responses in recent years have bracketed terrorism as part of a larger series of challenges facing Japan rather than a narrowly construed security threat that might deserve a more focused strategy.

In the remainder of this essay, we trace the evolution in the police and military roles in postwar Japanese politics, showing first that these two institutions operate in a constrained legal and political environment. We then discuss specific terrorist threats to Japan and the main legislative responses to them. After detailing the changing organizational structure of the Japanese government with regard to counterterrorism, we turn to some of the specific capabilities of these organizations, focusing especially on changes in intelligence analysis, law enforcement, and military potential. Finally, we examine the importance that the Japanese government places on its international relationships, which the government uses in part to offset its limitations and domestic challenges. Although these diplomatic efforts might normally be seen to be at best tangential aspects of a counterterrorism stance, Japan's political and legal environment enforces on decision makers constraints that can in some ways be overcome only through coordination and cooperation with other actors. Japan's security vulnerability thus pushes the government toward nuanced strategies that are designed to mitigate the consequences of a limited military and police role by making incremental improvements where possible and cooperating with other governments to the fullest extent possible.

THE POLICE AND THE MILITARY IN POSTWAR JAPANESE POLITICS

By 1947, when the Japanese Constitution was enacted, Japan was struggling to rise from the ashes of defeat. Written by the U.S. Occupation authorities with input from Japanese leaders, the Japanese Constitution aimed at both democratization and pacification. It established the concept that sovereignty resides with the people rather than the emperor (who is relegated to purely symbolic status), that the citizens of Japan would enjoy democratic civil liberties (which are actually more clearly articulated in the Japanese than in the U.S. Constitution, in part because of the progressive instincts of the Occupation authorities), and that—most famously—the Japanese government would forever renounce the right of war. Enshrined in Article IX of the Constitution, this aspect is one of the foundational elements of postwar Japan's political system. Between this renunciation and the guarantees of liberty (including freedom of religion, assembly, association, speech, press, and expression), the government faces significant constraints on the types of counterterrorism strategy it can pursue.

Japan's is a parliamentary system, with supreme legislative authority resting in the bicameral Diet, especially in its more powerful Lower House. The prime minister—chosen from the party or coalition with a majority of seats in the Lower House—selects a cabinet, which is constitutionally entrusted with the main administrative rights of the government. These cabinet ministers usually serve for short terms, generally of only a few years per position, limiting their expertise in comparison with the highly professional bureaucrats who work beneath them. And so, while the Constitution guarantees

that the Diet has supreme authority because of its ability to establish by proxy a cabinet that oversees the organs of the state, as a matter of course the bureaucrats are in a position to affect policy by writing the texts of the laws that are submitted to the Diet by cabinet ministers. This does not mean that they can run roughshod over the Diet; the Diet can, of course, reject laws as easily as it can pass them. The general pattern that has emerged in postwar Japan has been of a large, professional, organizationally oriented bureaucracy that proposes administrative solutions to problems but is mindful of key fault lines in the Diet that might lead to the embarrassing rejection of legislative proposals.

In the postwar period, no division has been more clear than that over the role of the military. In 1960, demonstrators took to the streets to protest the extension of the U.S.-Japan Security Treaty, which included in it guarantees of Japanese Self-Defense Forces' (SDF) involvement in the defense of Japan. The left-wing Socialist Party attempted to blockade the Diet floor, leading Prime Minister Kishi to order their arrest; the extension thus passed easily, with the largest opposition party out of the picture. Although successful, Kishi faced such condemnation that he had to step down, persuading subsequent Japanese prime ministers and cabinets that—whatever else they did—they would have to be very, very careful about extensions of military or police power.

The situation has not been purely static, of course. Japanese governments have successively encouraged reinterpretations of the Constitution to allow for a more expansive Japanese role in international security, particularly in response to the heavy criticism Japan faced due to its relative inaction in the Gulf War. Moreover, heavy criticism of fraud, waste, and mismanagement in the government generated calls for administrative reform, which involves the fundamental recasting and consolidation of key ministries. Even so, this pattern of policy-making and its bias against a more expansive role for the Japanese state in security are among the enduring features of postwar Japanese politics.

This modus operandi appeared to be highly stable during most of the thirty-eight-year reign of the Liberal Democratic Party (LDP), which fractured in 1993 and suffered its first Lower House defeat since 1955. Since then, the alignments of parties have been highly unstable and, although a new electoral law was predicted to create pressures toward the formation of a two-party system, Japanese lawmakers and bureaucrats alike have labored in the late 1990s and the early twenty-first century under conditions of intense instability. With the LDP recently in a curious and unwieldy coalition with New Komeito (a party tied to a religious sect with both conservative social views and strong pacifist tendencies) and the small Conservative Party, and confronted by growing but still ideologically diffuse parties like the Democratic Party, few seem willing to promote bold revisions of sensitive political topics such as military force or an extension of police powers. In particular, Prime Minister Mori's popularity has been so weak that potentially divisive political issues like these must seem like unacceptable risks for legislative action.

These divisions have been critical in recent developments in Japanese counterterrorism policy, which we will later examine in more detail. To give an illustrative example, however, the LDP tried to extend the government's counterterrorist capabilities after the Aum attack in 1995 by introducing new bills to enhance the country's security stance. By adding new laws and revising the Police Act (the basic law governing the National Police Agency), the LDP tried to strengthen the hand of law enforcement authorities against the possibility of future terrorist violence. Clearly, this would have been the time to make such changes (which were of course desirable to the bureaucrats helping to write the revisions), given the public mood toward Aum and terrorism in general. Even so, a government proposal to pass a wiretapping bill and to apply the Antisabotage Law to Aum met with intense criticism in the Diet. In particular, the Democrats and the Communist Party insisted that the bill would lead to abuses by the authorities, who would leap at the chance for more discretionary authority. Both parties explained that this growth in state authority would deprive Japanese citizens of fundamental political and human rights. The LDP countered that "wiretapping is part of public welfare" but said that it would "take fundamental human rights . . . into full consideration" by establishing stringent procedures governing the conditions under which the law could be invoked. When the LDP introduced a bill to curtail Aum's activities, informally dubbed the "Anti-Aum bill," opposition parties once again rallied against it. The LDP revised it substantially, narrowing its scope to only "those organizations that have committed indiscriminate mass murder," stating quite clearly that the law targeted Aum and no one else. We will return to this legal development.

The point here is not to castigate either side but simply to point out the tension involved in Japanese counterterrorism policy. Because of the memory of extensive police and military power in prewar Japan and the country's pride in a nonmilitarist Constitution that guarantees extensive democratic liberties, policymakers face tight limits on what they can do in the fight against terrorism.

JAPAN'S POSTWAR EXPERIENCE WITH TERRORISM

These limits strike many observers as mystifying, in part because Japan has faced significant terrorist threats that in other countries might have provoked more extensive revisions of counterterrorist doctrine. We turn now to Japanese terrorist violence as well as the threat of attacks against Japan, detailing particular public and legal responses to specific acts. The next section discusses in more depth the overall rubric of Japanese counterterrorism policy.

The Japanese Red Army's Early Violence

In particular, the Japanese Red Army (JRA) was long regarded as one of the world's most dangerous terrorist organizations because of the unpredictable and astonishingly violent nature of its attacks. Founded by Fusako Shigenobu, Tsuyoshi Okudaira, and others in Lebanon in 1970 as the Kyosando Sekigun-ha (Communist League—Red Army Faction), the early JRA began operating internationally immediately with its ambitious "Plan of International Bases," which were to be used in a conflict against global imperialism and capitalism.[3] The first terrorism attack caused by the Kyosando Sekigun-ha at this time was the Japan Airlines jetliner (Yodo-go) hijacking case.[4] From their Lebanese base, the group made contact with Palestinian terrorist organizations, like the Popular Front for the Liberation of Palestine (PFLP). By May 1971, the group had been joined by future leaders and strategists Koji Wakamatsu and Masao Adachi and would in 1972 form a coalition with another leftist organization in Japan itself. During a hostage crisis in Nagano Prefecture (where Aum would later test its sarin gas in its initial attack), the Japanese police arrested the members of the JRA's allies in Japan, discovering that the group had even killed twelve of its own members. Losing their organizational infrastructure in Japan, the nascent JRA temporarily renamed itself the Arab Red Army and issued a statement of farewell to its colleagues in Japan. Within days, it carried out the infamous Lod Airport Massacre in Tel Aviv on March 30, 1972, and would commemorate the date as the "birthday of the Japanese Red Army."[5]

The JRA's attacks have been legendary for their ambition and shock value, especially in the early to mid-1970s. In the Lod Airport Massacre, for example, JRA members sprayed the airport lobby with gunfire, also throwing grenades into the crowd. Fourteen people were killed, out of a total of roughly one hundred casualties. Two of the assailants were themselves killed in the attack, and the third was arrested by Israeli authorities and sentenced to life in prison, although he was released in a prisoner exchange deal with the PFLP; he then rejoined the JRA.

In 1973, JRA member Osamu Maruoka and four Palestinians hijacked a Japan Airlines (JAL) jetliner bound for Tokyo from Paris. After stopovers in the United Arab Emirates and Syria, the plane arrived at its final destination in Libya. Releasing the hostages, the group blew up the plane and surrendered to the Libyan government. At the same time, JAL headquarters received a ransom demand, although the crisis ended before the deal would have been made.

Using plastic explosives, two JRA and two PFLP members blew up storage tanks of a Shell Oil affiliate in Singapore and seized the company-owned ferry. They demanded that the Singaporean government provide an airplane for safe passage. A week later, five Palestinians, acting in concert with the terrorists in Singapore, stormed the Japanese embassy in Kuwait, taking sixteen embassy staff members hostage, including the ambassador. They demanded safe passage by air for the four people in Singapore and themselves. The Japanese government finally accepted the demands, claiming that its highest priority should be to secure the lives of the hostages. The government then sent a special JAL plane to pick up the terrorists in Singapore and Kuwait, flying them to South Yemen, where they all surrendered to local authorities.

Although the Japanese government had not been the target of either the Lod Airport Massacre or the Dubai incident, policymakers felt that they had no choice but to negotiate with the terrorists in the Singapore and Kuwait actions. Perhaps setting for itself a dangerous precedent, the Japanese government acceded to the demands. Although it may not have been considered part of Japanese doctrine on the issue, the government's willingness to negotiate established a pattern of protecting the lives of citizens, even at the expense of credibility or the ability to crush terrorism, that would have ramifications for future options.

Japan dodged a bullet in 1974 when the French government uncovered a plan to abduct Japanese diplomats and representatives of major trading firms in Europe; twelve JRA members were apprehended, and eight were deported by the French. In August, however, the Japanese government was forced to release five JRA prisoners in exchange for fifty-three hostages taken by the JRA at the consulate section of the American embassy in Kuala Lumpur. Together with their freed colleagues, the terrorists were flown to Tripoli, where they surrendered. The French government would have a less favorable encounter with the JRA later in 1974, when four of the group's members took eleven hostages, including the ambassador, at the French embassy in the Hague. The French government released one of the terrorists who had been taken in the earlier plot and provided an escape plane; the Dutch government paid a $300,000 ransom to the group, which ultimately had to fly to Syria to surrender to cooperative authorities.

In spite of these problems, it would take the hijacking of another JAL flight, this one from Paris to Tokyo via Bombay in September 1977, to initiate a fundamental rethinking of Japanese counterterrorism policy. The JRA members forced the plane to land in Dacca, Bangladesh, and demanded a $6 million ransom and the release of comrades held in prison in Japan. Fearing that the 151 passengers and crew would be killed, the Japanese government paid the ransom and attempted to release all of the JRA prisoners, although two refused to go. The JRA released most of the hostages and flew to Kuwait and Syria, where they freed several more. They released the remaining passengers and crew upon their arrival in Algeria.

A Tentative Shift in Policy

The willingness to pay ransom to ensure the safety of the hostages was publicly supported at the highest levels of the Japanese government. Prime Minister Takeo Fukuda, for example, remarked that "a life is heavier than the earth," meaning that the protection of life ought to be afforded nearly sacred priority. On one level, this seems like a natural response for a pacifist country trying to escape a militarist past. But Germany, with which Japan's behavior has often been compared, has adopted a different stance. When the West German Red Army Faction hijacked a Lufthansa airliner at roughly the same time as the Dacca incident, the West German government declared that, "for the sake of freedom and democracy," it would not negotiate with terrorists. It carried out a successful rescue operation with a special military unit, GSG9, saving all of the hostages. Although other governments negotiated with terrorists under certain conditions, the inability of the Japanese government to conceive of an alternative strategy suggests that the Japanese stance was distinctive.

The Dacca incident, however, represented a turning point. Justice Minister Hajime Fukuda resigned to take responsibility for the incident, and his successor, Minister Setoyama, said in his first press conference that "it is regrettable that our constitutional, law-abiding system, which has been established only with the enormous efforts of the Japanese people, would be destroyed by violent acts of small terrorist groups. We have to show our determination to protect our society at any cost in such cases." Pointing out that the release of prisoners clearly violated Japanese law, Fukuda told the Diet's Lower House Justice Committee that "as a law-abiding nation, we should never again make a decision that is inconsistent with our laws. We should stand by that policy even if it results in the sacrifice of some lives."

Setoyama's strident message was not necessarily popular among Japanese citizens, many of whom believed that the government really should protect life at all costs. In a poll conducted by the Prime Minister's Office after the Dacca incident, respondents were asked to comment on the government's decision to effect an extralegal release of prisoners and to pay ransom. In the poll, 64 percent of respondents supported the government's position, saying that it had had no choice. Only 23 percent argued that the government should not have made the concessions. With regard to government priorities in future hijacking cases, 62 percent said that "the government should make the lives of hostages its priority," while 24 percent said that "the government should take a stern approach to protect law and order, even though lives may be lost."[6]

The subsequent Bonn Summit in 1978 placed international terrorism, especially hijacking, onto the agendas of the world's leading industrialized democracies, leading them toward a more focused stance against terrorism. In an effort to bring Japan's standards and practices into line with those discussed at the summit, the government created a special task force on sabotage, including hijacking, and established a special policy "to act against hijacking and other violent activities." Stating clearly that Japan would not negotiate with terrorists, the government made a radical shift in its counterterrorism stance and was able to weld its position more tightly to those increasingly evident in the other advanced industrialized nations.[7] Subsequent summits (the sixth in Venice, the seventh in Ottawa, and the tenth in London) produced further statements and declarations of international cooperation against terrorism, and these have been made every year since the twelfth meeting in Tokyo. At the thirteenth summit, in Venice, the "no concessions" principle, which had been under discussion for years among the nations, was clearly articulated. This principle has formed the core of international cooperation against terrorism and has since underscored the basic approach of the Japanese government. But the view among Japanese citizens that the government should negotiate rather than lose lives would of course make the reaction to a hostage crisis more problematic for a Japanese administration.

The Fate of the JRA

Since the Dacca incident, which forced this fundamental shift in Japan's approach to terrorism, the Japanese government has been fortunate in that its resolution on the issue has not been tested. The JRA attempted to rename itself the Anti-imperialism International Brigade (AIIB) and fired projectiles into the Japanese and American embassies at Jakarta in 1986, also detonating a car bomb in front of the Canadian embassy. A year later, during the Venice Summit, the AIIB launched projectiles into the American and British embassies in Rome, also using another car bomb in a parking lot near the American embassy. In 1988, a car bomb outside of a United Service Organizations (USO) club in Naples exploded, killing five people, including an American serviceman, and injuring seventeen others. This time, a group calling itself the "Organization of Jihad Brigade" claimed responsibility. Although none of these has been linked definitively to the JRA, its members are the prime suspects in all three incidents. Moreover, the JRA is believed to have been involved in a November 1986 crisis with the communist New People's Army of the Philippines, when militants took hostage the general manager of the Manila office of a major Japanese trading firm.

The JRA has not disappeared. Although apparently it has not carried out any terrorist attacks since the bombing in Naples, a number of its members are at large. The U.S. State Department still lists the JRA as a "foreign terrorist organization," pursuant to the Antiterrorism and Effective Death Penalty Act of 1996, and its aging members still appear to be committed to the fight. Others, however, have been arrested around the world. One was seized in Tokyo as he tried to enter the country with a forged passport. Another was arrested in New Jersey in April 1988 and is still being held in the United States. The end of the Cold War, progress in the Middle East peace process, and the subsequent closing of the group's base camp on the Bekaa Heights, Lebanon together conspired against many of the remaining members. In 1995–96, three more were detained and/or arrested in Peru, Bolivia, and Nepal, with two returned to Japan for arrest and the other deported to the United States for trial.

In February 1997, the Lebanese government arrested five JRA members in Beirut on a number of charges unrelated to terrorism. After sentencing them to three years in prison and, in some cases, heavy fines, the Lebanese authorities decided that they would be deported upon their release. After several appeals, the Lebanese Supreme Court upheld the decision to deport them, although one of the members, Kozo Okamaoto, was given political asylum in Lebanon. In response to their deportation to Japan on March 18, 2000, a group supporting the JRA wrote on its Web site, "Our four comrades were deported to Japan by force. We will never forgive the Japanese government. Their return marks a beginning of a new round in the fight." Their anger was probably exacerbated by the November 2000 arrest of Fusako Shigenobu, the JRA's founder, in Osaka. This leaves only seven JRA members (Junzo Okudaira, Kunio Bando, Norio Sasaki, Hisashi Matsuda, Ayako Daidoji, Akira

Nihei, and political exile Okamoto), who are believed to be free in Lebanon.

Time has not been kind to the JRA. A changing international political context, one that is less tolerant of terrorism as a component of superpower rivalry, together with international cooperation has made life more difficult for the organization. The remaining members are in their fifties, and most of their terrorist acts are probably behind them. Even so, they are still apparently determined to fight and ought to be considered a threat.

The Reorientation of Japan's Stance toward Terrorism

The Japanese government's position vis-à-vis terrorism is stated in the 1995 edition of its *Gaikō Seishō* (Diplomatic Blue Book), published by the Ministry of Foreign Affairs. In a section entitled "Terrorism and Japan's Position," it clearly says:

> In the event that Japanese nationals are taken hostage by terrorists who make unlawful demands of the government of Japan, the government, of course, will make the utmost efforts to ensure the release of the hostages in cooperation with the foreign government [on whose soil the crisis takes place] that has primary responsibility. At the same time, in order to prevent similar incidents in the future, it is necessary to take a firm stand based on the "no concessions to terrorists" principle, which has been confirmed repeatedly at the G-7 Summit meetings.

In the twenty years after the Dacca incident, the Japanese government fortunately avoided any instances that might have put its resolution to the test. But the Lima crisis of 1996–97 challenged its convictions. Although the MRTA made no direct demands of the Japanese government, the large number of Japanese lives at stake affected the government's stance vis-à-vis the Peruvian government and its planned response. The Japanese government's basic position was that "securing the lives of the hostages, while not giving in to terrorism, is the highest priority. We will make the utmost efforts to achieve a peaceful solution with the release of all hostages as soon as possible, trusting that the Peruvian government is also committed to solving the crisis peacefully." Of course, the Peruvian government's stance was different, and it soon began planning a dramatic rescue operation. While it maintained an emphasis on its attitude against any negotiation with terrorists, the Japanese government seemed to place far more emphasis on "the safety of the hostages" and the importance of a "peaceful resolution."

To a large degree, its nervous stance reflected public opinion. A poll conducted by a television network in the early days of the hostage crisis revealed that 55.2 percent of respondents agreed with the statement that the government should "make concessions with terrorists to protect the lives of the hostages," while only 40 percent encouraged the government "to refuse to give in to terrorism and to carry out rescue operations."[8] A subsequent poll displayed a slight shift in favor of the latter position, but one cannot deny the marked tendency of citizens to prefer the protection of innocent life even at the expense of the "no concessions" principle.

In accordance with G-7 and G-8 agreements, the government's stance on terrorism is clear: that it is "opposed to all forms of terrorism, that it must fight against terrorism in a resolute manner, that it must not make concessions to terrorists, and that "it must bring terrorists to justice for their crimes." Japan's commitment to its no concessions policy, however, was sorely tested in late 1999, when members of the Islamic Movement of Uzbekistan (IMU) kidnapped four Japanese geologists, among other hostages, during a raid in Kyrgyzstan. The Japanese hostages were released unharmed after two months, and Japanese newspapers reported rumors of a ransom deal by the government. The Japanese Ministry of Foreign Affairs has adamantly denied that a ransom was paid and has pointed out that political contacts were made in order to ensure a peaceful resolution to the matter without violating Japan's core policy on concessions. Even so, the widespread belief among newspaper readers that a deal was made points out the difficulty the Japanese government faces in its counterterrorism stance. Because so many Japanese citizens believe that concessions are acceptable if they save the lives of citizens, peaceful resolutions to hostage crises will almost certainly involve questions of whether the government adhered to its stated policy or capitulated to a public preference for prioritizing the lives of hostages over abstract principles of counterterrorism policy.

Equally important, the Japanese government cannot prevent private citizens from making their own deals to rescue employees or loved ones. During the standoff in Peru, a number of hostages, including Americans and Europeans, were released by the MRTA, which claimed that it had no quarrel with these nations. Some Japanese hostages, mainly employees of Japanese companies, were also released, and there were unconfirmed reports that their firms had paid a ransom to release them. Although we cannot know what happened, Japan's no concessions policy, like similar policies in other countries, constrains only the activities of the government and not those of firms or families trying to rescue their employees or loved ones. In other words, even if the government faithfully holds the line on refusing concessions it cannot—in the absence of repressive laws—prevent private citizens from negotiating settlements in order to return their loved ones, especially because there is no social consensus that negotiating with terrorist groups to save lives is wrong. The Japanese government can try to make a credible commitment with regard to Japanese officials stationed abroad, but private citizens are another matter.

This is assuredly one of the continuing problems for Japan. Although Japan lacks the political profile of, for example, the United States, its citizens are vulnerable to attack overseas because of the country's position as a visible economic superpower. As businesspeople, tourists, scholars, and the like, private Japanese citizens live all over the world without any Japanese military or security presence; they are easy, visible targets. In fact, during the MRTA's siege of the Japanese ambassador's residence, its commander, Nestor Cerpa, reportedly spoke with the hostages about the role of the Japanese government in Peru; with the support of President Fujimori, he claimed, Japanese companies were exploiting Peruvian workers and sending their money to Japan. Moreover, Japan's role as a major aid donor will likely only increase its vulnerability because of the possible view among revolutionary organizations that "Japan is supporting our government" or "Japan is exploiting our citizens in sweatshops." With the possibility of easy scores through the kidnapping of Japanese, especially private citizens who might be ransomed by their employers or families, it is clear that Japan needs to think more cogently about international terrorism than its leaders have generally believed. At present, eight hundred thousand Japanese live overseas and annually more than sixteen million travel abroad, not only in Asia but across the globe. Japanese nationals are, more than ever, likely to be involved in cases of international terrorism for which the government is inadequately prepared.

THE ORGANIZATIONAL STRUCTURE OF JAPAN'S COUNTERTERRORISM PROGRAMS

Among the difficulties faced in Japan's efforts to combat terrorism is the way in which "terrorism" is, as a conceptual category, collapsed into other political and policy problems. Perhaps because of the postwar allergy to the use of military and police force, the Japanese government has not traditionally viewed terrorism as a discrete phenomenon requiring a special set of solutions. Instead, terrorism is perceived as an issue for "crisis management," and the structure of Japanese counterterrorism programs displays some of the peculiar consequences of this way of categorizing the threat. We discuss in this section not only the overall thrust of Japanese counterterrorism policy—which is integrated into larger crisis management concerns—but also the nature of recent changes in Japan's organizations that deal with terrorism. Some of the shifts have clearly been responses to the Aum incident and perceived shortcomings in Japan's counterterrorism capabilities. Other, more recent developments, however, reflect a larger public policy initiative toward administrative reform. Although the reform effort is not directly tied to concerns over the government's counterterrorism capabilities, the remarkable consolidation of Japan's public policy organizations in 2001 may have lasting effects on the way the government deals with terrorism.

The Aum attack was not the only calamity faced by Japan in 1995, and the release of sarin gas on the subway only served to deepen a sense of complete crisis among policymakers and citizens alike. In addition to the deepening economic recession and the continued problems of successive coalition governments, Japan also experienced the catastrophic Kobe earthquake, in which more than five thousand people were killed. Even more so than with the Aum attack—after which legal authorities would face tough questions over why they had failed to scrutinize the cult more effectively—the Hanshin earthquake raised alarms over the government's slow pace in dealing with the disaster. Its tardiness may have been partly responsible for the great loss of life. Interestingly, in part because the sarin attack and the earthquake occurred only months apart, the two have been almost inextricably linked in the Japanese public imagination. That is, for most people the Aum attack was not an example of inadequate public order or security policies and the earthquake's death toll was not accepted as the simple cost of residing along the seismically frenetic Pacific Rim. Instead, both events cemented among many the sense that the Japanese government was ill equipped to handle crises or deal with rapid, cataclysmic events in a way that might minimize the loss of life.

And so, in spite of the legislative proposals put forward after the Aum attack, many of the lasting changes in Japan's stance vis-à-vis terrorism reflect the government's efforts to handle crises more effectively and convincingly. In April 1997 (only three months after the government's appalling handling of a Russian oil spill in the Sea of Japan, which only placed further pressure on it), the new position of deputy chief cabinet secretary for crisis management was created in order to consolidate Japan's ability to deal with problems like these in the future. This new emergency secretariat was centered around the Cabinet Office for National Security Affairs and Crisis Management and includes the Cabinet Information Research Office, the Cabinet Councillors' Office on Internal Affairs, the Cabinet Councillors' Office on External Affairs, and the Cabinet Public Relations Office. In other words, in the event of another terrorism crisis these organizations were supposed to play a fundamental leadership role within the Japanese government, a capacity that the nation had essentially lacked during the 1995 Aum events. The secretariat, when not faced with emergencies, has conducted case study research, compiled crisis management manuals, and built networks with research institutes in Japan and abroad. A massive administrative reform program (to be discussed) has, however, shifted these functions so much that the shape of Japanese crisis management policy in the future is difficult to predict.

At present, the National Police Agency (NPA) and, on the sea, the Japan Coast Guard are the front-line organizations for gathering and analyzing information on terrorism and for responding to specific threats. The Aum Shinrikyo affair made the NPA painfully aware of its intelligence capabilities as well as its lack of knowledge regarding chemical and biological weapons. As a result, one of the NPA's key goals in the past few years has been the improvement of its information-gathering and analytical capabilities. Moreover, it has been trying to upgrade its equipment and criminal identification capabilities. It has also created Special Assault Teams (SATs), which can be dispatched in the event of a terrorist incident. Unlike special forces teams of other nations, however, the SATs probably cannot be used overseas given current constitutional restrictions against the use of Japanese force. The Japan Coast Guard has created a Special Security Team (SST) with similar capabilities.

Additionally, the Aum Shinrikyo attack produced calls for Japan's Self-Defense Forces (which it maintains in lieu of a true military) to take measures against terrorism. The Ground Self-Defense Forces (GSDF)—Japan's version of an army—is now establishing a special research headquarters to examine possible measures against, for example, terrorism with biological weapons as well as other nonconventional and asymmetric modes of warfare. There are also plans to establish a special team to deal with cyberterrorism and possibly others that will be specifically antiterrorist and antiguerrilla units.

The Aum attack also inspired other policy organizations to think about how they might be able to contribute to Japan's ability to handle these crises in the future. Like the First Responder program in the United States, these efforts have focused on the challenges that would face national and local administrative bodies in the event of a chemical, biological, radiological, and nuclear (CBRN) attack on the nation. For example, Japan's Ministry of Health and Welfare has created a research group to study ways of dealing with the large-scale biological infection that might result from a terrorist attack using bioagents. During the Okinawa G-8 Summit in July 2000, this group drew up a counterterrorism plan and conducted a simulation of biological and chemical terrorism. Moreover, the Tokyo Fire Department set up a program in 1996 to train personnel to handle chemical disasters. It currently provides information on sarin gas and other poisonous substances and has been preparing rescue equipment for these kinds of crises.

As noted, however, the loss of faith among Japanese citizens in the government's ability to handle crises has dovetailed with larger public concerns over the state's almost hallucinatory mismanagement of the economy in the 1990s and repeated corruption scandals that would have made even the most hardened member of Tammany Hall blush. And so these efforts to improve the government's ability to handle terrorist crises have been overshadowed by larger administrative reform initiatives. The most striking of these occurred in January 2001, with the twenty-one cabinet-led ministries and agencies being consolidated into a collection of only twelve ministries and agencies in total. The decisions about which functions would continue to exist and which would be absorbed into new administrative programs were of course subject to heated political debate and bargaining. We will now sketch some of the relevant changes in the structure of Japan's counterterrorism policy, but we cannot predict how the government's overall abilities will be modified by these shifts.

The cabinet crisis management offices have been radically altered. For example, the Cabinet Office for National Security Affairs and Crisis Management, the Cabinet Councillors' Office on Internal Affairs, and the Cabinet Councillors' Office on External Affairs have been abolished and their functions and personnel are supposed to be integrated into the larger Cabinet Councillors' Office. The Cabinet Public Relations Office and the Cabinet Information Research Office will continue to exist, but their personnel system will be shifted away from the linear/hierarchical form common to Japanese public policy organizations and will emphasize instead lateral postings among organizations in order to generate some "cross-pollination" for policies. The recently established office of the deputy chief cabinet secretary for crisis management will still handle emergencies, but it is supposed to be staffed in a "flexible" manner in response to circumstances.

The National Police Agency and the Defense Agency (which is in charge of the Self-Defense Forces) will both be placed under the Cabinet Office. The Japan Coast Guard will be absorbed into the new Ministry of Land, Infrastructure, and Transport, while the Ministry of Health and Welfare (which is responsible for some of Japan's programs with regard to the public health consequences of a CBRN terrorist attack) will be reorganized into the Ministry of Health, Labor, and Welfare. Other counterterrorism programs, including those related to responses to fire departments' handling of chemical weapons incidents, will be subsumed under the new Ministry of Public Management, Home Affairs, and Posts and Telecommunications.

One of the goals of the overall drive toward reform in Japan's public administration system has been to reduce the bureaucratic divisions that have hampered public policies in the past. Just as American bureaucracies have been described as "stovepiped," referring to the tendency to divide policy initiatives and administrative goals, Japan's bureaucracy has often been categorized as a *tatewari-gyōsei,* or "vertically segmented administration." In other words, the intense organizational loyalty and professionalism of Japanese bureaucracies have traditionally made it even more difficult for policymakers to overcome divisions between, for example, the Ministry of International Trade and Industry and the Ministry of Transport. If these administrative reforms are successful, the efforts to promote the posting of officials in organizations other than their career homes may help to facilitate the generation of better policy ideas, which will ostensibly be more manageable when the smaller number of large bureaucratic organizations can consolidate plans more quickly. That said, the program itself is too new for anyone to be able to judge its effectiveness, and the shifts in personnel chains, lines of command, control over budgets, and professional training may be so complex as to make responses to terrorist crises in the next few years more difficult rather than less so.

We raise these issues not only to make the usual caveat: that predictions are difficult. At a more fundamental level, we cannot know what effects the administrative responses to the Aum affair might have had because Japan has suffered from few terrorist events since the 1997 changes and none on Japanese soil. As a result, perhaps the instructive developments were not in the institutional responses but rather in the types of questions and concerns that were raised. That is, with new institutional homes some of the programs face uncertain futures. But the prevailing sense that the Japanese government must upgrade its crisis management capabilities has not disappeared, and it still seems to be an important element in critiques of Japanese administrative practices. In other words, bureaucratic reorganization can produce serious difficulties for any researcher attempting to predict how the government will react to events in the future, but the social and political pressures behind the various counterterrorism programs have not dissipated. There is reason to believe that the memory of the Aum incident is fresh enough to ensure that, even in new environments, policymakers will consider the improvement of the government's crisis management capabilities to be one of the paramount responsibilities of the Japanese state.

LIMITED INTELLIGENCE CAPABILITIES

Japanese officials dealing with terrorism will continue to operate in an environment that constrains their ability to create an aggressive counterterrorist stance. In addition to the constitutional limits on police and military authority, the government grapples with weak intelligence-gathering capabilities that hamper proactive efforts to track and defend against potential threats. Japan does not possess intelligence-gathering organizations that can perform the roles of America's Federal Bureau of Investigation or Central Intelligence Agency. In the prewar period, the police elements of the powerful Home Affairs Ministry worked in concert with the military government, cracking down on free expression and thought, and as a consequence they were abolished during the U.S. Occupation. After the return to political independence, a number of suggestions were made to improve Japan's investigative and intelligence-gathering capabilities, but a national "allergy" to such activities is clear in public opinion and in the strong statements made by opposition parties. As a result, Japan's intelligence-gathering capabilities are highly constrained.

The Japanese government does maintain some intelligence-gathering organs in the NPA, the Ministry of Justice, the Defense Agency, and the Ministry of Foreign Affairs (among others). The coordination and use of the intelligence are, however, tightly circumscribed by constitutional limits as well as public opinion. Because of these constraints, new legislation has appeared that proposes greater flexibility for the government to investigate private communications in the investigation of crimes. Furthermore, the kind of nationwide intelligence-gathering organization that the FBI in some ways represents in the United States is absent in Japan. And, with the constitutional limits on the military, the role of Japan's Self-Defense Forces is even more tightly controlled, with its intelligence-gathering office limited to a staff of one hundred. They even acknowledge that their most important source is "newspaper clippings." As a consequence, Japan's intelligence-gathering capabilities are extraordinarily insufficient, especially with regard to foreign countries. Japan has no choice but to rely on its global allies for primary intelligence support.

The primary intelligence resource for the government has been the Cabinet Research Office, which is legally mandated to gather and analyze information related to important policies of the cabinet. Many of these have taken the form of survey research on Japanese social and economic policy, but among the office's 120 staff members are security specialists and officials on loan from the National Police Agency and the Defense Agency.[9] In the event of an emergency, such as a terrorist event, the deputy chief cabinet secretary for crisis management is supposed to take charge of this office to coordinate the collection of information on the crisis. As of 1996, again in response to criticism over the Aum incident, the office has a Situation Center that is manned at all times and is responsible for communicating emergency information to the deputy chief cabinet secretary. Additionally, the office has been working to upgrade its intelligence-gathering capabilities; there are plans to launch, between 2002 and 2007, two information-gathering satellites, which will be used in part for national security and crisis management purposes.

Of rather more importance to Japan's counterterrorism programs, however, is the ability of the National Police Agency to gather and analyze information that might help in suppressing political violence against Japanese. In response to the Aum attack and the Peruvian hostage crisis, the NPA has implemented various organizational reforms and new counterterrorist measures within the agency. An internal review conducted by the NPA after the Aum attack concluded that the agency lacked adequate knowledge of science and technology (especially regarding sarin gas, VX gas, and so on) and had had little information regarding antisocial criminal organizations, at least those unrelated to the violent leftist groups of the 1960s and 1970s.

To correct these deficiencies, the NPA undertook a number of reforms.[10] First, as a way of strengthening its investigative capabilities pertaining to science, it established new forensics units and a chemistry section to study the properties of sarin gas and other poisonous substances. In accordance with tightened legislation on the use of chemical weapons, the NPA has also established an Investigation Office for Special Cases, which is responsible for incidents such as the one involving Aum. A new Office for Counterterrorism has been established in the NPA's Foreign Affairs Division, and it also gathers, classifies, and manages information regarding terrorism by foreign nationals or Japanese based overseas.[11] Moreover, the NPA's Security Bureau now has a new Special Investigation Office for Suspicious Groups, which monitors the activity of those organizations considered likely to turn toward terrorism. A new Psychology Section also provides research regarding the behavioral patterns of suspects and victims of terrorist assaults. This section is primarily designed to handle kidnapping and hostage situations, their investigations, and their aftermath. To manage the NPA's intelligence capabilities, a new position—chief executive analyst—was established in the Security Bureau, and this official is expected to handle the intelligence functions that previously had been highly decentralized.

The Ministry of Justice also maintains a Public Security Investigation Agency (PSIA), which contributes somewhat to Japan's intelligence capabilities in counterterrorism. Especially with regard to new legislation against organizations that have engaged in indiscriminate mass murder (the terminology used to write a law that would provide investigators with more power vis-à-vis Aum but narrowly enough construed to avoid a veto by left-leaning parties in the Diet), the PSIA collects information in urban areas and on groups like religious cults.[12] This marks a shift in its orientation, away from the rural and suburban investigations of radical leftist organizations of the 1970s and 1980s. Additionally, the agency is reported to have increased its investigations of the movements of foreign nationals who enter and remain in Japan illegally as well as the movements of members of international terrorist groups who have entered Japan. Besides providing information gained from these investigative activities to relevant parts of the government, at the end of each year the agency publishes "Public Security in Japan and Overseas," a summary of public security trends in Japan and abroad. It also compiles and makes public such materials as the "Survey of International Terrorism," "Public Security Worldwide," and "Trends in International Terrorism."

The Ministry of Foreign Affairs (MOFA) includes an Intelligence and Analysis Bureau. The Intelligence and Analysis Bureau was established in 1993, when the Information Research Bureau, which handled policy planning affairs, was reorganized to concentrate primarily on the collection and analysis of information. The new bureau includes three divisions and uses as its primary sources written reports and telegrams from embassies and other overseas posts, foreign newspapers, magazine articles, and the like. Its emphasis is on broad, mid- to long-range reports that differ from the daily administrative handling of policy decisions.

Finally, the Defense Agency also maintains limited intelligence capabilities in addition to those of the Self-Defense Forces. The agency established in 1997 an integrated Information Headquarters, which combines some of the intelligence functions of the SDF and the Defense Agency. Of its sixteen hundred personnel, roughly one thousand work at six communications facilities around Japan, primarily to monitor radio communications.

Again, most of these offices are rather broadly targeted at collecting information on all manner of threats, developments, political changes, and the like. Japan does not possess intelligence capabilities rivaling those of, say, the United States, and it lacks the specific counterterrorism abilities displayed in something like the Counterterrorism Center (CTC) at the CIA. Even so, the Aum affair and to a lesser degree the Peruvian crisis have instigated a fundamental rethinking of how far the Japanese state can go in monitoring its citizens and foreign nationals in the goal of protecting national security.

CHANGING LAW ENFORCEMENT AND MILITARY CAPABILITIES

Japan has never faced a terrorist challenge that has risen to the level of a crisis for the state itself, and, as noted, political realities there tend to constrain the state in its use of military or police power. Perhaps for these reasons, Japan has never passed a law like America's Anti-terrorism and Effective Death Penalty Act or the United Kingdom's Terrorism Countermeasures Act. With the power of public opinion and moderate and left-leaning parties to undermine political stability, the LDP has had a difficult time trying to change the environment in which law enforcement agencies and the military counters terrorism. This does not mean, of course, that the police and the military are powerless. For example, the Anti-subversive Activities Law enables police to prevent groups that are known to use political violence from demonstrating, holding assemblies, and the like. Promulgated largely to deal with left-wing threats in the 1960s and 1970s, however, this law turned out to be useless in preventing Aum from organizing and was almost equally so in cracking down on the cult even after the attack. According to the head of the PSIA, the government clearly needed new legal tools with which to fight Aum.

The outcome of this challenge is somewhat instructive. As noted, this legal initiative was informally dubbed the Anti-Aum law. In Japan, as in other democracies governed by the rule of law, it is of course improper to have a law that specifies one target and neglects others; it must classify and categorize if it is to have a lawlike quality rather than a simple directive of political or personal vengeance (President Bush cannot, e.g., push Congress to enact an "anti-Clinton" law). Yet the Japanese moderate and leftist parties displayed their usual allergy to the growth of state police and military power by pushing for a narrow law. In other words, it could neither be a law against religious cults (which might presumably have infringed upon the constitutionally guaranteed freedom of religion) or for sterner, more general counterterrorism capabilities. Instead, to pass the bill the LDP—along with NPA and Ministry of Justice analysts—was forced to narrow it to the point where, although Aum is not named, there could be little doubt as to the law's target. The Law to Control Organizations That Engage in Acts of Indiscriminate Mass Murder (a name every bit as unwieldy in the original Japanese as in translation) therefore gives police broad powers of investigation and control vis-à-vis groups like Aum, though fortunately there are no other groups like Aum in Japan.

In other words, Japanese parties are sufficiently distrustful of police authority to ensure that, at least for the time being, changes in the Japanese legal environment for the investigation and prosecution of terrorists will be incremental at best. To be sure, the constraints forced on the Japanese government help to ensure the maintenance of Japan's vibrant civil liberties. But earlier laws, narrowly tailored to deal with leftist organizations that had used political violence in the 1970s, were of virtually no help to the Japanese authorities in tracking a religious cult that had developed weapons of mass destruction and was able to use them at least twice, killing nearly twenty people and injuring hundreds. The legal developments in the wake of the Aum incident therefore leave us with an important question: will changes in the Japanese legal environment be similarly useless in preventing future attacks?

Although the Japan Coast Guard is responsible for counterterrorism measures at sea and the Japan Defense Agency has a limited but growing role as well, the NPA is clearly the first line of defense against terrorism, and it is the organization most affected by the stringent political environment of postwar Japan. Until recently, the NPA lacked both national investigative rights and special action units for terrorism, meaning that police units in local prefectures tended to have jurisdiction over terrorism cases. One of the lessons of the Aum example is that Japan's complicated prefectural systems are poorly suited to the task of dealing with large-scale terrorist attacks or criminal actions because of the "rough going" that attends any sort of large-scale investigation. As a result, in recent years there have been revisions in laws governing the NPA in order to grant it more investigative powers and also to create antiterrorism posts and special forces around the country to prepare for the further possibility of a large terrorist attack. There have been suggestions that the NPA should have direct control over special antiterrorist forces, but because of the role of the police in state repression in the prewar period there has also been considerable opposition to this idea. As a result, the NPA's capabilities are still limited.

Because it has been so difficult to strengthen the NPA's hand, it is unclear how Japan will react to unconventional terrorist attacks in the future. In its planning for these kinds of crises, however, the NPA has been creative, at least within the tight constraints of Japan's legal environment. In addition to the Special Action Teams (which have now been dispatched twice to deal with hijacking cases, though in neither case were they actually used in a takedown), the NPA has added newer units.[13] After the Peruvian hostage incident, the Emergency International Terrorism Team was established, and it can be dispatched to the site of crises involving Japanese nationals to consult with the host government. At other times, it prepares strategies for coping with hostage crises. The Aum attack served as a wake-up call regarding the possibility of future assaults using nuclear, biological, or chemical (NBC) weapons, provoking the development of special teams to handle such incidents in the future. For example, the NPA has established an investigative unit armed with the most advanced equipment to allow it to handle an NBC event. In the same vein, the NPA has begun to prepare for the possibility of cyberterrorism with the creation of a High-Tech Crime Division, and in 2001, a new unit called the Cyberforce will be established. The Cyberforce's responsibility will be the management of unauthorized computer access and cyberterrorist incidents. It will also coordinate prefectural and local responses to more contained threats in the future. In the event of genuine unconventional attacks, however, it is difficult to see how the NPA can handle them without coordination with and the participation of the Self-Defense Forces. But constitutional limits as well as the organizational dynamics between the two make it unclear whether or how this might be achieved. The NPA's capabilities in this regard have improved, but it is hard to know whether they have improved enough.

The Japan Coast Guard has also upgraded its abilities by combining preexisting teams (including a security unit from a plutonium transport ship and a counterterrorism unit from Kansai Airport) into its Special Security Team. The SST, created in 1996, is small: forty members, armed primarily with German-made MP5s and flash-stun grenades. Because of the Aum incident and the Peruvian hostage crisis, the SST now conducts a variety of counterterrorism drills, martial arts training, helicopter landing drills, and the like. It has also received training from the U.S. Navy.[14]

Under the Anti-subversive Activities Law and the Law to Control Organizations That Engage in Acts of Indiscriminate Mass Murder, the PSIA has some power to maintain surveillance over certain organizations that might commit acts of terrorism. Its authority under the Anti-subversive Activities Law was never used, but under the new law targeted at Aum it has conducted investigations by entering thirty-three Aum premises. Even here, however, the PSIA's law enforcement capability is limited at best. It must first apply to another body, the Public Security Examination Commission, for permission to keep the organization under surveillance, and it can enter the premises of the organization only if the commission has allowed it to. The PSIA lacks almost any genuine investigative authority that matches the abilities of its personnel, and it must even get permission from the owner or tenant before it can conduct a search.[15]

The Special Defense Forces, which operate in lieu of the constitutionally banned armed forces, are permitted to defend Japan to protect the nation from direct or indirect invasion and may engage in action to preserve public order when the need arises.[16] They have never been mobilized in a terrorist attack, however, nor have they ever been used to maintain public order. At the time of the Aum attack, the Ground Self-Defense Forces' Chemical Rescue Team was dispatched at the request of the government officials in Osaka and Tokyo, who were no doubt alarmed at the inability of the national government to dispatch SDF units even after the cataclysmic Kobe earthquake in January of that year. Their duties were confined, however, to the detection and analysis of the dispersed chemical substance, and the use of counteragents for removal and cleanup. This disaster operation—the closest the SDF has come to involvement in a terrorist incident—involved two hundred personnel and ten cleanup vehicles.[17]

Before the Aum attack, it had actually been Japanese defense doctrine that counterterrorism measures were strictly the responsibility of the police forces and that the SDF did not intend to establish special teams for this purpose in the future. After the sarin incident, however, an increasing number of observers began to argue that the police alone were not enough to protect the nation from terrorist assaults. With this push for the establishment of a counterterrorism mission for the SDF, the new "National Defense Guidelines," approved by the government in 1995, state unequivocally that one of the key functions of the SDF is to respond to terrorism. Particularly with the 1996–97 hostage crisis at the ambassador's residence in Peru, the SDF has been able to move toward a broader counterterrorism role.

The fiscal year 2000 budget of the Defense Agency demonstrated this shift in priorities. It provided additional funding to enhance defense capabilities by improving protective equipment, drills, and research to respond to suspicious vessels that might be involved in the transport of personnel or materials for terrorist assaults; making antiguerrilla preparations; preparing for terrorism with weapons of mass destruction; and so forth. The GSDF's Research Headquarters includes, for example, a new special weapons research commissioner, who works on protection against biological and chemical weapons. The Maritime Self-Defense Forces (MSDF) now have a Ship Investigation Team that might be used in counterterrorism missions. And a new institute is responsible for training the SDF in the handling of guerrilla tactics, street warfare, and the protection of sensitive facilities such as nuclear power plants from potential terrorist adversaries.[18] Additionally, the GSDF will add a Cyberterrorism Team sometime between 2001 and 2005, and it will be responsible for coordinating its activities with the MSDF and the Air Self-Defense Forces (ASDF) in the event of a terrorist attack on the information or communications infrastructure. Approved at the end of 2000, the plan demonstrates a new commitment to improving the SDF's capabilities against terrorism, particularly terrorist attacks with weapons of mass destruction.

These seem, of course, like fairly typical missions for the armed forces. But it bears repeating that Japan's SDF units are not ordinary armed forces and that the conception of terrorism has traditionally been quite different in Japan than in the other advanced industrialized nations. With a tightly circumscribed role for the SDF, even Japanese defense leaders have been reluctant to commit them to the protection of the nation against terrorist assaults. These changes, while muted in comparison with those evidenced in other nations, reflect important shifts in the way the government conceptualizes terrorism as a threat and a problem requiring a systematic response. Although it is too early to predict how the SDF would handle a bona fide terrorist event, and there is reason to doubt its ability to coordinate effectively with the NPA, its steps in the past few years suggest that its commanders have begun to think more seriously about the threat that terrorism presents and the ways in which the SDF can contribute to national security.

DIPLOMATIC STRATEGIES

Much has been made in the scholarly and journalistic literature on Japan of its small size, its resource dependence, and its consequential efforts to maintain strong international ties. This characterization of the nation is at best misleading. Indeed, with more than 125,000 million citizens, Japan is one of the world's ten most populous nations, and its gross national product is second only to that of the United States; in terms of economic power, it dwarfs all the other nations of East and Southeast Asia combined. Even so, there can be no doubt that a profound sense of vulnerability informs much of Japan's diplomatic orientation, which aims largely at building strong regional ties while protecting its crucial security alliance with the United States. Many Japanese and non-Japanese observers alike point to the government's interest in promoting multilateral agreements and institutions that can mitigate some of the concerns it has with the global environment. And perhaps to a larger degree than do many other nations the Japanese government clearly believes international cooperation to be one of its key tools in an overall counterterrorism strategy. International terrorism, practically by definition, requires international cooperation for lasting solutions. In the case of Japan—which is partly dependent on its allies for intelligence and security support—this is perhaps even more true.

Summits have played a particularly important role in setting Japan's vision of the global agenda and helping it to articulate in globally legible terms its understanding of security cooperation. At the G-5 Bonn Summit of 1978, for example, Prime Minister Fukuda—who had been deeply affected by Japan's inability to prevent or counter the Dacca hijacking—proposed a "Communiqué on Airline Hijackings," which was adopted by the summit participants. In successive G-5, G-7, and G-8 Summits, terrorism has been a major topic of discussion, and Japan is a signatory to its various communiqués and declarations on the subject. Following the resolutions adopted at the Halifax Summit, which was held after the 1995 sarin gas attack and the bombing of the U.S. Federal Building in Oklahoma, the nation's interior, justice, and foreign ministers participated in the Ministerial Conference on Terrorism in Ottawa. The chairman of the Public Security Examination Commission and the foreign minister represented Japan, reporting on the Aum Shinrikyo incident and proposing a meeting of experts on biological and chemical terrorism. This proposal was included in the "Ottawa Ministerial Declaration on Terrorism," which led to a conference of experts held in Paris in 1996. At the Denver Summit in June 1997, in the wake of the Peruvian crisis, Prime Minister Hashimoto expressed his determination to fight terrorism jointly with the international community

and vowed that Japan would never capitulate to terrorism. Among his proposals were improvements in capabilities vis-à-vis hostage situations, strengthened information exchange, and another experts meeting on terrorism and hostage-taking incidents. Japan is still making efforts to follow up on his proposals.

At the various working group meetings on counterterrorism, one of the main topics is always the effort to expand the use and recognition of international conventions against terrorism. At the July 2000 Okinawa Summit, the Japanese foreign minister called upon all nations to become signatories of the twelve counterterrorism conventions and to enforce them strictly. Japan has already ratified ten of the twelve, including those on hijacking, the taking of hostages, the protection of nuclear materials, and the like. It is working on the enabling legislation necessary to allow ratification of two more: the International Convention for the Suppression of Terrorist Bombings and the International Convention for the Suppression of the Financing of Terrorism.

The financing convention provides an illustrative glimpse at Japan's attempt to coordinate its efforts more effectively with the global community. To be sure, the problems with Aum should have alerted Japanese policymakers to their problems in investigating the financial transactions of terrorist groups. Aum had, after all, been able to support its vast network because it ran several profitable computer stores and other enterprises. Even so, the Japanese investigative agencies were ill prepared to track the growing financial resources of this radical cult. When the Financial Action Task Force (FATF), an international organization that is largely responsible for the investigation of money-laundering cases, conducted a survey in Japan in 1998, it informed Japanese leaders of the extent to which they were unaware of illicit financial transactions being carried out in the country. The FATF's Japanese representative pointedly remarked that Japan's criminal laws and regulations against organized crime were insufficient not only in their effectiveness but in their reflection of the seriousness of the problem of money laundering. In 1999, largely because of this criticism and the government's eagerness to meet international standards and demonstrate its commitment to global cooperation, Japan passed new legislation against money laundering and illicit financial transactions. Some experts have suggested that this financial infrastructure against money laundering may also be useful in implementing the requirements of the convention against the financing of terrorism. As the Japanese government investigates how it can best pass enabling legislation that will allow for the ratification of the convention, there can be little doubt that the government takes international cooperation against terrorism seriously. It is not an auxiliary element in the government's counterterrorism stance but one of its fundamental components. In related issue areas, the Japanese government has also passed legislation on the production of chemicals and unauthorized computer access, again in an effort to bring these up to international standards.

Although much of Japan's international cooperation on terrorism focuses on its collaboration with the other advanced industrial nations, it also maintains increasingly robust ties with its Asian neighbors. In January 1997, during the Peruvian crisis, Prime Minister Hashimoto visited the member states of the Association of Southeast Asian Nations (ASEAN), taking the opportunity to push for a network for the exchange of information and views on terrorism between Japan and the ASEAN nations as well as a regional experts' forum on terrorism. As a result, in June 1997 the Japan-ASEAN Information Network on Terrorism was created and in October Tokyo hosted the Japan-ASEAN Conference on Counterterrorism, which was attended by relevant personnel from Japan and all nine ASEAN countries. The conference concluded with an agreement for improved cooperation in intelligence, police protection, and communications during terrorist events. In 1999, Tokyo hosted a follow-up Asian–Middle East Conference on Counterterrorism, which was attended by representatives of a larger range of nations.

The Japanese government also uses some of its substantial Overseas Development Assistance (ODA) budget to support counterterrorism efforts among developing nations. Since 1995, the NPA has been holding seminars for personnel from developing countries on practical measures against terrorism. These seminars introduce counterterrorist equipment and tactics and operate as a kind of "technology transfer," especially with regard to the classification of analysis of intelligence, the detection of forged passports, and the like. The Japan International Cooperation Agency (JICA), one of the government's main foreign aid agencies, has also held annually since 1997 its Seminar for the Investigation of International Terror-

ist Incidents as a way of providing expertise on techniques that can be used to handle terrorist crises. Significantly, these programs work for both Japan and the visiting nations. That is, the Japanese government believes that its security is enhanced by the reduction of terrorist violence elsewhere, and these seminars are designed to provide the tools necessary to allow the governments of developing countries to prepare for and deal with terrorism.

Japan's overall ODA programs are perhaps a double-edged sword in its efforts to deal with international terrorism. Japan each year vies with the United States as the world's top donor of international aid, and its programs are designed in large part to enable developing nations to establish the kind of industrial infrastructure necessary to foster sustainable growth. In the absence of other tools for international engagement (e.g., a military that might more easily take part in collective security arrangements), Japan has turned toward ODA as one of the key aspects of its diplomatic orientation. As a nation committed to pacifist principles, Japan uses its aid in part to provide a basis for economic growth that can mitigate some of the potential causes of conflict. Although counterterrorism is hardly at the core of Japan's ODA charter—which focuses primarily on the humanitarian reasons for development assistance—these aid programs could presumably affect Japan's ability to deal with terrorism in two conflicting ways.

First, by providing development assistance to poor regions, Japan has tried to alleviate some of the worst suffering in developing nations, including some of those most affected by terrorism. The late Prime Minister Obuchi, for example, proposed enhanced ODA contributions to the Philippines, which has in recent years suffered from terrorist attacks by leftist revolutionaries as well as Muslim separatists. Whether economic development fostered by such assistance can be part of a long-term strategy to undermine the causes of conflict is still unclear, but if an improvement in people's lives is visible there might be a reduction in public support in poor areas for groups posing a violent challenge to the government. Second, however, Japan's ODA programs almost inevitably establish ties between it and the government of the developing region. That is to say, Japanese ODA—which is often accompanied by Japanese private investment and Japan-related joint ventures—becomes a symbol of Japan's relationship with a government under attack. For example, Japan's ties with Peru have grown in the past decade, a fact not lost on the MRTA rebels who stormed the ambassador's compound. As noted previously, the leader of the rebels told the hostages that Japanese firms were in part responsible for the misery of Peruvian workers and peasants.

As one of the world's leading industrial democracies, Japan is not going to turn away from its ODA programs. And in the absence of other military tools Japan's economic strength could conceivably be one of its most important assets in its efforts to contribute to international counterterrorism priorities. In the long run, the economic growth generated by Japan's ODA programs might alleviate some of the suffering that no doubt can be mobilized as support for violent rebel groups that use terrorist tactics. Even so, in the short run, Japan's development assistance ties make it a symbolic target and inevitably put Japanese workers in harm's way.

CONCLUSION

Because of the vexing nature of terrorism, governments are perhaps better equipped to deal with it when they have options rather than when they are institutionally forced onto one path. An Israeli refusal to deal with organizations that have used terrorist violence in the past, for example, would have scuttled the Middle East peace process from the start. Israel's flexibility—a combination of tough-minded security measures and a realistic assessment of how to generate political solutions—has at least allowed it to move with the Palestinian Authority toward a resolution of one of the world's most terrorism-ridden conflicts. In contrast, Japan's counterterrorism policymakers operate within a tightly constrained environment, one that by and large rejects expansion of police or military power and relies instead on narrowly construed responses to specific terrorist incidents and on broad diplomatic cooperation to mitigate Japan's vulnerabilities.

This discussion of the evolution of Japan's counterterrorism policies demonstrates how incidents such as the Aum Shinrikyo attack and the crisis in Lima have led to reforms. Without an understanding of the constitutional, legal, and political limits on decision makers, however, observers will likely find the nature of Japan's re-

sponses incomprehensible. After all, among the advanced industrial nations Japan is alone in having actually suffered from a bona fide terrorist attack using weapons of mass destruction, one that fortunately killed only a few but could have been far worse. Why has the Japanese government's response been so muted, not only against the religious cult but also against the possibility of future acts of terrorist violence?

Simply put, Japanese decision makers have had to learn how to negotiate in a narrow environment, trying to balance the complex security issues engendered by domestic and international terrorism and a social mistrust of the police and the military. There have been limited, qualified improvements in Japan's counterterrorist capabilities in the past few years, and clearly there has been a subtle shift in the public mood toward a belief that social and political threats do exist and it is the state's responsibility to protect citizens. The shift has not gone far enough to overcome political opposition toward more expansive roles for the police and the SDF, but it suggests that Japanese policymakers can feel more confident than before about their role in trying to prepare for the possibility of terrorist events in the future. After all, the terrible events of 1995 and 1996, including the Aum and MRTA incidents as well as the catastrophic earthquake in Kobe, have increased the expectations of Japanese citizens that the government must have enhanced capabilities for dealing with crises. Within the constitutional and political restraints that prevent a more aggressive policy orientation, Japanese counterterrorism policymakers have been working quietly to make such improvements.

POSTSCRIPT

WITHIN DAYS OF THE terrorist attacks on the World Trade Center and the Pentagon, Japan's new prime minister, Junichiro Koizumi, spoke in unusually harsh terms, calling them "unforgivable." Unwilling to sit on the sidelines, he rapidly proposed a seven-point plan to ensure that Japan would be engaged in the U.S. war on terrorism. Although proposals like this have often foundered in the Diet, Koizumi's popularity and his reputation as a free-thinking maverick encouraged many supporters of action to believe that Japan would play a far more active role than it traditionally has in international conflicts. His success—the legislation passed the Diet after only a few weeks of debate—might be seen as evidence of a radical rethinking of Japan's counterterrorism policies. But in many ways, counterterrorism was largely beside the point. Although some officials now seem interested in pursuing certain issues on the counterterrorism agenda, this bill was focused on military support for the United States in a specific conflict, not on a change in priorities over the nation's approach to terrorism.

The U.S.-Japan Security Treaty does not compel the Japanese government to come to America's defense in the event of an attack on American soil. But with vivid memories of the criticism the nation faced for its failure to participate more quickly in the international coalition in the Gulf War, Prime Minister Koizumi recognized that Japan simply could not stand idly by while the United States emphasized cooperation against terrorism. And so he took the controversial step of proposing that Japanese troops be sent overseas to take part in the coalition. Although they would not be used in combat—primarily offering logistical support, providing intelligence assistance through the deployment to the Indian Ocean of Aegis-equipped cruisers, and perhaps manning field hospitals in Pakistan—members of the Self-Defense Forces would be authorized to fire their weapons to defend themselves and those under their care. This was undoubtedly an ambitious proposal, and perhaps only Koizumi had the popularity and the devil-may-care attitude to make it work. But its focus on military assistance near the Afghani theater reflected a belief that this was a military strike on the United States and was not emblematic of a growing terrorist threat that Japan might itself face.

To be sure, officials in Japan have moved to align the nation's practices more firmly with those of other G-8 nations in the war on terrorism. The Diet, for example, has committed itself to ratifying the International Convention on the Suppression of Terrorist Financing sometime in 2002, far more quickly than it might have without the catalyst of the September 11 attacks. And Japan's diplomats with expertise in South Asia, the Middle East, and Southeast Asia have no doubt about working with local governments to promote cooperation with U.S. initiatives. Japanese police also arrested eight Uzbeks in Japan, all of whom were suspected of having ties to Al Qaeda.

Even so, the Koizumi proposal and the immediate shifts after the September 11 attacks do not yet imply that Japan will undergo a transformation in its counterterrorism policies. The nation's muted international posture and tight immigration controls together suggest to policymakers that the country is neither the target nor the safe haven of members of the Al Qaeda network. Although twenty-four Japanese were killed in the September 11 attacks—twice as many as in Aum Shinrikyo's sarin gas attack in Tokyo—no one believes that groups affiliated with Osama bin Laden are primarily interested in attacking Japan. The Aum attacks provoked narrow, specific, legislative and administrative changes in keeping with the government's emphasis on civil liberties and strict limits on police and military power. Although the new legislation stretches those boundaries, it does not offer carte blanche to policymakers to expand the state's counterterrorism role.

Japan might prove in the long run to make a greater contribution to the U.S. war on terrorism if it systematically upgrades its intelligence-gathering and sharing activities. This will be particularly true if American activities spread—as many believe they will—to Southeast Asia. Islamist movements in the Philippines and Indonesia are known to have been affiliated with Al Qaeda, and the network might spread into Malaysia as well. Japanese knowledge of the region is both deep and expansive, and it might be of considerable assistance. The emphasis on military support is worrisome, however, because it is less likely that the Diet will support a direct Japanese military role in any actions in Southeast Asia. Moreover, if Japan adopts a role that is highly visible it might have to contend with the anger of Islamist movements in the region. The Diet seems to understand that the Self-Defense Forces will face danger abroad, but it seems less aware that Japanese civilians might themselves become targets throughout the region should terrorist groups believe that they can undermine the war on terrorism by attacking Japan. Though bold, Japan's new counterterrorism legislation might then prove to be woefully inadequate to face the challenges of this new, highly uncertain endeavor.

Conclusion

Yonah Alexander

ON SEPTEMBER 12, 2001, the day after the most brutal terrorist attacks in history took place in New York, Washington, D.C., and Pennsylvania, the United Nations (UN) Security Council passed Resolution 1368 (2001) in which it unequivocally condemned the operation as a threat to international peace and security and expressed its readiness to combat all forms of terrorism. Subsequently, the world organization took other action, such as the adoption on September 28 of Security Council Resolution 1373 (2001), which required states to undertake a range of responses to the challenge of international terrorism. The following are some of the steps that were outlined.

1. [All UN member states] shall:
   (a) Prevent and suppress the financing of terrorist acts; . . .
2. [All member states also] shall:
   (a) Refrain from providing any form of support, active or passive, to entities or persons involved in terrorist acts, including by suppressing recruitment of members of terrorist groups and eliminating the supply of weapons to terrorists;
   (b) Take the necessary steps to prevent the commission of terrorist acts, including by provision of early warning to other States by exchange of information; . . .
   (d) Prevent those who finance, plan, facilitate or commit terrorist acts from using their respective territories for those purposes against other States or their citizens; . . .

(f) Afford one another the greatest measure of assistance in connection with criminal investigations or criminal proceedings relating to the financing or support of terrorist acts, including assistance in obtaining evidence in their possession necessary for the proceedings;

(g) Prevent the movement of terrorists or terrorist groups by effective border controls and controls on issuance of identity papers and travel documents, and through measures for preventing counterfeiting, forgery or fraudulent use of identity papers and travel documents.

Similarly, other international bodies condemned the September 11 attacks and outlined various recommendations to cope with the growing threats of terrorism. For instance, the North Atlantic Treaty Organization (NATO) implemented Article 5 of the NATO Treaty, which asserts that an attack on one NATO member is an attack on all. This was the first time that the collective self-defense article of NATO was implemented.

Also on September 21, 2001, the foreign ministers of Latin America adopted a resolution calling for Organization of American States (OAS) members to "take effective measures to deny terrorist groups the ability to operate within their territories." They called on countries to work together to pursue those responsible for the attacks and bring them to justice, strengthening cooperation in such areas as extradition, mutual legal assistance, and information exchange. The ministers also directed the OAS Permanent Council to begin drafting a hemispheric antiterrorism treaty and convene a meeting of the Inter-American Committee against Terrorism (CICTE).

Finally, on December 4, 2001, the Ministerial Council of the Organization for Security and Cooperation in Europe (OSCE) agreed on the Bucharest Plan of Action for Consulting Terrorism in that:

> The OSCE stands ready to make its contribution to the fight against terrorism in close cooperation with other organizations and forums. This contribution will be consistent with the Platform for Cooperative Security and will benefit from interaction between global and regional anti-terrorism efforts under the aegis of the United Nations. The OSCE participating States commit their political will, resources, and practical means to the implementation of their obligations under existing international terrorism conventions and pledge them-

selves to intensify national, bilateral, and multilateral efforts to combat terrorism. (MC 9. Dec./1 Annex)

The aforementioned global and regional responses are only illustrative of the emerging trend of heightened concerns about terrorism in the post–September 11 era. This essay focuses on selected past counterterrorism strategies, summarizes the experiences of the ten countries examined in this volume, and provides some "best practices" lessons to be considered in developing future responses on the national and international levels.

PAST GOVERNMENTAL RESPONSES TO TERRORISM

The vulnerability of modern society and its infrastructure, coupled with the opportunities for the utilization of sophisticated high-level conventional and mass destruction weaponry, requires nations, both unilaterally and in concert, to develop credible response strategies and capabilities to minimize future threats. The stunning success of terrorist bombings, kidnappings, hijackings, facility attacks, and assassinations often results in a popular awareness of the important counterterrorist measures that states apply. After all, states possess enormous legal, economic, police, and military resources that terrorists cannot match. Governments have taken domestic and international measures to deal with conventional acts of terrorism, and they have taken special precautions to deal with mass destruction threats.

Since it is generally easier to take steps at home than it is to promote international action, states have taken a wide variety of domestic measures. Most notably, they have given great public attention to terrorism; improved intelligence-gathering resources against terrorists; enacted appropriate legislation; apprehended, prosecuted, and punished terrorists; and provided greater protection to government facilities and officials than they had furnished earlier. Moreover, certain counterterrorist measures have been taken in places where terrorists have been able to do great damage—most notably at airports.

Most governments have drawn attention to the barbarous nature of terrorism. It is not uncommon for political leaders to speak out publicly in denouncing terrorist acts. In choosing civilians as targets, terrorists have often undermined their own case, as the random slaughter of men, women, and children in the Oklahoma City bombing in 1995 indicates. Political leaders have been able to use such cases as examples of atrocities committed by terrorists. The most dramatic illustration of this approach relates to the September 11 events.

Intelligence agencies are alert to terrorism to an increasing extent. Timely collection, analysis, and dissemination of relevant information about the perpetrators, their ideologies, their modus operandi, and other aspects of their activities help to prevent incidents from occurring. In 1983, for example, a plot to firebomb a Seattle theater filled with hundreds of innocent people was foiled. In 1991 European intelligence agencies prevented Iraq-initiated terrorism in connection with the Gulf crisis. Finally, a number of suspects were arrested in the United States and abroad in December 1999 in an alleged plot to conduct terrorist activities on or around the New Year's holiday.

Statutory loopholes in domestic law have been closed, as the experience of the United States suggests. A case in point is congressional action to pass the "long arm" statute, which makes it a federal crime for a terrorist to threaten, detain, seize, injure, or kill an American citizen abroad. Thus, in a sting operation in international waters off the coast of Cyprus, the Federal Bureau of Investigation (FBI) arrested Fawaz Younis, a Lebanese operative, in the 1985 hijacking of a Jordanian airliner that included American hostages. He was subsequently convicted and sentenced. In 1995, Ramzi Yousef, the conspirator behind the 1993 World Trade Center bombing, was arrested in Pakistan and extradited to the United States. Also, Mohambedou Ould Slahi was arrested and later released in Nouakchott, Mauritania, upon the request of the United States. He was suspected of being the head of the Montreal terrorist cell that conspired to attack the United States around the 2000 New Year.

Governments have taken steps to protect their representatives abroad. Embassies are now constructed with security considerations heavily in mind, and diplomats are given training in thwarting terrorist acts such as kidnapping. Aviation throughout the world has become alert to the dangers posed by terrorists. Because of extensive hijackings of airplanes in the 1970s and 1980s, airlines today require security check-ins, with X-ray machines scanning passengers and their baggage. Although not foolproof, as was demonstrated by the Lockerbie disaster, which destroyed a Pan Am flight over Scotland, killing 270 people, the surveillance system has had its share of successes.

Regarding weapons of mass destruction, government agents are responsible for preventing and responding to threats of their use. For example, these agents must employ the specific means and tools needed to manage the consequences of biological attacks. In general, government teams that must deter such threats will need greater capabilities in order to detect and identify the biological agents involved, disarm or destroy the device responsible if it has not yet completed dispersing the agent, protect victims and themselves from further contamination, track the agent cloud or otherwise delimit the contaminated area, decontaminate and treat victims, and decontaminate the affected site.

Special measures have been taken to deal with nuclear explosives and materials. Interagency cooperation in the United States is reflected in the fact that the FBI has contingency plans with every nuclear facility. Furthermore, states have engaged in a variety of measures to deal with the international aspects of terrorism. Among the most prominent are the use of diplomacy, implementation of economic sanctions, cooperation in law enforcement, ratification of international conventions, and employment of military force.

States can break diplomatic relations with countries sponsoring terrorist actions. They can, moreover, expel diplomats believed to be implicated in such matters. Western European countries and the United States have expelled Libyan diplomats suspected of engaging in terrorist activities. Economic sanctions are a lever against terrorism, although they are difficult to impose because they require widespread international cooperation. But the United States imposed an economic embargo against Iran and Libya in the 1980s and 1990s, as did the United Nations against Afghanistan in 1999 and 2000.

Many international conventions have been concluded to deal with terrorism. Some of the instruments include the 1988 Rome Convention for the Suppression of Violence against the Safety of Maritime Navigation, the 1991 Montreal Convention on the Market of Plastic Explosives for the Purpose of Detection, and the International Convention for the Suppression of the Financing of Terrorism.

Finally, military force has been used by countries experiencing terrorism. Thus, Israel retaliated against Hizbullah in Lebanon in 2000 and the United States bombed Sudan and Afghanistan in 1998 in response to the attacks against American embassies in East Africa. As a consequence of the September 2001 attacks, the United States and its coalition destroyed the Al Qaeda network in Afghanistan and the Taliban regime, which had supported Osama bin Laden's group.

EXPERIENCES OF COUNTERTERRORISM STRATEGIES IN TEN COUNTRIES

Each of the ten countries selected for analysis in this volume recorded different experiences of counterterrorism strategies. The following discussion summarizes research findings prior to the September 11, 2001, attacks by Al Qaeda's terrorists.

United States

Since the 1970s, all U.S. administrations have viewed terrorism, especially international terrorism, as a serious threat to national security that requires a strong response. Although the average annual incidence of terrorist attacks reached a peak in 1986 and has since been declining, several massive terrorist bombings of U.S. targets in recent years suggest a trend toward more lethal attacks that cause larger numbers of casualties. Also, today's terrorists are more likely to be associated with loose networks than established groups, and many are motivated by religious fanaticism and messianic goals rather than coherent political causes of the kind pursued by former terrorist organizations.

These modern terrorist elements present a particular challenge. The United States is especially concerned that terrorists may acquire biological, chemical, or radiological materials for attacks that would inflict catastrophic destruction. While this threat is sometimes sensationalized, it is nevertheless real. The United States combats state-sponsored terrorism, principally through sanctions, but it has had mixed success in co-opting allies for sanctions. Nevertheless, state terrorism has declined sharply.

The United States defines *terrorism*, in general, as "premeditated violence against noncombatants to influence an audience" and regards terrorist acts as crimes that should be prosecuted and punished. The United States has greatly expanded its antiterrorism laws and has supported a growing body of international antiterrorism treaties. It also seeks to enhance the physical security of U.S. installations and infrastructure. American policy opposes concessions to terrorists. The United States has occasionally retaliated against terrorists with military force, but this option is problematical and seldom available. Counterterrorism policy stresses close cooperation with foreign governments and has helped forge a growing international consensus against terrorism. To avoid the mistakes of former decades, the United States today pursues careful coordination of counterterrorism policy and operations among diplomatic, law enforcement, and intelligence agencies and the Department of State. These policies have resulted in the apprehension of a growing number of international terrorists. In the U.S. public affairs policy on terrorism, officials strive for a balanced approach that avoids creating unnecessary fear to the advantage of terrorists. But politicians and the media do not always do likewise.

Argentina

Argentina's war on terrorism was not a good war. No one should make excuses for the various terrorist groups that set Argentina ablaze in the 1970s. Their war was not a just one, but the response of the government went far beyond that needed to defeat such groups as the Montoneros and the People's Guerrilla Army. The security forces did too much and too little and always erred on the side of excess. Quite rightly, the government response has been called "the dirty war" (*la guerra sucia*). The cost in human lives—especially innocent ones—was enormous, and the consequences of how that war was waged by the authorities continue to haunt Argentina today, twenty years after the conflict ended.

Why did things go so wrong? In part, Argentina was simply unprepared for what was a largely urban battle against terrorist groups, often of a Marxist bent, but with only marginal contacts with the Soviet camp. While nations like Peru and Venezuela faced both urban and rural violence in the early 1960s in the wake of the

Cuban revolution, Argentina was left largely untouched. Only when the focus of guerrilla strategy shifted to the cities, as it did in Brazil and Uruguay beginning in the late 1960s and early 1970s, was Argentina drawn into what was intended to be a continentwide insurgency that the violent Left in Latin America believed was the only way to defeat "U.S. imperialism."

Despite Che Guevara's vision, that strategy fell short, as Guevara himself experienced in the lonely wilds of Bolivia in October 1967. The Argentine terrorist groups launched their struggle anyway. Their campaign of terror peaked during the brief presidency of Isabel Perón who succeeded her husband, Juan Perón, upon his death in July 1974. The second Perón proved to be utterly inept and confused in office, leaving decisions to shadowy figures like José López Rega, who was the government's chief sponsor of counterterrorism. Unfortunately, López Rega had no scruples about waging war and used the Argentine Anticommunist Alliance (Alianza Anticommunista Argentina) as his chief tool of repression. The Triple A, as it was called, followed no rules, kidnapping and killing anyone suspected of links with the terrorist groups. Many of the victims were innocent, and all would disappear without a trace.

Although the Triple A was disbanded shortly after the military ousted Mrs. Perón, the armed forces carried out its counterterror measures with the same disregard for human rights. In the traditional Argentine manner, each service was itself ridden with factions and acted independent of the high command. How much the junta leaders knew or ordered is still open to debate. But the results are apparent. Without good intelligence and a proper chain of command, the military and police were free to wage war as they saw fit. Some thirty thousand Argentines lost their lives, and most have never been accounted for. The questions of guilt, responsibility, and the ways in which the war's victims met their end still haunt Argentine politics fifteen years after civilian rule was reestablished.

The terrorist groups of the 1970s may be broken permanently, but there is little sign that Argentina's security services are any better equipped to deal with terrorism today. The fact that no one has yet solved the terrorist bombings of the Israeli embassy and a Jewish community center in Buenos Aires some years ago only confirms that belief.

Primarily, the conflict in Peru involved the Sendero Luminoso (SL, or Shining Path), the smaller Movimiento Revolucionario Tupac Amaru (MRTA), and the Peruvian state. Both insurgent and state forces made serious and decisive mistakes during the conflict. But in the end the former were defeated because they committed more mistakes and also because the latter, almost a decade after the beginning of the armed struggle on May 17, 1980, developed a different and more or less efficient counterinsurgency strategy than they previously had devised.

The strategic defeat of SL and the MRTA would not have been possible without the critical participation of the rural civil population, which forged an alliance with the security forces as part of that new approach in the late 1980s. This was, of course, the organization of self-defense committees (*rondas campesinas*), which in the end broke the Sendero's strategic backbone.

In the late 1980s and early 1990s, Peru was on the brink of collapse. The existence of a state, the survival of a nation, and the stability of a region were at stake. A small, ruthless, but organized and dedicated revolutionary organization almost destroyed the country. How could this have happened? Why was the response so ineffectual until almost 1988–89? Carlos Tapia, a Peruvian counterinsurgency expert, says that in only a few instances in Latin American history has frivolity, inaction, or covert conciliation in the face of terrorist subversion taken a country to the edge of collapse. Also there have been only a few cases in which one can find so many mistakes committed by politicians and military leaders who had the responsibility for fighting the subversion and facilitated its expansion and development over several years.

From the beginning of the insurgency, both the civilian and military leaders failed to understand the real nature of the threat as a revolutionary war machine whose main objectives were political, although the primary symptoms felt were the military actions of the Ejército Guerrillero del Pueblo (EGP, or Popular Guerrilla Army), the armed branch of the SL. The Sendero's leader, Abimael Guzmán, structured the SL like an iceberg: the EGP acted on the surface, but the most important action took place under the surface. The Peruvian security establishment failed to understand that this insurgency was different from the one that took place in 1965, which was easily infiltrated and destroyed. Consequently, it required a new counterinsurgency approach. As this study demonstrates, the Sendero also managed to wage a very efficient, asymmetrical war, which provoked and made the state's initial response late, disproportionate, flawed, and counterproductive.

Colombia

Over the last forty years, terrorism in Colombia has gradually increased to the level at which many Colombians today are leaving the country, expressing the sentiment that "it is impossible to live here anymore." This comment can be viewed as an indication of a level of fear that most terrorists only dream of achieving. Some analysts also assert that the migration from Colombia indicates an almost catastrophic failure of counterterrorism strategies by the government, private security forces, and society in general. But these are simplistic views of terrorism and counterterrorism strategies in Colombia. This intense fear is the result not of the impact of a single group of terrorists but of the cumulative effect of many manifestations of violence, crime, political unrest, and weak government efforts to take action against these negative elements.

The groups involved in imposing the violence include Marxist-inspired insurgent groups, such as the Revolutionary Armed Forces of Colombia and the Army of National Liberation, and several other groups that over the years were formed and defeated or negotiated settlements with the government. At the other end of the political spectrum are the self-defense forces, such as the Autodefensas Unidas de Colombia, which use terrorism in an effort to eradicate the Marxist groups. Further confusing the picture are criminal groups such as the drug mafias, the kidnapping mafias, and other common criminal groups, organized and unorganized. Such a mixture would be devastating for any nation.

The Colombian government and society have adopted many strategies over the past fifty years or so to deal with the various manifestations of violence and terrorism in their country. Most of these strategies have been abysmal failures. Some worked in the short run, and a few showed signs of minimal success. The principal failure of all is that there is a complete lack of consensus within the country on what a peaceful Colombia should look like.

The most significant fact is that Colombia has never developed a doctrine of national security, despite the almost forty years of open warfare with at least two Marxist insurgencies at any given time. In the absence of such a doctrine, the military and police are incapable of developing strategies to stop the rampant disregard for law and order. So various groups, such as the armed forces, paramilitary self-defense groups, churches, nongovernmental organizations, and the police, have developed tactics on their own, with various degrees of success. The military's strategic reliance on the illegal paramilitary groups has worked temporarily as a force multiplier but reduces respect for the law. Churches work out strategies for accommodation, but these depend on the goodwill of the oppressors. Colombia's presidents rely on foreign governments for strategies and funding, irrespective of national interests.

The worst effect of this cumulative volume of terror is that throughout Colombian society, almost to the individual level, there is a total lack of trust in government. The past five Colombian administrations have proved incapable of stemming the violence, and the current one shows almost no capacity to develop a successful, long-term counterterrorism strategy. As a case study in counterterrorism strategies for the twenty-first century, with few exceptions Colombia is primarily an example of what not to do.

Spain

Spanish counterterrorist policies include: (1) police and judicial action, (2) negotiation, (3) a program of integration for the members of the Euskadi ta Askatasuna (ETA) who renounce violence, (4) dispersion of prisoners, and (5) international cooperation. Although some specific policies, such as the dispersion of prisoners, have harmed the cohesion of ETA, counterterrorist policies have not been fully successful from a general perspective.

Two negative lessons from the Spanish experience should be stressed. First, the rule of law should always be respected in combating terrorism. Second, one should not be ingenuous and suppose that a transition to democracy will change the radical demands of a terrorist group. In fact, the Basque people have achieved a unique degree of self-government within Spain; participation, recognition, and access to the democratic system are already available to Basque citizens. Therefore, it is suitable to conclude that Basque national separatism, as defended by ETA, has nothing to do with the fight for individual rights and liberties or the democratic regulation of states.

United Kingdom

The United Kingdom provides an informative case study on the effectiveness of counterterrorism measures in that the same measures were applied to both international and domestic terrorism with differing results. It shows that where there is no domestic support for the cause of the terrorists—as in the case of international terrorism in Britain—firm counterterrorism measures coupled with effective procedures can virtually eliminate terrorism. For domestic terrorism, absent a genuine political process in which there is a determined support, albeit from a minority composed of a small number of activists and a larger number of tacit supporters, the most that such policies can achieve is to contain the terrorist threat and damage within "acceptable" limits.

In the case of Northern Ireland, the situation is further complicated by intercommunal strife and is not a case of a terrorist group operating against a central government. Such terrorism cannot be eradicated by means of counterterrorism methods alone: political measures by the respective communities as well as the government are also needed. Even in this case of domestic terrorism, international mediation proved essential to a peace process. In spite of the setbacks, as far as Northern Ireland is concerned, the U.K. government's security and political measures, with some exceptions, generally struck a balance between maintaining democratic and legal rights and avoiding continuous recourse to draconian military measures.

A key ingredient in which there has been success in counterterrorism measures is an obdurate stand on not making concessions to acts of violence and vigorous intelligence gathering. As the Northern Ireland case demonstrates, concessions may have to be made to complete a peace process but only in a context in which the parties concerned have stopped using terrorism as the principal means of achieving their objectives.

Israel

In its war against terrorism, Israel has defined four strategic objectives. The first is a comprehensive strategy based on a multidimensional front for an ongoing battle rather than ad hoc tactical operations. The second is a combination of offensive and defensive operations and psychological and political elements. It is important to note Israel's unequivocal concept, which claims that there is no strictly political solution to terrorism. Third, the most important weapons in this long war are patience, determination, and cunning and not necessarily firepower, military courage, and operational and tactical daring. Fourth, the cooperation of all "players" is imperative in this complex war. Cooperation is particularly important among the defense forces themselves (e.g., intelligence and the military), the political system, the general public, and the media.

The experience of Israel in its war against terrorism contains a singular character that prevents copying exactly its counterterrorism strategies and applying in other countries. At the same time, it is doubtful whether any other country has acquired such rich experience and myriad lessons—good and bad—in this cruel and difficult war.

The summary of Israel's war against Arab terrorism since the Six Day War in 1967 is very important. Israel has learned that there is no military solution to terrorism, that sooner or later a political agreement will be reached, and that only such an agreement will bring an end to the terrorist war. At the same time, and in spite of this fundamental assumption, Israel maintains that it will not be possible to reach a political agreement unless the leadership of the Arab terrorist organizations comes to recognize that Israel cannot be defeated by force.

Turkey

Turkey has been a prime victim of terrorism over the last thirty years and will continue to suffer from it in the foreseeable future. With the changing global and regional political environment, the

Turkish regime has been attacked by virtually every kind of terrorism present in today's world—ideological, religious, and ethnic. Flourishing in the impoverished parts of the country and supported by foreign powers at odds with Turkey, Kurdish ethnic nationalist terrorism has inflicted much damage on the Turkish people in the last decade and a half. However, as this particular terrorist threat has been neutralized, at least for the time being, Marxist (always in fashion in Turkey) and Islamic fundamentalist terrorists are accelerating their assaults.

When terrorism turned into a low-intensity conflict in Turkey toward the end of the twentieth century, the government was forced to develop new military and legal methods to fight it, while still determined not to negotiate with or make concessions to the terrorists. This, in turn, led to legal and diplomatic problems that came close to making Turkey a pariah state on account of its human rights record. Fortunately, the victory over the separatists provided an environment of reconciliation and peace, which made it possible to improve human rights and democratic practices. In the future, Turkey's terrorism problem is expected to mutate into a transitional narcocriminal one, which will be harder to fight than its previous form due to its economic dimension. Nevertheless, the determination of the civilian and military authorities to overcome this new form of terrorism is promising better days for Turkey.

India

Terrorism in India can be broadly classified under three categories: (1) cross-border terrorism in Jammu and Kashmir; (2) terrorism with internal roots, but supported by external forces in the Northeastern states and Punjab; and (3) domestic terrorism, with no external links, in Bihar and Andhra Pradesh. In Jammu and Kashmir, the situation is complicated because the terrorist movement is spearheaded by Islamic fundamentalists from Pakistan. This type of international terrorism can be effectively dealt with through closer international cooperation. Terrorism in the second and third categories can be eradicated only if more attention is paid to tackling its internal root causes.

The counterterrorism strategy has to be multidimensional. Economic and political measures are as important as, if not more important than, military measures. Military measures, although an essential component, cannot deal with this complex problem alone, as is clearly demonstrated by the Indian experience in Punjab and Mizoram. But making concessions under duress does not lead to an improvement in the situation either. Terrorist groups are unlikely to come to the negotiating table unless they are put under pressure. At the same time, excessive use of military force can be counterproductive. Public support is crucial. Only a balanced approach that does not unnecessarily alienate the people is likely to succeed. Special forces, such as the National Security Guard, and antiterrorism law, such as the Terrorist and Disruptive Activities Act, can play vital roles in curbing terrorism.

Japan

Before the Aum Shinrikyo's 1995 sarin gas attack, Japan's gravest terrorist threat emerged from the leftist Japanese Red Army. Because of the Japanese Constitution's stringent civil liberties guarantees as well as its famous Article IX, in which the nation gives up the right to war as well as participation in most forms of armed conflict, Japanese police and security forces faced a tough environment in which to crack down on the group. Because of some badly handled crises in the 1970s, Japan acquired a reputation for being a "bargainer" with terrorist groups and has had to work with the international community in order to compensate for its relatively underequipped counterterrorist capabilities. Even so, because of Japan's restrained international presence, this approach has worked reasonably well.

The Aum attack changed all that. Suffering from the only major use of chemical weapons by a terrorist group against a civilian population, the Japanese government was quickly criticized by citizens who were angry about its failure to have done more to prevent the attack. Because the attack was quickly followed by the Tupac Amaru siege of the Japanese ambassador's compound in Peru, a palpable sense of crisis emerged among policymakers who deal with terrorism.

Their response has been muted but has signaled important institutional innovations. Because of constitutional proscriptions against the use of force as well as a public expectation that the government should take a conciliatory approach with terrorists in order to save lives, the Japanese government must work within tight constraints. Even so, the National Police Agency, the Self-Defense Forces, and other elements of the Japanese government have begun to coordinate their efforts more closely in order to enhance their counterterrorism capabilities. The radical reorganization of the Japanese bureaucracy in early 2001 makes it too early to determine how effectively the government will handle the next terrorist crisis.

SELECTED "BEST PRACTICES" LESSONS

This volume, in focusing on the experiences of ten countries, provides ample evidence of counterterrorism strategy failures and successes. The record is unmistakable. The main question is: what are the lessons to be learned in terms of developing more effective responses in the future so that the threat of primitive, spectacular, super-, and cyberterrorism can be reduced and brought under manageable levels?

Analysis of this perspective requires an examination of two major areas. The first focuses on policies of governments vis-à-vis terrorism. Included in this framework are issues such as the political environment in the country concerned; the perception of the nature of the terrorist threat, domestically and internationally; low-, medium-, and high-priority counterterrorism policies developed by governments; and the legal environment. The second area deals with the structure, resources, and implementation of counterterrorism policies. This cluster covers counterterrorist organizational structures, intelligence, law enforcement and diplomatic methods, economic measures, and military responses.

Among the successes relevant to some of these themes, it is noteworthy to mention that a positive political environment is critical. For instance, the government of Peru won against the Sendero Luminoso terrorists in part because the military did not interfere in the daily lives of the people in the countryside. In fact, the armed forces followed a constructive policy: while the Sendero became more distant toward peasant society, the military forged closer ties with all sectors of Peruvian society. As the Sendero grew more external to peasant society, the armed forces became more tied to the population.

Similarly, Turkey has revised its criminal procedure laws, which are now mostly in accord with human rights norms. Among these are shorter detention periods prior to detainment and the right to counsel during detention. Turkish citizens have access to the European Court of Human Rights if citizens feel that their rights have been violated.

Another useful lesson relates to successful counterterrorism policies. The Israeli experience is instructive. Essentially, in its long war against terrorism, Israel has defined four strategic objectives: a comprehensive strategic concept presenting a multidimensional front for the ongoing battle rather than an ad hoc operation comprising only tactical and fragmented actions; a combination of various elements such as offensive and defensive actions, patience, determination, and cunning (and not necessarily firepower); and the cooperation of all the "players"—both civilian and military.

Effective legal policies, such as national legislation, are also notable. For instance, in the United Kingdom, terrorism laws were initially temporary because legislation evolved in response to Irish violence and later to international terrorism. Out of a concern for civil rights protection, Britain's counterterrorist laws had to be reviewed on an annual basis.

"Best practices" lessons related to implementation of counterterrorism strategies are also evident. Within the organizational structure, the role of intelligence is particularly significant. In the Israeli experience, for example, intelligence is critical for operational purposes and therefore it has to be almost exclusively of a tactical nature.

Military forces must be specially trained for counterterrorism operations. In India in 1987, the National Security Guard, a professional force of commandos, succeeded in flushing the terrorists from the Golden Temple without undue loss of life. It was a highly successful operation.

Negotiations between governments and insurgent organizations have mixed results. Sometimes, as in the case of Northern Ireland, they may lead to movement toward a consensus and a willingness to work peacefully within the political system. At other times, however, they are unsuccessful. Although the Basque people are assured political representation and respect for human rights in Spain, negotiations have not succeeded in ending separatist violence in that country. Negotiations between Israel and the Palestinian Authority have broken down, leading to escalating terrorist activities by groups such as Hamas and Islamic Jihad and expanding military responses by the Israel Defense Forces.

Developing good "best practices" policy in counterterrorism requires coming to terms with the mistakes made by governments. The most fundamental reason why Argentina's experience with counterterrorism was less than satisfactory was Argentina's lack of preparation among the security forces and their inability to learn from past mistakes. A lesson learned from the U.S. failure in Iran-Contra is that close teamwork among many agencies must be integrated in a coordinated process. The failure of the Indian central government to strengthen the Punjab police in 1983 resulted in forces that were neither organized nor trained to effectively counter terrorist attacks. Similarly, coordination and information sharing among the various intelligence and security services in Turkey, especially in the 1980s and early 1990s, were far from satisfactory, resulting in a duplication of effort and setbacks for the common cause.

Because Spain had a poor system of information on terrorism toward foreign countries in its transition to democracy, it had much trouble in its war against ETA. The inability of Colombia to devise a comprehensive counterterrorism strategy has contributed to the breakdown of law and order in that country and a reliance on paramilitary forces to perform the functions of the government.

In sum, many governments and people have failed to appreciate the magnitude and implications of the terrorist threat. Some countries have tended to regard terrorism as a minor nuisance or irritant. As a result, a large number of states have not yet developed a strong commitment to deal effectively with the problem of terrorism.

The policy implications are therefore threefold. First, there are no simplistic or complete solutions to the problem of terrorism. As the tactics utilized to challenge the authority of the state are, and continue to be, novel, so, too, must be the response by the instruments of the state. We must also be cautious to avoid the kinds of overreaction that could lead to repression and the ultimate weakening of the democratic institutions we seek to protect.

Second, having achieved considerable tactical success during the past three decades, terrorists sometimes find it politically expedient to restrain the level of political violence. These self-imposed restraints will not persist indefinitely, and future incidents may continue to be costly in terms of human lives and property. Certain conditions, such as religious extremism or perceptions that the "cause" is lost, could provide terrorists with an incentive to escalate their attacks dramatically.

Third, the vulnerability of modern society and its infrastructure, coupled with opportunities for the utilization of sophisticated, high-leverage, conventional and unconventional weaponry, requires states both unilaterally and in concert to develop credible responses and capabilities to minimize future threats.

These policy implications are more relevant in the post–September 11 era than ever before. The United States and the international coalition have recognized that the future terrorist challenge demands from them no less resolve than was required to combat Nazism and Fascism during the last century. The message communicated by Sir Winston Churchill at the House of Commons on May 13, 1940, will therefore continue to be instructive well into the twenty-first century: "Victory at all costs, victory in spite of all terror, victory however long and hard the road may be; for without victory there is no survival."

Notes

UNITED STATES

1. Office of the Secretary of State, Office of the Coordinator for Counterterrorism, *Patterns of Global Terrorism, 1991* (Washington, D.C.: U.S. Department of State, 1992) (hereafter *Patterns of Global Terrorism, 1991*); and Office of the Secretary of State, Office of the Coordinator for Counterterrorism, *Patterns of Global Terrorism, 1999* (Washington, D.C.: U.S. Department of State, 2000) (hereafter *Patterns of Global Terrorism, 1999*).

2. Information provided by the Office of the Coordinator for Counterterrorism, U.S. Department of State.

3. Office of the Secretary of State, Office of the Coordinator for Counterterrorism, *Patterns of Global Terrorism, 1998* (Washington, D.C.: Government Printing Office, 1999) (hereafter *Patterns of Global Terrorism, 1998*); *Patterns of Global Terrorism, 1999*. Of the 111 attacks against U.S. targets in 1998, 77 were nonlethal bombings of a multinational pipeline in Colombia that terrorists regarded as a U.S. target. The number of international terrorist attacks worldwide and the number of attacks against U.S. targets rose sharply in 1999 to 392 and 169, respectively. The significant increase in 1999 runs counter to the previous trend. It was due primarily to 91 nonlethal attacks on American-owned oil pipelines in Colombia; dozens of nonlethal attacks on property of various nations in Europe in protest against the North Atlantic Treaty Organization (NATO) bombing in Serbia; and the capture of Abdullah Ocalan, the leader of the Kurdish Workers' Party (PKK).

4. *Patterns of Global Terrorism*, various editions, and information obtained from the Office of the Coordinator for Counterterrorism. Statistics are one measure of the harm caused by terrorism, but trend lines are uneven. For example, a single catastrophic act of terrorism, like the bombing of Pan American Flight 103 in 1988, which killed 193 Americans, can significantly alter the averages.

5. Title 22, *U.S. Code,* sec. 2656f(d).

6. U.S. Department of State, *Report of the Accountability Review Boards on the Embassy Bombings in Nairobi and Dar es Salaam* (Washington, D.C.: U.S. Department of State, January 1999).

7. U.S. Department of State, *Report to the Congress on Actions Taken by the Department of State in Response to the Program Recommendations of the Accountability Review Boards on the Bombings in Nairobi and Dar es Salaam* (Washington, D.C.: U.S. Department of State, April 1999).

8. Export Administration Act of 1979, 50 *U.S. Code,* app. 2405, sec. 6j.

9. Ibid.; see also 22 *U.S. Code,* secs. 2780, 2371.

10. *U.S. Code,* sec. 2339B.

11. *Patterns of Global Terrorism, 1999,* app. B, 65.

12. Michael Collins Dunn, "Usama Bin Laden: The Nature of the Challenge," *Middle East Policy* 6, no. 2 (October 1998): 23.

13. *Islamist* is a term often used in the current literature. It means Muslims who promote the idea of an Islamic state.

14. Bruce Hoffman, *Inside Terrorism* (New York: Columbia University Press, 1998).

15. James Zogby, "Are Arab Americans People Like Us?" *Foreign Service Journal* (May 2000): 32.

16. *Attorney General: Guidelines* is quite strict and prohibits surveillance on grounds of suspicion based on radical views. These guidelines are policy, but they are also based on the right to privacy and freedom from search and seizure, rights that are protected by the Constitution and the laws thereunder.

17. Walter Laqueur, *The New Terrorism: Fanaticism and the Arms of Mass Destruction* (New York: Oxford University Press, 1998).

18. Most U.S. antiterrorism statutes are found in Title 18, *U.S. Code.*

19. 50 *U.S. Code,* sec. 2405; 22 *U.S. Code,* secs. 286e-11, 2371, 2377, 2378, 2780, 2781.

20. The Iran-Libya Sanctions Act is 50 *U.S. Code,* sec. 1701. The Helms-Burton Act is 22 *U.S. Code,* sec. 6201.

21. *Patterns of Global Terrorism, 1999,* 107.

22. David C. Martin and John Walcott, *Best Laid Plans: The Inside Story of America's War against Terrorism* (New York: Harper and Row, 1988).

23. *Patterns of Global Terrorism, 1999,* vii.

24. 22 *U.S. Code,* sec. 2708.

25. Jane C. Loeffler, chap. 11 in *The Architecture of Diplomacy: Building America's Embassies* (New York: Princeton Architectural Press, 1998).

26. U.S. Department of State, *Report of the Advisory Board on Overseas Security* (Washington, D.C.: U.S. Department of State, 1985).

27. U.S. Department of State, *Report of the Accountability Review Boards on the Embassy Bombings in Dar es Salaam and Nairobi* (Washington, D.C.: U.S. Department of State, April 1999).

28. Ibid.

29. As of March 18, 2002, OSAC bulletins could be obtained at <www.ds-osac.org>.

30. Travel advisories, as of March 18, 2002, could be obtained at <www.travel.state.gov/travel>.

1. A *Washington Post* op-ed piece provides recent examples of the last point: Noga Tarnopolsky, "Up against Argentina's Stonewall," *Washington Post*, August 28, 2000, A19. Tarnopolsky is a journalist currently at work on a book about family members who disappeared during the *guerra sucia*, the "dirty war." The author argues for the declassification of U.S. and Argentine documents that would shed light on the thirty thousand who "disappeared" between 1976 and 1983, a quest, of course, that leaves out those who were illegally liquidated before the military coup in March 1976. Still, the point made in the piece remains valid. After more than twenty-five years, Argentine and possibly U.S. government documents regarding the fates of thousands of individuals remain hidden and unobtainable, with no adequate explanation as to why, a clear and present indication of the war's political legacy, which has haunted at least the last three civilian governments and no doubt will trouble governments to come. Also see Tim Weiner and Ginger Thompson, "Wide Net in Argentine Torture Case," *New York Times*, September 11, 2000, A6. The *Times* story recounts the arrest in Mexico of a reputed torturer who plied his trade during the 1970s at the Argentine Navy's New Mechanics School (see the discussion in text at note 24), where as many as five thousand Argentines may have disappeared.

2. As we shall see, years after the bombing of the Israeli embassy in Buenos Aires in March 1992 and the Asociación Mutual Israelita Argentina (AMIA, or the Argentine Israelite Mutual Association) Jewish Cultural Center in July 1994, also in Buenos Aires, the perpetrators are still at large. Although clues and suspects abound, Argentina's authorities have made no high-level arrests, and the country's intelligence-collecting abilities regarding these terrorist acts remain scanty and ineffective despite extensive U.S. assistance.

3. See, for example, Marguerite Feitlowitz, *A Lexicon of Terror: Argentina and the Legacies of Torture* (New York: Oxford University Press, 1998). For a much more sympathetic account of the Argentine insurgents, see Donald C. Hodges, *Argentina, 1943–1976: The National Revolution and Resistance* (Albuquerque: University of New Mexico Press, 1976), passim.

4. Roger W. Fontaine, "Communist Revolutionaries in Argentina," in *Argentina, OAS, and Hemispheric Security* (Washington, D.C.: American Foreign Policy Institute, 1979), 44.

The Ejército Guerrillero del Pueblo (EGP) spent eight months preparing for its first and last battle—time enough for the local police to thoroughly infiltrate this small band of adventurers led by journalist Ricardo Masetti, none of whom had the slightest knowledge of operational security. In a grim pattern that would be repeated, however, neither the body of Masetti nor those of his followers was ever produced by the authorities.

5. For a keen sociological analysis of Uruguay in the 1970s during the era of the Tupamaro, see Ernst Halperin, *Terrorism in Latin America* (Washington, D.C.: Center for Strategic and International Studies, 1976), 37–45. It should be pointed out that while groups like the Montoneros did resemble the Tupamaros in social background and educational levels, the Trotskyite Ejército Revolucionario del Pueblo (People's Revolutionary Army, or ERP)

leaders were older, were less university oriented, and had received training in Cuba. Overall, the ERP chiefs were more "professional" in conducting their war against the Argentine government.

6. Ibid., 40.

7. Geoffrey Jackson, *Surviving the Long Night* (New York: Vanguard, 1974). Like the contemporaneous Brazilian urban guerrillas and their leader, Carlos Marighela, the Tupamaros in reality often hit civilian targets that had little to do with the military or police, a taste for gunplay for the sake of gunplay that rapidly lost them public support. For a sense of the Marighela style, see his *Minimanual of the Urban Guerrilla* (London: International Institute for Strategic Studies, 1971).

8. Halperin, *Terrorism in Latin America,* 17. See also William E. Ratliff, *Castroism and Communism in Latin America, 1959–1976* (Washington, D.C.: American Enterprise Institute–Hoover Policy Studies, 1976), 143–46. The ERP after 1974 would shift its focus from urban- to rural-based insurgency but with as little success as its 1963 EGP predecessors enjoyed. In addition to the two principals, the ERP and the Montoneros, Argentines of a Maoist bent formed the Fuerzas Argentinas de Liberación Nacional (FALN) while the ERP spawned a splinter group, the ERP–22 de Augusto. See O. Carlos Stoetzer, "The Political Situation in Argentina," in *Argentina, OAS, and Hemispheric Security* (Washington, D.C.: American Foreign Policy Institute, 1979) 18. It should be added that all of these groups, with their penchant for violence, were self-consciously at cross-purposes with the Argentine Communist Party (PCA), which was thoroughly pro-Soviet in ideology and patronage and had long lost its taste for *revolutionary* adventurism. The armed Left's final toll in human lives is still open to debate. At a minimum, however, it murdered 697 persons, including 400 policemen and 143 military, mostly officers. That figure is taken from Daniel Frontalini and Maria Cristina Caiati, *El Mito de la Guerra Sucia* (Buenos Aires: Ed. CEL, 1984), quoted in Feitlowitz, *Lexicon of Terror,* 6. It is generally agreed that Montonero violence began in May 1970 with the kidnapping and subsequent murder of former president Pedro Eugenio Aramburu, the hardline anti-Peronist successor of Juan Perón. In a bit of grim Grand Guignol, the Montoneros would later steal Aramburu's coffin from a Buenos Aires cemetery. See Fontaine, "Communist Revolutionaries in Argentina," 52.

9. Ratliff, *Castroism and Communism in Latin America,* 143–44.

10. Guillén's best-known work is his *Estratégica de la Guerrilla Urbana* (Montevideo: Liberación, 1969). For a brief time, he became popular, a Spanish version of Herbert Marcuse, that is, a Marxist who truly believed in revolution but was not tied directly to the Soviet Union.

11. Ratliff, *Castroism and Communism in Latin America,* 146–54. See also Donald C. Hodges, *Philosophy of the Urban Guerrilla: The Revolutionary Writings of Abraham Guillén* (New York: Morrow, 1973). Guillén had a direct connection to Argentine terrorism. As early as the late 1950s, the Spaniard drew up a plan of insurrection after Juan Perón's fall from power in 1955. Later, in Cuba, Guillén would train Montonero militants. See Hodges, *Argentina,* x–xi.

12. One of the Triple A's favorite and indiscriminate targets was students, both university and secondary. In Latin America, students have a

well-earned reputation for their wholesale adoption of left-wing causes. That apparently was enough for the Triple A. At the School of Architecture and Urban Planning in La Plata (the capital of Buenos Aires Province and an hour's drive from the city of Buenos Aires), reportedly one hundred students were murdered by the Triple A. The murders were supplemented by the bombing of the school's cafeteria. See Feitlowitz, *Lexicon of Terror*, 179, 184. The Triple A's branch organization in Córdoba, the Comando Liberador de América, was particularly violent and antisemitic to boot (214). It should be noted that López Rega was ousted from Isabel Perón's cabinet at the insistence of the military. See also Hodges, *Argentina*, 110–12.

13. According to Gen. Ramon Díaz Bessone, the Triple A ceased activities toward the end of 1975. He provides no documentation, however. See Ramon Genaro Díaz Bessone, *Guerra Revolucionaria en la Argentina (1959–1978)* (Buenos Aires: Editorial Fraterna, 1986), 211–12.

14. For her account of that conflict, see Margaret Thatcher, *The Downing Street Years* (New York: HarperCollins, 1993), 173–235.

15. Stoetzer, "Political Situation in Argentina," 20.

16. Feitlowitz, *Lexicon of Terror*, 6.

17. John J. Johnson, *The Military and Society in Latin America* (Stanford: Stanford University Press, 1964), 102, 126, 129. In a sense, Argentina continues to face that problem. Violent crime is increasing, leading to what some analysts have described as a "soft civil war." Armed robberies, kidnappings, and extortion—all the evils of the 1970s—are reappearing and often are the work of security force agents themselves. The only difference is that the current kind of crime is purely criminal in nature rather than political. But even the political terror was not pure since individuals did well in acquiring ill-gotten wealth during the *guerra sucia*.

18. To be sure, Argentina and Chile nearly came to blows on a number of occasions, especially over the Beagle Channel Islands—a dispute that was only resolved through the good offices of Pope John Paul II in 1984–85.

19. See Max Hastings and Simon Jenkins, *The Battle for the Falklands* (New York: Norton, 1983).

20. Alexander M. Haig Jr., *Caveat: Realism, Reagan, and Foreign Policy* (New York: Macmillan 1984), 261–302.

21. See Thomas Skidmore and Peter H. Smith, *Modern Latin America*, 4th ed. (New York: Oxford University Press, 1997), 100–103.

22. Harry Shlaudeman, who was U.S. ambassador before and during the Falklands War, observed that the dirty war "was to be a decentralized operation. The army was not about to take on the job alone and the opprobrium that would come with it. All three services and all their elements had to be involved in the responsibility for the repression. So the regime ended up as a strange mixture of repressive police-state style government with a weak hierarchy of authority and a general inability to control things from the center" (quoted in Hans Binnendijk, ed., *Authoritarian Regimes in Transition* [Washington, D.C.: Foreign Service Institute, Center for the Study of Foreign Affairs, 1987], 235).

23. The ambiguity thickens. Massera, for example, was found to be responsible for the navy's crimes but in his words was found "not guilty." Precisely what this means remains unclear. The process took place under the

auspices of the National Commission on the Disappeared (CONADEP), appointed by President Alfonsín. For a year, the commission took evidence from witnesses, documenting nearly nine thousand victims. Its report was turned over by Alfonsín to the armed forces' Supreme Tribunal for trial of the ex-commanders at the end of 1985. At trials' end, Alfonsín sponsored two new laws that ended further prosecutions after February 23, 1987 (ibid., 13–14). The cessation of prosecution, of course, applies only to Argentina. Recently, the government of Mexico detained an Argentine citizen, Ricardo Miguel Cavallo, who has been accused of being a torturer at the navy's New Mechanics School (ESMA). He is being held at the request of a Spanish magistrate, Baltasar Garzón, for possible trial in Spain for the crimes of torturing Spanish citizens in Argentina. Garzón is the same magistrate who sought Chile's former dictator, Gen. Augusto Pinochet. Incidentally, Argentine president Fernando de la Rua (who resigned in December 2001) has already registered his objection to this process as an act of extraterritoriality, the precise view the Chilean government took of the attempted prosecution of Pinochet. See Weiner and Thompson, "Wide Net in Argentine Torture Case." As for the former terrorists, they were given a blanket pardon by President Menem at the end of 1990. See Jorge G. Castañeda, *Utopia Unarmed: The Latin American Left after the Cold War* (New York: Knopf, 1992), 15.

24. Feitlowitz, *Lexicon of Terror,* 46–47. The body count of five thousand can never be proved to be entirely accurate. But if some object that the figure is exaggerated, it is hardly the fault of those who came up with that number. Apparently, neither the Argentine Navy nor the country's other security services bothered to keep an accurate count or follow even the minimum legal procedures. To this day, the argument goes on as to whether a list exists of the victims of the navy as well as of the other security forces. Various governments have claimed that such a list no longer exists—if it ever did. Even human rights organizations are divided on the question. Some believe, for example, that the list survives and remains hidden within the intelligence services; others claim such depositories as a Swiss vault (215–16).

25. As a good example of the authorities' confusion as to who the real enemy was, consider the case of Jacobo Timmermann. A newspaper editor and gadfly, Timmermann initially welcomed the 1976 military coup, which, among other things, put him in the black book of the Far Left. Nevertheless, Timmermann would be arrested a year later and held without charge until he was released in 1979. See his *Preso sin Nombre, Celda sin Número* (Buenos Aires: El Cid Ediciones 1981). Since Timmermann's release, he has succeeded in outraging the Israeli and Cuban governments with his trenchant criticism.

26. Feitlowitz, *Lexicon of Terror,* 6.

27. Robert Cox, former editor of the *Buenos Aires Herald,* makes precisely that point upon first supporting the military intervention after the chaos of the *peronista* interlude. See Binnendijk, *Authoritarian Regimes in Transition,* 244–46.

28. Domingo Cavallo, Roberto Domenech, and Yair Mundlak, *La Argentina que Pudo Ser: Los Costos de la Represíon Económica* (Buenos Aires: Ediciones Manatial, 1989). A summary of this valuable work in English has been prepared by the International Center for Economic Growth, San Fran-

cisco, California, under the title *The Argentina That Could Have Been: The Costs of Economic Repression*, published in 1992.

29. It should come as no surprise that an economist (and an Argentine to boot), Raúl Prebisch, provided the rationale for these policies beginning in the 1940s. His emphasis on abandoning liberal policies for statist ones came as a reaction to the world depression of the 1930s. His influence was eventually felt throughout Latin America, but Argentina probably remained under the Prebisch spell longer than any other country. See, for example, Raúl Prebisch, "El Desarollo Económico de América Latina y Algunos de Sus Principales Problemas," *El Trimestre Económico* (July–September 1949): 359–61. For a recent appreciation and critique of Prebisch, see Leopoldo Solis, *Raúl Prebisch at ECLA: Years of Creative Intellectual Effort* (San Francisco: International Center for Economic Growth, 1988).

PERU

1. Carlos Tapia, *Las Fuerzas Armadas y Sendero Luminoso: Dos Estrategias y un Final* (Lima: Instituto de Estudios Peruanos, 1997), 21.

2. Alberto Bolivar, "Insurgency and Counterinsurgency in Peru, 1980–1990," *Low Intensity Conflict and Law Enforcement Journal* 6, no. 1 (summer 1997): 8.

3. Ibid., 22–23.

4. J. Bowyer Bell, *The Dynamics of the Armed Struggle* (London: Frank Cass: 1998), 36.

5. William Ratcliff, "Revolutionary Warfare," in *Violence and the Latin American Revolutionaries*, edited by Michael Radu (New Brunswick, N.J.: Transaction Books, 1988), 25.

6. Cynthia McClintock, *Revolutionary Movements in Latin America: El Salvador's FMLN and Peru's Shining Path* (Washington, D.C.: U.S. Institute of Peace, 1998), 13.

7. Robin Kirk, *Las Mujeres de Sendero Luminoso* (Lima: Instituto de Estudios Peruanos, 1992), 33.

8. Alberto Bolivar, "Intelligence and Subversion in Peru," *Low Intensity Conflict and Law Enforcement Journal* 3, no. 3 (winter 1994): 418–19.

9. Bell, *Dynamics*, 7, 9, 54.

10. Carlos Iván Degregori, "Harvesting Storms: Rondas and the Defeat of Sendero Luminoso in Ayacucho," in *Shining and Other Paths: War and Society in Peru, 1980–1995*, edited by Steve J. Stern (Durham: Duke University Press, 1998), 131.

11. Bell, *Dynamics*, 12, 31.

12. Carlos Iván Degregori, "After the Fall of Abimael Guzmán," in *The Peruvian Labyrinth: Polity, Society, Economy*, edited by Maxwell A. Cameron and Philip Mauceri (University Park: Pennsylvania State University Press, 1997), 180.

13. Raj Desai and Harry Eckstein, "Insurgency: The Transformation of Peasant Rebellion," *World Politics* 42, no. 4 (July 1990): 441–65, quoted in McClintock, *Revolutionary Movements*, 34.

14. Alan Hoe and Eric Morris, *Re-enter the SAS: The Special Air Service and the Malayan Emergency* (London: Leo Cooper, 1994), 142.

15. Robert Thompson, *Revolutionary War in World Strategy, 1945–1960* (New York: Taplinger, 1970), 9.

16. Bard E. O'Neill, *Insurgency and Terrorism: Inside Revolutionary Warfare* (Washington, D.C.: Brassey's, 1990), 142.

17. John Simpson, *In the Forests of Night: Encounters in Peru with Terrorism, Drug-Running, and Military Oppression* (New York: Random House, 1993), 78–79.

18. Michael Radu, "Revolutionary Elites" in Radu, *Violence,* 109–10.

19. Michael Radu and Vladimir Tismaneanu, *Latin American Revolutionaries: Groups, Goals, Methods* (New York: Pergamon and Brassey's, International Defense Publishers, 1990), 52, 326.

20. O'Neill, *Insurgency and Terrorism,* 75.

21. William A. Hazleton and Sandra Joy-Hazleton, "Sendero Luminoso: A Communist Party Crosses a River of Blood," in *Political Parties and Terrorist Groups,* edited by Leonard Weinberg (London: Frank Cass, 1992), 71.

22. David Scott Palmer, "The Revolutionary Terrorism of Peru's Shining Path," in *Terrorism in Context,* edited by Martha Crenshaw (University Park: Pennsylvania State University Press, 1995), 303.

23. Gordon H. McCormick, *The Shining Path and the Future of Peru* (Santa Monica: Rand Corporation, 1990), 7; Ann Ruth Willner, *The Spellbinders* (New Haven: Yale University Press, 1984), 18–19, quoted in McCormick, *Shining Path,* 7.

24. Quoted in Thompson, *Revolutionary War,* 5.

25. Robin Kirk, *The Monkey's Paw: New Chronicles from Peru* (Amherst: University of Massachusetts Press, 1997), 2.

26. Gerónimo Inca, *El ABC de Sendero Luminoso y del MRTA* (Lima: Grupo Editorial Gerónimo Inca, 1994), 29. Here I have to say something about Gerónimo Inca. He does not exist. The name is a play on words. If one takes the first two letters of the first name and the first two letters of the last name, one has GEIN (for Grupo Especial de Inteligencia), the DINCOTE unit directly in charge of capturing Guzmán. The address of Grupo Editorial Gerónimo Inca does not exist either: Av. Los Libertadores no. 1509 (Liberator's Avenue, no. 1509). This is Guzmán's number in prison. *El ABC de Sendero* was a semiofficial book published by DINCOTE.

27. See Sendero's newspaper, *El Diario,* November 22, 1991.

28. Carlos Tapia, *Autodefensa Armada del Campesinado* (Lima: Centro de Estudios para el Desarrollo y la Participación, 1995), 19.

29. Thompson, *Revolutionary War,* 4.

30. Cited in Peter Paret, *French Revolutionary Warfare from Indochina to Algeria* (New York: Praeger, 1964), 16–17, quoted in Richard H. Shultz Jr., "Political Strategies for Revolutionary War," in *Political Warfare and Psychological Operations: Rethinking the U.S. Approach,* edited by Carnes Lord and Frank R. Barnett (Washington, D.C.: National Defense University Press in cooperation with the National Strategy Information Center, 1989), 114.

31. Richard Clutterbuck, *Terrorism and Guerrilla Warfare: Forecasts and Remedies* (London and New York: Routledge, 1990), 143.

32. Ernst Halperin, "Ernesto 'Che' Guevara and the Reality of Guerrilla Warfare," in Radu, *Violence,* 40, 42–43.

33. O'Neill, *Insurgency and Terrorism,* 24.

34. Radu and Tismaneanu, *Latin American Revolutionaries,* 26.

35. See Alberto Bolivar, "La Geopolítica y los Orígenes de la Subversión en el Perú," *Defensa Nacional Journal* 13 (October 1993): 57–66. This practice was not new. In Algeria, it was the *petit fonctionaires,* symbol of the French presence, that the assassins seemed particularly bent on finding. See Alistair Horne, *A Savage War of Peace: Algeria, 1954–1962* (New York: Viking, 1978), 26. For John McCuen, the resulting administrative vacuums have encouraged and continue to encourage revolutionary movements. See his *The Art of Counter-revolutionary War* (Harrisburg: Stackpole, 1966), 97.

36. Kirk, *Monkey's Paw,* 54.

37. O'Neill, *Insurgency and Terrorism,* 79.

38. Quoted in McCuen, *Art of Counter-revolutionary War,* 32–33.

39. Degregori, "Harvesting Storms," 147.

40. Nelson Manrique, "The War for the Central Sierra," in Stern, *Shining and Other Paths,* 217.

41. Ponciano del Pino, "Family, Culture, and Revolution: Everyday Life with Sendero Luminoso," in Stern, *Shining and Other Paths,* 186. On the Asháninkas tragedy, see Simpson, *In the Forests,* 243–62; and Friar Mariano Gragnon, with William and Marilyn Hoffa, *Warrior in Eden* (New York: Morrow, 1993). Asháninka *rondas* are still active against Sendero's attempts to rebuild its forces in the Ene Valley. See Orazio Potestá, "*En Nombre de Gedión:* Tras la muerte de su líder Gedión Charrete, los Asháninkas están dispuestos a buscar y derrotar a los terroristas con el apoyo del Ejército o sin él," *Caretas,* November 25, 1999, 56–60.

42. Carlos Iván Degregori and Carlos Rivera, *Fuerzas Armadas, Subversión y Democracia, 1980–1993* (Lima: Instituto de Estudios Peruanos, 1993), 10.

43. Palmer, *Revolutionary Terrorism,* 253.

44. Santiago Pedraglio, *Seguridad Democrática Integral: Armas para la Paz* (Lima: Instituto de Defensa Legal, 1990), 87.

45. Michael Don Ward, Introduction to *The New Geopolitics,* edited by Michael Don Ward (Gordon and Breach, 1992), viii.

46. Bolivar, "Insurgency and Counterinsurgency," 5.

47. Philip Mauceri, *State under Siege: Development and Policymaking in Peru* (Boulder: Westview, 1996), 25, 115.

48. Charles Dunlap Jr., "Preliminary Observations: Asymmetrical Warfare and the Western Mindset," in *Challenging the U.S. Symmetrically and Asymmetrically: Can America Be Defeated?* edited by Lloyd J. Matthews (Carlisle Barracks, Pa.: U.S. Army War College, 1998), 7.

49. Loren B. Thompson, "Introduction," in *Low-Intensity Conflict: The Pattern of Warfare in the Modern World,* edited by Loren B. Thompson (New York and Ontario: Lexington, 1989), 23.

50. Neil Livingstone, "A New U.S. Antiterrorism Strategy for the 1990s," in Thompson, *Low-Intensity Conflict,* 93.

51. O'Neill, *Insurgency and Terrorism,* 130.

52. Quoted in Noel Barber, *The War of the Running Dogs: The Malayan Emergency, 1948–1960* (New York: Weybright and Talley, 1972), 63.

53. Iván Hinojosa, "On Power Relations and the Nouveau Riche: Shining Path and the Radical Peruvian Left," in Stern, *Shining and Other Paths,* 77.

54. Lloyd J. Matthews, introduction to "Part I, Symmetries and Asymmetries: A Historical Perspective," in Matthews, *Challenging the U.S.*, 34.

55. Paul F. Herman Jr., "Asymmetrical Warfare: Sizing the Threat," *Low Intensity Conflict and Law Enforcement Journal* 6, no. 1 (summer 1997): 176. Dunlap, in *Preliminary Observations,* says that in broad terms it simply means warfare that seeks to avoid an opponent's strengths; it is an approach that tries to focus whatever may be one side's comparative advantages against its enemy's relative weaknesses. In a way, seeking asymmetries is fundamental to fighting all wars. But in the modern context asymmetrical warfare emphasizes what are popularly perceived as unconventional or nontraditional methodologies. Sendero was a nontraditional revolutionary organization.

56. Belaunde decided that the Sinchis, a supposed counterinsurgency unit of the Civil Guard created during his first administration (1963–68), which played an important role in combating the 1965 insurgency, would cope with Sendero in Ayacucho. The Sinchis, as was going to be the case with the armed forces, were trained to fight classical insurgents, something the members of Sendero were not. Frustration and impotence led to abuse of the population.

57. *El Comercio,* June 16, 1965, quoted in Pedraglio, *Seguridad Democrática Integra,* 57.

58. Donald Mackay, *The Malayan Emergency, 1948–60: The Domino That Stood* (London and Washington, D.C.: Brassey's, 1997), 162.

59. Tapia, *Las Fuerzas Armadas,* 101.

60. Barber, *War of the Running Dogs,* 193.

61. O'Neill, *Insurgency and Terrorism,* 125–26.

62. Quoted in Harry Summers, "A War Is a War Is a War Is a War," in Thompson, *Low-Intensity Conflict,* 31. Peruvian intelligence did not perform badly prior to the ILA; actually, it correctly anticipated it but the consumers did not pay much attention. In spite of this relative success, it failed to assess what kind of insurgency the Sendero represented. See Gustavo Gorriti, *Historia de la Guerra Milenaria en el Perú-I* (Lima: Editorial Apoyo, 1990), 80–93.

63. McCuen, *Art of Counter-revolutionary War,* 29.

64. Shultz, "Political Strategies," 129.

65. Barber, *War of the Running Dogs,* 62.

66. Mauceri, *State under Siege,* 136.

67. Degregori and Rivera, *Fuerzas Armadas,* 11.

68. McCuen, *Art of Counter-revolutionary War,* 143.

69. Clutterbuck, *Terrorism and Guerrilla Warfare,* 129.

70. Barber, *War of the Running Dogs,* 96, 160.

71. Mackay, *Malayan Emergency,* 117.

72. McCuen, *Art of Counter-revolutionary War,* 57.

73. Clutterbuck, *Terrorism and Guerrilla Warfare,* 149.

74. McCuen, *Art of Counter-revolutionary War,* 176, 204.

75. Clutterbuck, *Terrorism and Guerrilla Warfare,* 10.

76. O'Neill, *Insurgency and Terrorism,* 80–81. In Algeria, Ben Boulaid, a National Liberation Front (FLN) leader, said that the French *ratissages* operations (*razzias*) were its best recruiting agent. One French officer, in the

face of excesses by the paras, said, "I am Captain Bottier; I fought myself; I did thirty jumps with the resistance. . . . You band of little idiots—you are doing exactly what the FLN terrorists count on you doing." The journalist Herb Greer, reporting on a particularly brutal French reprisal in which women were killed, quotes a member of the FLN as declaring, "Voilà, we've won another battle. They hate the French a little more now. The stupid bastards are winning the war for us." Both quotes are from Horne, *Savage War of Peace,* 110, 173–74.

77. Thompson, *Revolutionary War,* 96.

78. Quoted in Horne, *Savage War of Peace,* 107.

79. Edward Luttwak, "Notes on Low Intensity Warfare," in *Defense Planning for the 1990s,* edited by William A. Buckingham Jr. (Washington, D.C.: National Defense University Press, 1984), 206–7, quoted in Thompson, *Low-Intensity Conflict,* 3–4.

80. McCuen, *Art of Counter-revolutionary War,* 60.

81. Paul Seabury and Angello Codevilla, *War: Ends and Means* (New York: Basic Books, 1989), 186, quoted in J. I. Bakker, "The Aceh War and the Creation of the Netherlands East Indies State," in *Great Powers and Little Wars: The Limits of Power,* edited by A. Hamish Ion and E. S. Errington (Westport and London: Praeger, 1993), 60.

82. Clutterbuck, *Terrorism and Guerrilla Warfare,* 193.

83. Ibid., 12.

84. Mackay, *Malayan Emergency,* 93.

85. McCuen, *Art of Counter-revolutionary War,* 253.

86. McClintock, *Revolutionary Movements,* 77.

87. Ibid., 290.

88. O'Neill, *Insurgency and Terrorism,* 72, 77.

89. Kirk, *Monkey's Paw,* 174.

90. O'Neill, *Insurgency and Terrorism,* 84–85.

91. Timothy Lomperis, *From People's War to People's Rule: Insurgency, Intervention, and the Lessons of Vietnam* (Chapel Hill: University of North Carolina Press, 1996), 301.

92. Thomas A. Marks, *Maoist Insurgency since Vietnam* (London and Portland: Frank Cass, 1996), 254.

93. Simpson, *In the Forests of the Night,* 84.

94. Stern, *Shining and Other Paths,* 4. Guzmán also seemed not to have read history: in 1949, the Greeks defeated the communist insurgency, among other reasons because the population had been alienated by rebel excesses. The population defended itself and supported the government without special counterorganizational measures other than the formation of a militia. So far, no one but the Greeks, says McCuen, and obviously after them the Peruvians, has accomplished the feat—and they did it with assistance from the rebels themselves (*Art of Counter-revolutionary War,* 309).

95. Degregori, "Harvesting Storms," 146–47.

96. Bolivar, *Insurgency and Counterinsurgency,* 12–13.

97. Mauceri, *State under Siege,* 138.

98. Instituto de Defensa Legal, *Perú: En La Espiral de Violencia* (Lima, Instituto de Defensa Legal, 1990), 10.

99. Marks, *Maoist Insurgencies,* 277.

100. Gagnon, *Warrior in Eden,* 159.

101. Francisco Reyes, "Los Neutrales han Muerto," in *Hablan los Ronderos,* edited by Orin Starn (Lima: Instituto de Estudios Peruanos, 1992), 59.

102. Tapia, *Las Fuerzas Armadas,* 127.

103. Manrique, *The War for the Central Sierra,* 226, 236.

104. McCuen, *Art of Counter-revolutionary War,* 103–4.

105. José Luis Rénique, "Apogee and Crisis of a Third Path: Mariateguismo, People's War, and Counterinsurgency in Puno, 1987–1994, in Stern, *Shining and Other Paths,* 332.

106. Kirk, *Monkey's Paw,* 192.

107. Stern, *Shining and Other Paths,* 126.

108. C. I. Degregori, "Ayacucho despues de la Violencia," in C. I. Degregori et al., *Las Rondas Campesinas y la Derrota de Sendero Luminoso* (Lima: Instituto de Estudios Peruanos, 1996), 26.

109. Michael Schoelwer, "The Failure of the U.S. Intelligence Community in LIC," in Thompson, *Low-Intensity Conflict,* 148.

110. Hoe and Morris, *Re-enter the SAS,* 205.

111. Maurice Tugwell and David Charters, "Special Operations and the Threats to United States Interests in the 1980s," in *Special Operations in U.S. Strategy,* edited by Frank R. Barnett (Washington, D.C.: National Defense University Press and National Strategy Information Center, 1984), 34–35.

112. Donald J. Mrozek, "Asymmetric Response to American Air Supremacy in Vietnam," in Matthews, *Challenging the U.S.,* 85.

113. Quoted in McCuen, *Art of Counter-revolutionary War,* 206.

114. Horne, *Savage War of Peace,* 254, 335.

115. Mackay, *Malayan Emergency,* 152.

116. Hoe and Morris, *Re-enter the SAS,* 169.

117. Matthews, *Challenging the U.S.,* 20.

118. Quoted in McCuen, *Art of Counter-revolutionary War,* 62.

119. Mackay, *Malayan Emergency,* 129.

120. Quoted in Barber, *War of the Running Dogs,* 118–19.

121. See "El Topo (The Mole)," *Caretas,* August 1, 1991.

122. Paul A. Smith Jr., *On Political War* (Washington, D.C.: National Defense University Press, 1989), 21–22.

123. Shultz, "Political Strategies," 131.

124. Clutterbuck, *Terrorism and Guerrilla Warfare,* 13.

125. McCuen, *Art of Counter-revolutionary War,* 56.

COLOMBIA

1. Gran Colombia was the name given to the newly independent republic that had been the Spanish Viceroyalty of Nueva Granada, which encompassed what is today Panama, Colombia, Venezuela, and Ecuador.

2. There are many good historical studies of Colombia, including David Bushnell's many publications on the subject; Paul Oquist, *Violence, Conflict, and Politics in Colombia* (Bogotá: Instituto de Estudios Colombianos, 1978); and Alfredo Ranguel Suarez, *Colombia: Guerra en el fin de siglo* (Bogotá: Universidad de los Andes, 1999). A brief sketch of Colombia's history is available in U.S. Department of State, "Background Notes," on the Internet at

<www.state.gov/www/background_notes/Colombia_1999_bgn.html> (accessed March 18, 2002).

3. This was one of the first uses of the term *terrorism* in the Colombian lexicon of violence and thus an acknowledgment that terrorism exists in the country, protestations presented in the introduction to this study notwithstanding. However, it was only used in relation to Escobar's bombing campaign.

4. Francisco Santos, "The Colombian Nightmare," *Chicago Tribune*, July 16, 2000.

5. "Confidenciales," *Semana*, June 24, 2000, Internet edition.

6. Government of Colombia Executive Order 180 of 1988, adopted as permanent legislation in 1991.

7. *1999 Country Reports on Human Rights Practices: Colombia*. Washington, D.C.: U.S. Department of State, February 25, 2000. Internet version: <http://www.state.gov/www/global/human_rights/1999_hrp_report/colombia.html> (accessed March 18, 2002).

8. Andres Oppenheimer, "Hugo Chavez, Colombia's Marulanda Enriching Miami," *Miami Herald*, July 2, 2000, Internet edition.

9. "RCN Poll Results," *Semana*, August 1999, Internet edition.

10. Kimberley L. Thachuk, "Colombian Drug Policy: Crisis Decision-Making," in *Crisis? What Crisis? Security Issues in Colombia*, edited by James L. Zackrison (Washington, D.C.: National Defense University Press, 1999).

11. For a detailed account of this effort, see Rafael Pardo Rueda, *De primera mano, Colombia, 1986–1994: Entre conflictos y esperanzas* (Bogotá: CEREC, Grupo Editorial Norma, 1996).

12. Francisco Leal Buitrago, "Las utopias de la paz," in *Los laberintos de la guerra*, edited by Francisco Leal Buitrago (Bogotá: TM Editores, 1999).

13. Josiah M. Heyman and Alan Smart, "States and Illegal Practices: An Overview," in *States and Illegal Practices*, edited by Josiah M. Heyman (New York: Berg, 1999), 3.

14. Interview with Dr. Eduardo Pizarro, July 18, 2000.

15. The guerrillas set up mobile roadblocks, searching for detainees with sufficient money to merit kidnapping for ransom. These roadblocks are called "miraculous fishing expeditions," or *pescas milagrosas*.

16. Interview with Pastor Climaco Hoya, retired SDA minister, Cali, Colombia, March 12, 1999.

17. A good source on the structure and history of the Colombian forces in terms of counterterrorism and police forces (unfortunately available only in Spanish) is Malcolm Deas and Maria Victoria Llorente, eds., *Reconocer la Guerra para Construir la Paz* (Bogotá: CEREC, Ediciones Uniandes, and Editorial Norma, 1999). A second source, primarily descriptive of the current force structure, is Policia Nacional Direccion de Inteligencia, *Reflexiones de Inteligencia #4: Vision panoramica de los servicios de inteligencia* (Santa Fe de Bogota: Policia Nacional Direccion de Inteligencia, 1999).

18. Policia Nacional Direccion de Inteligencia, *Reflexiones de Inteligencia #4*.

19. Some of this material is based on an interview with a Colombian military official who requested anonymity, February 2000. The description

of the GAULA's organization was obtained from an interview with Col. Jesus Bohorquez, director of the military (army) GAULAs, in Bogotá, March 1999. The number of hostages and rescue efforts were compiled from various government sources.

20. Eduardo Pizarro, "Toward an Institutional Collapse?" in Zackrison, *Crisis?*

21. Interview with Jorge Alberto Londono, General Manager, Invamer Gallup, February 2000.

22. Steve Salisbury, "Rebels Vow to Seize Power at Any Price," *Washington Times*, January 17, 2002, A14.

SPAIN

1. Of course, this is not the only possible definition of *terrorism* but a working one adopted for the benefit of the whole project. The director of this project, Yonah Alexander, gave us the example of a much more general definition, which is the one used by the U.S. Department of Defense: "The calculated use of violence or threat of violence to inculcate fear; intended to coerce or try to intimidate governments or societies in the pursuit of goals that are generally political, religious, or ideological." Another example may simply be "coercive intimidation used for political ends," proposed in Richard E. Friedman, "In Search of a Counterterrorism Strategy," *Terrorism* 12, no. 6 (1989): 417–18.

2. See, for example, Fernando Reinares, *Terrorismo y antiterrorismo* (Barcelona: Paidós, 1998).

3. For example, ETA had close relations with the Provisional Irish Republican Army (PIRA) and other terrorist groups. See generally ibid., 175.

4. The GRAPO acknowledged its responsibility for a frustrated attempt to rob a money van in late June 2000 in Vigo (Galicia), which resulted in the death of two guards. Other terrorist groups, particularly Catalonian groups demanding independence from Spain, such as Terra Lliure (Free Land), had some relevance during the transition to democracy.

5. See Fernando Reinares, "Sociogénesis y evolución del terrorismo en España," in *España: sociedad y política*, edited by Salvador Giner (Madrid: Espasa Calpe, 1990), 366–70.

6. For a recent and excellent book covering relevant aspects of ETA, see Antonio Elorza, José María Garmendia, Gurutz Jáuregui, Florencio Domínguez Iribarren, and Paxto Unzueta, *La historia de ETA* (Madrid: Temas de Hoy, 2000). See also the comprehensive article by Goldie Shabad and Francisco José Llera Ramo, "Political Violence in a Democratic State: Basque Terrorism in Spain," in *Terrorism in Context*, edited by Martha Crenshaw (University Park: Pennsylvania State University Press, 1995), 410–69.

7. Antonio Elorza has edited a selection of Arana's texts in Sabino Arana Goiri, *La patria de los vascos: Antología de escritos políticos* (San Sebastián: Haramburu, 1995). For a critique of his ideology, see Jon Juaristi, *El bucle melancólico* (Madrid: Espasa, 1997), particularly chapters 4 and 5.

8. This new foundation of Basque nationalism in the Basque language is largely due to the effort of Federico Krutwig. He had an ethnically mixed origin and was a militant of ETA from 1966 to 1968. Krutwig wrote a very in-

fluential book (published under the pseudonym Fernando Sarrailh) called *Vasconia: Estudio dialéctico de una nacionalidad* (Buenos Aires: Norbait, [ca. 1963]). Some authors contend that this book was of material importance for ETA in its first years as a clandestine group (Reinares, *Terrorismo y antiterrorismo,* 44); others deny this direct influence (Juaristi, *El bucle melancólico,* 285). The important fact is not whether *Vasconia* directly influenced ETA. The key was the renewal of the whole approach that the book implied, that language, rather than race, is the defining feature of Basque nationalism. From an ethnic perspective, language is the soul of a people. See Elorza et al., *La historia de ETA,* 59.

If one considers the mixed demographic composition of the Basque Land in the time of Arana, but also when ETA was set up, the turn to Euskera becomes a necessary step toward the construction of a realistic nationalism. Of course, as the sociologist Gurutz Júaregui notes, Euskera itself is a language that was not spoken by most Basques ("ETA: Orígenes y evolución ideológica y política," in Elorza et al., *La historia de ETA,* 175).

9. The boundaries of the Basque region are a source of controversy even among radical Basque groups. Today, the Basque Autonomy includes three provinces: Vizcaya, Guipúzcoa, and Alava. However, the Basque Movement of National Liberation pretends at least that the seven historical provinces of the Basque country (the three already mentioned plus Navarra in Spain and Laourd, Basse Navarre, and Soule in France [also known as the French Basque Land]) constitute the Basque nation. One should take into account that Basque nationalism is of low priority in the French Basque Land and that there are no expectations for growth of Basque nationalism in Navarra.

10. See Gurutz Jáuregui, "ETA," in Elorza et al., *La historia de ETA,* 171.

11. The Burgos trial occurred in December 1970. In that trial, three members of ETA were found guilty and sentenced to death but were finally pardoned by Franco. However, all the resistance to the trial and the coverage by the media helped ETA to acquire an international name and also to be recognized as a fighter for democracy against Franco. See, for example, Sagrario Morán, *ETA entre España y Francia* (Madrid: Universidad Complutense de Madrid, 1998), 76. Another famous trial with charges of terrorism took place in 1975 and ended with a death sentence for five terrorists, including two members of ETA and three members of the Frente Revolucionario Antifascista y Patriótico (FRAP). On this occasion, the sentence was enforced. See J. L. Piñuel, *El terrorismo en la transición española, 1972–1982* (Madrid: Fundamentos, 1986). After the restoration of democracy in Spain following the death of Franco in 1975, the Spanish legal order abolished capital punishment.

12. An accurate portrayal of these quarrels may be found in the history of ETA's assemblies. For an account of the ideological and political problems in the Fifth and Sixth Assemblies, see Gurutz Jáuregui, "ETA," in Elorza et al., *La historia de ETA,* 233.

13. For instance, Jáuregui affirms that ETA has been ideologically dead from 1971 to the present (ibid., 260).

14. It has been reported that ETA has earned approximately 6.7 billion pesetas from its kidnappings. This calculation is made from the abduction

of Felipe Huarte, a businessman from Navarra, in 1973 to the abduction of Cosme Delclaux, a Basque businessman, in 1997. See Florencio Domínguez Iribarren, "El enfrentamiento de ETA con la democracia," in Elorza et al., *La historia de ETA,* 360. Of the seventy-seven people kidnapped by ETA between 1972 and 1997, two were elected officials, one was a prison official, and the other seventy-four were civilians. As to the place where the kidnappings happened, sixty-three were in the Basque Land (Vizcaya, Guipuzcoa, and Alava) and fourteen in the rest of Spain.

15. The MLNV consists of legal and illegal organizations, including a political party, Herri Batasuna (HB); a labor union, Langillen Abertzalen Batzordea (LAB); groups of young militants, for example, Jarrai and Taldes Y; and ETA.

16. A relevant member of the Socialist Party (Partido Socialista Obrero Español, or PSOE) said that precisely that moment should have witnessed the beginning of the end of violence. See José María Benegas, *Euskadi: Sin la paz nada es posible* (Barcelona: Argos Vergara, 1984), 50 (quoted in Morán, *ETA entre España y Francia,* 105).

17. See Juan Aranzadi, Jon Juaristi, and Paxto Unzueta, *Auto de terminación* (Madrid: El Pais, 1994), quoted in Jáuregui, "ETA," 267.

18. Actually, the French police were following the trail of two wired Russian missiles that Spanish intelligence had sold to the terrorist band.

19. We will discuss this collaboration further in the next section.

20. See Iribarren, "El enfrentamiento," 419.

21. The Forum of Ermua, already mentioned, was an initiative born at that time.

22. The Ajuría Enea Pact was an agreement against violence signed on January 12, 1988, by the Partido Socialista Obrero Español, Alianza Popular (AP) [now Partido Popular], Centro Democrático y Social (CDS), Partido Liberal (PL), Convergencia i Unió (CIU), Partido Nacionalista Vasco, and Euskadiko Ezkerra. Two Basque parties—HB and Eusko Alkartasuna (EA)—did not sign. The Lizarra Pact of August 1998 brought the Ajuría Enea Pact to an end because the PNV agreed to be associated with Euskal Herritarrok (just a new name for HB) and therefore with ETA. ETA's cease-fire, begun in September 1998, ended in December 1999 because the terrorist band believed that the PNV did not go far enough in its compromise with both the "national construction" of the Basque country and the interruption of any relationship with "the Spanish people."

23. For an analysis focused on this issue, see Benjamín Tejerina, "Civil Society, Political Violence, and Social Movements: The Case of the Basque Country," in *State and Societal Reactions to Terrorism,* edited by Fernando Reinares (Oñati: International Institute for the Sociology of Law, 1997), 121–48. Tejerina's article attempts to prove that "the success or failure of an organization using political violence does not depend so directly on its military efficiency, but on its capacity to create a social movement around itself, or to attract organizations from different social movements to its objectives" (122).

24. On the military, see Oscar Jaime-Jiménez, "Control social y violencia colectiva: Un estudio comparado de la respuesta policial al terrorismo en sociedades avanzadas," *Sistema,* no. 134 (1996): 95–108.

25. Yonah Alexander, remarks at "Conference Report on Legal Aspects of Terrorism," *Terrorism* 12, no. 4 (1989): 298–99.

26. Santiago Sánchez, "Spain: Have We Learned Anything from Our Experience?" in Reinares, *State and Societal Reactions to Terrorism*, 43.

27. For a general account, see Oscar Jaime-Jiménez, "Avatares políticos y organizativos de la respuesta policial al terrorismo en España (1976–1996)," in Reinares, *State and Societal Reactions to Terrorism*, 59–81.

28. See table 2.

29. Article 52(2) is a provision that governs the exceptional derogation of fundamental rights. It says: "An organic law may determine the manner and the circumstances in which, on an individual basis and with the necessary participation of the courts and proper parliamentary control, the rights recognized in section 17, clause 2, and section 18, clauses 2 and 3, may be suspended as regards specific persons in connection with investigation of the activities of armed bands or terrorists groups." For a commentary on this provision, see Francisco Fernández Segado, in *Comentarios a la Constitution Española de 1978*, edited by Oscar Alzaga Villamil, vol. 4 (Madrid: Cortes Generales, 1996), 627. A critique of the provision may be found in Sánchez, "Spain," 43–45. The laws allowing special procedures have been challenged before the Constitutional Court, which declared them partially unconstitutional. See cases STC 25/1981, of July 14, 1981, *Boletín Oficial del Estado* (BOE) of August 13, 1981; STC 199/1987, of December 16, 1987, BOE of January 8, 1988; STC 89/1993, of March 12, 1993, BOE of April 15, 1993; and STC 71/1994, of March 3, 1994, BOE of March 24, 1994. See also, for example, José Carlos Remotti Carbonell, *Constitución y medidas contra el terrorismo* (Madrid: Colex, 1998), 247–327.

30. All of these reforms were undermined by the activities of the Grupos Antiterrorista de Liberación (GAL), which we will describe subsequently.

31. See Reinares, *Terrorismo y antiterrorismo*, 132–40.

32. Sánchez, "Have We Learned Anything from Our Experience?" 50.

33. Some specific studies on the subject are Robert Clark, *Negotiating with ETA: Obstacles to Peace in the Basque Country, 1975–1988* (Reno: University of Nevada Press, 1990); and Carlos López Fonseca, *Negociar con ETA: De Argel al Gobierno del Partido Popular* (Madrid: Temas de Hoy, 1996).

34. The present policy differs from the one defended by the PNV under the Lizarra Pact.

35. As a matter of fact, the government only requires a statement by a member of ETA that he or she renounces violence. Moreover, that person must have no record of having been accused of a crime of blood.

36. Art. 62(j) CE.

37. For a view from the courts, see, among others, Juan Carlos Campo Moreno, *Represión penal del terrorismo: Una visión jurisprudencial* (Valencia: Tirant lo Blanch, 1997). On the matter of law enforcement, we are thinking mainly of the Spanish Criminal Code of 1995, which has a special provision, Title XXII, sec. 2, that sanctions terrorist activities (Arts. 571–80). There are many commentaries on these articles. See, for example, Gonzalo Rodríguez Mourullo, *Comentarios al Código penal* (Madrid: Civitas, 1997).

38. Sánchez, "Spain," 51.

39. Other Basques have been ministers of the interior, such as the socialist José Luis Corcuera and the present minister, Jaime Mayor Oreja, who has served since 1996.

40. Alexander notes that it may be misleading to conclude that a decline in terrorist incidents shows that counterterrorist policies have worked. If the government makes political or economic concessions to terrorists, for example, the number of incidents may decline but the influence of terrorists may have been strengthened. Similarly, one incident may have a greater political, psychological, and strategic impact than hundreds of small attacks.

41. Ley 32/1999, October 8, Solidaridad con las víctimas del terrorismo, BOE, no. 242, October 9, 1999. In 2000, U.S. $1 was worth approximately 175 pesetas.

42. See, generally, José Ramón Recalde, "Problemas de legitimidad: Provocación terrorista y respuesta del Estado," in Reinares, *State and Societal Reactions to Terrorism,* 31–39 (analyzing the lack of a proper state response to terrorism, the problem of illegitimate violence, and the failure of the democrats to fight antidemocrats). See also Melchor Miralles and Ricardo Arques, *Amedo: El estado contra ETA* (Barcelona: Plaza Janes, 1989).

43. Morán, *ETA entre España y Francia,* 186–87. Newspapers such as EGIN denounced the GAL as a group created by the Spanish government with the tacit acceptance of French authorities.

44. Judgment of the Second Chamber of the Supreme Court, July 29, 1998.

45. Judgment of the Audiencia Nacional, April 26, 2000.

46. See Fernando Reinares, "Fundamentos para una política gubernamental antiterrorista en el contexto de regímenes democráticos," *Sistema,* nos. 132–33 (1996): 111–28. This article is included as chapter 4 in his book *Terrorismo y antiterrorismo.*

47. See Morán, *ETA entre España y Francia.*

48. See Reinares, *Terrorismo y antiterrorismo,* 140–43, which emphasizes this poor system of information dispersal.

49. Gaston Deferre declared at that time that "un terroriste n'est pas un refugié politique" (a terrorist is not a political refugee).

50. Philip Bidart, the leader of Iparretarrak, was arrested in France on February 20, 1988.

51. See Antonio Cassese, *Terrorism, Politics, and Law* (Cambridge: Cambridge University Press, 1989). See also Alfred P. Rubin, "Current Legal Approaches to International Terrorism," *Terrorism* 13, nos. 4–5 (July–October 1990): 277–97 (Rubin defends an expansion of the humanitarian element that has become part of the law of war treaties to which nearly all states are parties; the application of the general rules of international law forbidding states to permit their territory to be used as a base for armed bands of whatever nature to operate in the territory of another state; and the refining of the law of self-defense and neutrality. These approaches are preferred to those that focus on the extension of national jurisdiction in disregard of the limits inherent in the international legal order because it is "the one most likely to lead to unmanageable political complications." Writing in 1989, Rubin erroneously thought that an "international criminal court" was "inconsistent

with both law and reality.") Richard Friedman also favors self-help as legitimate under international law ("In Search of a Counterterrorism Strategy").

The treaties to which Spain is a party are available on the Internet from any major source (such as the United Nations treaties data base). For a Spanish collection of treaties related to terrorism, see, for example, Jorge Pueyo Losa and M. Teresa Ponte Iglesias, *Derecho internacional público: Recopilación de instrumentos jurídicos fundamentales* (Santiago de Compostela: Tórculo, 1998), 191–231. See also Yonah Alexander, ed., *International Terrorism: Political and Legal Documents* (Dordrecht: Kluwer, 1992).

52. The European Convention on the Suppression of Terrorism, concluded at Strasbourg on January 27, 1977, is available at <http://conventions.coe.int/Treaty/EN/Treaties/HTML/090.htm>. Spain ratified the convention on May 9, 1980. For a Spanish commentary on the convention, see Eduardo Vilariño, "El convenio europeo sobre represión del terrorismo," *Revista de Instituciones Europeas*, no. 4 (1978): 427–34.

53. The European Convention on Extradition was concluded in Paris on December 13, 1957. It is available at <http://www.coe.fr/eng/legaltxt/24e.htm> (March 18, 2002). The new provisions of the French criminal code made it possible for the judiciary to extradite ETA members just for belonging to the terrorist organization. The first case occurred on June 8, 1994, when the Appellate Court of Paris authorized the extradition of Oroitz Salegi García on the grounds of being a member of ETA. See Morán, *ETA entre España y Francia*, 372, which emphasizes the symbolic meaning of this change.

54. European Union Treaty, as reformed by the Treaty of Amsterdam in 1997.

55. The negotiation of the Treaty of Amsterdam became very difficult when the problem of asylum was discussed. Indeed, the Spanish government, spurred by the controversial decision of a Belgian authority not to extradite two Spanish citizens accused of complicity with ETA, presented a proposal to add a new paragraph on asylum to Article 8 of the Treaty Establishing the European Community. That paragraph was intended to exclude the nationals of the members of the European Union from the right to asylum and the status of refugee. When the scope of Spain's first proposal proved to be too wide, a second proposal intended to limit the right of asylum was presented. Finally, the member states decided to annex Protocol 29 to the European Community Treaty on asylum for nationals of member states of the European Union (1997), which is a compromise intended to accommodate the Spanish view with the international obligations and opinions of other European Union members.

56. Article 29, European Union Treaty. On the third pillar after the Treaty of Amsterdam, see Jaap de Zwaan and Mireille Vrouenraets, "The Future of the Third Pillar: An Evaluation of the Treaty of Amsterdam," in *The European Union after Amsterdam*, edited by Ton Heukels, Niels Blokker, and Maecel Brus (The Hague: Kluwer, 1998), 203–14. See also Carlos Espósito, "The EU Response toward Racism," *Revue des Affaires Européens*, nos. 1–2 (2000): 118–27. For a study of the third pillar as established by the Treaty of Maastricht, see J. Monar and R. Morgan, eds., *The Third Pillar of the European Union* (Brussels: European Interuniversity Press, 1994).

57. Title IV, European Community Treaty. See Henry Labayle, "Un espace de liberté, de sécurité, et de justice," *Revue trimestrielle de droit européen* 33, no. 4 (1997): 813–82; and Hervé Bribosia, "Liberté, securité, et justice: L'imbroglio d'un nouvel espace," *Revue du Marché Unique Européen*, no. 1 (1998): 27–54. See also Kay Hailbronner, "The Treaty of Amsterdam and Migration Law," *European Journal of Migration and Law* 1 (1999): 1–7; and J. D. M. Steenbergen, "All the King's Horses . . . : Probabilities and Possibilities for the Implementation of the New Title IV EC Treaty," *European Journal of Migration and Law* 2, no. 1 (1999): 29–60.

The transfer of subjects is usually called "communitarization." A noteworthy example here would be the Schengen Agreements of June 19, 1990, which provides for police transboundary vigilance and pursuit and judicial cooperation in cases of terrorism. See, generally, Council Decision of May 1, 1999, which laid down the detailed arrangements for the integration of the Schengen Secretariat into the General Secretariat of the Council, OJ L 119, 7.5.1999, p. 49.

58. OJ C 78, 30.3.1995, p. 1.

59. OJ L 273, 25.10.1996, p. 1.

60. OJ C 313, 23.10.1996, p. 11.

61. OJ C 26, 30.1.1999, p. 22.

62. OJ C 373, 23.12.1999, p. 1.

63. See Peter Chalk, "EU Counter-terrorism, the Maastricht Third Pillar, and Liberal Democratic Acceptability," *Terrorism and Political Violence* 6, no. 2 (1994): 103–45.

64. On the second pillar after the Treaty of Amsterdam, see Antonio Remiro-Brotóns, "¿Qué ha significado el Tratado de Amsterdam para la PESC?" *Gaceta Jurídica de la CE*, series D, no. 29 (1999): 71–104. The overlapping problem is mentioned by Reinares (*Terrorismo y antiterrorismo*, 209), who cites a paper by Monica den Boer presented at the conference European Democracies against Terrorism, International Institute for the Sociology of Law, Oñati, 1996.

65. See Reinares, *Terrorismo y antiterrorismo*, 145–46.

66. See Judgment of the Second Chamber of the Supreme Court, July 29, 1998; and Judgment of the Audiencia Nacional, April 26, 2000.

67. See the Joint Declaration by the Heads of State and Government of the European Union, the President of the European Parliament, the President of the European Commission, and the High Representative for the Common Foreign and Security Policy, September 14, 2001.

UNITED KINGDOM

1. Emergency Powers Act 1920, Sec. 2(1).

2. PTA, Sec. 20.

3. William Best was in the Royal Irish Rangers but was originally from Derry. He was visiting friends at the time of his kidnapping. Four hundred women attacked the offices of the official IRA the next day, expressing the outrage of the local community over the murder.

4. For example, the IRA set off a bomb outside the Chelsea Barracks in London on October 10, 1981, which killed two civilians and injured twenty-

three soldiers. On October 12, 1984, it set off a bomb at the hotel being used for the Conservative Party's annual conference—the Grand Hotel in Brighton. This bomb was intended to kill the entire British cabinet in one go. It killed five people and injured many more but missed its principal target, Margaret Thatcher, then prime minister, and members of her cabinet. In the spring of 1993, IRA bombs at Warrington and Bishopsgate, respectively, killed two and one persons and injured fifty-one and forty-five others. After the collapse of the IRA cease-fire in February 1996, large bombs at Canary Wharf in London (two dead and more than one hundred injured) and in Manchester (more than two hundred injured) rocked the business communities there.

5. The security services are popularly known, respectively, as MI5 and MI6.

6. On Tuesday, June 8, 1971, Harry Tuzo, then general officer commanding the British Army, said that a permanent military solution to the conflict could not be achieved.

7. Various authors have worked on chronologies of the Troubles. Most accessible is a series of chronologies on the Web at <http://cain.ulst.ac.uk/othelem/chron.htm>, accessed March 18, 2000, prepared by Paul Bew and Gordon Gillespie, both of Queen's University Belfast, who coauthored two books: *Northern Ireland: A Chronology of the Troubles, 1968–1993* (Dublin: Gill and Macmillan, 1993); and *The Northern Ireland Peace Process, 1993–1996: A Chronology* (London: Serif, 1996). In addition, there are Sydney Elliott and W. D. Flackes, *Northern Ireland: A Political Directory, 1968–1999* (Belfast: Blackstaff, 1999); and Malcolm Sutton, *An Index of Deaths from the Conflict in Ireland, 1969–1993* (Belfast: Beyond the Pale, 1994).

8. The UDR was a locally recruited branch of the British Army.

9. One example is the demonstrations and riots in Seattle during the G-8 meeting in early 2000.

10. This was in the Downing Street Declaration of August 1969.

11. Efforts to foster dialogue included the Downing Street Declaration of 1969, Tripartite talks in 1971, meetings with the IRA in London in 1972, the Darlington Conference in 1972, the Sunningdale Agreement in 1973, Constitutional Elections and Assembly in 1975, the Aitkins talks in 1980, the Anglo-Irish Intergovernmental Council in 1981, and the Anglo-Irish Agreement in 1985.

12. Physical abuse and harsh intimidation were allegedly used by the police in the early 1970s as a means of obtaining confessions.

13. This operation had an important legal background in that the denial of continuous control over parts of Ulster by the paramilitaries was a major factor in effectively preventing them from succeeding in claiming combatant status under the international laws of armed conflict.

ISRAEL

1. The government of Israel adopted a resolution making it the legal heir of the Jordanian government with regard to all of Judaea and Samaria (the West Bank) and the legal heir of the Egyptian military administration with regard to the Gaza Strip. The government regarded all of the lands as

belonging to the state, with all public lands designated for the establishment of Israeli settlements in those areas. It also saw no obligation to preserve any tracts for the needs of the indigenous Palestinian populace.

2. The acronym SHABAK stands for Hebrew *shin-beth-kaff,* the initials of Sherut Bitachon Kelali, which translates as General Security Service.

3. Black September was the name given by the Palestinians to the grim military confrontation that erupted in September 1970 between the Jordanian army and Palestine Liberation Organization (PLO) militias in Jordan (with even Syrian forces penetrating Jordan at a given point with the assistance of PLO fighters).

4. Israel enjoys an extremely high level of alertness among the Israeli public to possible terrorist bombs and any other suspicious phenomena. Every citizen has the ability to immediately call in a police patrol or bomb squad, and this has frequently resulted in the early detection and neutralization of bombs before they could cause harm. Such successful outcomes would not be achievable if it were not for the willingness of the public to tolerate hundreds of false alarms and the unhesitating readiness of the various bomb squads to speed to the site of suspicious objects. The Israeli public and the security services have proven that "crying wolf" does not always diminish vigilance.

5. In February 1999, in the wake of severe military clashes in southern Lebanon, Israel anticipated that Hizbullah would launch Katyusha rockets against Israeli civilian targets, towns, and villages along the Lebanese border. As a precaution, the military authorities of the Israeli Northern Command ordered the local populace to take to the shelters (prompting many civilians to take their families to different locales). The rocket attacks never came, and it was several days before the "all clear" signal was given. Thus, Hizbullah was able to achieve its goal of terrorizing Israelis without launching a single rocket.

6. To this day, Israel has not been able to resolve this difficult dilemma. From the legal, moral, and operational standpoints, Israel must choose between exerting physical pressure during the interrogation of a terrorist for the sake of extracting vital and urgent intelligence and the desire to adhere to the conventional norms of a democratic state that is founded on laws and recognizes the rights of the individual.

7. It is noteworthy that the decision to suspend security measures of one sort or another, a decision that clearly establishes who is to be held responsible if anything goes awry, is a sensitive political-psychological issue.

8. In the interest of preventing, as much as possible, a disruption of the employment of Palestinian workers in Israel, and a similar interest in disturbing the local populace as little as possible, the Israeli government adopted a new policy in 1998. This permitted the entry of workers into Israeli territory, in spite of any closure that might be in effect, as long as such workers had had special permits issued to them on the responsibility of their employers. The functional effectiveness of this decision has not yet been tested in application.

9. The relatively new phenomenon of Palestinian suicide-bombers in 2001–2 has significantly changed this criticism. On one hand, these terror-

ists are clearly choosing closed civilian targets, like restaurants, hotels, shops, malls, or passenger buses. On the other hand, the presence of a security-warden at the entrance of such places did, in numerous cases, deter the terrorist from trying to enter the closed target and brought them to commit suicide at the entrance, thus bringing down significantly the number of Israeli casualties.

10. In keeping with the Oslo Declaration of Principles, Israel and the Palestinians are currently (April 2000) implementing an interim agreement whereby Israel is gradually handing over sections of Judaea, Samaria, and the Gaza Strip to Palestinian control. The occupied territories have been segmented into three categories: Area C, which continues to be under full Israeli military control; Area A, which already has been handed over in its entirety to the Palestinians; and Area B, which has been handed over to the Palestinians in terms of total civil administration but with Israel continuing to be exclusively responsible for collective security.

11. In the past, during the period preceding the peace process, Israel possessed a clear and diametric policy. The strategy in the battle against Palestinian terrorism was expressed in efforts to persuade neighboring countries not to cooperate with Palestinian terrorist organizations and to take initiatives for inhibiting and dampening cross-border attacks; otherwise, their own civil and military facilities might be vulnerable to Israeli attack. During that period, Israel was not deterred by the threat of escalation, even at the risk of war. During the 1950s, such Israeli military actions led to the Sinai Campaign against Egypt. In the 1960s, Israel's actions were directed against Jordan and Syria, which served as no small factor in the backdrop of the Six Day War. The battles of Black September in Jordan of the 1970s had a similar backdrop. Finally, the situation in southern Lebanon led to Operation Peace for Galilee in 1982.

12. Among the prominent examples are the following:

July 1956. Mustafa Hafez, head of Egyptian intelligence in the Gaza Strip, was killed by a letter bomb; two days later, Salah Mustafa, who was responsible for initiating and organizing Fidayun attacks against Israel, was killed in a similar manner.

April 1988. A commando force in Tunis killed Abu Jihad, head of the PLO military arm.

January 1996. Yehya Ayash, the "Engineer," who was behind a string of painful terrorist attacks in Israel, was killed in Gaza (which was under full PA control).

September 1997. There was an unsuccessful attempt to kill Khaled Mashal, one of the key figures of the Hamas movement, in Jordan.

13. An unusual occurrence was the mistaken killing of Ahmad Bushelki, an Arab of Palestinian origin, in Lillehammer, Norway. He was mistakenly identified as a member of the terrorist cell that had carried out the grim massacre of the Israeli athletes at the Munich Olympics in 1972. The resulting political storm over the mistaken identity and the subsequent arrest of some of the Israelis involved in the action led to the revelation that Israel had been behind it.

14. On this point, it is important to bear in mind that until recently Israel did not have a National Security Council. Therefore, such recommendations for action are not examined or analyzed by a neutral and objective body, exploring and weighing the full spectrum of political, legal, moral, and operational considerations for the benefit of the government leadership that has to approve implementation.

15. This assertion does not discount the option of eliminating figures with regard to whom the direct operational effect is negligible. The main contribution in such a case is in reinforcing the concept that Israel has "long arms that can reach anywhere." The goal is to reflect positively on Israel's intelligence services, sending a message that traitors among the senior figures of the terrorist organizations had supplied the information and data to Israeli intelligence and, of course, acknowledging the operational daring and imagination that enabled such a successful attack.

16. On a number of occasions, I was personally involved in situations wherein Israeli intelligence received data that would have justified planning an operation for the elimination of the head of the PLO, Yasser Arafat. Furthermore, in each case it was clear that an operation of this sort would have to be an open one, wherein it would be impossible to hide Israel's direct responsibility. I was of the opinion that the elimination of Arafat would have yielded no real operational benefits; moreover, it would have caused severe damage in the form of the harshest possible reactions both on the political plane and in the form of retaliatory terrorist attacks. In such cases, it was my practice to appear before the IDF chief of staff and the minister of defense, presenting them with the information and functional options for planning a military action along with clear arguments for my ultimate recommendation against initiating such an action. These recommendations were accepted without objection.

17. Israel did not forget the important lessons of its own experience during the British Mandate period. When the mandatory authority began issuing and carrying out death sentences, the Jewish Etzel underground (Irgun Tzva'i Le'umi) instituted a policy of taking British hostages and clearly threatening that, if the British authorities were to carry out further death penalties, the Etzel would hang them. Following the hanging of two such hostages, the Mandate authorities put an end to implementation of the death sentence. In view of this experience, the consideration that deterred Israel more from levying the death penalty than any other was concern over causing harm to potential Israeli hostages or even innocent Jews in other countries.

18. At the end of 1992, following a string of terrorist attacks carried out by Hamas and the Palestinian Islamic Jihad organizations, the government of Israel decided upon a mass expulsion of some four hundred Palestinians to Lebanese territory. Because of judicial delays, and in spite of the fact that Israel's High Court of Justice had approved the expulsion orders, the Lebanese government was able to prevent the deportees from entering its territory, leaving them in a sort of no-man's land adjacent to the border. This area for months saw numerous politicians and media people making pilgrimages to it. Ultimately, in a "thin, small voice," Israel canceled the expulsion orders.

19. Ron Ben-Ishai, "Coping with Terror," public lecture delivered at Tel Aviv University, May 8, 1996, published in *Dapei Elazar 19,* Yad David Elazar Publishing and Tel Aviv University's Jaffee Center for Strategic Studies, 62.

20. The only exception to this is tourism, which has suffered in the wake of every act of terrorism, causing a critical drop in the number of international tourists.

21. From September 29, 2000, to April 22, 2002, there were 102 terrorist acts initiated by Palestinian suicide-bombers. In these acts, a total of 430 Iraelis were killed and some 1,600 were wounded.

TURKEY

1. Terrorists in Turkey murdered more than three hundred such officials and professionals between 1990 and 2000.

2. Approximately six thousand security force members, five thousand civilians (five hundred of them children), and twenty-four thousand terrorists were killed in Turkey during this time period.

3. This group was a Cold War aberration that aimed to create an independent Armenian homeland in eastern Turkey.

4. Kurds are estimated to represent approximately 20 percent of Turkey's 65 million people.

5. Ely Karmon, "Islamic Terrorist Activities in Turkey in the 1990s," *Terrorism and Political Violence* (Tel Aviv) 10, no. 4 (winter 1998), electronic edition.

6. Ibid.

7. Rusen Cakir, "Iddianameye gore Hizbullah" (Hizbullah according to the Indictment), *MAG NTV Magazin,* February 2001, 25.

8. F. Bulut and M. Farac, *Kod Adi: Hizbullah* (Code Name: Hizbullah) (Istanbul: Ozan, 1999), 9.

9. "Birlesemeden Yakalandilar" (Caught before Unification), *Milliyet,* October 3, 2000, electronic ed.

10. Emin Demirel, *Teror,* 4th ed. (Istanbul: Alfa, 1999), 616.

11. Karmon, "Islamic Terrorist Activities."

12. Demirel, *Teror,* 661.

13. "Turk Teroristin Sasirtan Profili" (Surprising Profile of the Turkish Terrorist), *Hurriyet,* July 30, 2000, electronic ed.

14. C. Ozunder, untitled paper presented at the symposium The Terror Problem and Elements of National Power, Turkish War College, Istanbul, 1997, 22.

15. Ismet Imset, *PKK* (Ankara: Turkish Daily News Publications, 1993).

16. USIP (U.S. Institute of Peace), *Special Report: How Terrorism Ends* (Washington, D.C.: USIP, 1999), 1.

17. James L. Gallagher, *Low Intensity Conflict* (Harrisburg, Pa.: Stackpole, 1992), 36.

18. Ali M. Koknar, "The Internationalists: PKK's German Legion," in *First International Symposium on Security and Peace in Eastern and Southeastern Anatolia* (Elazig: Firat University Press, 2000), 199–209.

19. In December 2000, the Turkish Parliament enacted a law granting

early release to approximately twenty thousand inmates convicted of nonpolitical or nonviolent political offenses. In January 2001, the chairman of the Turkish General Staff, Gen. Huseyin Kivrikoglu, claimed that approximately sixteen hundred of those released under the amnesty were PKK members who should have been left behind bars.

20. Gunduz Aktan, "The European Parliament and Turkey," *Perceptions* (Ankara), 3, no. 4 (December 1998–February 1999): 5–10.

21. Turkish Democracy Foundation, *Fact Book on Turkey, Kurds, and PKK Terrorism* (Ankara: Koreks, 1996), 21.

22. Gallagher, *Low Intensity Conflict,* 79.

23. USIP, *Special Report,* 2.

24. Ibid.

25. Ibid., 3.

26. Ibid., 2.

27. Ibid., 4.

28. Ibid., 2.

29. Nese Duzel, "Interview with Turkish State Minister Salih Yildirim," *Yeni Yuzyil,* April 27, 1998, electronic ed.

30. "Vali: Terör Azaldi" (Governor: Less Terror), *Radikal,* November 15, 2000, electronic ed.

31. Mehmet Ali Kislali, untitled column in the newspaper *Turkiye,* October 3, 2000, electronic ed.

32. Ali M. Koknar, "Threats from Above," *Armed Forces Journal International* 137, no. 6 (January 2000): 18.

33. After leaving Syria in the fall of 1998, Ocalan traveled to Russia, Italy, and Greece before he was secretly taken to Kenya by his Greek hosts in February 1999. Soon Turkish intelligence agents found him in Nairobi, Kenya, and took him back to Turkey.

34. The use of "pseudo" insurgents (i.e., members of the counterinsurgency forces posing as insurgents) is a well-established, if lesser-known, method of gathering intelligence and one often used by police units involved in crime detection.

35. These turned terrorists (or "repentant informers" as they were often called) were deployed in a fashion similar to the South African security police deployment of the *askari,* that is, former terrorists from the Umkhonto we Sizwe and Azanian People's Liberation Army.

36. Approximately ten thousand armed terrorists were captured alive between 1984 and 2000.

37. For example, DEVSOL shot antitank rockets at American diplomatic missions as well as Turkish police buildings, tried to bomb a large American air base in Turkey, and attacked and/or assassinated American diplomats, military officers, and civilians in Turkey as well as Turkish military, law enforcement, and intelligence personnel.

38. Aktan, "European Parliament and Turkey."

39. Stephen Button, "Interview with Turkish Minister of Defense Nahit Mentese," *Military Review,* December 1994.

40. Koknar, "Internationalists," 200.

41. Suat Ilhan, *Teror: Neden Turkiye?* (Terror: Why Turkey?) (Ankara: Nu-Do, 1998), 319–20.

42. Ibid.

43. "Diyarbakir'da Teror Azaldi" (Less Terror in Diyarbakir), *Cumhuriyet,* November 15, 2000, electronic ed.

44. Necip Torumtay, *Degisen Stratejilerin Odaginda Turkiye* (Turkey at the Center of Changing Strategies) (Istanbul: Milliyet, 1996), 233.

45. Turkish Democracy Foundation, *Fact Book,* 39–40.

46. "GAP to Fill the Gap in Southeastern Anatolia," *Turkish Daily News,* October 4, 2000, electronic ed.

47. Mehmet Ali Kislali, *Guneydogu: Dusuk Yogunluklu Catisma* (The Southeast: Low-Intensity Conflict) (Ankara: Umit, 1996), 8.

48. Gallagher, *Low Intensity Conflict,* 10.

49. Bulut and Farac, *Kod Adi,* 70–71.

50. Kislali, *Guneydogu,* 223.

51. USIP, *Special Report,* 1.

52. Mahmut Bulut, "Kislaya Donus" (Back to the Barracks), *Sabah,* October 15, 2000, electronic ed.

53. "Tehdit Degerlendirmesi" (Threat Evaluation), <www.ntvmsnbc.com>, November 15, 2000, electronic edition.

54. "Bati'da PKK Usulu Irtica" (PKK-Style Fundamentalism in the West), *Hurriyet,* October 2, 2000, electronic ed.

55. "Vali: Terör Azaldi."

56. "Solcu Partilerden Filistinlilere Destek" (Support from the Leftist Parties to the Palestinians), *Zaman,* October 15, 2000, electronic ed.

57. Koray Dugencioglu, "Buyuyen Bir Tehdit: Uluslararasi Orgutlu Suc" (A Growing Threat: International Organized Crime), *Strateji* 4, no. 11 (Ankara: Strateji Publishing Group, 1999), 131.

58. Sue Pleming, "U.S. Concerned by Rise in International Crime," Reuters, December 15, 2000.

59. In the mid-1990s, PKK's revenue was estimated to be anywhere from $80 to $200 million.

60. F. Haut, J. C. Salomon, and J. L. Vanner, *Two Typical Degenerate Guerrilla Groups: The Liberation Tigers of Tamil Eelam and the Kurdistan Workers' Party* (Paris: Paris Criminology Institute, 1996), 30.

61. F. Gullapoglu, untitled column in *Hurriyet,* April 4, 1998, electronic ed.

62. Ceyhan Mumcu, *Ugur Mumcu Cinayetinin Bilinmeyen Yonleri* (Unknown Aspects of the Ugur Mumcu Assassination) (Ankara: Kuvayi Medya, 1996).

63. Dugencioglu, *Buyuyen Bir Tehdit,* 131.

64. *Cumhuriyet,* October 9, 2000, electronic ed.

65. Bulut and Farac, *Kod Adi,* 70–71.

66. The General Staff created a new unit called Ekonomik ve Mali Izleme Merkezi (Economic and Financial Monitoring Center, or EMIM) for this purpose.

67. Mutlu Colgecen, "Yolsuzluk Resmi Oncelikli Tehdit" (Corruption Is the Official Primary Threat), *Yeni Safak,* November 23, 2000, electronic ed.

68. Approximately forty thousand Turks have died as a result of terrorism since the 1970s, which cost the Turkish economy more than 250 billion dollars.

1. See Yossef Bodansky, *Bin Laden: The Man Who Declared War on America* (Rocklin, Calif.: Prima, 1999), 195.

2. Ibid., 319–20.

3. Ibid., 339–40.

4. See Human Rights Watch, *India: Arms and Abuses in Indian Punjab and Kashmir,* 6, no. 10 (September 1994).

5. In 1947, Pakistan consisted of two parts—West Pakistan and East Pakistan—which were divided by fifteen hundred kilometers of Indian territory. East Pakistan seceded in 1971, after a civil war with West Pakistan, and was renamed Bangladesh.

6. See Ved Marwah, *Uncivil Wars: Pathology of Terrorism in India* (New Delhi: Indus, 1995), 390.

7. Ibid.

8. Ibid., 194.

9. Ibid., 390.

10. Ibid., 65.

11. Ibid., 120.

12. See *India Today* (New Delhi), December 11, 1994.

13. See *North East Sun* (Guwahati), May 15–31, 2000, 8.

14. Quoted in the English daily *Matamgi Yakairol* (Imphal), March 2, 2000.

JAPAN

1. This essay is not primarily about the Aum affair, although we use it to examine shifts in Japan's counterterrorism policy. For English-language examinations of the attack, see such works as Ian Reader, *Religious Violence in Contemporary Japan: The Case of Aum Shinrikyo* (Honolulu: University of Hawaii Press, 2000); David E. Kaplan and Andrew Marshall, *The Cult at the End of the World* (New York: Crown, 1996); and, in comparative perspective, Mark Juergensmeyer, *Terror in the Mind of God* (Berkeley: University of California Press, 2000).

2. For another English-language source that discusses the Japanese government's position on military and police violence, relating it to overall security politics, see Peter J. Katzenstein, *Cultural Norms and National Security* (Ithaca: Cornell University Press, 1996). Katzenstein and Yutaka Tsujinaka are coauthors of *Defending the Japanese State* (Ithaca: Cornell University, East Asia Program, 1992).

3. The Plan for International Bases was aimed at establishing international bases in socialist countries such as North Korea and Cuba, using them to train JRA members, and then sending them back to Japan to achieve communist revolution through armed struggle. See Japan National Police Agency, "White Paper on Police," 1997, 11.

4. On March 31, 1970, Japan Airlines jetliner Flight 351 (Yodo-go), bound for Fukuoka from Tokyo, was flying over Mount Fuji when it was hijacked by nine armed members of Kyosando Sekigun-ha. The terrorists took 129 passengers and crew members hostage and demanded that the plane be flown to North Korea. They surrendered to North Korean author-

ities, although the North Korean government had not been in on the plan. This was the first hijacking case in Japan.

Among the hijackers, two died in North Korea (Kintaro Yoshida in 1985 and the leader, Takamaro Tamiya, in 1995). Yoshimi Tanaka was detained by the Cambodian authorities in March 1996, transported to Thailand, and arrested there. In June 2000, he was extradited to Japan, where he is now detained. Five other members are believed to still be in North Korea, although unconfirmed reports suggest that one is dead. The last member was arrested in Japan in 1988 after returning and hiding in the country. He was found guilty and sentenced to five years in prison. He was discharged from prison after serving his term.

5. Japan Red Army, *The Japan Red Army's History of 20 Years* (Feature Stories, 1993), 142–209.

6. The opinion poll was entitled "The Japan Air Lines' Hijacking Case" by the Office of Public Relations of the Prime Minister's Office. The survey had more than 3,500 respondents, based on a stratified two-stage random sample, taken from 4,400 requests made between October 19 and October 23, 1977.

7. The following statement, the first major one from the Japanese government on the topic, was released by a special task force on August 25, 1978.

Counter-Measure Policies against Hijacking and Others

1. In order to confront with international terrorism such as hijacking, it is particularly important to enhance international cooperation. For this reason, "a statement on hijacking" was made in the G7 Summit Meeting held in Bonn in West Germany. In this statement, 7 industrial nations, including Japan, expressed their resolution to jointly take specific countermeasures against a country which would refuse to extradite criminals in dealing with international hijacking case. The Japanese government, in cooperation with other countries, is to make necessary arrangements to promptly put all procedures in the statement into practice, and to earnestly request other nations to participate in enforcing these measures.
2. To deal with terrorism such as hijacking, it is important to take complete preventive measures and to allow terrorists no opportunities of which they may take advantage, and the Japanese government will continue its efforts in this regard. Should an incident unfortunately take place, however, the government is to make all possible efforts to rescue hostages safely. Furthermore in such a case, based upon the aforementioned international cooperation and enhanced cooperative relations, the Japanese government is ready to take a stern stance against any unlawful demands from terrorists, to maintain the order of law.
3. We request that the public support this stance.

8. Survey conducted by *Press 2001* (Fuji TV network), published in *Sankei Shimbun*, December 12, 1996.

9. Organization Regulations of the Cabinet Information Research Office, Articles 3–7.

10. Japan National Police Agency, "White Paper on Police" 1996, 54–57.

11. For details, see the Enforcement Regulations of Police Law, Article 1, clause 24.

12. Establishment Law of Public Security Investigation Agency, Article 4.

13. On the hijacking incidents, see *Chunichi Shinbun,* May 5, 2000.

14. Ibid., April 29, 1998.

15. Laws to Control Organizations That Engage in Acts of Indiscriminate Mass Murder, Article 5–30; Anti-subversive Activities Law, Article 11–34.

16. The Self-Defense Forces were established as the National Police Reserve in 1950. After the promulgation of the Self-Defense Forces Law, they were reorganized as the Ground, Maritime, and Air Self-Defense Forces in 1954. On their range of action, see Self-Defense Forces Law, Article 3.

17. Japan National Defense Agency, "Defense White Paper" 1995, 172.

18. *Yomiuri Shinbun,* August 19, 1999; *Asahi Shinbun,* January 27, 2000. The Ground Self-Defense Forces have already carried out a large-scale drill in response to mock terrorist incidents and armed guerrilla attacks (*Nihonkeizai Shinbun,* November 28, 1999).

Select Bibliography

Alexander, Yonah. *Middle East Terrorism: Selected Group Profiles*. Washington, D.C.: Jewish Institute for National Security Affairs, 1994.

———. *Political and Legal Documents*. Dordrecht: Martinus Nijhoff, 1992.

Alexander, Yonah, and Edgar H. Brenner, eds. *Legal Aspects of Terrorism in the United States*. Vols. 1–4. Dobbs Ferry, N.Y.: Oceana, 2000.

———. *Terrorism and the Law*. Ardsley, N.Y.: Transnational, 2001.

Alexander, Yonah, and Milton Hoenig, eds. *Super Terrorism: Biological, Chemical, Nuclear*. Ardsley, N.Y.: Transnational, 2001.

Alexander, Yonah, Michael S. Swetnam, and Herbert M. Levine, eds. *ETA: Profile of a Terrorist Group*. Ardsley, N.Y.: Transnational, 2001.

Alexander, Yonah, and Donald J. Musch, eds. *Terrorism: Documents of International and Local Control—U.S. Perspectives*. Vols. 15–30. Dobbs Ferry, N.Y.: Oceana, 1997–2001.

Alexander, Yonah, and Alan O'Day, eds. *The Irish Terrorism Experience*. Brookfield, Vt.: Dartmouth, 1991.

Alexander, Yonah, and Dennis A. Pluchinsky, eds. *European Terrorism: Today and Tomorrow*. Washington, D.C.: Brassey's, 1992.

Alexander, Yonah, and Michael S. Swetnam, eds. *Cyber Terrorism and Information Warfare: Threats and Responses*. Ardsley, N.Y.: Transnational, 2001.

———. *Usama bin Laden's al-Qaida: Profile of a Terrorist Network*. Ardsley, N.Y.: Transnational, 2001.

Alibek, Ken. *Biohazard: The Chilling True Story of the Largest Covert Biological Weapons Program in the World, Told from the Inside by the Man Who Ran It*. New York: Random House, 1999.

Beckwith, Charlie A. *Delta Force: The Army's Elite Counterterrorist Unit*. New York: Avon, 2000.

Bell, Bowyer J. *The Dynamics of Armed Struggle*. London: Frank Cass, 1998.

Bergen, Peter L. *Holy War, Inc.: Inside the Secret World of Osama bin Laden*. New York: Free Press, 2001.

Clark, Robert P. *Basque Insurgents: ETA, 1952–1980.* Madison: University of Wisconsin Press, 1984.

Clutterbuck, Richard. *Terrorism and Guerrilla Warfare: Forecasts and Remedies.* London and New York: Routledge, 1990.

Cohen, Susan, and Daniel Cohen. *Pan Am 103: The Bombing, the Betrayals, and a Bereaved Family's Search for Justice.* New York: Signet, 2001.

Cooley, John K. *Unholy Wars: Afghanistan, America, and International Terrorism.* London: Pluto Press, 1999.

Cordesman, Anthony H. *Terrorism, Asymmetric Warfare, and Weapons of Mass Destruction: Defending the U.S. Homeland.* Westport, Conn.: Praeger, 2002.

Farrell, William. *Blood and Rage: The Story of the Japanese Red Army.* Toronto: Lexington, 1990.

Feitlowitz, Marguerite. *A Lexicon of Terror: Argentina and the Legacies of Torture.* New York: Oxford University Press, 1998.

Gay, Kathlyn. *Silent Death: The Threat of Chemical and Biological Terrorism.* Brookfield, Conn.: Twenty-First Century Books, 2001.

Gurr, Nadine, and Benjamin Cole. *The New Face of Terrorism: Threats from Weapons of Mass Destruction.* New York: St. Martin's, 2000.

Harmon, Christopher C. *Terrorism Today.* Portland: Frank Cass, 2000.

Heymann, Philip B. *Terrorism and America: A Commonsense Strategy for a Democratic Society.* Cambridge, Mass.: MIT Press, 1998.

Higgins, Rosalyn, and Maurice Flory, eds. *Terrorism and International Law.* London and New York: Routledge, 1997.

Hoffman, Bruce. *Inside Terrorism.* New York: Columbia University Press, 1998.

Holmes, Jennifer S. *Terrorism and Democratic Stability (Perspectives on Democratization).* Manchester: Manchester University Press, 2001.

Jackson, Geoffrey. *Surviving the Long Night.* New York: Vanguard, 1974.

Juergensmeyer, Mark. *Terror in the Mind of God: The Global Rise of Religious Violence.* Berkeley: University of California Press, 2000.

Kassimeris, George. *Europe's Last Red Terrorists: The Revolutionary Organization 17 November.* New York: New York University Press, 2001.

Kushner, Harvey W. *Terrorism in America: A Structured Approach to Understanding the Terrorist Threat.* Springfield, Ill.: Charles C. Thomas, 1998.

Laqueur, Walter. *A History of Terrorism.* New Brunswick, N.J.: Transaction, 2001.

———. *The Age of Terrorism.* New Brunswick, N.J.: Transaction, 2000.

———. *The New Terrorism: Fanaticism and the Arms of Mass Destruction.* New York: Oxford University Press, 1999.

Lifton, Robert Jay. *Destroying the World to Save It: Aum Shinrikyo, Apocalyptic Violence, and the New Global Terrorism.* New York: Henry Holt, 1999.

Linenthal, Edward Tabor. *The Unfinished Bombing: Oklahoma City in American Memory.* New York: Oxford University Press, 2001.

Maniscalco, Paul M., and Hank T. Christen. *Understanding Terrorism and Managing the Consequences.* Upper Saddle River, N.J.: Prentice-Hall, 2002.

Martin, David C., and John Walcott. *Best Laid Plans: The Inside Story of America's War against Terrorism.* New York: Harper and Row, 1988.

Marwah, Ved. *Uncivil Wars: Pathology of Terrorism in India.* New Delhi: Indus, 1995.

McClintock, Cynthia. *Revolutionary Movements in Latin America: El Salvador's FMLN and Peru's Shining Path.* Washington, D.C.: U.S. Institute of Peace, 1998.

Miller, Judith, Stephen Engelberg, and William Broad. *Germs: Biological Weapons and America's Secret War.* New York: Simon and Schuster, 2001.

Mishal, Shaul, and Avraham Sela. *The Palestinian Hamas: Vision, Violence, and Coexistence.* New York: Columbia University Press, 2000.

Noone, Michael F. and Yonah Alexander, eds. *Cases and Materials on Terrorism: Three Nations' Response.* Boston: Kluwer Academic, 1997.

O'Ballance, Edgar. *Sudan: Civil War and Terrorism, 1956–99.* New York: St. Martin's, 2000.

O'Neil, Bard E. *Insurgency and Terrorism: Inside Revolutionary Warfare.* Washington, D.C.: Brassey's, 1990.

Pillar, Paul R., and Michael H. Armacost. *Terrorism and U.S. Foreign Policy.* Washington, D.C.: Brookings Institution, 2001.

Rapoport, David C. *Inside Terrorist Organizations.* 2d ed. London: Frank Cass, 2001.

Reinares, Fernando, ed. *European Democracies against Terrorism: Governmental Policies and Intergovernmental Cooperation.* Brookfield, Vt.: Ashgate, 2000.

Reuters, eds. *September 11: A Testimony.* New York: Financial Times and Prentice-Hall, 2002.

Rose, Gideon, and James F. Hoge Jr. *How Did This Happen? Terrorism and the New War.* New York: Public Affairs, 2001.

Simon, Jeffrey D. *The Terrorist Trap: America's Experience with Terrorism.* 2d ed. Bloomington: Indiana University Press, 2001.

Sofaer, Abraham D., and Seymour E. Goodman, eds. *The Transnational Dimension of Cyber Crime Terrorism.* Stanford: Hoover Institution Press, 2001.

Stern, Jessica. *The Ultimate Terrorists.* Cambridge: Harvard University Press, 2001.

Taillon, J. Paul de B. *The Evolution of Special Forces in Counter-Terrorism: The British and American Experiences.* Westport, Conn.: Praeger, 2001.

Tanter, Raymond. *Rogue Regimes: Terrorism and Proliferation.* New York: St. Martin's, 1999.

Tucker, Jonathan B. ed. *Toxic Terror: Assessing Terrorist Use of Chemical and Biological Weapons.* Cambridge: MIT Press, 2000.

Wallis, Rodney. *Lockerbie: The Story and the Lessons.* Westport, Conn.: Praeger, 2001.

Wilkinson, Paul. *Terrorism Versus Democracy: The Liberal State Response.* London: Frank Cass, 2001.

Woodworth, Paddy. *Dirty War, Clean Hands: ETA, the Gal and Spanish Democracy.* Crosses Green Cork, Ireland: Cork University Press, 2001.

Contributors

GUNDUZ S. AKTAN is a former Turkish Ambassador and columnist.

YONAH ALEXANDER is Professor and Director, Inter-University Center for Terrorism Studies; Senior Fellow and Director, International Center for Terrorism Studies, Potomac Institute for Policy Studies; and Co-Director, Inter-University Center for Legal Studies, International Law Institute.

ALBERTO BOLIVAR is at the Peruvian Institute for Geopolitical and Strategic Studies, Lima, Peru.

CARLOS ESPÓSITO is Professor of International Law and Relations at the School of Law, Universidad Autonoma de Madrid, Spain.

ROGER W. FONTAINE is a journalist, formerly with the U.S. National Security Council.

SHLOMO GAZIT is at the Jaffee Center for Strategic Studies, Tel Aviv University, Israel. He is former Head of Military Intelligence, Israel Defense Force.

ISAO ITABASHI is Senior Analyst at the Council for Public Policy, Tokyo, Japan.

ALI M. KOKNAR is a security consultant in Washington, D.C.

DAVID LEHENY is Assistant Professor in the Department of Political Science, University of Wisconsin–Madison.

VED MARWAH is Governor of the State of Manipur, India. He is a former Research Professor at the Center for Policy Research, New Delhi, India.

MASAMICHI OGAWARA is Visiting Researcher at the Council for Public Policy, Tokyo, Japan.

ANTONIO REMIRO BROTÓNS is Professor of International Law and Relations at the School of Law, Universidad Autonoma de Madrid, Spain.

TERENCE TAYLOR is President and Executive Director of the International Institute for Strategic Studies (IISS–US), Washington, D.C., and Assistant Director of the IISS, London.

PHILIP C. WILCOX JR. is President of the Foundation for Middle East Peace, Washington, D.C. He is a former Ambassador and Coordinator for Counterterrorism, U.S. Department of State.

JAMES ZACKRISON is at Oxford University, United Kingdom.

Index